SIXTH EDITION

UNDERSTANDING READING

A Psycholinguistic Analysis of
Reading and Learning to Read

SIXTH EDITION

UNDERSTANDING READING

A Psycholinguistic Analysis of Reading and Learning to Read

FRANK SMITH

2004

LAWRENCE ERLBAUM ASSOCIATES, PUBLISHERS

Mahwah, New Jersey   London

Lawrence Erlbaum Associates, Inc., Publishers
10 Industrial Avenue
Mahwah, New Jersey 07430

Cover design by Kathryn Houghtaling Lacey

Library of Congress Cataloging-in-Publication Data

Smith, Frank, 1928– .
    Understanding reading / Frank Smith.—6th ed.
p. cm.
Includes bibliographical references and index.
ISBN 0-8058-4711-1 (cloth : alk. paper)
ISBN 0-8058-4712-X (pbk. : alk. paper)
1. Reading.   2. Learning, Psychology of.   3. Written communi-
    cation.   I. Title.
LB1050.S574   2003
372.4—dc22   2003060718
                                                    CIP

Books published by Lawrence Erlbaum Associates are printed on acid-free paper, and their bindings are chosen for strength and durability.

Printed in the United States of America
10 9 8 7 6 5 4 3 2

Contents

Preface
to the Sixth Edition

Here are extracts from the reports of two anonymous reviewers of the fifth edition of *Understanding Reading*:

> Reviewer 1: *"Frank Smith's research summarizes a generation of investigations across disciplines .... In one succinct, readable volume it comprises what I consider a thorough and incisive summation of core research, theory and interpretation. It represents a new mainstream in progressive reading research .... Its major strength is its straightforward, compelling presentation of approaches to reading and writing that are meaningful and salient to children."*

> Reviewer 2: *"This volume contains partial truths, contradictions, and cites only references that support the author's view. Either the author is not familiar with the current research literature, or he deliberately avoids citing evidence that is contrary to his point of view .... This book is no recipe for improving reading skills of children, especially beginning readers and poor readers; it is a recipe for disaster."*

Both reviewers are professors at university schools of education, experts in the field, with access to the same professional literature and with the same professional concerns. Yet a chasm separates their points of view, one of which is expressed with vehemence and indignation.

This head-on clash of attitudes currently permeates every aspect of theory and research into reading and reading instruction, among practitioners, politicians, and the general public. It has become a focus of legislation and litigation. One has to turn to religious fundamentalism to find another issue that arouses such bitter controversy. There is no other academic discipline where so many people claim sole possession of truth and declare those with a different point of view "unscientific."

The first edition of this book, in 1971, set out to be an objective (and scientific) review of every field of study that had anything relevant to say about reading and about learning to read, with the uncomplicated aim of "understanding reading." Every edition, including the present one, has steadfastly resisted giving teachers a recipe for teaching reading while aiming to help them make their own decisions, based on research about reading, which is accessible to anyone, and their experience and personal knowledge of their students, which only they possess.

But it is impossible to write a book about reading, however detached the intention, without being caught in the cross fire of how reading should be taught. I have never professed any doctrinal allegiance, yet people who believe one thing accept this book as support for their point of view while those who take an opposing position anathematize it.

Who is right? I don't think that's a useful question at present. Each side believes it has the monopoly on truth, and few of the major protagonists would even consider the possibility of being wrong. If a crucial experiment or unanswerable argument existed, one side would have disappeared from the scene years ago.

A better question might be, what constitutes the grounds for people on both sides to feel so sure they are right and the other side wrong? That is the issue I focus on as I endeavor to bring the latest edition of *Understanding Reading* up to date.

But because of the clamor of the controversy it is not enough for me to lay out the facts of reading and learning to read as I see them. The controversy itself must be examined, to ascertain why such extreme divergences of opinion can come about. All teachers of reading, and ultimately all parents and other interested observers, must make up their own minds about why these conflicting points of view exist, unless they blindly submit to the assertions of the people who shout loudest or wield the biggest sticks (or carrots). That is the reason I include a brief statement of "issues" at the end of every chapter.

THE GREAT DEBATE

The fifth edition of *Understanding Reading*, published in 1994, included a lengthy summary of the "Great Debate" then raging between proponents of "whole language" and those of "direct instruction." I commented that it would be comforting not to have to include the section in a sixth edition, but that the portents were not auspicious.

My prognostication was correct, but not quite for the reasons I anticipated. If the great debate no longer has the same intensity, it is because direct instruction carried the day. Whole language has been sidelined rather than vanquished. The direct instructional view, with its assumption that reading is a matter of decoding letters to sounds, has been taken for granted by those arguing for accountability, standardization, high-stakes testing, and external control of classroom instruction and teacher education, from the highest political levels down. In many parts of the English-speaking world—particularly the United States, Britain, Canada, Australia, and New Zealand—whole language (or "real reading") has become a subversive, underground movement. Resistence to the control exercised by mandated tests and curriculums has become more of a confrontation over teachers' freedom in classrooms than over technical and philosophical issues related to reading instruction. Proponents of direct instruction concede that there must be a place—usually late in the course of instruction—for meaningful reading and for "teaching comprehension," and whole-language teachers and theorists deny that they ever proposed abolishing all reference to phonics in teaching reading, only against giving phonics priority and predominance. The old schisms have been papered over, and a new dispute—it can hardly be called a debate—has arisen over political issues.

WHAT'S NEW?

What justifies a sixth edition of *Understanding Reading*? The facts are the same, but the perspectives are different. Many of the basic facts about the nature of reading have been known for at least a century but, as Edmund Burke Huey observed in 1908, disputes over them seem always fresh.

My regular excursions through mountains of related literature reveal that little of substance has changed since the first edition of *Understanding Reading* was published in 1971. The main controversies persist (what it means to be a reader, how written words are recognized, and how reading should be taught), and the only consequence of continued research seems to be a hardening of positions. It is unnerving to discover that what were once seen as fresh approaches are now ancient dogmas, adopted or rejected by waves of new champions, sometimes with immoderate enthusiasm or intemperate scorn. No wonder teachers and students can be confused, if they expect either side of controversies to be proved right or to admit to being wrong.

This is clearly not a matter of "facts." There is more evidence than anyone knows what to do with, but it comes into educational theorizing and policy as raw material, to be analyzed in different ways for different purposes. What matters is how facts are gathered, which facts are considered relevant, and how they are interpreted—all subject to personal predilection. There are no "pure facts"—their place in any theory is always determined by broader theoretical and political intentions. One issue that has particularly attracted my attention is the assertion, which I regard as ominous, that there is something unnatural about reading. I give this early attention.

Substantial portions of the present volume have remained unchanged through all six editions. I have again examined every word carefully and consider that these portions are indeed unchallengeable, at least without argument at the level of "Of course the world is flat. It's obvious, isn't it?" Other portions are, I think, equally supportable, but give rise to opposing points of view because of perceived instructional implications. I don't want to claim absolute truth, because I am sure others will find better and more insightful ways of understanding reading in the future, although not, I suspect, in the way some current participants in the controversy vociferously claim that they are indubitably and everlastingly "right."

I have added about 220 new references (having scrutinized perhaps 10 times that number) and removed about 500 of the older references. But I have refrained from replacing the old with the new just for the sake of "updating." Where earlier studies remain unique or have been copied but not improved on, I have let them stand—they have stood the test of time. I don't support claims that the "latest" research is always the most significant or the most reliable. Often it simply reflects current enthusiasms, special interests, and the predispositions of funding sources.

Apart from the introduction of a new chapter 1, I have not found it necessary to alter the order of chapters or the general thrust of the discussion. Most of the major changes have been to the notes rather than to the chapters. Writing remains a major topic that has not been covered to the extent that it warrants, primarily because I discuss the subject at length in a companion volume, *Writing and the Writer* (Smith, 1994a).

I have continued to resist the tendency of new editions to put on weight with age, and the final product is 25,000 words slimmer than its predecessor. In the notes (starting on page 233) there is an explanation for why I have retained the word *psycholinguistic* in the subtitle to this book, despite considerable changes in its use since I first employed it. There is also an important acknowledgment.

TEACHERS MUST DECIDE

In acknowledging alternative points of view, I have not concealed my own position, and I certainly cannot claim to give opposing beliefs a comprehensive hearing in this book (although there are plenty of other books around that do that). But when it comes to the point, teachers and students must make up their own minds, which is something I said way back in the first edition.

We live and learn in a world where no final answers are guaranteed, and must make profound decisions for ourselves (even if only to accept unquestioningly the opinions or decisions of someone else). Throughout their professional lives, teachers are confronted by conflicting points of view, frequently urged with compelling authority and conviction, and they must be able to take a position. The first responsibility and right of all teachers and students must be to exercise independent thought—although in their own education they are often denied that opportunity with rationalizations that they "aren't ready," "shouldn't be confused," or "lack thinking experience" (Smith, 1990, 1993).

Reading is complex, but so also are walking, talking, and making sense of the world in general—and children are capable of achieving all of these, provided the environmental circumstances are appropriate. What is difficult to describe is not necessarily difficult to learn. One consideration that this book emphasizes is that children are not as helpless in the face of learning to read as often is thought.

Because an understanding of reading requires acquaintance with research in a variety of disciplines, more than half of the book is devoted to such general topics as language, memory, learning, the development of spoken language ability, and the physiology of the eye and brain. The aim is to make these topics comprehensible, with the assumption that many readers will have neither the time nor the experience to undertake deep or specialized study in these areas. At the risk of offending specialists, diverse subject areas have been covered only to the extent that they are relevant to reading.

Not all readers automatically consult notes that are mentioned in the text, and few probably go on to plough through the mass of notes at the end. But I have preferred to keep the main part of the book compact and coherent, without lengthy digressions. The notes remain supplementary resources.

In general, this book is designed to serve as a handbook for language arts teachers, a college text for a basic course on the psychology of reading, a guide to relevant research literature on reading, and an introduction to reading as an aspect of thinking and learning.

—*Frank Smith*

Notes to the Preface begin on page 233 covering:
Psycholinguistics and cognitive science
Research
Acknowledgment

1 The Essence of Reading

Proponents of direct, intensive, and early phonics training for teaching reading (like Reviewer 2 in the preface) partly justify their beliefs by asserting that unlike learning spoken language, learning to read is not "natural" and that reading itself is an unnatural activity. This book takes a contrary position.

READING THE WORLD

I'll start my discussion of reading with a psychological point. Nothing is unnatural in the eyes of infants. Everything they encounter in the world is natural, even if they find it aversive. The arbitrary division of the world into what nature once provided and what people have subsequently done to it is something that has to be learned. Other creatures never make such a distinction. I doubt whether crows have different categories for cars and houses than they do for rocks and trees. Deer are unlikely to think "Here's where nature ends" when they cross from forest glade to cement highway. "Unnatural" is a concept that doesn't exist outside language.

So what is written language? For a child, print is just another facet of the world, not yet comprehended perhaps, but not different from all the complex sights, sounds, smells, tastes, and textures in the environment—not especially mysterious or intimidating.

1

And what do infants do when they are born into this wholly natural world? They do as they will for the rest of their lives: They try to make sense of it, to discover how it relates to everything else that they know, to understand its relationship to them, its "meaning." Trying to make sense of any facet of the environment, including print, is a natural activity.

How exactly do infants (and adults) strive continually to make sense of everything they encounter in the world? They *read* it. Reading is the most natural activity in the world.

I am not taking liberties with language here. The word "reading" is properly employed for all manner of activities when we endeavor to make sense of circumstances; its original meaning was "interpretation." We read the weather, the state of the tides, people's feelings and intentions, stock market trends, animal tracks, maps, signals, signs, symbols, hands, tea leaves, the law, music, mathematics, minds, body language, between the lines, and above all—a point I must come back to—we read faces. "Reading," when employed to refer to interpretation of a piece of writing, is just a special use of the term. We have been reading—interpreting experience—constantly since birth and we all continue to do so.

What is this basic reading or "making sense" that we all engage in? I don't think it needs to be explained, or even can be explained. It is what we are. Anyone who didn't try continually to make sense of the world could not be considered a functioning human being. Making sense is a matter of interpreting, relating the situation you are in to everything you know already. Not to part of what you know, but everything, because all our knowledge hangs together. Our understanding of the world, all of the world, is coherent, consistent, and immediate. Once you know that a flame burns, you don't have to say to yourself, "That is a flame, therefore it burns." You know that flames burn. Once you can recognize a truck, you don't have to say to yourself "That is a truck" and consult some inner encyclopedia. Once you can read the written word "dog," you don't have to say to yourself, "That word says *dog*, I must look up what it means." You know what it means.

What do children do when they encounter a dog? They don't say "I recognize that animal with a particular juxtaposition of wet nose, sad eyes, and floppy ears as a certain kind of dog," nor do they say "There's a dog" to themselves and look up its meaning in a library in the brain. They certainly don't wait to hear the animal bark to decide what it is. Recognition, whether of dogs and cats or written words, is not a matter of breaking something down to its components, but of integrating it into a larger context.

All learning and comprehension is interpretation, understanding an event from its context (or putting the event into a context). All reading of print is interpretation, making sense of print. You don't worry about specific letters or even words when you read, any more than you care particularly about headlights and tires when you identify a car.

The best strategy for determining the identity of meaning of an unfamiliar word is to work out what it is from context. As we shall see, this happens very quickly. An equally good way in different circumstances is simply to ask someone what it is. Often we don't have to ask. A very poor strategy is to try to "sound it out."

Some people seem to believe that learning to read is a particularly challenging undertaking—despite the ease with which many children accomplish it, and despite how much children have learned in other contexts. Learning to read is not rocket science.

No one could catalogue all the things a human being, even a young child, has been able to make sense of in the world; it would be an impossible task. We live in an enormously complex and complicated world, but the times when individuals are actually confused, even babies, are remarkably few. Children aren't usually confused by written language—until someone tries to *instruct* them on how to read. When people *help* children to read, by reading to them and with them, there is rarely confusion. It is not reading that many children find difficult, but the instruction.

Most of our learning is unsuspected. Perhaps the most complex learning of all involves the human face. Researcher Daniel McNeill (1998) explained how 22 pairs of facial muscles are constantly orchestrated to display at least four thousand different expressions, all produced and universally understood without any instruction at all. Some basic expressions of emotion—like fear, anger, surprise, disgust, sadness, and enjoyment—may be instinctive, but the majority are learned early in life. These expressions, involving the entire face from the corners of the mouth to the eyebrows, with each element operating individually, communicate not just physical states, but agreement, disagreement, encouragement, puzzlement, disbelief, collusion, threat, challenge—and of course interest and desire. When was anyone taught to interpret all this, to read faces? (Or to write on faces, for that matter.)

It is natural for children, and adults, to strive always to make sense of the world, to interpret what everything must mean. So why should language written in an alphabetic script be particularly difficult? The answer is that it isn't. Reading print is no more complex than reading faces, and other things in the world. Making sense of print can't be more complicated than making sense of speech, which begins much earlier. Written words and spoken words share the same kind of grammar, meanings, and other structures. If we can make sense of all the words of spoken language that we know, we can do the same for written words. The actual numbers involved fade before the vast numbers of faces, places, objects, events, expressions, and relationships that we can make sense of in the world. Memory is hardly a problem. Written words are actually easier to discriminate than speech—we can mishear what someone says, or be unable to recover from a lapse in concentration; in writing we can always check back. Some written words are easier to discriminate than the objects they refer to. Participants in a scientific experiment could identify words flashed on a screen faster than they could identify drawings of the objects the words referred to (like house, dog, flower, and so forth), even after extensive practice on the limited set of alternative words and pictures that were presented.

There is nothing unnatural about any of this, as I have maintained. Written language is no more opaque or impenetrable than anything else in the world, once we have made sense of it (because we have encountered it in circumstances that make sense to us).

So why do some people have so much trouble learning to read? The first reason might be that they are confronted by reading when it is not the best time for them to learn, just as not everyone learns to play the piano, to swim, or to play chess at the same time. They may be too involved in other things, or trying to recover from some trauma. Learning to read is not necessarily a problem at any age—unless there are years of reading confusion and failure in the past. Which leads to the second reason why some people have so much trouble learning to read. They've been confused. Instead of being helped, they've been handicapped.

People can be confused by anything. Difficulty in learning to read doesn't mean that it is unnatural (unless everything else that humans do that is not instinctual is regarded as unnatural).

Allusions to "scientific" studies don't prove a thing. If phonics is an impossible system, even for computers, then any experimental study claiming to show that phonic drills have helped children to read must have been looking at something else. In fact, many studies of phonics and phonemic awareness acknowledge that they *are* looking at something else. Instead of looking at reading as a matter of making sense of text, they look at how well children can put sounds to isolated words, and even to meaningless sequences of letters, to confirm that they use the alphabetic code. This is like tying children's feet together to prove they must jump before walking.

References to mythical brain disabilities (diagnosed circularly in relation to perceived reading difficulties) explain nothing. Such phantasms are conjured up in the absence of understanding or coherent theory. And even if there were rare brain malfunctions that make it difficult for a few children and adults to read, that doesn't mean that such individuals should be subjected to regimes of unnatural treatment. Such individuals must still be helped to make sense of print—but it will take more time and patience. Calling them disabled is hardly likely to help.

Reading print is as natural as reading faces. Learning to read should be as natural as any other comprehensible aspect of existence. How reading is naturally accomplished, and what can go wrong, are the twin concerns of this book.

DISENTANGLING THE UNDERGROWTH

To clear the ground for the rest of the book, I must deal with several matters that in my view contribute to confusions or misconceptions about the nature of reading. They concern (1) the alphabet, (2) language, and (3) the brain. I raise these issues now because to some extent they contradict what often seems obvious, and there is no point in trying to understand reading without first examining critically what many people may take for granted. The remainder of the book will develop the arguments.

The Alphabet

Ever since an alphabetic writing system was invented by the Greeks over two thousand years ago, the 26 or so letters have had a profound influence on human thought. Many people through the centuries have been fascinated by the letters that make up words, and the putative relationships of these letters to the sounds of speech. They cannot imagine reading without a central role for the letters that make up individual words. Reading instruction from Greek and Roman times has focused on letters and sounds, despite continual efforts by critics to emphasize the vital role of meaning in reading (Mathews, 1966) and to demonstrate that letters play only a small, redundant, and often confusing part. Letters have become a fetish. People transfixed by the alphabet ask incredulously what the purpose of letters might be if not to make it possible for readers to read.

But the alphabet was never designed to help readers. It was not invented or developed for that purpose. Nor was it intended to be of any particular help to writers. The alphabet's true function has always been to help people cope with technical problems of reproducing written language, for scribes, copyists, inscribers, and printers. I'll call them transcribers. Tolchinsky (2003) provided an excellent summary of this, adding that a particular motivation for trying to make writing reflect sound was so that people's names would appear consistent in print (pp. 42–44).

The prime importance of the alphabet is that it enables people to make marks on paper (and other surfaces) in a simple and consistent manner, so that to speakers of a language, the written words will always look the same. In a sense, the 26 letters are convenient alternatives to thousands of drawings. They are building blocks for the construction of visible words, like the wooden tablets used in many board games. "Decoding to sound" has nothing to do with it. Readers have coped with nonalphabetic languages like Chinese for centuries, and continue to do so. Learning to read an ideographic script has never been a particularly complicated or traumatic process. Even in alphabetic cultures today we all understand a multitude of symbols that don't decompose into individual sounds, like the ubiquitous ⊘ ("don't even think about it"), the icons on washroom doors, dashboards, and laundry machines, numerical symbols like 1, 2, 3, and so forth, and such characters as @ # $ % ^ & * ( ) + = ? on keyboards. They have names, but they can't be decoded into sounds. Nor has the alphabet anything to do with *encoding*, for that matter. Letters correspond to sounds only coincidentally; they are guidelines that keep transcribers from representing words in an idiosyncratic and arbitrary manner. Letters cut down on arguments. No one can claim that C-O-W is a better way of writing "horse" than H-O-R-S-E. But this was far more important for the transcriber than for the writer. In fact, it was not until after the Gutenberg revolution, when texts began to be mass produced, that printers began to worry particularly about consistency. They didn't want spellings that sounded right, just ones that weren't contentious.

The alphabet is a construction kit for putting words together— much like the set used by a person who constantly changes the billboards for movie theaters or supermarkets, assembling one letter at a time from a stock (for the English language) of 26 alternatives. This is an enormous advantage. From just 26 basic shapes, a unique visual representation of every word in the language can be produced. The sign writer doesn't even need to be literate, as he copies one letter at a time from his script. And contrast the cost-effectiveness of having 26 basic shapes from which to build words,

wouldn't it help writers if people were consistant?

compared with the complexity of Chinese script, which for formal purposes has to be drawn by an artist. (A standardized alphabetic form of Chinese became imperative with the advent of keyboards for typewriters and computers.)

The second advantage of the alphabet is that each of these shapes, and their variants, has been given a name—Ay, Bee, Sea, etc.—so that the illiterate sign writer can be *told* how to construct every word in the language. Instead of "Use a circle, a zigzag, and a right-angle" he can be told to put up an O, a W, and an L.

When a child asks "How do I write cat?" we don't have to say "There's an open circle at the beginning, then a closed circle with a tail, and finally a ..." (I can't even think how to describe a "T"), we simply say "Cat is written C A T." We can do that for every word in the language.

This far from exhausts the utility of the alphabet. The 26 letters have been assigned a conventional order, so that every word in the language, including names, can be put into easily sorted, easily searched, sequences. Think of the utility of alphabetical order in dictionaries, directories, libraries, and other information storage and retrieval systems. Imagine the organizational chaos if alphabetical order didn't exist. (How could I construct an author and subject index for this book?)

So the alphabet earns its keep; it is one of our most useful inventions. But it is not essential. We could have visible language without it. People can learn to read without a phonetic alphabet without great difficulty. Chapter 9 examines why the sounds associated with letters are largely irrelevant and frequently misleading for readers and writers. But here's a quick demonstration of that fact. Computer programs that "read" by producing sounds from text that is keyboarded in, and that "write" by transforming speech input into text, don't use phonics. The programs won't work at the letter-sound level. And as for "phonemic awareness," the detection of distinct sounds in spoken language that are supposed to correspond to letters, computers can't do it at all. Computers do best with words, especially when grouped in meaningful sequences.

Language

I don't propose to enter into a lengthy disquisition on the nature of language, or on its uses in society, communication, and expression. I just want to focus here on one narrow aspect of language, which has a considerable impact on the way everyone thinks. I want to consider how language *creates* worlds, objects and relationships, which in no other sense exist. Language makes us think something is there when it isn't. It deceives us.

The human race is always prone to give names to aspects of experience, and then to take for granted that whatever corresponds to those names exists. Give something a name (like intelligence, or perseverance, or wickedness), and many people will think that it exists, not as a kind of behavior that fits a certain description, but as the cause or underpinning of the behavior. Thus for example *reading*, which in general is easily identifiable behavior, has become transmuted into *the reading process*, which is assumed (by many) to actually exist within the human brain (which is also supposed to contain a writing process, a grammatical process, and a phonemic awareness process).

Learning and comprehension are particularly interesting examples of this drive to construct fictitious entities. Both are widely regarded as *skills*, reflecting learning and comprehension processes in the brain. Instructional programs are devised to augment these processes, and standardized tests to calibrate their effectiveness. But a different point of view can be taken that learning and comprehension are simply states of the human organism. They are neither skills nor processes, but a consequence of being alive. Their presence in human beings doesn't have to be explained, only their absence, or rather the consequences of their suppression. Any human in a position of being unable to learn is bored. No one would claim that boredom was a process; it is the opposite of learning, an alternative state. Similarly absence of comprehension is not a lack of skills, nor the shutting down of a process; it is a state, to which we normally give the name of confusion. It might be tempting to consider confusion as a chaotic disorganization of certain structures of the brain, but it is not. It is simply a state that is the opposite of comprehension. I should perhaps note that both boredom and confusion are aversive; they are not natural states to be in. All human beings strive naturally to be in a continuous state of learning and comprehending, just as they continually strive to breathe.

So there are two problems with language. It enables us to think about things that don't actually exist, and then to devise unseen processes that bring these things into being.

I don't want to belittle language in any way; it has many beautiful and useful characteristics. It enables us to think and to create. Language is particularly useful for *description*—a few well-chosen words can give a powerful image of people or objects, and of many associated characteristics (whether or not the person or object actually exists). But language is distinctly lacking in *explanatory* power. Whether we try to explain a person, a group, or an activity like reading, we quickly fall back on fiction and metaphor. Rather than describe the circumstances in which individuals demonstrate literacy, or learn to become literate, we *invent* explanations. We put mechanisms and processes into their heads (see "Making a Mystery Out of a Marvel," in Smith, 2003, chap. 2).

Little of this explanation-through-fantasy would matter if we put two little words into our diagnostic and referential statements— the words *as if*. To say the human brain sometimes functions *as if* it were a computer is altogether less misleading than to say that the brain *is* a computer. The statement that some people read *as if* they employ knowledge of letter–sound correspondences is easier to comprehend, and much easier to discuss rationally, than the blunt assertion that people can read because they employ phonic skills.

Language can be used for the careful dissection and analysis of complex human behavior—but not if wielded like a blunt instrument.

The Brain

My point about the brain is simply stated. Despite extravagant claims—usually by people who are not neurologists—no one knows how the brain is ultimately related to anything we see or do in the world. Brain research tells us nothing about anything except the brain itself. We may point to various irregularities in the brain to try to account for why things occasionally go wrong, but we cannot use the architecture of the brain to explain why anything we do or think goes right, or even why it occurs.

We can take the brain apart and see how all the bits are joined together. We can poke and prod at parts of the living brain and see how a person reacts. We can see what goes wrong when bits are missing. We can take various kinds of pictures of the brain and see how it heats up as people engage in various kinds of activity or as they think about particular things. But none of this *explains* why we have the kinds of thoughts or sensations that we do. If a blow to a particular part of my brain makes me see stars, or hear a symphony, I have to tell someone of that fact. No neuroscientist can look inside my brain and say, "He's hearing Mahler's Second right now." No neuroscientist can explain why I see green, or taste salt, or experience the scent of a rose. Neuroscientists might claim to have produced a complete wiring diagram of the parts of the brain that seem to be involved in anything I do or experience, but they can never say why I have that particular experience. They can't find a map in my head if I claim to know my way around the university, nor can they find why I might decide to walk from one part of campus to another.

The neuroscientist's situation is no different from that of the television technician who can tell you how the various components of your system work together, and who can explain why sometimes you don't get sound or a picture, but who has no way of explaining why the various electromagnetic events that take place on the screen should make you laugh, cry, or switch channels in abject boredom.

We'd think it absurd if our technician told us he had detected a sitcom-sensitive area in the television receiver, or that a particular module accounted for the upbeat attitudes of weather reporters, even though a misdirected screwdriver could certainly interfere with both. Yet neuroscientists have no trouble labeling a reading process in the brain. They will draw diagrams of the inside of the brain with arrows and little boxes labeled <input> <output> <phonemic processing> <memory> and even <understanding>. But they can't explain what goes on in those boxes, or the nature of the "information" assumed to pass along the routes indicated by the arrows.

No neuroscientist has ever been able to find any of the 26 letters of the alphabet in the brain, nor the connections they are supposed to have with particular sounds, although we are assured that such structures exist (although not in people afflicted with "dyslexia"). The alphabet is doubtless a consequence of something in the brain, but not anything that could be regarded as specialized and dedicated for the purpose of producing and making use of letters. The parts of the brain involved in handling letters could very well be the same parts that are involved in identifying birds or cooking omelettes. I see no reason why they should not be. The same applies to phonics skills and phonemic awareness. Even if these things have any real existence in the brain (which I doubt), I have encountered no evidence that they would be any different from processes that enable us to listen to jazz or enjoy a movie.

And because there is absolutely no evidence of how any neurological or chemical processes in the brain might produce reading, it makes no sense to say that there are specialized centers or processes in the brain responsible for reading. Obviously there are parts of the brain involved in reading, and a good number of other activities too, but that is no reason to claim that these areas are *for* reading, any more than you can say that one part of an automobile engine is responsible for getting you to the supermarket and another part for driving to the beach.

I have to admit that "brain" used to be one of my favorite words; I held it responsible for almost everything we do. I still regard the brain as an astonishing instrument, far more remarkable than it is often given credit for, but it makes sense much of the time to refer to the whole person rather than to the individual's cranial contents, although it may sound less scientific. Reading, for example, is best regarded as something done by people rather than by brains. To say the brain "looks," "thinks," or "remembers" is about as appropriate as saying that the stomach enjoys a good meal. I have not been able to remove the brain from chapter 5 ("Between Eye and Brain") because that is what the chapter is about, although I have tried to keep the discussion on as literal a level as possible. The brain reappears in later chapters but always when I am referring specifically to the organ, not to the person as a whole. My problem in trying to avoid talking about the brain as if it "learns" or "makes decisions" emphasizes the metaphorical nature of the language we must use when trying to relate physiological structures to feelings or behavior (see chap. 2 notes.)

ISSUES

Just about every statement I make in this chapter can be challenged by some people, especially those who prefer to believe that learning to read is simply a matter of subjection to a rigorous regime of *phonics* instruction. The statements will not necessarily be challenged because they are refutable or inappropriate, but because they conflict with preconceptions about how reading should be taught.

SUMMARY

The alphabet was designed as a technology to simplify making language visible, not as an aid to readers or writers. Reading is as natural as recognizing and interpreting facial expressions. Understanding reading becomes complicated when certain metaphorical states of affairs are taken as being literally true.

Notes to chapter 1 begin on page 238 covering:

Matters of interpretation

Alphabets

Writing systems

2 Comprehension and Knowledge

Most people would say they know what the word *comprehension* means, at least in a general sense, although it is not a term that occurs often in everyday speech. In fact, it is almost exclusively found in the context of reading. In everyday speech we are much more likely to use the term *understanding* (as I have done in the title of this book) or even my preferred alternative of *making sense*. The word comprehension was rarely used in the research literature on reading before the 1950s, when systems analysts and behavioral engineers were first recruited to design reading programs (Smith, 1998, p. 116).

In other words, *comprehension* is a kind of up-market synonym for *understanding* in discussions that are (or are intended to appear) technical and scientific. In such contexts the word frequently doesn't appear alone, but in such combinations as *comprehension skills* or *the comprehension process*, even by people who would never use expressions like *understanding skills* or *the understanding process*.

I can't avoid the word comprehension in this book—it is too well established in the world of reading to be ignored. But I don't regard comprehension as some kind of special or unusual process. As I said in chapter 1, I see comprehension as a state rather than a set of skills or a process.

Comprehension may be regarded as relating aspects of the world around us—including what we read—to the knowledge, intentions, and expectations we already have in our head. It is clearly the purpose of reading and of learning to read. What is the point of any activity that causes confusion?

We don't have to know something in advance in order to comprehend it. But we must be able to relate new things to what we already know if we are to comprehend them. And relating something new to what we already know is of course learning. We learn to read, and we learn through reading, by elaborating what we know already. This is natural.

Thus, comprehension and learning are fundamentally the same, relating the new to the already known. To understand all this, we must begin by considering what it is that "we already have in our heads" that enables us to understand the world. We must begin by comprehending comprehension.

Cognitive Structure

Several terms may be used to refer to the knowledge we carry around in our heads all the time. *Prior knowledge* and "*nonvisual information*" are synonyms for the mental resources that enable us to make sense of "visual information" arriving through the eyes. *Long-term memory* is our permanent source of understanding of the world. *Cognitive structure* and *theory of the world* are two other terms that I am about to introduce. But the italicized terms do not refer to different things; they are synonymous. The knowledge we must already possess in order to understand written language (like the knowledge we need for understanding speech) must be part of our long-term memory. And remembrance of the sense we have made of past experience is the foundation of all new understanding of language and the world. In more general contexts, this basis of understanding is referred to by psychologists as *cognitive structure*. The term is apt because "cognitive" means "knowledge" and "structure" implies organization, and that indeed is what we possess—an organization of knowledge.

Certainly, it would be simplistic to suggest that what we carry around in our heads is just "memories." The brain is not filled with an assortment of snapshots, videos, and recordings of bits of the past. At the very least we would have to say that all our memories have a meaning; they are related to everything else that we know.

Cognitive structure is more like a summary of past experience. I don't want to remember that on 16 July I sat on a chair, on 17 July I sat on a chair, and on 18 July I sat on a chair. I want to remember that chairs are for sitting on, a summary of my experience. We remember specific events only when they are exceptions to our summary rules or when they have some particularly dramatic or emotional significance. And even then our memories, when we "recall" them, turn out to be highly colored by our present intentions and perspectives about the world (Bartlett, 1932). Specific memories that can't be related to our summary, to our present general understanding, will make little sense, which may be the reason we can recall so little of our childhood.

But it would also be an oversimplification to suggest that our heads are filled with an accumulation of facts and summaries. The brain is not like a library where useful information is filed away under appropriate headings for possible future reference. And it is certainly not like a bank in which we save nuggets of information deposited by teachers and textbooks. Instead, the knowledge we possess is organized into an intricate and internally consistent working model of the world, built up through our imagination and our experiences in the world, and integrated into a coherent whole. We know far more than we were ever taught.

THEORIES OF THE WORLD

Everything that we know and believe is organized into a personal *theory* of what the world is like, a theory that is the basis of all our perceptions and understanding of the world, the root of all learning, the source of hopes and fears, motives and expectancies, reasoning and creativity. And this theory is all we have. If we can make sense of the world at all, it is by interpreting our experience with the world in the light of our theory. The theory is our shield against bewilderment.

As I look around my world, I distinguish a multiplicity of meaningful objects that have all kinds of complicated relationships with each other and with me. But neither these objects nor their interrelations are self-evident. A chair does not announce itself to me as a chair; I have to recognize it as such. Chairs are a part of my theory. I recognize a chair when I decide that a chair is what I am looking at. A chair does not tell me that I can sit on it, or put my coat or books or feet on it, or stand on it to reach a high shelf, or wedge it against a door that I do not wish to be opened. All this is also part of my theory. I can only make sense of the world in terms of what I know already. All of the order and complexity that I perceive in the world

Sort of suggests that we don't learn anything

around me must reflect an order and complexity in my own mind. Anything I can't relate to my theory of the world will not make sense to me. I am bewildered.

The fact that bewilderment is an unusual condition for most of us despite the complexity of our lives is a clear indication that our theory of the world is very efficient. The reason we are usually not aware of the theory is that it works so well. Just as we take the air we breathe for granted until deprived of it, so we become aware of our dependence on our theory only when it proves inadequate, and the world fails to make sense. That we can occasionally be bewildered only serves to demonstrate how efficiently our theory usually functions. When were you last bewildered by something that you heard or read? Our theory of the world seems ready even to make sense of almost everything we are likely to experience in spoken and written language—a powerful theory indeed.

And yet, when was the last time you saw a bewildered baby? Infants have theories of the world too, not as complex as those of adults, but then children have not had as much time to make their theories complex. But children's theories seem to work very well for their needs. Even the smallest children seem able most of the time to make sense of their world in their own terms; they rarely appear confused or uncertain. The first time many children run into a situation that they cannot possibly relate to anything they know already is when they arrive at school, a time when they may be consistently bewildered if they are confronted by situations that make no sense to them. Children are often denied credit for knowing very much. But, in fact, most of our knowledge of the world—of the kinds of objects it contains and the way they can be related—and most of our knowledge of language have been organized before we arrive at school. At age 5 or 6 the framework is there, and the rest is mainly a matter of filling in details.

In chapter 12 I look more closely at three quite remarkable characteristics of our theory of the word: that it is *coherent* (it all hangs together), *consistent* (it doesn't need radical changes every day), and *consensual* (it is largely compatible with other people's theory). For the remainder of this chapter, I talk a little more about how the theory is organized and then discuss how it is used so that we can comprehend the world.

THE STRUCTURE OF KNOWLEDGE

The system of knowledge that is our theory of the world may be regarded as a structure just like any other theory or system of organizing information, such as a library or an encyclopedia.

Information systems have three basic components—a set of categories, some rules for specifying membership of the categories, and a network of interrelations among the categories. I briefly examine each component in turn.

Categories

To categorize means to treat some objects or events as the same yet as different from other objects or events. All human beings categorize, instinctively, starting at birth. There is nothing remarkable about this innate propensity to categorize, because living organisms could not survive if they did not treat some objects or events as the same yet as different from other objects and events.

No living organism could survive if it treated everything in its experience as the same; there would be no basis for differentiation and therefore no basis for learning. There would be no possibility of being systematic. Just as a librarian can't treat all books as the same when putting them on the stacks, so all human beings must differentiate throughout their lives. In our culture at least, everyone is expected to be able to distinguish dogs from cats, tables from chairs, and the letter A from the letter B.

But similarly, no living organism could survive if it treated everything in its experience as different. If there is no basis for similarity, there is still no basis for learning. Thus the librarian must treat some books as the same in some senses—so that all chemistry books are stacked in the same area—even though these books may differ in size, color, and author's name. In the same way everyone, in our culture at least, is expected to ignore many differences in order to treat all dogs as the same, all cats as the same, and many different shapes like A, A, a, and a as the letter "a."

In other words, the basis of survival and of learning is the ability to ignore many potential differences so that certain objects[1] will be treated as the same yet as different from other objects. All objects that belong to one category are treated as the same yet as different from objects belonging to other categories.

The categories that we all observe, which are part of our theories of the world, are quite arbitrary; they are not generally imposed on us by the world itself. The world doesn't force us to categorize animals into dogs and cats and so forth—we could divide them up in

---

[1]From this point on, I refrain from the cumbersome practice of talking all the time about "objects or events." But every reference to "objects" applies in general to "events" as well.

other ways, for example, treating all green-eyed animals as the same, in contrast to those with other eye colors, or differentiating those over 15 inches in height from those under 15 inches. The librarian could organize books on the basis of the color of their covers, or their size, or the number of pages. But we can't usually invent categories for ourselves—hence the qualification "in our culture at least" in previous paragraphs. The reason we divide animals on a cat and dog basis and not on the basis of size or eye color is that the categories we have are part of our culture. Categories are *conventions*. To share a culture means in part to share the same categorical basis for organizing experience. Language reflects the way a culture organizes experience, which is why many of the words in our language are a clue to the categories in our shared theories of the world. We have the words *dog* and *cat* but not a word for animals with green eyes or less than 15 inches in height. When we have to learn new categories, the existence of a name in the language is often the first clue that a category exists.

Not that words are prerequisites for the establishment of categories. Quite the reverse—categories can exist for which we have no names. I can easily distinguish certain mottled brown and grey birds that come to my garden every morning, but I do not know a name for them. To know a name without an understanding of the category that it labels is meaningless. In fact, the existence of a category is a prerequisite for learning how to use words, because words label categories rather than specific objects. What we call a dog is any individual animal that we put in the category with the name *dog*.

The category system that is part of our theory of the world is essential for making sense of the world. Any situation that we cannot relate to a category does not make sense; we are bewildered. Our categories, in other words, are the basis of our perception of the world. Perception must be regarded as decision making. We "see" what we decide we are looking at, which means the category to which an experience is allocated. If I see a chair in front of me, then I must have a category for chairs in my theory of the world, and I must have decided that what I am looking at belongs in that category. If I can see the word *cat* when I read, then I must have a category for that word quite independent of my knowledge of its name or possible meanings, just as I must have categories for the letters *c*, *a*, and *t* if I can distinguish those letters in the word. Interestingly, we cannot see things in more than one category at a time; it is not possible to see the letters *c*, *a*, and *t* and the word *cat* simultaneously in the visual configuration *cat*, which is why children may find learning to read more difficult if they are required to concentrate on the individual letters in words. Usually you only see what you are looking for and remain quite unaware of other possibilities. If I ask you to read the address *4IO LION STREET,* you will probably not notice that the numerals *IO* in *4IO* are the same characters as the letters *IO* in *LION.* When you look for the category of numerals you see numerals, and when you look for the category of letters you see letters. Even now that you are aware of what I am doing, you cannot look at *IO* and see both letters and numerals simultaneously, any more than you can see the faces and the vase simultaneously in the ambiguous illustration of Fig. 2.1. We can make decisions about only one category at a time in relation to a single visual configuration (although we could see the face and vase in Fig. 2.1 simultaneously if they did not share a common contour). And if there is no category to which we can relate an object to which we are exposed, we can make no decision at all; the world will not make sense to us. We must have categories in order to make decisions, categories that embrace not only sights and sounds but also tastes, odors, feelings, and sensations, as well as many kinds of events, patterns, and relationships.

Rules for Category Membership

Categories in themselves are not enough. The category "chemistry books" is useless if a librarian has no way of recognizing a chemistry book when encountering one, just as a child can make no use of the information that there are cats and dogs in the world without some notion of how to distinguish one from the other. A child who can recite the alphabet has established a set of 26 categories but may not be able to recognize a single letter. For every category that we employ there must be at least one way of recognizing members of that category. Every category must have at least one set of rules, a

FIG. 2.1.   Ambiguous visual information.

specification, that determines whether an object belongs in that category. Sometimes a single category may have more than one set of rules—we can distinguish an object as an orange by its appearance, feel, smell, and taste. We can recognize the letter *a* in a number of different guises. But just as we must have a category for every object we can distinguish in the world, so we must have at least one set of rules—a list of significant attributes or *distinctive features*—for allocating that object to a particular category. These are not usually rules that we can put into words. Knowledge of this kind is implicit—we can only infer that we have the categories or rules by the fact that we can make use of them.

The question of what constitutes the rules that differentiate the various categories that we employ in reading and language generally demands a good deal of attention in later chapters—especially when we see that "teaching" is often little more than telling children that a category exists, leaving them to discover for themselves what the rules are.

Category Interrelations

Rules permit the categories in a system to be used, but they don't ensure that the system makes sense. A library doesn't make sense simply because all the chemistry books are stacked in one place and all the poetry books in another. What makes a library a system is the way in which the various categories are related to each other, and this is the way our personal systems of knowledge make sense as well.

It is impossible to list all the different interrelations among the categories in our theory of the world. To do so would be to document the complexity of the world as we perceive it. Everything that we know is directly or indirectly related to everything else, and any attempt to illustrate these relationships risks becoming interminable.

For example, consider an onion. We know what that particular object is called—in more than one language perhaps—and also the names of several kinds of onion. All these are relations of the particular object to language. We also know what an onion looks, feels, smells, and tastes like, again perhaps in more than one way. We know where an onion comes from—how it is grown—and we probably have a good idea about how it gets to the place where we can buy one. We know roughly what onions cost. We know how an onion can be used in cooking and we probably know some other uses as well. We may know half a dozen different ways of cooking onions (with different names), and we certainly know a number of things that can be eaten with onions. We know a number of instruments for dealing with onions—knives, graters, and blenders, for example. We not only know what we can do with onions, we also know what onions can do to us. We know people who love onions and people who hate them; people who can cook them and people who can't. We may even know something about the role of onions in history. One enormous ramification of our knowledge of onions is related to the fact that we can call them by more than one name. An onion can also be called a vegetable, which means that everything we know about vegetables in general applies to onions in particular. Indeed, every time we relate an onion to something else—to a knife, a frying pan, or a particular person—then we discover that what we know about onions is part of what we know about knives, frying pans, and people. There is no end.

Many cognitive interrelations pertain to the system of language that is such an important part of everyone's theory of the world. One complex set of interrelations is called *syntax* and describes how elements of language should be related to each other in speech and writing. Syntax enables us to put words together in ways that are "grammatical" (although people whose language is often characterized as "ungrammatical" don't normally lack syntactic knowledge; they observe different conventions). Another set of interrelations is called *semantics*, concerned with the way language is related to the world at large or rather, to our perception of the world. The semantic richness of words indicates to some extent the complexity we perceive in the world (Whorf, 1956), or at least how easily we can talk about it (Hunt & Agnoli, 1991). Knowledge of language must also include extensive understanding of the conventional ways in which language and other systems of communication are used on particular occasions, sometimes referred to as *pragmatics* or as *semiotics*. And a good deal of our knowledge of the world is actually held in the form of language, in verbal *descriptions* of things that we know. Our heads can also contain a host of *propositions*, ranging from simple facts (Paris is the capital of France, two times two is four), through proverbs and other compact bundles of ideas or common sense, to complex verbal formulas and even entire segments of prose or poetry. All of this verbal prior knowledge can become available to us at relevant times to help us to comprehend and even to bring about particular sets of circumstances.

Schemes, Scenarios, and Stories

Many important sets of cognitive relations relate to places and scenes with which we are familiar. We know the spatial organization of familiar landscapes and locations—the beach where we played as children, the family living room, or our first classroom. We are quickly aware if something in a familiar setting has changed (even if we cannot immediately determine what exactly is different). In addition, our theory also contains many more symbolic representations, such as maps (which is the primary way most of us understand the geography of the world) and diagrams.

Our theories also contain (or can construct) extensive representations of more general patterns or regularities that occur in our experience. These representations are metaphorically called *schemes* (or occasionally *schemas* or *schemata*). Most of us have a complex generic scheme for what classrooms are like, for example. We can recognize and make sense of classrooms we have never been in before, just because they contain familiar arrangements of familiar elements. Our cognitive structures similarly include schemes of department stores and restaurants, for example, which enable us to make sense of new experiences and to behave appropriately. Many experiments have demonstrated that our ability to recognize scenes and to remember them depends on the extent to which they conform to our expectations of what such scenes should be like, to the schemes that we already possess.

Readers develop and require a large number of spatially organized schemes related to the way in which books and other kinds of written texts are organized. Among such schemes are those of specific *genres*—newspapers are not set out in the way that magazines, novels, or textbooks are. All of these schemes, or specifications for various kinds of text, are conventional. The appearance and organization of a book or a newspaper can vary considerably from one community or culture to another, and their schemes have to be known to us if we are to make sense of them. Other conventional rules of written *discourse structure* include organization into paragraphs, chapters, or sections, with titles and other kinds of headings, which readers as well as writers have to observe and expect.

The examples of schemes I have so far given have all been spatial, the way things are laid out, primarily for comprehension visually. But we also possess innumerable schemes for other sense modalities—for arrangements of sounds, tastes, smells, and a variety of tactile sensations, many of them closely related to each other and to patterns of events in the visual world.

Many of our most important schemes are laid out in *time*; they have a serial or temporal organization. Time and change are essential aspects of the way we perceive the world—how otherwise could we understand language, music, or a football game? Schemes that have a temporal as well as a spatial basis are often referred to as *scenarios* or *scripts*. A department store script sets out expected and conventional patterns of behavior for ourselves and for others when we go out to shop, even when we are purchasing unfamiliar items in stores we have never been to before. An absence or mismatch of scripts can result in confusion, embarrassment, and misunderstanding. Collectively, scripts, scenarios, and schemes are sometimes referred to as *event knowledge* (Nelson, 1986).

Knowledge of relevant schemes is obviously essential if we are to read any kind of text with comprehension. A child who doesn't have a scenario about farming is unlikely to understand a story about farming or references to farming in a textbook. But there are special kinds of language schemes that readers particularly require. If we are readers, or if we hope to become readers, our theories of the world must include *story schemes*, specifications of how stories are organized and how they unfold. We must know that stories comprise particular kinds of plots, characters, and episodes. How well a story is understood and remembered depends on how well it conforms to conventional schemes for stories and on how well the reader is familiar with those schemes.

The complexity of cognitive structure is indeed astounding. Our prior knowledge resists all efforts to catalog it or to reduce it to a few simple categories. Attempts to "simplify" its organization or operation can only mislead, especially if made the basis of instructional or diagnostic practices in education. The enormous cognitive power of every individual is frequently overlooked if there is an emphasis on "needs" or "disabilities." Our ability to make sense of the world, like our ability to remember events, to act appropriately, and to predict the future, is determined by the complexity of the knowledge we already possess.

THE DYNAMICS OF COGNITIVE STRUCTURE

Cognitive structure, our personal theory of the world, may so far have seemed rather a crowded and static place, not very different in essence from a collection of facts and procedures. But the theory is *dynamic*, and not just in the sense that it is constantly being added to and modified, particularly during that lively period of intense exploration and learning we call childhood. We can do much more with the theory of the world than use it to make sense of experience. We can *live* in the theory, in worlds that exist only in the imagination. Within the theory we can imagine and create, testing

provisional solutions to problems and examining the consequences of possible behaviors. We can explore new worlds of our
own and can be led into other worlds by writers and artists.

But the aspect of imagination with which we will be most concerned is more mundane, although at first encounter it may sound
quite exotic. We can use the theory of the world to *predict* the future. This ability to predict is both pervasive and profound, because it is the basis of our comprehension of the world, including
our understanding of spoken and written language. Reading depends on prediction.

The Pervasiveness of Prediction

Everyone predicts—including children—all the time. Our lives
would be impossible, we would be reluctant even to leave our beds
in the morning, if we had no expectation about what the day might
bring. We would never go through a door if we had no idea of what
might be on the other side. And all our expectations, our predictions, can be derived from only one source, our theory of the world.

We are generally unaware of our constant state of anticipation
for the simple reason once again that our theory of the world works
so well. Our theory is so efficient that when our predictions fail, we
are surprised. We don't go through life predicting that anything
might happen—indeed, that would be contrary to prediction, and
in that case rhinoceros could surprise us. The fact that something
always could take us by surprise—like the word *rhinoceros* a few
words ago—is evidence that indeed we always predict and that our
predictions are usually accurate. It is always possible that we could
be surprised, yet our predictions are usually so appropriate that
surprise is a very rare occurrence. When was the last time you were
surprised?

We drive through a town we have never visited before, and nothing we see surprises us. There is nothing surprising about the
buses and cars and pedestrians in the main street; they are predictable. But we don't predict that we might see anything—we
would be surprised to see camels or submarines in the main street.
Not that there is anything very surprising or unpredictable about
camels or submarines in themselves—we would not be surprised
to see camels if we were visiting a zoo or to see submarines at a na-
val base. In other words, our predictions are very specific to situations. We don't predict that anything will happen, nor do we predict
that something is *bound* to happen if it is only *likely* to happen (we
are no more surprised by the absence of a bus than we are by the

presence of one), and we predict that many things are unlikely to happen. Our predictions are remarkably accurate—and so are those of children. It is rare to see a child who is surprised.

The Need for Prediction

Why should we predict? Why not expect that anything could happen all the time, and thus free ourselves from any possibility of surprise? I can think of three reasons. The first reason is that our position in the world in which we live changes constantly, and we are usually far more concerned with what is likely to happen in the near and distant future than we are with what is actually happening right now. An important difference between an experienced driver and a novice is that the experienced driver is able to project the car into the future and the novice's mind is more closely anchored to where the car is now—when it may be too late to avoid accidents. The same difference tends to distinguish experienced readers from beginners, or from anyone having difficulty with a particular piece of reading. In fluent reading aloud, the eye is always ahead of the voice, checking for possible obstacles to a particular understanding. Readers concerned with the word directly in front of their noses will have trouble predicting, and they will have trouble comprehending.

The second reason for prediction is that there is too much ambiguity in the world; there are too many ways of interpreting just about anything that confronts us. Unless we exclude some alternatives in advance, we are likely to be overwhelmed with possibilities. Of the many things I know about onions, I don't want to be concerned with the fact that they are pulled from the ground or that they bring my cousin George out in spots if all I want is garnish for a hamburger. What I see is related to what I am looking for, not to all possible interpretations. Words have many meanings—*table* can be several kinds of verb as well as several kinds of noun—but there is only one meaning that I am concerned with, that I predict, if someone tells me to put my books on the table. All the everyday words of our language have many meanings and often several grammatical functions—*table, chair, house, shoe, time, walk, open, close*—but by predicting the range of possibilities that a word is likely to be, we are just not aware of the potential ambiguities.

The final reason for prediction is that there would otherwise be far too many alternatives from which to choose. It takes time to make decisions about what the eyes are looking at, and the time that is required depends on the number of alternatives. We take longer to decide that we are looking at the letter *A* when it could be any one of the 26 letters of the alphabet than when we are told in advance that it is a vowel. We take longer to identify a word in isolation compared with a word in a meaningful sentence. The fewer the alternatives, the quicker is the recognition. If there are too many alternatives confronting the eyes, then it is much harder to see or to comprehend.

Prediction is the core of reading. All of our schemes, scripts, and scenarios—our prior knowledge of places and situations, of written discourse, genres, and stories—enable us to predict when we read and thus to comprehend, experience, and enjoy what we read. Prediction brings potential meaning to texts, reducing ambiguity and eliminating in advance irrelevant alternatives. Thus, we are able to generate comprehensible experience from inert pages of print.

Prediction is not reckless guessing, nor does it involve taking chances by betting everything on the most likely outcome. We don't go through life saying "I'll see a bus round the next corner," or "The next word I read will be *rhinoceros*." We predict by opening our minds to the probable and by disregarding the unlikely. Here is a formal definition: *Prediction is the prior elimination of unlikely alternatives*. It is the projection of possibilities. We predict to reduce any uncertainty we might have, and therefore to reduce the amount of external information that we require. Our theory of the world tells us the most probable occurrences, and we decide among those remaining alternatives until uncertainty is reduced to zero. And we are so good at predicting only the most likely alternatives that we are rarely surprised.

Put more informally, prediction is a matter of asking specific questions. We don't ask "What is that object over there?" but "Is that something I can put my books on?" or whatever we want to do. We don't look at a page of print with no expectation about what we shall read next; instead we ask, "What is the hero going to do?" "Where is the villain going to hide?" and "Will there be an explosion when liquid A is mixed with powder B?" And provided the answer lies within the expected range of alternatives—which it usually does if we are reading with comprehension—then we are not aware of any doubt or ambiguity. We are neither bewildered nor surprised.

Prediction and Comprehension Related

Now at last prediction and comprehension can be tied together. Prediction means asking questions, and comprehension means being able to get some of the questions answered. Comprehension, as I have said, is the absence of confusion. As we read, as we listen to someone talking, as we go through life, we are constantly asking implicit questions, and if we are able to find answers to those questions, then we comprehend. The person who doesn't comprehend how to repair a bicycle is the one who can't ask and find answers to such questions as "Which of these nuts and bolts goes where?" at appropriate times. And the person who doesn't comprehend a book or newspaper article is the one who can't find relevant questions and answers concerning the next part of the text. There is a *flow* to comprehension, with new questions constantly being generated from the answers that are sought. This flow, especially in the imagination, is a significant part of what is usually regarded as *thought*.

Such a view of comprehension differs from the way the word is often used in school. So-called comprehension tests in school are usually given after a book has been read and as a consequence are more like tests of memory. (And because the effort to memorize can drastically interfere with comprehension, the test may destroy what it sets out to measure.) If I say that I comprehended a certain book, it doesn't make sense to give me a test and argue that I didn't understand it, although I may have understood it differently from the test constructor. And a high score on a test certainly would not convince me that I had really understood a book or a speaker if my feeling is that I did not.

The very notion that comprehension is relative, that it depends on the questions that an individual happens to ask, is not one that all educators find easy to accept. Some want to argue that you may not have understood a book even if you have no unanswered questions at the end. They will ask, "But did you understand that the spy's failure to steal the secret plans was really a symbol of humanity's ineluctable helplessness in the face of manifest destiny?" And if you say "No, I just thought it was a jolly good story," they will tell you that you didn't *really* comprehend what the story was about. But basically what they are saying is that you were not asking the kind of questions they think you should have asked.

THINKING AND "META-THINKING"

Thinking has become a focus of attention for many educators. In part, this concentration of interest has been generated by *cognitive scientists* trying to develop models of thought that might serve in the development of "thinking computers," and also by *cognitive psychologists* involved with human thinking who nevertheless want to simulate or test their theories on computers. As a result, thinking has tended to be fragmented into distinct clusters of "information-processing" procedures, more appropriate to the programmed sequential operations of electronic technology than to humans whose flow of thought and actions are based primarily on their intentions, interests, and values.

It could also be argued that another reason for the sudden concern about thinking is the tendency to fragment reading and reading instruction into packages of decontextualized "basic skills," none of which particularly engage thinking.

Yet reading cannot be separated from thinking. Reading is a thought-full activity. There is no difference between reading and any other kind of thought, except that with reading, thought is engendered by a written text. Reading might be defined as thought stimulated and directed by written language. This entire book could be considered to be a disquisition on thinking from a reading point of view.

Particular characteristics of the thinking ideally engaged in by readers must be separated into two categories, not always clearly recognized. The first is the thinking involved in the *act* of reading—such as drawing appropriate inferences in order to comprehend—and the other is thinking that is a *consequence* of reading, that might transpire in concurrent or subsequent reflection. Reading involves no special kind of thought that is not already displayed in other aspects of mental life.

Thinking should not be regarded as a set of specialized processes that are superimposed on the organization of knowledge, our theory of the world discussed earlier in this chapter. Thinking—including reading—is not a distinct faculty or set of skills, different from comprehension, prediction, or imagination; rather, it is our theory of the world in action (Smith, 1990). The theory of the world constantly modifies itself in relation to our current concerns and state of affairs. Thinking is the normal operation of our dynamic theory of the world. The flow of thought is powered by our intentions and expectations, guided by the consequent experience. It is creative and constructive, not passive and reactive.

All aspects of thought that language distinguishes can be seen as the dynamic interplay of cognitive relationships. *Reasoning* usually refers to relationships within a series of statements or states of affairs: the way one thing follows another. *Inference* involves relationships between particular statements or states of affairs and some more general circumstances, and *problem solving* relates existing states of affairs to desired states. *Classification, categorization, concept formation*, and other manifestations of what are sometimes called *higher order* or *abstract* thinking all impose and examine relationships among statements or states of affairs. The terms I have italicized are just *words*, not different kinds of thinking. We are not doing different things when we reason, draw inferences, or solve problems; they only appear different because of the context in which they are done or the consequences of doing them.

We are constantly engaged in relational thought, in our everyday transactions of comprehending and learning about the world around us. What differs among individuals is not so much the general ability to think as the possibility of demonstrating aspects of thought on particular occasions. Three constraints bear on how well individuals can appear to think on particular occasions, none of them dependent on the acquisition of specialized or exotic skills. All of us on occasion find ourselves in situations in which we are unable to think—especially in "educational" contexts—but this is not because no one has taught us specific "thinking skills."

Constraints on Thinking

The first constraint on thinking is *prior knowledge*. Like language, thought always has a subject. And just as we cannot talk or write competently if we don't know what we are talking about, so it is not possible to demonstrate thought in any way if we don't understand what we are expected to think about. If I have difficulty understanding an article on nuclear physics, it is not because I'm unable to draw conclusions, make inferences, follow arguments, or solve problems, but because I don't know enough about nuclear physics.

The second constraint on thinking is *disposition*. Philosopher John McPeck (1981) asserts that the "judicious suspension of belief," which is his definition of critical thinking, is a disposition rather than a skill. Whether or not we take something for granted, whether we challenge other people's assertions or question our own opinions in the light of new evidence, depends on individual propensities to behave in those ways, not on the acquisition of abilities that can be developed through instruction or even practice. Dispositions can be innate, aspects of personality we are born with, or they can be the result of experience—"once bitten, twice shy."

And finally, whether or not anyone will exercise thought, particularly of the critical variety, depends on possession of the *authority* to do so. Challenging conventional thought or other people's opinions, or even drawing one's own conclusions, is not something everyone is in a position to do, certainly not in every situation. In many institutions and in many patterns of personal relations, the authority for engaging in thought of a significant nature (as opposed to accepting or providing "right answers") is not distributed equally. Thinking can upset applecarts.

Metacognition

One other topic related to thinking that receives considerable attention from educational researchers is *metacognition*—literally "cognition about cognition" or thought about our own thought. *Metacognitive processes* are presumed to take place when we think about our own thinking, for example, when we reflect on whether we know something, whether we are learning, or whether we have made a mistake.

Some researchers are inclined to regard metacognitive processes as yet another special set of skills which have to be taught and learned. On the other hand, children learn many things, including talking and much of literacy, without awareness of learning. And we are usually aware when we are confused by something, or when we don't know something at a time when some knowledge is personally relevant and important to us. Metacognition could be regarded as a newfangled label for the old-fashioned concept of "reflection."

ISSUES

There is a widespread assumption that thinking can be broken down into sets of skills—like comprehension skills or information acquisition skills—that must be taught, rather than being a natural human capacity. This is the instructional issue again, with proponents of the skills point of view arguing that children won't be able to think without specific instruction. Their opponents argue that children (and adults) simply need experience of seeing others exercising thought in various circumstances and opportunity to do the same themselves. The role of prediction in reading has also been disputed (see Notes).

The metaphorical nature of terms like scheme and script is often overlooked. The use of computers as an analogy for the brain in educational theorizing has led to a belief that schemes, scripts, and cognitive structure itself are "data" or "programs" that people must "acquire" through instruction. The alternative view is that the distillation of experience into forms that might be conceptualized as schemes or scripts is natural for humans of any age.

SUMMARY

(Terms printed in *italics* in the summaries are key terms that can be found in the glossary.)

Nonvisual information, long-term memory, and *prior knowledge* are alternative terms for describing *cognitive structure*, each individual's *theory of the world*. The theory includes *schemes*, or generalized representations of familiar settings and situations, essential in all understanding and remembering. The theory of the world is the source of *comprehension*, as we continually generate and examine possibilities about situations in real and imaginary worlds. The basis of comprehension is *prediction*, the prior elimination of unlikely alternatives. Predictions are questions that we ask, and comprehension is receiving relevant answers to those questions. If we cannot predict, we are confused. If our predictions fail, we are surprised. And if we have no interest or uncertainty as a basis for prediction, we are bored. Thinking—including *metacognition*, or "thinking about thinking"—is not a special set of skills but constant reflective activity, subject only to constraints of individual prior knowledge, disposition, and authority.

Notes to chapter 2 begin on page 240 covering:
Knowledge and constructivism
Prediction
Categories
Schemes
The narrative basis of thought
Thinking

3 Spoken and Written Language

Language, naturally, constitutes a substantial part of any person's theory of the world. It obviously plays a central role in reading. The present chapter is concerned with language from a number of perspectives, including the relationships between the sounds of speech and their meaning, between the printed marks of written language and their meaning, between productive aspects of language (talking and writing) and receptive aspects (listening and reading), and between spoken and written language. The chapter also refers briefly to grammar and to other conventions of language.

All of these aspects of language are relevant for an understanding of reading, yet each is a complex area of study in its own right. It isn't possible here to study any topic to the same theoretical depth as the professional linguist or cognitive psychologist would, but fortunately such detail is also unnecessary. The basic insights that a student of reading must grasp are relatively few and easy to explain and to demonstrate. These insights, however, are not always part of the general awareness of educators in the field of reading; they are widely disregarded in many instructional programs and materials and in a good deal of reading research, so that they may appear to be new and even unfamiliar ideas.

For example, one basic but neglected insight is that the statements that people utter or write do not convey meaning in any simple fashion. Meaning is not contained within the sounds of speech or the printed marks of writing, conveniently waiting to be extracted or decoded, but rather must be constructed by the listener or reader. As a consequence, an understanding of reading requires a more complex theory of comprehension than one that simplistically assumes that meaning takes care of itself if a reader names individual words correctly. Most of this chapter is concerned with the fundamental issue of how language is comprehended.

TWO ASPECTS OF LANGUAGE

Surface Structure and Deep Structure

There are two quite different ways of talking about language, whether spoken or written. On the one hand, you can talk about its physical aspect, about characteristics that can be measured, such as the loudness, duration, or pitch of the sounds of speech, or the number, size, or contrast of the printed marks of writing. All of these observable characteristics of language that exist in the world around us may be called *surface structure*. They are the part of language accessible through the ears and eyes. Surface structure is a useful term because it is not restricted to a particular form of language, either spoken or written. Surface structure is the "visual information" of written language—the source of information that is lost to the reader when the lights go out—but it is also a part of spoken language—the part that is lost when a telephone connection is broken.

On the other hand, there is a part of language that can neither be directly observed nor measured, and that is *meaning*. In contrast to surface structure, the meaning of language, whether spoken or written, can be referred to as *deep structure*. The term is apt. Meanings do not lie at the surface of language but far more profoundly in the minds of users of language, in the intentions of speakers and writers and in the interpretations of listeners or readers.

These two different aspects of language, the physical surface structure and the meaningful deep structure, can in fact be completely separated; it is quite possible to talk about one without reference to the other. We can say that someone is talking loudly or softly, or fast or slowly, without reference to what is being said. We can say that a line of print is five inches wide, or has eight characters to the inch, without fear that someone will contradict us by saying that we haven't understood the meaning of the text. Conversely, meaning is not directly affected by the form of the surface structure. If we are told that a certain city will host the next Olympic Games, we can't reply that it depends on whether the speaker's source of information was spoken or written. The truth of an utterance is not related to its loudness or the number of repetitions.

All of this may seem obvious, trite even, but the distinction between the surface and the deep structure of language is crucial for an understanding of reading for one simple reason: the two aspects of language are separated by a chasm. Surface and deep structures are not opposite sides of the same coin; they are not mirror reflections of each other. They are not directly and unambiguously related. In technical jargon, there is no one-to-one correspondence between the surface structure of language and meaning. Meaning lies beyond the mere sounds or printed marks of language and can't be derived from surface structure by any simple or mechanistic process.

One way of exemplifying this absence of a one-to-one relationship between the two aspects of language is by showing that differences can occur in surface structure that make no difference to meaning and that there can be differences in meaning that are not represented in surface structure (Miller, 1965). For example, here are some radically different surface structures that don't correspond to radical differences in meaning: (a) *the cat is chasing a bird*; (b) *a bird is chased by the cat*; (c) *a warm-blooded feathered vertebrate is pursued by the domesticated feline quadruped*; (d) *le chat chasse un oiseau*. Four quite different sequences of marks on paper, but all represent (in general terms at least) the same meaning. When we try to say what words mean, all we can do is offer other words (a synonym or a paraphrase) that reflect the same meaning. The actual meaning always lies beyond words. It makes sense to say that *bachelor* means (or conveys the same meaning as) *unmarried man*, but it doesn't make sense to ask what the meaning is that *bachelor* and *unmarried man* have in common. Alternative verbal definitions or descriptions simply compound the problem. They are additional surface structures.

On the other hand, it isn't difficult to find individual surface structures that have at least two possible meanings or interpretations—for example, *flying planes can be dangerous; visiting professors may be tedious; the chicken was too hot to eat; she runs through the spray and waves; he enjoys talking with old men and women* (all women?); *Cleopatra was rarely prone to talk (and Mark Antony wasn't inclined to argue).*

The examples just quoted represent a particular kind of ambiguity, namely puns. Puns are often difficult to comprehend immediately—you may not have seen at first glance the alternative meanings in all of the previous examples—and therein lies an important theoretical issue: Why are we so rarely aware of the potential ambiguity of language? It's not just puns but every possible sequence of words in our language, and just about every individual word for that matter, that is a source of potential misinterpretation. To understand why we are so rarely aware of the multiple meanings that might be attributed to surface structure of our language, we must look at a more basic question. If there is this chasm between surface structure and deep structure, how then is language comprehended in the first place? The question is of considerable relevance to reading, because if meaning isn't immediately and unambiguously given by the surface structure of speech, then there's no point in expecting a reader to "decode" written language to speech in order for comprehension to occur. Speech itself needs to be comprehended, and print can't be read aloud in a comprehensible way unless it is comprehended in the first place. Written language doesn't require decoding to sound in order to be comprehended; the manner in which we bring meaning to print is just as direct as the manner in which we understand speech. Comprehension is the same for all aspects of language. Reading aloud is more complex, and therefore more demanding, than silent reading.

The Trouble With Words

How then is language understood, whether spoken or written? The answer is not that we put together the meaning of individual words and thereby understand entire sentences. For a start, it seems doubtful whether words can be said to exist in spoken language at all. Scientific instruments can't isolate the beginning and ending of many sounds—or even words—that we hear as quite separate. The actual flow of speech is relatively continuous and smoothly changing, like the colors of a rainbow, and the segmentation into distinct sounds and words is largely something that listeners contribute. You can get some indication of this by listening carefully while you repeat the two words *west end*. You will probably find that if you introduce any pause at all in the utterance, it will be between the /s/ and the /t/—that actually you are saying *"wes tend"* rather than *"west end."* Of course, English speakers would never think that you really said *wes tend*. But that is only because they speak the language and are able to work out—and hear—the sounds you *thought* you were producing. The fact that you need to *know* a language in order to be able to *hear* it properly becomes apparent when you listen to a foreign language. Not only can you not distinguish what the distinctive sounds of the language are, you can't even distinguish the number of words in an utterance. Speakers of other languages have exactly the same trouble with English.

The very existence of words may be an artifact of the writing system. At least in writing we can provide a definition of a word—as something with a space on either side. Children learning to talk either produce groups of words that they use as one long word—*allgone, drinkamilk, gowalk, alot*—or else they use single words as entire sentences—*drink, tired, no.* Beginning readers often cannot say how many words are in a sentence, either spoken or written. They need to be experienced readers to understand the question.

Words and Meanings

Another reason why it is difficult to argue that the meanings of sentences are made up of the meanings of words is that it would appear that words often get meaning by virtue of occurring in sentences. In fact, it is difficult to see what meaning a word in isolation might have. Even nouns, which might seem the easiest class of words to account for, present difficulties. It is certainly far from true that every object has one name and every word one meaning. Every object has more than one name. The family pet, for example, can be called *an animal, a canine, a dog, a retriever, "Rover,"* and a variety of other titles, including, of course, *"family pet"* and *"that slavering brute."* What is the "real name" of the animal? There isn't one. The appropriate name for the speaker to use depends on the listener and the prior knowledge of the listener. In talking to a member of the family, the name *"Rover"* is adequate, or simply *"the dog"*; on other occasions no single word would be adequate, and the name would have to be qualified as *"that brown dog over there"* or *"the large retriever."* Everything depends on the knowledge of the listener or reader and the alternatives from among which Rover has to be distinguished. The same animal will be described in different ways to the same person depending on the characteristics of other dogs that are around. What then does a word like *dog* mean? The dictionary tells us that it is "any of a large and varied group of domesticated animals related to the fox, wolf, and jackal." But that surely is not the meaning of dog in the sentence *"Beware of the dog,"* let alone such expressions as *hot dog,*

[handwritten marginal note: More than one meaning, word, sentences provide to a context]

top dog, putting on the dog, dirty dog, dog-eared, dog tired, or *going to the dogs*.

All the common words of our language have a multiplicity of meanings, with the most common words being the most ambiguous. To test what I say, just look up a few words in the dictionary. Words that come most immediately to mind—the everyday words like *table, chair, shoe, sock, dog, field, file, take, look, go, run, raise, narrow*—require many inches and even columns of "definition." Less familiar words like *frugal, gossamer*, or *tergiversation* are disposed of in a crisp line or two. Prepositions, which are among the most common words of our language, have so many different senses that they are sometimes maligned as having "function" rather than "content." But it makes a difference whether something is in the box rather than on the box; prepositions have meanings—in great number. The linguist Fries (1945), for example, located in the *Oxford Dictionary* no fewer than 39 separate senses for *at* and *by*, 40 each for *in* and *with*, and 63 for *of*. You would surely have no difficulty in understanding my saying that I found the book by Charles Dickens by the tree by chance; I shall return it by mail by Friday—but it would be difficult for you to tell me the meaning (or meanings) of the word *by* on all or any of its five occurrences. Prepositions in context seem full of meaning, but in isolation it is impossible to say what the meaning might be. That is why it is so difficult to translate prepositions from one language to another.

It's not necessary to pursue the argument about the nature of words or their meaning, because it is quite clear that sentences aren't understood by trying to put together meanings of individual words. *The man ate the fish* and *The fish ate the man* comprise exactly the same words, yet they have quite different meanings. *A Maltese cross* is not the same as *a cross Maltese*, nor is *a Venetian blind* the same as *a blind Venetian*. A house that is pretty ugly is not exactly ugly but is certainly not pretty. Obviously, the words in all these examples don't combine in any simple fashion to form the meaning of the whole.

Perhaps then word order is the key—the word *cross* has one meaning before *Maltese* and another meaning after it. But words in the same position can represent different meanings—compare the final words of *She went down the drive* and *She went for a drive*—and words in different positions in a sentence may reflect the same meaning. Words that often seem to have a similar meaning, such as *look* and *see* may suddenly acquire quite different meanings when an identical prefix is added, as in *overlook* and *oversee*.

A common explanation is that grammar makes the difference; syntax (word order) is the bridge between the surface structure of language and its deep structure. But the problem with this point of view is that often it is impossible to say what a word's grammatical function is before the sentence in which it occurs is understood. Formal grammar, of the kind often taught in school, is a *descriptive* grammar. It never helps anyone to say anything or to understand what anyone else is saying. It is simply a way of talking about surface structure. Grammar, in other words, doesn't reveal meaning; meaning must precede grammatical analysis. Consider again the familiar words that I have been citing like *table, chair, shoe, sock, file, dog, field, take, go*, and so forth; these are all words that not only have a multiplicity of meanings but also a variety of grammatical functions. To ask anyone to identify such words when they are written in isolation is pointless because they can commonly be both noun and adjective, or noun and verb, or adjective and verb, or perhaps all three. How do we understand a simple statement like *Open the empty bottle*? It is not by taking into account the fact that *open* is a verb and *empty* an adjective, because in the equally comprehensible sentence *Empty the open bottle*, the two words switch grammatical roles without any difference in surface structure. This complicated ambiguity of language is one reason it is difficult to program computers to translate language or make abstracts, even when they are equipped with a "dictionary" and a "grammar." Computers lack the knowledge of the world that is required to make sense of language. Thus, a computer is befuddled by over a dozen different possible meanings of a simple expression like *time flies*. Is *time* a noun, or a verb (as in *time the racehorses*), or an adjective (like the word *fruit* in *fruit flies*)? Is *flies* a noun or a verb? A computer is said to have interpreted *out of sight, out of mind* as *invisible and insane*.

Not only is it impossible to state the grammatical function of individual words outside of a meaningful context, it can also be impossible to state the grammatical structure of entire sentences without prior understanding of their meaning. Most English teachers would parse *The onions are planted by the farmer* as a passive sentence, because it contains the three grammatical markers of the passive form—the auxiliary *are*, the participle ending *-ed*, and the preposition *by*. But the sentence *The onions are planted by the tree* is not a passive sentence, although its surface structure would appear to contain the appropriate three grammatical markers. Meaning determines the grammatical structure of these sentences, not the surface structure markers. In fact, *The onions are planted* *by the farmer* need not be a passive sentence, because it is just as ambiguous grammatically as *She was seated by the minister*; the grammar depends on the meaning.

In other words—and this must be the answer to the question at the beginning of this section—there is only one way in which language can be understood, that print can be comprehended, and that is by having meaning brought to it.

Comprehension Through Prediction

The statement that language is understood by having meaning brought to it shouldn't be taken to imply that any particular utterance or sentence can mean anything. Usually there would be some broad general agreement about the main implications of statements, at least when they are made in real-world situations. If someone in an elevator remarks "It's raining outside," few people would want to claim that it could mean that the streets are dry. And by the same argument, the meanings that listeners and readers bring to language can't be wild guesses; the usual broad general agreement about implications makes the reckless attribution of meaning unlikely as well. If most people seem to be in agreement about the kind of meaning that can be attributed to a particular sequence of words, then some explanation must be found as to why such agreement exists.

The explanation that can be offered should not be unfamiliar. Language tends to be understood in the same way on similar occasions because listeners or readers must have a pretty good idea about the meaning that was intended in the first place. To be more precise, meaning is brought to language through prediction, which you will remember from the previous chapter means the prior elimination of unlikely alternatives. Prediction doesn't mean staking everything on one wild guess (which would indeed run the risk of frequent error), nor does it mean that the precise meaning is known in advance (which would of course make attention to language unnecessary in the first place). Prediction simply means that uncertainty in the listener or reader is limited to a few probable alternatives, and provided that information can be found in the surface structure of the utterance to dispose of the remaining doubt—to indicate which predicted alternative is appropriate—then comprehension occurs.

Prediction is the reason we aren't normally overwhelmed by the possible number of alternatives in language; there are actually very few alternatives in our minds at any time that we are comprehending what is being said. And prediction is the reason we are so rarely aware of ambiguity: We expect what the writer or speaker is likely to say and just don't contemplate alternative interpretations. We interpret *The thieves decided to head for the bank* in one way if we know they were sitting in a car and in another way if they were swimming in a river. When language is comprehended, the recipient is usually no more aware of possible ambiguity than the producer. The first interpretation that comes to us is the one that makes the most sense to us at the particular time, and alternative and less likely interpretations will not be considered unless subsequent interpretations fail to be consistent or to make sense, in which case we realize our probable error and try to recapitulate. One interpretation usually satisfies us, provided it makes sense, so we don't waste time looking for a second. This is the reason that puns may be difficult to see, and also why they may be mildly irritating. We don't expect to find more than one meaning for the same sequence of words.

As I indicated in the previous chapter, there is nothing remarkable or particularly clever about this process of prediction; it goes on all the time. Prediction enables us to make sense of all the events in our daily lives. And we are no more aware of our predictions when we read than we are at any other time for the simple reason that our predictions are usually so good. We are rarely surprised because our predictions rarely let us down, even when we read a book for the first time.

What exactly do we predict when we read? The fundamental answer is meaning, although of course we may look at particular words to find evidence that will confirm or disconfirm particular interpretations. In other words, we look for sense. A number of detailed predictions may be made and tested simultaneously—and constantly modified—as we make our way through the text. Every specific prediction, however, no matter how detailed and transient, will be derived from our more general expectations about where the text as a whole might be leading.

Some Practical Implications

The preceding discussion should make it clear that it is misleading if not inaccurate to regard reading as a matter of "following the text" or to say that a listener "follows" the meaning of a speaker. Language is understood by keeping ahead of the incoming detail. By having some expectation of what the speaker or writer is likely to say, by making use of what we know already, we protect ourselves against being overwhelmed by irrelevant information. We avoid the confusion of ambiguity and succeed in bridging the gap between the surface structure of the text and the writer's intention.

It is easy to demonstrate how we keep ahead of any words that we identify as we read. Ask a friend to turn out the light while you read aloud, so that you are suddenly deprived of visual information, and you will find that your voice is able to continue "reading" another four or five words. Your eyes were a second or more ahead of the point your voice had reached when the lights went out. This phenomenon is known as the *eye–voice span*, a term that is rather misleading because it might suggest that we need more than a second to organize in speech the sounds of the particular word that we are looking at. But this is incorrect. We don't need a second to identify a word; the difference in time is not so much a reflection of how far thought lags behind the eye as of how far thought is ahead of the voice. We use our eyes to scout ahead so that we can make decisions about meaning, and thus about individual words, in advance. Indeed, the eye–voice span exists only when we can make sense of what we read. If we read nonsense— *dog lazy the over jumps fox quick the* rather than *The quick brown fox jumps over the lazy dog*—then eye and voice tend to converge on the same point, and the eye–voice span disappears. The span, in fact, reflects rather precisely the sense that we make of text, because it tends to extend to the end of a meaningful phrase. The four- or five-word span is merely an average. If the lights go out just as we are about to read ... *and drove off into the night*, we are likely to continue aloud as far as *off* or as far as *night*, but not stop at *into* or *the*.

It is because a reader must keep ahead of the text that it is so hard for children to learn to read from material that doesn't make sense to them or is so disconnected and fragmentary that prediction is impossible. Reading is similarly much more difficult for children who have been taught that they should get the words right rather than try to make sense of what is being read. Not only is "getting the words right" harder and slower unless meaning is brought to the text in the first place, identifying each successive word on the line one after the other will not, in itself, give meaning. Reading is never a matter of decoding the surface structure of print to the surface structure of speech; the sounds will not make sense of their own accord.

The difficulty of many high school "problem readers" is not that they have failed over the years to learn how to sound out words correctly, nor that they are careless about getting every word right, but rather that they read one word at a time as if meaning should be the last concern. They expect that meaning will take care of itself, although this is the reverse of the way in which sense is made of reading.

WHY WRITTEN AND SPOKEN LANGUAGE DIFFER

Obviously, spoken language and written language are not the same. It is not difficult to detect when a speaker reads from a prepared text or when a passage that we read is the unedited transcription of spontaneous talk. Speech and print aren't different languages—they share a common vocabulary and the same grammatical structures—but they have different conventions for using vocabulary and grammar. It shouldn't be considered surprising or anomalous that differences exist between spoken and written language; they are generally used for different purposes and addressed to different audiences. The way we talk always varies depending on the reason we are talking and the circumstances we are in, and the same variation occurs with written language.

Written language is different from spoken language for the good reason that spoken language has adapted itself to being heard but written language is more appropriately read. Written language is not made more comprehensible by being translated into "speech."

The Specialization of Language

To understand why such a specialized adaptation of spoken and written language might have come about, consider the different demands the two aspects of language make on their recipients. There is, for example, the obvious fact that the spoken word dies the moment it is uttered and can only be recaptured if held in the listener's fallible memory or as the result of a good deal of mutual inconvenience as the speaker recapitulates. Even tape recording does little to mitigate the essential transience of speech in contrast to the facile way in which the eyes can move forward (and backward) through a written text. The reader has control over time, can decide which parts of the text to attend to, the order in which they will be selected, and the amount of time that will be spent on them. In other words, spoken language may make considerable demands on attention which written language does not.

On the other hand, written language might seem to place a far greater burden on memory—on what we already know about language and the world—than our everyday speech. To bring meaning to spoken language, all we need consider may be the circumstances in which an utterance is made. Much of our everyday spoken language is directly related to the immediate situation in which it is uttered. We may pay little attention to the actual words the speaker is using. The relevance of the utterance is as ephemeral as the words themselves—"Pass the salt, please"—and there is little involvement of memory. Written language, by contrast, generally depends on nothing but what we can and do remember.

There is the question of how the meaning of language is verified: How do we confirm that information we are receiving is likely to be true, that it makes sense, or that we are understanding it correctly? What is the source of the predictions that can cut through all the ambiguity inherent in language so that we make the most reasonable and reliable interpretation? For the kind of everyday spoken language I have been talking about, the answer is simple: Look around. Any uncertainty we have can probably be removed by what we know already of the speaker's nature, interests, and likely intentions. Anyone who asks "Pass the salt" is probably looking at the salt. But the language of texts offers no such shortcuts. There is only one final recourse if we aren't sure of what we have read, and that is to return to the text itself. For verification, for disambiguation, and to avoid error, a difficult and possibly unfamiliar kind of ability is required. That is the ability to pursue a line of thought, looking for internal consistencies, and evaluating arguments. Both the source and the test of many of the changing predictions that are necessary for the comprehension of written language must lie in the text itself, informed by the more general expectations that readers bring from their prior knowledge. The text determines what the actual alternatives might be and whether they have been successfully predicted. For that reason alone, spoken language and written language can rarely be the same.

A Different Difference in Language

The previous section began by considering some fairly obvious differences between spoken and written language. But it quickly became necessary to acknowledge that the general distinctions being made were between a particular kind of speech, the "everyday spoken language directly related to the situation in which it is uttered," and a particular kind of written language, namely, that of "texts." To present the complete picture I must now explain that there is another distinction that slices right across the spoken–written dimension.

The issue basically concerns how the spoken or written words are selected and organized in the first place. Obviously words are rarely produced at random. There is usually a necessity or reason for every word we use, related in part to the intention we want to fulfill and to the language with which we propose to fulfill it. Both of these considerations, the reason for saying something and the linguistic vehicle we select for saying it, place considerable constraints on what we say and write. But there is a third important constraint, the one with which I am at present most concerned, and that is the environment in which the language is produced. To use language rather arbitrarily myself for the moment, I shall use the term *situation* to refer to the physical environment in which words are produced—the position in which you are standing when you say something or the location in which written words happen to be written or printed—and I shall use the word *context* to refer to the language environment in which spoken or written words occur. The context for the word *context* in the previous sentence, for example, is all the other words in that sentence and in the chapter as a whole. A distinction must be made between *situation-dependent* and *context-dependent* language.

Situation-dependent speech is the spoken language with which infants first become familiar, and it is the basis on which they begin all their learning about language. By situation-dependent I mean that the speech is directly related to the physical and social situation in which it is uttered. If someone says "Pass the salt, please," then there is likely to be some salt around, a person who would like some salt, and another person in a position to pass it. If someone says "It's raining again," then the streets are likely to be wet. Given the physical situation and the speaker's intentions, it would not be possible to say anything much different, like "It's raining again," if the speaker really wanted the salt passed, or vice versa.

The fact that such speech and the situation in which it is uttered (including the speaker's intentions) are closely related is the basis of children's language learning. It is the way in which language is first comprehended and verified. Normally we think that such language describes the situation in which it occurs. We hear someone say "Pass the salt, please," and we can construct the probable cast of characters and the major props, even if we can't see what is going on. But the clues also work in the other direction; the situation can make sense of the language. A child who doesn't yet understand what "Pass the salt, please" means can work it out from the situation in which the language is uttered. Indeed, if someone actually said "It's raining again," and another person passed the speaker the salt, then the child might assume that "It's raining again" meant "Pass the salt."

This strategy of using the situation for clues to how unfamiliar language works is not uncommon. We all tend to use the strategy when confronted by someone speaking a foreign language or in any other situation when we don't understand what is being said. If the waiter says something incomprehensible, we look to see if we are being offered the menu, the wine, or the bill. Because most of the meaning and the verification of such language rests in the particular situation in which it is uttered, it tends to be elliptical and brief—"Coffee?" "Thanks"—without much evident grammar about it.

Just as there is a good deal of situation-dependent spoken language in the environment of most children, who use it to make their first sense of speech, so there is a good deal of situation-dependent *written* language in most contemporary environments, which children can again employ to make sense of reading. I am referring now to the written language of signs and labels, the ubiquitous language that we find on every product we buy, festooned around every store, on every wrapper, on every street sign, and as part of every television commercial. We do not have a convenient word in our language for such situation-dependent writing, so I refer to it as *ambient* print. It functions in exactly the same way as situation-dependent speech, because it is also closely tied to the situation in which it occurs. The situation provides learners with a clue to its meaning, and it can't be arbitrarily changed or moved without losing its sense. The word *toothpaste* tells the reader what is in the tube and the contents of the tube tell the learner what the printed word is likely to be. Indeed, some children think the printed word *Crest* says toothpaste just as they may think that the sign *McDonald's* says hamburgers. (And the advertisers of Crest and McDonald's will tell you that these are indeed what their brand names are supposed to say.) Certainly a child who finds he is brushing his teeth with shampoo or that she has poured herself a bowl of detergent doesn't need an adult to point out the reading error. If you don't understand what the sign or label means, look at the situation in which it occurs. Like situation-dependent speech, ambient print is tied to where it occurs. The sign *Exit* can't be moved to the middle of the wall because we are tired of seeing it over the door. Like situation-dependent speech, such print tends to be elliptical and independent of grammar. The situation takes the place of complexity of language.

Quite different from the situation-dependent written language of signs and labels, however, is the continuous written language of texts, of books, magazines, newspapers, and every kind of reference material. This language is more complex and has to be. It doesn't derive or convey its meaning from the situation in which it occurs; its location offers no clues to its sense. If you don't understand something in a newspaper or novel, it won't help you to look at where the text is located in the room or into the face of the person who gave it to you. The appropriate meaning of the text remains constant, whether you look at it now in the room or an hour later in the street. It can't be elliptical. It is grammatically complex.

Despite this independence from the specific location in which it is produced and read, however, there is just as much necessity about the written language of texts as there is about situation-dependent writing and speech. The writer is still not free to produce words arbitrarily or at random. A writer can't decide to make the next word *rhinoceros* or *platitudinous* just because it is a long time since these words were last used. Now, however, the constraints on the words are determined by just two things: the topic that the writer is talking about (what the writer wants to say) and the language the writer is employing (how the writer wants to say it). In other words, all of the constraints on what is written occur within the context of the language itself. That's why I call such language *context dependent*. Not only does the intricate texture of a written context give every component word its meaning, but because of the redundancy in the text, it is usually possible to replace a word that has been left out or to work out the meaning of an unfamiliar word.

For anyone learning to read, the ability to make use of contextual clues to meaning is crucial. But the clues embedded in the immediate language environment of context-dependent writing are not the same as those in situation-dependent writing (which is one reason why children who have essential insights into reading from ambient print may still have difficulty with continuous text). Nor are the clues of context-dependent writing those of situation-dependent speech (which is one reason why being read to is such an enormous advantage in learning to read).

The particular requirements of context-dependent writing have so impressed some theorists (Goody & Watt, 1972; Havelock, 1976; Olson, 1977) that they have argued that written language has introduced a whole new mode of thought to our basic human repertoire of intellectual skills. But context-dependent written language is not unique. Not all our spoken language is of the "everyday," situationally verifiable kind that has been discussed. Some of our spoken language can be as abstract, argumentative, and unrelated to the circumstances in which it is comprehended as an article in a scientific journal. There is also context-dependent speech. "Academic language" is a particular variety of this detached way of talking. Experience in reading makes it possible for us to understand abstract spoken language, which in its form is more like writing than everyday speech. But the contrary also applies; by hearing such speech, a child becomes better equipped to read.

THE ORGANIZATION OF TEXTS

Texts are not all written in the same way, even if they are written differently from the way spoken language is produced. Instead, different kinds of text are organized and presented in distinctive and characteristic ways. Each kind of text has its own conventions of layout, typography, and style—called *genre schemes*—which distinguish it from other genres or kinds of text. Novels don't have the same genre schemes as textbooks, poems, newspapers, letters, or telephone directories. E-mails and web sites have developed their own genre schemes. Furthermore, various kinds of text may have quite different genre schemes in different cultures. Newspapers or novels produced in France for French readers aren't written and presented in the same way as those for readers elsewhere. Often we can *see* that texts are different from culture to culture, even though we can't read the language. There is nothing particularly logical or necessary about specific genre schemes—they could be different, as they usually are from one culture to another—but they have become conventional where they are employed, and they serve their purposes because they are conventional.

Genre schemes help both readers and writers. Their characteristic forms help readers by giving them a basis for predicting what a text will be like, that a novel will be constructed in a particular way, that a scientific article will follow a certain format, that a letter will observe typical conventions. Readers become so accustomed to the genre schemes of the texts with which they are familiar that they assume they are natural, inevitable, and universal. A text that is produced differently in a different culture may be regarded as odd. Genre schemes also help writers (if they know them), because they provide a framework for organizing what writers want to say and more importantly for anticipating and respecting what readers are likely to expect. Genre schemes facilitate communication.

Similarly, every kind of text, and every form of spoken-language interaction, too, has characteristic internal relationships, called *discourse structures*, which are again largely arbitrary and accidental but which serve their purposes because they are conventional. Discourse structures in conversation tell us when we may interrupt (at the end of a sentence) and when we may not; they protect speakers from interruption while allowing others the opportunity to take a turn. In written language, readers can expect writers to observe conventional discourse structures and writers can expect readers to understand them. The structures form another basis for prediction. The manner in which chapters and paragraphs are arranged in books is a matter of discourse structure.

Even stories have their conventions, whether they are spoken or written. These conventional ways of telling a story, of relating sequences of events, are known as *story grammars*. They are the framework upon which various characters, plots, motives, and resolutions are linked in related episodes and represented in ways that will be intelligible. If a story makes sense to us, if it *sounds* like a story, this is not just because the story is told in an appropriate way but also because we know the appropriate way in which stories are told, at least in our culture. Stories must reflect the story schemes with which readers are familiar, if writers and readers are to connect.

The important function served for readers by all these conventional and characteristic structures of texts is underlined by evidence that the structures are the basis of our comprehension of texts. If we don't know the relevant structures, then we won't understand the text, or our reading of it will be distorted. Researchers have noted that readers' comprehension of texts is similar to the structures in the text itself. Ask people to recapitulate what they have read in a story, and they will tend to do so with the same structural form as the story rather than with the same words or even "their own" words. Novice readers have been shown to insert into their retelling of stories conventional aspects that have been omitted in the telling but that are part of their own story grammars. They put more into the story than was in it originally, because this is their way of making sense of stories.

It is also the structures in the head rather than those in the text that determine our *memory* for texts; they are the forms in which texts are remembered. Discourse structures and story grammars are part of our own cognitive structure, part of the way we organize our knowledge of the world (and therefore a reason that reading is important—it provides us with new frameworks for perceiving the world and organizing experience). The more we can anticipate and employ the formal structures that an author uses, the more we can understand and remember what we read, because the structures also form the basis of our understanding and remembering. And the more an author knows and respects the structures that the reader will predict, the more the text will be readable and memorable.

None of this is new. The British psychologist Frederick Bartlett (1932) demonstrated experimentally more than 70 years ago that the way stories are interpreted and remembered varies with the cultural backgrounds and expectations of their readers and listeners. Who would expect otherwise? But experiments and theoretical work into these matters demonstrate convincingly what in the past has perhaps been only intuitively obvious (or should have been intuitively obvious).

Two brief qualifications must be added. First, the structures of texts should be seen as the basis for comprehension but not for comprehension itself. Some researchers assume that we have understood a story if we can repeat large parts of it. But comprehension is less a matter of being able to reproduce the facts in a text than of what one is able to do as a consequence of interacting with the text. You don't prove that you have understood anything by repeating it. Second, these structures that can be observed and analyzed in the organization of texts aren't structures that require our conscious attention. We don't need to be able to talk about a particular grammatical construction or other convention in order to understand and use it. The knowledge that enables us to make sense of the world and of language is not knowledge of which we are aware, even if we are psychologists or linguists.

There is no evidence that making text structures explicit improves comprehension, or that teaching such structures explicitly to children helps them understand. In fact, without the prior understanding, such "explanations" are themselves meaningless. Children learn the structures by being helped to understand the texts in which the structures are employed.

THE CONVENTIONS OF LANGUAGE

There is one final characteristic of language, both spoken and written, situation-dependent and context-dependent, that I must emphasize. It is that all language is conventional. *Semiotics*—an area of study that interests a number of reading researchers—is specifically concerned with the nature of all different kinds of communicative conventions, their use, and how they develop. This is an enormous topic with multiple ramifications, but I must try to deal with it briefly, first by explaining what it means to say that all language is conventional, then why the statement is critical.

All language is conventional in the sense that every aspect of language is a matter of chance and of mutual respect. All the various forms of language must work, they must fulfill a function, but the nature of the forms themselves is always arbitrary, a matter of historical accident; they could always be different. There is no particular logic or necessity about the specific forms employed in any of the 6,000 or more different languages that exist in the world. That is what the word "conventional" means, arbitrary forms that could be different, functioning in the way they do because their form is mutually respected among the users of each language.

The use of red to mean stop in traffic signs is a matter of convention. The convention works because it is mutually accepted that red should mean stop (in those cultures where red means stop). But things could have worked out differently. Green could mean stop tomorrow, provided everyone agreed on the change. In some cultures, in certain circumstances, it is a mark of respect to remove your hat. In other cultures, the mark of respect is to keep it on. What makes removing your hat (or putting it on) a mark of respect has nothing to do with the act itself but with the mutual understanding that this is how the act is to be interpreted, the intention that it reflects.

Every aspect of language is conventional, starting from the very sounds and meanings of words we use. In English, *yes* means *yes*, but this is only a convention. *No* could mean *yes*. In other languages, other words mean *yes*. The same applies to all the words in every language. No one has a free choice with words. No one can call anything something different from everyone else in their language community, not if they want to be understood.

Words are conventional, and so is grammar. Different languages have different grammatical structures and there is nothing more logical or rational or efficient about one grammar than another. All languages solve the same kind of problems, but they solve them in different ways. I have already noted that story grammars, discourse structures, and genre schemes are conventions. They could be different, they are different in different languages and cultures, and they function despite their arbitrary nature because they are all matters of mutual agreement among the people who employ them.

There is an enormous range of conventions in language, many of which have not yet been mentioned. For example, there are the conventions of *idiom*. Language is far more than grammar and vocabulary (although a good deal of instruction in reading, in English, and in other languages, seems to assume that this is what language consists of). Knowledge of grammar and vocabulary gives no one a mastery of language, either in producing or in understanding it. By

far the greatest part of any language, the "working" part of it, is idiom, the way people actually speak, and by definition idiom can't be
accounted for by vocabulary and grammar. Idiom is the way words
in the vocabulary and structures in the grammar are actually used
in a particular language community, and this usage is a complex
and constantly changing system of conventions. Idioms usually
can't be translated word for word from one language to another.

There are conventions of *cohesion*. Speech doesn't consist of
one statement after another, and paragraphs are more than a simple succession of sentences. Statements and sentences are inter-
locked; they cohere. I can say "*I looked for John. But he had
gone*" but not "*But he had gone. I looked for John.*" I would have
to change the sentences to something like "*John had gone. I
looked for him.*" The pronoun and the *but* are two of a number of
cohesive devices that lock sentences together in English, but they
are conventions because different languages cohere in different
ways. You can't change the order of sentences in any language
without having to change the sentences themselves, at least not in
meaningful text. (This is a useful way of finding out whether material prepared for beginning readers is meaningful. If the order of
sentences can be arbitrarily changed without anyone noticing the
difference, then they don't make sense; they aren't normally functioning language.)

There are tremendously subtle and intricate conventions of
language, both spoken and written, concerned with *register*. This
term refers to the fact that you must choose and put your words
together differently depending on the subject you are talking
about, the person you are talking to, and the circumstances in
which you are talking. You can't speak a language unless you employ the forms of vocabulary, grammar, idiom, and cohesion appropriate to the relevant register. Children quickly learn they
must speak in one way to younger children, another way to their
peers, another way to teachers, and another way to other adults.
All of the differences of register are conventional; there is no intrinsic logic about the particular form that comes to be appropriate at a particular time. You can't carry your own conventions of
language with you when you travel, not if you want to understand
and be understood. Not even the nonverbal conventions of language, like how close you should stand to another person in conversation or how long you should look someone directly in the
eye, are consistent from one culture to another.

Written language has its own substantial set of conventions.
There are conventions of spelling, punctuation, letter formation,

the size of handwriting or type, capitalization, paragraphing, page layout, and bookbinding—and in e-mails and web chat. All of these could be different, and all of them are, in other languages, other cultures. Every aspect of language is conventional.

Why should I bother to point all this out? Because it is important to understand that language isn't just vocabulary and grammar. Familiarity with written language conventions is essential for readers and writers because conventions make prediction possible. The forms of particular conventions can't be predicted; they vary by chance or historical accident from one language community to another, and they also change with time. But knowledge of what to expect makes the conventions that will be used on particular occasions predictable. To be able to read a text, we must be able to anticipate the conventions that its writer will employ. This understanding of the appropriate conventions, together with prior knowledge related to the subject matter, is the essential contribution of readers to the act of reading. But the understanding must be mutual. To be comprehensible, the writer must anticipate and respect the conventions that the reader will predict. Conventions are the common currency of every language transaction.

There is a tendency to think of language as "logical," as "rational," even as if it could be in our genes. But language is enormously complex, and all of its complexity is arbitrary and accidental. It could all be different. The implication of this is that no one ever learns language by sitting down and thinking about it, by anticipating what it will be like, or even by learning a few rules. Learning a language or learning to read involves learning a tremendous number of conventions. And these can't be learned by rule or by rote, nor are they instinctive in any way. They must be experienced, one at a time, in ways that are most meaningful for every learner.

There is one other important implication of the conventional nature of language. It is that language is *social* in all its aspects. Language does things for *people*, and its particular conventions—the way it does things—are matters of social contract and social identification. We talk the way people around us talk—provided we can identify with that kind of person. We use language in the ways that it is used by the people around us, again provided we don't see ourselves as different from them. Above and beyond all the technical aspects of reading discussed in this book and in many other books on the same topic, reading is a social activity, learned (or not learned) in a social rather than an intellectual context.

Language About Language

An interesting question about all the complexities of language that I have discussed in this chapter concerns how much they need to be consciously known by a learner. Is it necessary for beginning readers to be *instructed* in the difference between surface structure and meaning, in the fine points of grammar, or in all the other essential conventions of language, both spoken and written? Should they be able to talk about language as well as be able to use it?

There is a special word for language about language—the word is *metalanguage*. In a general sense, this entire chapter has been written in metalanguage, because it has been on the topic of language. More specifically, there are a number of *metalinguistic* terms that are frequently central to any discussion involving language—terms like *noun, verb, word, syllable, phrase,* and *sentence.*

The word *metalanguage* may remind you of the word *metacognition*, which was introduced in chapter 2. Metacognition is thinking (or language) about thinking, just as metalanguage is language (or thinking) about language. And there is a controversy in psychology and educational research about how important ability in both metacognition and metalanguage is for learning to read and to write.

Some researchers argue that children must be aware of their own learning processes and able to talk about specific aspects of spoken and written language, if they are to learn to read. Downing (1979), for example, asserted that children who don't have metalinguistic competence are in a state of "cognitive confusion" when someone tries to teach them about reading. (Downing himself uses technical metacognitive language here. Instead of saying that children may be "in a state of cognitive confusion," he could simply describe them as "confused.") Other theorists argue that children are obviously capable of learning without being able to talk about learning—how else would babies learn to talk in the first place? We have all learned many things in our lives without being able to talk about what we were learning or, indeed, being aware at the time that we were learning. Many people can read and write phrases and paragraphs without being able to provide a linguistic definition for them or to parse a sentence.

As for being able to understand the language of language, it is also evident that many people learn to read without understanding the meaning of many metalinguistic terms. Indeed, terms like *word, sentence, comma,* and *period* have no meaning until we can read. They are not parts of spoken language, certainly not in any direct or conspicuous way. Like Molière's *bourgeois gentilhomme* we all speak prose without knowing we are doing so until someone points it out to us (and explains the technical meaning of the word).

Why then should knowledge of metalinguistic terminology be thought to be so critical in reading instruction? The explanation seems to be that children need to understand what teachers are talking about, and if teachers find it necessary to use metalinguistic or metacognitive language, then children are in difficulty if they don't understand such language themselves. Cognitive confusion is caused by instruction that is not comprehensible. Whether it is essential for classroom teachers to employ the abstract technical language of linguistics and other specialized disciplines in teaching reading is another matter.

ISSUES

Many of the topics in this chapter are subject to endless dispute among specialists—including the nature of language, the role of grammar, and the meaning of meaning. Such issues have resisted solution or agreement for over 2,000 years, and there are no reasonable grounds for believing they can ever be resolved. The issues are abstract and need have little bearing on the teaching of reading. More central is the controversy over the "relationship" of written to spoken language, which comes up frequently in this book. Some people regard written language as "parasitical" on speech, or "unnatural" in some other way. Historical, linguistic, or philosophical speculation is unlikely to settle the arguments, and the convictions of various specialists reflect faith rather than infallibility. Another matter of preference rather than evidence concerns the nature of metalinguistic discourse (is language about language any different from language about anything else?) and its role in instruction.

SUMMARY

The sounds of language and the *visual information* of print are *surface structures* of language that do not represent meaning directly. Meaning resides in the *deep structure* of language, in the intentions of speakers and writers, and in the interpretations of listeners and readers. Written language and spoken language are not the same, and language also differs to the extent that it is *situation-dependent* or *context-dependent*. The basis of comprehension is prediction, made possible by the complex conventional nature of language.

Notes to chapter 3 begin on page 245 covering:

Surface structure and deep structure

Semiotics

Discourse and genre

Text organization and comprehension

Some technical terms

Speech, writing, and "language"

More about words

4 Information and Experience

If reading is a natural activity, then literacy education should obviously center on aspects of reading that are most natural to us. The most natural activity for human beings is to engage in interesting *experience*, the absence of which leads to boredom and withdrawal. But experience is not a topic that has much currency in education, except for the absurd suggestion that some students don't do as well as others because they haven't had many experiences. Instead the focus is on the *information* students are supposed to acquire. And the deliberate acquisition of information is *not* a particularly natural activity. People usually accumulate information without trying, in the course of engaging in interesting experiences. The interest is always in the experience, rather than in the information. The intentional acquisition of information, especially at the arbitrary behest of others, is one of the most tedious and unnatural activities anyone can engage in.

Louise Rosenblatt made the crucial distinction as long ago as 1978. She says there are two ways to read—for information or for experience—and it is easy to tell the difference between the two. When information is what we want, we are perfectly content to get it in any way we can. No one ever says, "Don't tell me that telephone

55

number, I want the pleasure of looking it up for myself." But when we read for experience, said Rosenblatt, we are reluctant to be deprived of even a moment. I can't imagine anyone saying "I can't be bothered to read the last chapter—tell me if the butler did it." Often we slow down as we near the end of a novel, as we might at the end of a good meal, to protract the experience.

The distinction between information and experience is usually disregarded in education. Books or other texts that should be read for experience are treated only as sources of information. Rosenblatt said this is because it is easier to grade readers on the information they might be expected to acquire than on the experience they might enjoy. She satirized such an approach in an article entitled "What Facts Does This Poem Teach You?" (Rosenblatt, 1980).

It is often said that we live in an "information age"—but the word *information* is used very loosely. Usually it is taken to be synonymous with "facts" or "data." Despite its vagueness and ambiguity, the word has become ubiquitous in education. Reading and learning are both referred to as "the acquisition of information" and writing (and teaching) as its "transmission." But this is a vacuous misuse of the word information.

Information has been given a precise technical definition that most people in education are not aware of, although it has enabled some aspects of reading to be accurately measured. I shall use the word in this strict technical sense when I examine how the visual system solves complex problems of identifying letters and words in print. On the other hand, the widespread use of the word in a more general sense in educational and psychological research—for example, in the characterization of the brain as an "information-processing device"—distorts rather than facilitates efforts to understand literacy and learning. And information, when the word is used in a more general sense, can't be measured.

First, I examine the technical definition of information and its relationship to another general term that can also be used technically in a very precise sense—*uncertainty*. I also look at how information can be related to comprehension and to another important concept in reading, *redundancy*. I then refer to some limitations on the way in which individuals can make use of information and also on the contrast between information and experience.

INFORMATION AND UNCERTAINTY

We shouldn't expect to be able to measure information the way we measure height and weight. Information can be found in a multitude of guises—in marks on paper, facial expressions and other bodily gestures, the configuration of clouds, trees (and sometimes tea leaves), and in the sounds of speech. Obviously sources of information do not have much in common, and neither do the channels through which information passes.

Consider the mutations of information when we listen to a broadcast recording of someone talking. What we hear begins as an intention in the speaker's mind, represented in some deeply mysterious way in the flux of chemical and bioelectrical activities in the structures of the brain. This intention is then translated into bursts of neural energy, dispatched from the brain at different times, rates, and directions to the musculature of the jaw, mouth, lips, tongue, vocal cords, and chest, orchestrating the expulsion of breath in such a manner that distinctive pressure waves of contrasting intensity and frequency radiate through the surrounding atmosphere. These fleeting disturbances in the molecules of the air cause the tiny diaphragm of a microphone to resonate in sympathy, triggering a flow of electrical energy along a wire quite unlike the corresponding patterns of neural energy in the nervous systems of the speaker or listener. Amplified and modulated, the electrical impulses from the microphone impress subtle combinations of magnetic forces onto a plastic tape or etch wavy lines into a plastic disk, often after being "digitized." Through further mechanical and electronic incarnations, the information may then be diffused by radio transmission (perhaps diverting through the transistors of earth-orbiting satellites) before being reconstituted by an electronic receiver and loudspeaker into airborne pressure waves that lap against the listener's ear. And still the transformations are not done. The oscillations of the eardrum are conveyed to another resonating membrane across a tiny bridge of three articulating bones—the hammer, the anvil, and the stirrup of the listener's inner ear. And then, perhaps most bizarrely, a pressure wave pulses back and forth through liquid in the coiling canals of the inner ear, a labyrinth carved into the skull itself, where microscopic hair cells wave like reeds with the movement of the fluid in which they are contained. The roots of these fronds are the tiny beginnings of the mighty auditory nerve, and they generate the final relays of neural impulses that travel the hundreds of thousands of separate fibers of the auditory nerve, through half a dozen booster and transformer stations in various recesses of the brain, to become at last subjective experiences of meaningfulness and sound. And this meaningfulness of acoustic events can be congruent with a subjective meaningfulness and visual experience from perhaps the same

words written down and reaching the brain by a completely different route through the eyes. How can all or even part of this complexity be identified and evaluated as "information"?

On Making Decisions

The technical answer is that information can be evaluated by looking at what it enables the "receiver"—the listener or the reader—to
do. Information enables a person to make decisions, to choose
among alternative possibilities or competing courses of action. Information can be assessed, not from its source or from the various
forms that it can take during transmission, but from what it enables the receiver to do. Reading requires decisions, whether by a
child striving to understand a brief story or by a scholar struggling
to decipher an obscure medieval text. And anything that helps a
reader to make a decision is information.

Put into other words again, *information reduces uncertainty*.
The change of focus from the facilitation of decisions to the reduction of uncertainty may not seem to be much of a conceptual gain,
but it permits information to be measured, or at least estimated
comparatively. Information can't be quantified directly, any more
than the size or weight of a decision can be calculated directly. But
it is possible to put a number to uncertainty and thus indirectly to
the amount of information that eliminates or reduces that uncertainty. The trick is accomplished by defining uncertainty in terms
of the number of alternatives confronting the decision maker. If
you are confronted by a lot of alternatives, you have a great deal of
uncertainty; there are many different decisions you could make. If
you have fewer alternatives, it may be just as hard for you to make
up your mind but theoretically your uncertainty is less; there are
fewer alternative decisions you might make. The argument has
nothing to do with the importance of the decisions to you, only with
the number of alternatives. Theoretically, your uncertainty is the
same whether you must decide for or against major surgery or for
having your eggs scrambled or fried. The number of alternatives is
the same in each case, and so therefore is your uncertainty.

And now information can be defined more precisely: *Information reduces uncertainty by the elimination of alternatives*. Information, very reasonably, is anything that moves you closer to a
decision. It is beside the point whether the decision concerns the
identification of particular objects or events or the selection among
various choices of action. Uncertainty and information are defined
in terms of the *number* of alternative decisions that could be made

no matter what the alternatives are. However, it is easier to reach an understanding of these concepts if particular situations are taken as examples.

Suppose that the information sought involves a single letter of the alphabet, say, someone's middle initial. There are 26 letters of the alphabet, and the uncertainty requires a decision or choice among 26 alternatives. If the situation involves bidding in a bridge game, and the uncertainty concerns a partner's strongest suit, then the number of alternatives will be 4. For the simple toss of a coin, the number of alternatives is 2; for the roll of a die, it is 6. Sometimes the exact number of alternatives is not immediately apparent—for example, if a word rather than a letter is involved. But it may still be possible to determine when this indefinite amount of uncertainty has been reduced—for example, if a reader learns that a word begins with a particular letter or is of a particular length. Either of these pieces of information will reduce the number of alternative possibilities of what the word might be.

We can now return to the definition of information as the reduction of uncertainty. Just as the measure of uncertainty is concerned with the number of alternatives among which the decision maker has to choose, so information is concerned with the number of alternatives that are eliminated. If the decision maker is able to eliminate all alternatives except one and thus can make a fully informed decision, then the amount of information is equal to the amount of uncertainty that existed. A bridge player who receives the information that the partner's strongest suit is red has had uncertainty reduced by one half; if the information is that the strongest suit is hearts, uncertainty is reduced completely. Similarly, a child who knows the alphabet well enough to decide that a particular letter is a vowel has acquired information reducing uncertainty from 26 alternatives to 5. If the letter is correctly identified, then the information gained from the letter must have been equal to the original uncertainty.

Some aspects of reading involve the acquisition of information in order to make decisions, to reduce uncertainty. For the visual identification of letters and words and possibly some aspects of "reading for meaning," uncertainty can be calculated and therefore also the amount of information required to make a decision. The exact number of alternatives can be specified for letters, an approximate figure can be put to the number of words, but the number of alternatives for a meaning, if it can be estimated at all, must obviously be closely related both to the text being read and to the particular individual who is doing the reading. Examples are given in the notes.

COMPREHENSION AND INFORMATION

Comprehension can't be measured in the way that some aspects of information can. Comprehension can't be measured at all, despite constant educational efforts to do so, because it is not a quantity of anything. Comprehension doesn't have dimension or weight; it is not incremental. Comprehension is not the opposite of uncertainty or even of ignorance, and therefore is not quantifiable as the accumulation of a number of facts or items of information. As I proposed in chapter 2, comprehension is the condition of relating whatever we are attending to in the world around us to knowledge, intentions, and expectations we already have in our head.

We comprehend the situation that we are in if we are not confused by it, whether we are reading a book, repairing an appliance, or trying to find our way through the streets of an unfamiliar city. Absence of comprehension means not knowing what to do next or which way to turn. When we can't comprehend, we can't predict, we can't ask questions. Absence of comprehension makes itself immediately evident to the person involved and to anyone looking on, even if it can't be measured. I don't need a numerical test to detect confusion in myself or in others; bewilderment doesn't conceal itself. If I see your brows furrow and your eyes glaze, then I know that all is not well with your comprehension. Without comprehension, there can be no reduction of uncertainty. The rote memorization of "facts" without comprehension is not uncertainty reduction. What we learn—with difficulty—under such conditions becomes informative to us only in the future, if by chance we should suddenly discover the sense it is supposed to make. Conversely, when uncertainty reduction is taking place, there must be some comprehension.

Comprehension doesn't entail that all uncertainty is eliminated. As readers, we comprehend when we can relate potential answers to actual questions that we are asking of the text. We usually have unanswered questions when we read a newspaper—there wouldn't be much point in reading it if we knew everything in advance. And we don't need to have all our uncertainty reduced in order to comprehend. In fact, as we acquire information that reduces uncertainty in some ways, we usually expand our uncertainty in other ways. We find new questions to ask.

Absence of uncertainty is not a condition that we tolerate for very long; we find it boring. There is no "experience" to it. We seek uncertainty, provided we can keep it under control and clear of confusion. We comprehend when we can "make sense" of experience. Throughout this book, I usually refer to comprehension in reading as "making sense of text," relating written language to what we know already and to what we want to know or experience.

Errors and Noise

Of course we may think we comprehend, and look as if we comprehend, but nevertheless make a mistake. Comprehension doesn't come with an unconditional guarantee. The way we understand something now may prove to be inappropriate later. To have a wrong idea about something is a constant possibility, but again not something that can be measured. And no one else can decide for us whether we are in a state of comprehension or confusion, though they can dispute whether we are in such a state for good reason and even help us to move from one state to the other. Comprehension and confusion are the consequences of how well we cope with the particular situation that we happen to be in, with whether or not we feel we know what to do next. What may be comprehensible to you may not be comprehensible to me.

Similarly, what is information for you may not be information for me, if it doesn't contribute to my comprehension. And such negative information can have more than just a neutral, inconsequential effect. It can be positively disruptive.

A technical term for a signal or message that does not convey information is *noise*. The term is not restricted to acoustic events but can be applied to anything that makes communication less clear or effective, such as poorly printed material, or inadequate illumination, or distraction of the reader's attention. The *static* that sometimes interferes with television reception is visual noise. Any part of a text that a reader lacks the skill or knowledge to comprehend becomes noise. The present chapter offers information to readers who understand its language and general theme, but is noise for anyone else. And noise can't easily be ignored; it is not an absence of information so much as interference that increases uncertainty.

Because anything becomes noise if one lacks the familiarity or knowledge to understand it, reading may be intrinsically more difficult for the novice than for the experienced reader. On the other hand, reading can be made so difficult for experienced readers that they behave no differently from beginners.

The Relativity of Information and Comprehension

What is commonly called information can't always be measured. Facts are often called information, but the informativeness of facts depends on the prior knowledge of the person receiving them. "Paris is the capital of France" is a fact, but it is not informative to Tom, who knows it already, nor to Dick, who doesn't understand what the word "capital" means. And although the statement is informative to Harry, who wasn't aware of the fact before, it is not possible to say how informative it is because Harry's uncertainty can't be calculated. We don't know how many alternative cities Harry thought might be the capital of France or how many countries he thought Paris might be the capital of. We don't even know if he cares. Quite possibly, "Paris is the capital of France" is a fact with no information value to Harry when he learns it, although it may be useful to him later in his life. On the other hand, information that serves only to clutter the mind is really noise.

Information exists only when it reduces uncertainty, which is relative to the knowledge and purposes of the individual receiving it. And comprehension also depends on what an individual already knows and needs or wants to know. Comprehension doesn't entail assimilating or even examining all of the information in a text, but rather being able to make sense of the text in terms of the reader's expectations and intentions. Even fluent readers must read some texts more than once in order to comprehend them or to remember a lot of detail. Reading always involves asking questions of a text, and comprehension ensues to the extent that such questions are answered. I may not comprehend a particular text in the same way as you, but then I may not be asking the same questions. Arguments about how a novel, poem, or any other text is most appropriately or "correctly" comprehended are usually arguments about the most relevant kind of questions to ask. A child who claims to have understood a story may not have understood it in the same way as the teacher, but the child was probably not asking the same questions as the teacher. The teacher's questions may be noise to the child. A large part of comprehending literature in any conventional manner is knowing the conventional questions to ask and how to find their answers.

All the preceding discussion of information and comprehension underlines the importance in reading of what goes on behind the eyes, where prior knowledge, purposes, uncertainty, and questions reside. So also do the next two major topics that are discussed, the matter of information that is available from more than one source and the importance of having more than one source of information available.

Redundancy

Redundancy exists whenever the same information is available from more than one source, when the same alternatives can be eliminated in more than one way. And one of the basic skills of reading is the selective elimination of alternatives through the use of redundancy.

An obvious type of redundancy is repetition, for example, when the alternative sources of information are two identical successive sentences. A different means of having the same information twice would be its concurrent presentation to the eye and to the ear—an audiovisual or multimedia situation. Repetition is an eminently popular technique in advertising, especially in television commercials, exemplifying one of the practical advantages of redundancy—that it reduces the likelihood that recipients will unwittingly make a mistake, or overlook anything, in their comprehension of the message. There are other aspects of redundancy, however, that are not always as obvious but that play a more important role in reading.

The fact that the same alternatives are eliminated by two sources of information is often not apparent. Consider the following pair of sentences:

1. The letter of the alphabet that I am thinking of is a vowel.
2. The letter I am thinking of is from the first half of the alphabet.

At first glance the statements might appear to provide complementary pieces of information telling us that the letter is a vowel in the first half of the alphabet. However, if we look at the alternatives eliminated by each of the two statements, we can see that they actually contain a good deal of overlapping information. Statement 1 tells us that the letter is not $b, c, d, f, g, h, j, k, l, m, n, p, q, r, s, t, v, w, x, y, z$, and statement 2 tells us that it is not $n, o, p, q, r, s, t, u, v, w, x, y, z$. Both statements tell us that the letter is not $n, p, q, r, s, t, v, w, x, y, z$, and it is to this extent (the extent to which the excluded sets of alternatives intersect) that the statements are redundant. In fact, the only new information provided by statement 2 is that the letter is not o or u; all the other information is already provided in statement 1.

There are frequent examples of redundancy in reading. As an illustration, consider the unfinished sentence (which could perhaps be the bottom line of a right-hand page of a book):

The captain ordered the mate to drop the an-

There are four ways of reducing uncertainty about the remainder of that sentence, four alternative and therefore redundant sources of information. First, we could turn the page and see how the last word finished—this would be *visual* information. But we could also make some reasonable predictions about how the sentence will continue without turning the page. For example, we could say that the next letter is unlikely to be *b, f, j, m, p, q, r, w*, or *z* because these letters just don't occur after *an* in common words of the English language; we can therefore attribute the elimination of these alternatives to *orthographic* (or spelling) information. There are also some things that can be said about the entire word before turning the page. We know that it is most likely to be an adjective or a noun because other types of words such as articles, conjunctions, verbs, and prepositions, for example, are most unlikely to follow the word *the*; the elimination of all these additional alternatives can be attributed to *syntactic* (or grammatical) information. Finally, we can continue to eliminate alternatives even if we consider as candidates for the last word only nouns or adjectives that begin with *an* plus one of the letters not eliminated by the orthographic information already discussed. We can eliminate words like *answer* and *anagram* and *antibody* even though they are not excluded by our other criteria because our knowledge of the world tells us these are not the kinds of things that captains normally order mates to drop. The elimination of these alternatives can be attributed to *semantic* information.

Obviously, the four alternative sources of information about the incomplete word in the previous example, visual, orthographic, syntactic, and semantic, to some extent provide overlapping information. We don't need as much visual information about the next word as we would if it occurred in isolation because the other sources of information eliminate many alternatives. The four sources of information, therefore, are all to some extent redundant. The skilled reader who can make use of the three other sources needs much less visual information than the less fluent reader. The more redundancy there is, the less visual information the skilled reader requires. In passages of continuous text, provided that the language is familiar and the content not too difficult, every other letter can be eliminated from most words, or about one word in five omitted altogether, without making the passage too difficult for a reader to comprehend.

One last point. I have talked of redundancy in reading as if it exists in the written words themselves, which of course in a sense it does. But in a more important sense, redundancy is information that is available from more than one source only when one of the alternative sources is the reader's own prior knowledge. Put another way, there is no utility in redundancy in the text if it doesn't reflect something the reader knows already, whether it involves the visual, orthographic, syntactic, or semantic structure of written language. The reader must know that *b* is unlikely to follow *an-* and that *anchors* are ordered dropped by captains. In making use of redundancy, the reader makes use of prior knowledge, using something that is already known to eliminate some alternatives and thus reduce the amount of visual information that is required. Redundancy represents information you don't need because you have it already.

LIMITS TO THE UTILITY OF INFORMATION

The reason for the importance of redundancy, and of prior knowledge in general, is that there are severe limits to the amount of new information we can cope with at any one time, whether through the eyes or any other sense modality. We may have questions that we want answered and potential answers to those questions may be in front of our eyes, but if our uncertainty is extensive or if we are trying to make sense of too much information, then we may not be able to handle all the information we need to reduce our uncertainty. We may fail to comprehend.

In plain language, we can try so hard to understand and to remember more of what we read that we succeed only in confusing ourselves and learning less. Limitations of the visual system and of memory are discussed in the following chapters. But there is another factor to be taken into account that may sound rather paradoxical—the more we strive to avoid error, the less likely we are to be right. We always have a choice about how wrong we will be.

Hits, Misses, and Criteria

There's not a fixed amount of information that readers require in order to identify a letter or a word, no matter how much redundancy is involved. Exactly how much information a reader will seek before making a decision about a particular letter, word, or meaning depends on the difficulty of the task (which must always be defined with respect to a particular reader) and on the "cost" of making a decision.

A useful term for the amount of information that individuals require before coming to a decision is their *criterion level*. If the amount of information about a particular letter, word, or meaning meets a reader's criterion level for making a decision, then a choice will be made at that point, whether or not the reader has enough information to make a decision correctly. We see a letter or word when we are ready and willing to decide what it is.

Individuals vary in the way they establish a criterion—ranging from a supercautious attitude requiring almost an absolute certainty to willingness to take a chance on minimal information, even at the risk of making a mistake. To understand why a particular criterion level is established, it is necessary to understand what the effect of setting a high or low criterion might be.

The concept of criterion levels for perception developed in an area of study called *signal detection theory*, which upset a number of venerable ideas. It is traditional to think, for example, that one either sees something or one does not and that there is no area of freedom between within which the perceiver can choose whether something is seen or not. Signal detection theory, however, shows that in many circumstances the question of whether an object is perceived depends less on the intensity of the object—on its "clarity," if you like—than on the attitude of the observer. It is also traditional to think that there is an inverse relationship between correct responses and errors, that the more correct responses there are on any particular task, the lower the number of errors must be. Signal detection theory, however, shows that the cost of increasing the proportion of correct responses will be an increase in the number of errors. In other words, the more often you want to be right, the more often you must tolerate being wrong. The paradox can be explained by examining in a little more detail how the theory originated.

Signal detection theory was originally concerned with the ability of radar operators to distinguish between the "signals" and "noise" on their radar screens when they wanted to identify aircraft presumed to be hostile. As far as the actual situation is concerned, there are only two possibilities: A particular blip on the screen is either a signal or noise; an aircraft is present, or it is not. As far as the operator is concerned, there are also only two possibilities: a decision that the blip on the screen is an aircraft or a decision that it is not. In an ideal world, the combination of the actual situation and the operator's decision would still permit only two possibilities: Either the blip is a signal, in which case the operator decides that there is an aircraft, or the blip is merely noise, in which case the decision is that no aircraft is involved. We may call each of these two alternatives *hits* in the sense that they are both correct identifications. However, there are two other possibilities, of quite different kinds, that must be considered errors. The first type of error occurs when no aircraft is present but the operator decides that there is—this situation may be called a *false alarm*. And the other type of error occurs when there is an aircraft present but the operator decides that there is not, that the signal is actually noise—a situation that can be termed a *miss*.

The problem for the operator is that the numbers of hits, false alarms, and misses are not independent; the number of one can't be changed without a change in the number of another. If the operator is anxious to avoid false alarms and wants to get maximum information before deciding to report an aircraft, then there will be more misses. If, on the other hand, the operator wants to maximize the number of hits, reducing the possibility of a miss by deciding in favor of an aircraft on less information, then there will also be more false alarms.

Of course, with increased skills of discrimination radar operators can improve their level of efficiency and increase the ratio of hits to false alarms, just as increased clarity of the situation will make the task easier. But in any given situation the choice is always the same between maximizing hits and minimizing false alarms. Always the perceiver has to make the choice, to decide where to set the criterion for distinguishing signal from noise, friend from foe, *a* from *b*. The higher the criterion, the fewer will be the false alarms but the fewer also will be the hits. There will be more hits if the criterion is set lower, if decisions are made on less information, but there will also be more false alarms.

Now we can approach the question of the basis on which the criterion is established: What makes the perceiver decide to set a criterion high or low? The answer lies in the relative costs and rewards of hits, misses, and false alarms. A radar operator who is heavily penalized for false alarms will set the criterion high, risking an occasional missed identification. One who is highly rewarded for the identification of a possible enemy and excused for the occasional mistake will set the criterion low.

Readers can't afford to set a criterion level too high before making decisions. A reader who demands too much visual information will often be unable to get it fast enough to read for sense. Readiness to take chances is critical for beginning readers who may be forced to pay too high a price for making "errors." The child who stays silent (who "misses") rather than risk a "false alarm" may please the teacher but develop a habit of setting a criterion too high for efficient reading. Poor readers often are afraid to take a chance;

they may be so concerned about getting words wrong that they miss meaning altogether.

INFORMATION AND EXPERIENCE

I have gone to some length to present a technical consideration of the nature of information and its relevance in the study of reading. But my qualification must be emphasized. *The information-processing point of view is useful for thinking about decision-making aspects of reading, but not about reading in general.* Readers need to make sense of the visual information in a text in order to be able to read that text, but reading is much more than the identification of visual information. In a sense, reading is what you do after you get visual information; the visual information is just the raw material.

I am again arguing against the view that reading is the "acquisition of information" from text or, even more specifically, that reading is a matter of receiving particular messages or facts put into a text by the writer. This is the common "communication model," which sees text as some kind of channel along which information passes from writers to readers. Sometimes the communication metaphor becomes even more specific, with writers "encoding" messages in texts, which readers in their turn must then "decode."

However, many kinds of text and considerations of reading are distorted if not fundamentally misperceived if the communication and information-processing metaphors are applied too generally. As Rosenblatt (1978) pointed out, there is reading done for the sake of experience, which is usually the case with novels and poetry, and also for the stimulation and exploration of ideas. In these cases what the reader brings to the text, looks for in the text, and does as a consequence of this interaction with the text are far more important and relevant than being able to "identify" and recall the actual content of the text. Indeed, I suspect that very little reading is done for purely factual purposes, where information provided by the text is of primary importance. Such reading (outside of formal school tasks) is rarely "cover-to-cover," but rather is extremely selective and localized, limited by the specific intentions of the reader. I am referring to the occasions on which we consult encyclopedias, dictionaries, catalogs, web pages, television guides, and telephone directories. At other times—even with newspapers and magazines—we read more for the experience generated by the reading, for the satisfaction of the act, than for the specific information that the reading provides.

The information-transmission metaphor is widespread in education, where all aspects of literacy are likely to be categorized and perceived as "communication skills." The metaphor comes, of course, from the ubiquitous electronic technology in our environment, from radio, television, telephone, and computers. But even in these contexts the information and communication perspective is limited and narrow. For example, television is often seen as a source of either "information" or "entertainment." But there is another alternative. Most of the so-called informational and entertainment programs also present the possibility of *experience*, far more relative to each individual's knowledge and purposes than either of the other two supposed categories and probably far more important. Indeed, the view that education is a matter of acquiring information leads to misconceptions not only about reading (and television watching) but also about learning itself, culminating in the dubious belief that children will soon be able to do all their learning (acquire all the necessary facts) at the consoles of computers. This exclusive emphasis on information acquisition overlooks the critical importance in education, and in life in general, of experience and self-directed exploration.

The decision-making part of reading is usually only a minor part of the act as a whole, involving the identification of occasional letters, individual words, and possibly from time to time one of a limited range of meanings. Research has tended to concentrate on these restricted aspects of reading. But the information that enables you to make such identifications is not the same as the "message" that you interpret from the text, or the understanding that you bring to it, and certainly not the same as the experience that it might generate for you.

It might be best to regard the information offered by texts in a more general sense as *evidence* rather than as a message, the basis for a response or understanding rather than the content of comprehension. Information may be what the brain looks for in reading, through the eyes, but it is not the end of reading. It is the basis on which a meaning is interpreted, an experience constructed, or the exploration of an idea launched.

In this book, I don't use the term *information* in its broad and imprecise sense at all. The term is used fairly extensively in the next few chapters, but only in the strictly technical sense, in discussions of how uncertainty related to visual "input" from the eyes is resolved. Despite the time I have spent discussing information, I don't regard it as the greatest or most important aspect of reading.

What is experience? It can't be measured and isn't easily defined (see "As-if" in the notes to chapter 1, page 238). Perhaps experience doesn't need definition. It is synonymous with *being*, with creating, exploring, and interacting with worlds—real, possible, and invented. It is engagement and participation, always involving the emotions and often including a deliberate quest for uncertainty. It is an essential condition for being human and alive.

Reading is experience. Reading about a storm is not the same thing as being in a storm, but both are experiences. We respond emotionally to both, and can learn from both. The learning in each case is a by-product of the experience. We don't live to acquire information, but information, like knowledge, wisdom, abilities, attitudes, and values, comes with the experience of living.

ISSUES

The chapter has been almost entirely about one of the most crucial (although often unspoken) sources of contention in education—whether teaching and learning should focus on acquisition of information or quality of experience. Almost all systematic instruction in schools (including tertiary institutions) is based on information transmission, and almost all evaluation is based on information assimilation. Whether more specific emphasis should be placed on experience, both for teachers and for students, is an issue involving values, not research.

SUMMARY

There are two fundamental reasons for reading—for information and for experience. Although it has a clearly defined meaning in a narrow technical sense, the word *information* is widely overused and misused. Information may be regarded as the reduction of uncertainty concerning the alternatives among which a reader must decide. How much visual information a reader will require is affected by the reader's willingness to risk an erroneous decision. Readers who set too high a *criterion level* for information before making decisions will find comprehension more difficult. Because there are limits to how much information the brain can cope with in making sense of texts, readers must make use of all forms of *redundancy* in written language—*orthographic, syntactic,* and *semantic*. Because reading is more than a matter of making decisions, the relevance of the information-processing perspective is limited.

Notes to chapter 4 begin on page 255 covering:

Measuring information and uncertainty

Measuring redundancy

Limitations of information theory

Computers and people

5 Between Eye and Brain

The eyes are given altogether too much credit for seeing. Their role in reading is frequently overemphasized. The eyes don't see at all, in a strictly literal sense. The eyes *look;* they are devices for collecting information for the brain, largely under the direction of the brain, and it is the brain that determines what we see and how we see it. Our perceptual decisions are based only partly on information from the eyes, greatly augmented by knowledge we already possess.

The present chapter is not intended to be a comprehensive physiology of the visual system, but it does outline a few characteristics of eye-brain function that make critical differences to reading. Three particular features of the visual system are considered:

1. We don't see everything that is in front of our eyes.
2. We don't see anything that is in front of our eyes immediately.
3. We don't receive information from our eyes continuously.

Together these three considerations lead to three important implications for reading, and for learning to read:

1. Reading must be fast.
2. Reading must be selective.
3. Reading depends on what the reader already knows.

The remainder of this chapter discusses the preceding six points in order, after considering the importance of what goes on behind the eyes in reading.

TWO SIDES OF READING

Obviously, reading is not an activity that can be conducted in the dark. To read you need illumination, some print in front of you, your eyes open, and possibly your spectacles on. In other words, reading depends on some information getting through the eyes to the brain. This can be called *visual information*. It's easy to characterize the general nature of visual information—it goes away when the lights go out.

Access to visual information is a necessary part of reading, but not sufficient. You could have a wealth of visual information in a text before your open eyes and still not be able to read. For example, the text might be written in a language you don't understand. Knowledge of the relevant language is essential for reading, but you can't expect to find it on the printed page. Rather it is information that you must have already, behind the eyeballs. It can be distinguished from the visual information that comes through the eyes by being called *nonvisual information* or *"prior knowledge."*

There are other kinds of nonvisual information apart from knowledge of language. Knowledge of subject matter is equally important. Give many people an article on deconstructionism, subatomic physics, or the differential calculus, and they will not be able to read—not because of some inadequacy in the text, which specialists can read perfectly well, nor because there is anything wrong with their eyes, but because they lack appropriate nonvisual information. Experience in reading is another kind of nonvisual information of evident importance in making reading possible, although it has nothing to do with the lighting, the print, or the state of one's eyes. Nonvisual information is easily distinguished from visual information—it is carried around by the reader all the time; it doesn't go away when the lights go out.

The Trade-Off Between Visual and Nonvisual Information

The distinction between visual and nonvisual information may seem obvious; nevertheless, it is so critical in reading and learning to read that I put it into diagram form (Fig. 5.1).

The reason that the distinction between visual and nonvisual information is so important is simply stated—there is a reciprocal

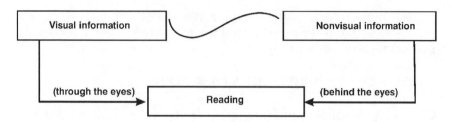

FIG. 5.1.   Two sources of information in reading.

relationship between the two. Within certain limits, one can be traded off for the other. The more nonvisual information a reader has, the less visual information the reader needs. The less nonvisual information that is available from behind the eyes, the more visual information is required. This reciprocal relationship is represented by the curved line between the two kinds of information in Fig. 5.1.

Reading always involves a combination of visual and nonvisual information. Informal demonstrations of the trade-off between the two sources of information are not difficult to give. Popular novels and newspaper articles tend to be easy to read—they can be read relatively quickly, in poor light, despite small type and poor quality printing. They are easy to read because of what we know already; we have a minimal need for visual information. On the other hand, technical materials or difficult novels—or even the same material when read by someone not as familiar with the language or the conventions of the text—require more time and more effort, larger type, clearer print, and superior physical conditions. The names of familiar towns on traffic signs can be read from further away than the same size place names of unfamiliar localities. It is easier to read letters on a wall when they are arranged into meaningful words and phrases than the same size letters in the random order of an optometrist's test chart. In each case the difference has nothing to do with the quality of the visual information available in the print but with the amount of nonvisual information that the reader can bring to bear. The less nonvisual information the reader can employ, the harder it is to read.

Making Reading Difficult

Now we can see one reason why reading can be so very much harder for children, quite independently of their actual reading ability. They may have little relevant nonvisual information. Some beginning reading materials are perversely designed to prevent the use of prior knowledge. At other times, adults may unwittingly or even deliberately discourage its use, by prohibiting "guessing." For whatever cause, insufficient nonvisual information makes reading more difficult.

Insufficient nonvisual information can even make reading impossible, because there is a limit to how much visual information the brain can handle at any one time. There is a bottleneck in the visual system between the eye and the brain, as indicated in Fig. 5.2. Because of this bottleneck a reader can temporarily become functionally blind. It is possible to look but not to see, no matter how good the physical conditions. A line of print that is transparently obvious to a teacher (who knows what it says in the first place) may be almost completely illegible to a child whose dependence on visual information can limit perception to just two or three letters in the middle of the line.

Being unable to discern the words for the print is not a handicap that is restricted to children. Experienced readers may find themselves in exactly the same situation for essentially the same reasons—by being given difficult material to read, by being required to pay a lot of attention to every word, or by being put into a condition of anxiety, all of which increase the demand for visual information and have the paradoxical consequence of making it harder to see the text.

Later in this chapter, I show how the relative proportions of visual and nonvisual information required in reading can be estimated and also indicate how narrow the bottleneck is, so narrow that at least three quarters of the visual information available in text must usually be ignored. In the words of psychologist Paul Kolers (1967), "Reading is only incidentally visual."

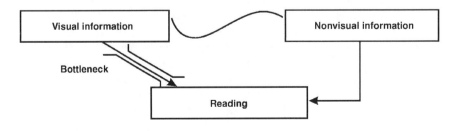

FIG. 5.2.   The bottleneck in reading.

LIMITATIONS OF VISION

We Don't See Everything

The fact that the eyes are open is not an indication that visual information from the world around is being received and interpreted by the brain. We don't *see* the world as its image falls on our eyes. How could we, when that image must often be a kaleidoscopic blur as the eyes flick from place to place in their fitful investigations of the world? But the argument is more complex than the relatively simple fact that the world we see is stable although the eyes are frequently in movement. The scene we perceive has very little in common with the information the eyes receive from the surrounding world.

No single nerve fiber runs directly from the eye to the brain; instead, there are at least six interchanges where impulses along one nerve may start—or inhibit—propagation of a further pattern of impulses along the next section of the pathway. At each of these neural relay stations there are large numbers of interconnections, some of which determine that a single impulse arriving along one section may set off a complex pattern of impulses in the next, while others may relay the message only if a particular combination of signals arrives. Each interconnection point is, in fact, a place where a complex analysis and transformation take place.

Three layers of interconnections are located in the retina of the eyes, which is, in terms of both function and embryonic development, an extension of the brain. A tremendous compression takes place within the retina itself. When the nerve fibers eventually leave the eye on their journey to the brain (the pencil-thick bundle of nerve fibers is collectively called the *optic nerve*), the impulses from about 120 million light-sensitive cells in the retina where the neural messages originate have been thinned out over a hundredfold; the optic nerve consists of barely a million neural pathways.

The actual nature of the impulses that pass along this complex cable of nerves is also very different from our perception or belief of what the visual stimulus is like. Every nerve in our body is limited to conveying only one type of signal—either it fires, or it doesn't. The speed of the impulse may vary from nerve to nerve, but for any one nerve it is fixed; the response is "all or none." The nerve impulse is relatively slow: The fastest rate, for some of the long thick nerve fibers that travel several feet along the body, is perhaps 300 feet per second (about 200 miles per hour). The smaller nerves, such as those in the visual system and brain, transmit at only a tenth of that speed (about 20 miles per hour).

Many examples of the way in which the brain imposes stability on the ever-changing perspective of the eyes are provided by what psychologists call the visual constancies. For example, we always see a known object as a constant size; we don't think that a person or automobile moving away from us gets smaller as the distance increases, although the actual size of the image on the retina is halved as the distance doubles. We don't think the world changes color just because the sun goes in, nor do we see a lawn as being different shades of green because parts of it are in the shade. We "see" plates and coins as circular, although from the angle at which such objects are usually viewed, the image hitting the eye is almost invariably ovoid.

One might think that at least the perception of movement is determined by whether or not the image that falls on the retina is moving, but that is not the case. If our eyes are stationary and a moving image falls across them, we do indeed normally see movement. But if a similar movement across the eyes occurs because we move our eyes voluntarily—when we look around a room, for example—we don't see the world moving. Our perception of whether or not something is moving depends as much on the knowledge we have about what our eye muscles are doing as on the visual information being received by the eye. We can easily fool our own brain by sending it false information. If we "voluntarily" move an eye up or down the page of a book by the use of our eye muscles, we don't see the book move, but if we move the eye in the same way by poking it with a finger—moving the eye without moving the eye muscles—then we do see the book in movement. The brain "thinks" that if the eye muscles haven't been actively involved, then the changing image on the eye must mean external movement, and constructs our perception accordingly.

Tachistoscopes and Tunnel Vision

Seeing is not a simple matter of an inner eye in the brain examining snapshots or video images of complete scenes from the outside world. The brain may generate a feeling that we are able to see most of what is in front of our eyes most of the time, but that is what it is—a *feeling*, generated by the brain. Upon analysis we may find that in fact we see very little. The eyes are not windows, and the brain doesn't look through them. No pictures pass between the eye and brain, and no little person (no *homunculus*) sits inside the brain inspecting them. Not only what we see, but our conviction of seeing, is a fabrication of the brain.

Take the case of reading. When we look at a page of print we may feel that we see entire lines at a time. In practice, we probably see very much less. And in extreme circumstances we may be almost blind. Paradoxically, the harder we try to look, the less we may actually see. To understand the research that underlies these assertions, it is necessary to acquire some familiarity with a venerable piece of psychological instrumentation and with a rather precise way of talking about very small units of time. The small unit of time is the *millisecond*, usually abbreviated to *msec*. One millisecond is a thousandth part of a second; 10 milliseconds is a hundredth of a second; 100 msec is a tenth; 250 msec, a quarter; 500 msec, a half a second; and so forth. Ten milliseconds is about the amount of time the shutter of a camera requires to be open in normal conditions to get a reasonable image on a film. It can also be sufficient time for information to be available to the eye for a single perceptual experience to result. Much more time is required for neural impulses to get from the eye to the brain or for the brain to make a perceptual decision.

The venerable piece of psychological equipment is the *tachistoscope*, a device that presents information to the eyes for very brief periods of time. In other words, a tachistoscope discloses how much we can see at any one time. It doesn't allow the reader a second look.

In its simplest form, a tachistoscope is a slide projector that throws a picture on a screen for a limited amount of time, usually only a fraction of a second. In experimental laboratories today, brief presentations are usually controlled with great precision by computers. One of the first discoveries made through the use of tachistoscopic devices during the 1890s was that the eye had to be exposed to visual information for very much less time than generally thought. If there is sufficient intensity, an exposure of 50 msec is more than adequate for all the information the brain can manage on any one occasion. This doesn't mean that 50 msec is adequate for identifying everything in a single glance; obviously it is not. You can't inspect a page of a book for less than a second and expect to have seen every word. But 50 msec is a sufficient exposure for all the visual information that can be gained in a single fixation. It will make no difference if the source of the visual information is removed after 50 msec or left for 250 msec; nothing more will be seen. Eyes pick up usable information for only a fraction of the time that they are open.

The second significant finding from the tachistoscopic and other studies was that what could be perceived in a single brief presentation, in one glance, depended on what was presented and on the viewer's prior knowledge. If random letters of the alphabet were presented—a sequence like *KYBVOD*—then only four or five letters might be reported. But if words were presented for the same amount of time, two or three might be reported, comprising a total of perhaps 12 letters. And if the words happened to be organized into a short sentence, then four or five words, a total of perhaps 25 letters, might be perceived from the same exposure duration.

The preceding paragraph reports a finding that is central to an understanding of reading. To underline its importance, the main points are reiterated in the form of a diagram (Fig. 5.3).

In the Notes section at the end of this book, it is shown that the eye and brain are doing the same amount of work in each of the three situations depicted in Fig. 5.3. The eyes are sending the same amount of visual information to the brain and the brain is making sense of the same proportion of it. But the more sense the letters make—which means the more the brain is able to use nonvisual information—the more can be seen. The difference lies in the number of alternatives confronting the brain in making perceptual decisions. If the letters are random—or as good as random to the person trying to read them—they are basically unpredictable and demand a good deal of visual information for each identification decision. The reader consequently sees very little and is in a condition known as "tunnel vision" (Mackworth, 1965), very similar to trying to examine the world through a narrow paper tube. Everyone can have tunnel vision; it has nothing to do with the health or efficiency of the eyes. Tunnel vision is a result of trying to handle too much visual information. Airline pilots can suffer from tunnel

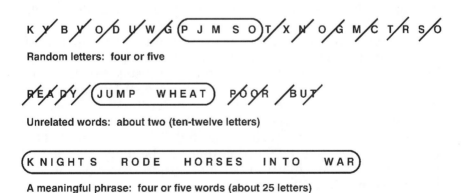

Random letters: four or five

Unrelated words: about two (ten-twelve letters)

A meaningful phrase: four or five words (about 25 letters)

FIG. 5.3.   What can be seen in one glance.

vision, especially during takeoff and landing. That is why it takes more than one pilot to fly large planes. All readers can be afflicted with tunnel vision when the material they are trying to read is unfamiliar, opaque, or otherwise difficult—or when through the particular demands of the task or sheer anxiety they try to handle too much visual information. Beginning readers are prime candidates for having tunnel vision much of the time, especially if the books they are supposed to read make little sense to them. Tunnel vision, in other words, is caused by information overload.

On the other hand, if the text is easily comprehended, entire lines can be seen at one time. So for a teacher who points to some words in a book and says to a child, "There, you can see that clearly enough, can't you?" the answer is probably "No." The teacher who can see the entire line knows what the words are in the first place. The fact that the teacher is pointing can make the situation even worse and ensure that the child sees nothing very much beyond the tip of a finger.

You can't read if you see only a few letters at a time. Tunnel vision makes reading impossible. And the situation can't be retrieved by trying to look at the words more often. Seeing takes time, and there is a limit to the rate at which the brain can make its visual decisions.

Seeing Takes Time

We usually feel that we see what we are looking at immediately. But this is another illusion generated by the brain. It takes time to see anything because the brain requires time to make perceptual decisions. And the time that is required is again directly related to the number of alternatives confronting us. The more alternatives we have to consider and discard, the longer it takes the brain to make up its mind, so to speak, and for seeing to occur.

The tachistoscope can again be used for an experimental demonstration. If a single letter of the alphabet is briefly but clearly displayed, say, *A*, the delay before the viewer succeeds in saying "A" will depend on the number of letters that could have occurred instead of *A*. Give the viewer no clue, so that the letter might be any one of 26 alternatives, and the delay—the "reaction time"—can be as long as 500 msec, half a second. Say in advance that the letter is a vowel, and the reaction time will be much briefer. Tell the viewer that the letter is either *A* or *B*, and reaction time may drop to as little as 200 msec. With fewer alternatives the brain of the viewer has much less work to do, and the decision comes very much faster.

In reading, it is imperative that the brain should make use of anything relevant that we already know in order to reduce the number of alternatives. The rather slow rate at which the brain can make decisions can be extremely disruptive. If the brain has to spend too long deciding among the alternatives, the visual information that the eye makes available to the brain will be gone. That is the explanation of tunnel vision—the brain loses access to visual information before it has had time to make many decisions about it.

Visual information doesn't stay available to the brain for very long after being picked up by the eye. Obviously, visual information remains somewhere in the head for a short period of time, while the brain works on the information collected by the eye in the first few milliseconds of each look. Psychologists have even coined a name for the place where this information is supposed to reside between the time it has been sent back from the eye and the time the brain has made its decisions. This place is known as the *sensory store*, although it so far has remained a purely theoretical construct without any actual known location in the brain. But wherever and whatever the sensory store might be, it doesn't last very long. Estimates of its persistence vary from half a second to—under optimum conditions—2 seconds. But it is just as well that sensory store does persist briefly because a full second is required for the brain to decide even about the limited amount that it is usually able to perceive in a single glance. The visual information that can be utilized in a single glance or tachistoscopic exposure—resulting in the identification of four or five random letters, a couple of unrelated words, or a meaningful sequence of four or five words—in fact requires a full second. The caption to Fig. 5.3 could be amended to read not just *"What can be seen in one glance"* but also *"What can be seen in one second."* The basic physiological limitation on the rate at which the brain can decide among alternatives seems to put the limit on the speed at which most people can read meaningful text *aloud*, which is usually not much more than 250 words a minute (about 4 words a second). People who read very much faster than that rate are generally not reading aloud and certainly not delaying to identify every word.

Information isn't usually allowed to stay in sensory store for its full term of a second or so. Every time the eyes send another portion of visual information to the brain—which means every time we shift our gaze to a new focal point or at least blink to take a second look at the same place—then the arrival of new visual information erases the previous contents of sensory store. This phenomenon is referred to as *masking*. It is by the controlled use of masking in tachistoscopic experiments that psychologists have determined that the brain does indeed require a substantial amount of time to make perceptual decisions. The experiments illustrating how much can be seen in a single glance only work if a second exposure to visual information doesn't follow the first before the brain has had time to make sense of it. If a second exposure is presented less than half a second after the first, the viewer is unlikely to report the full four or five random letters or words that would otherwise be perceived. If the two events occur too close together—say within 50 msec of each other—then the second can completely obliterate the first. Because masking occurs before the brain has time even to decide that something has taken place, the viewer will be completely unaware of a visual event that would otherwise be seen quite clearly. Seeing is a relatively slow process.

On the other hand, because information in sensory store doesn't persist more than about a second under most conditions, we can't see more simply by looking longer at one spot. The eyes must be constantly active to replenish the fading stock of visual information in sensory store. A person who stares is not seeing more, but rather is having difficulty deciding what was looked at in the first place. Because the contents of sensory store decay rapidly and cannot be replenished from an eye that remains fixed in the same position, the eyes of anyone alert to the visual environment tend to be constantly on the move, even though the brain attends to only the first few moments of every new look. Visual information is constantly subject to interruption.

Seeing Is Episodic

Our eyes are continually in movement—with our knowledge and without it. If we pause to think about it, we know that our eyes are scanning a page of text, or glancing around a room, or following a moving object. These are the eye movements we observe if we watch another person's face. These movements are rarely random—we would be quickly alarmed if our own eyes or someone else's began rolling around uncontrollably—but instead the eyes move systematically to where there is the most information or interest for us. The movements of the eye are controlled by the brain, and by examining how the brain directs the eye, we can get a basis for understanding what the brain is looking for, in general terms at least.

But first, we must consider quite a different kind of eye movement, one not apparently under the direct control of the brain nor one that is noticeable either in ourselves or others, but that none-theless can help to underline a point about the constructive nature of vision. Regardless of whether we are glancing around the environment, following a moving object, or maintaining a single fixation, the eyeball is in a constant state of very fast movement. This movement, or *tremor*, occurs at the rate of 50 oscillations a second. We don't notice the tremor in other people, partly because it is so fast, but also because the movement covers only a very short distance; it is more a vibration than a movement from one place to another. But although the movement is normally unnoticeable, it does have a significant role in the visual process; the tremor ensures that more than one group of retinal cells is involved in even a single glance. The tremor provides another illustration of the now familiar point that if the perceptual experience were a simple reproduction of whatever fell on the retina, then all we should ever see would be a giddy blur.

The constant tremor of the eye is essential for vision—cancel it and we are quickly blinded. The cancelation has been accomplished by an ingenious experimental procedure called "stabilizing the image" (Heckenmueller, 1965; Pritchard, 1961). Information coming to the eye is made to oscillate at the same rate and over the same distance as the movement of the eye itself by being reflected through a small mirror mounted directly on the eyeball. The consequence of stabilizing the image is not that the viewer suddenly perceives a super-sharp picture of the world; on the contrary, perception disappears.

The image doesn't seem to disappear instantaneously, nor does it fade slowly like a movie scene. Instead, entire parts drop away in a systematic fashion. If the outline of a face has been presented, meaningful parts will vanish, one by one, first perhaps the hair, then an ear, then perhaps the eyes, the nose, until the only thing remaining may be, like the Cheshire cat, the smile. The word *BEAT* might disintegrate by the loss of its initial letter, leaving *EAT*, and then by dissolution to *AT* and *A*. By itself, the letter *B* might lose one loop to become *P* and then another to leave *I*. The phenomenon shows that the brain holds on to a disappearing image in the most meaningful way possible. Presumably the overworked retinal cells, deprived of the momentary respite the tremor can give them, become fatigued and send less and less information back to the brain, while the brain continues to construct as much of a percept as it can from the diminishing material that it receives.

Other kinds of eye movement need not detain us. There is a kind of slow drift, a tendency of the eye to wander from the point of focus, which is probably not very important because the eye has picked up all the useful information it is going to get during the first few milliseconds. There are "pursuit" movements that the eye makes when it follows a moving object. The only time that the eyes move smoothly and continuously from one position to another is in the course of a pursuit movement. Looking a person up and down with a single sweep of the eyes occurs only in fiction.

The eye movement that is really of concern in reading is, in fact, a rapid, irregular, spasmodic, but surprisingly accurate jump from one focal position to another. It is perhaps a little inappropriate to call such an important movement a jump, so it is dignified by the far more elegant-sounding French word *saccade* (which literally translated into English, however, means "jerk").

Fixations and Regressions

A saccade is by no means a special characteristic of reading, but rather the way we normally sample our visual environment for information about the world. We are skilled in making saccadic movements of the eye. Guided by information received in its periphery, the eye can move very rapidly and accurately from one side of the visual field to the other, from left to right, up and down, even though we may be unaware of the point or object upon which we will focus before the movement begins. Every time the eye pauses in this erratic progression, a *fixation* is said to occur.

For reading English text, fixations are generally regarded as proceeding from left to right across the page, although, of course, our eye movements must also take us from the top of the page toward the bottom and from right to left as we proceed from one line to the next. Experienced readers often don't read "from left to right" at all—they may not make more than one fixation a line and may skip lines in reading down the page. We consider in a later chapter how such a method of reading can be possible. All readers make another kind of movement that is just another saccade but has got itself something of a bad name—a *regression*. A regression is simply a saccade that goes in the opposite direction from the line of type—from right to left along a line or from one line to an earlier one. Regressions can be just as productive as saccades in a forward, progressive direction.

During the saccade, while the eye is moving from one position to another, very little is seen at all. The leaping eye is functionally blind. Information is picked up between saccades when the eye is relatively still—during fixations. The sole purpose of a saccade, in whatever direction, is to move the eye from one position to another to pick up more visual information, like a bee foraging for pollen. The information collection occurs only once during a fixation—for the few hundredths of a second at the beginning, when information is being loaded into the sensory store. After that time, the back-room parts of the visual system are busy, perhaps for the next quarter of a second, making sense of the information.

Saccades are fast as well as precise. The larger saccades are faster than the short ones. The movement of the eyes through 100 degrees, say from the extreme left to the extreme right of the visual field, takes about 100 msec, a 10th of a second. A movement of only a 20th of that distance—about two or three words at a normal reading distance—might take 50 msec. But the fact that a saccade can be made in 50 msec doesn't mean that we can take in new information by moving the eye 20 times a second. The limit on the rate at which we can usefully move from one fixation to another is set by the time required by the brain to make sense of every new input. That is why there can be little "improvement" in the rate at which fixations are made during reading. You can't accelerate reading by hurrying the eyes along.

The number of fixations varies with both the skill of the reader and the difficulty of the passage being read, but not to any remarkable extent. In fact, fixation rate settles down by about Grade 4. There is a slight tendency for skilled readers to change fixations faster than unskilled readers, but the difference is only about one extra fixation a second; adults may average four and children just starting to read change fixation about three times a second. For any reader, experienced or novice, reading a difficult passage may cut about one fixation a second off the fastest reading rate.

Children tend to make more regressions than fluent readers, but not so many more, perhaps one for every four progressive fixations compared with one in six for adults. Once again, the rate of occurrence is determined as much by the difficulty of the passage as by the skill of the reader. Faced with a moderately difficult passage, skilled readers will produce as many regressions as beginning readers with a passage that they find relatively easy. Readers who don't make any regressions may be reading too slowly, too cautiously. When children make a lot of regressions, it is a signal that they are having difficulty, not a cause of difficulty. The number of regressions that readers make is an indication of the complexity to them of the passage they are trying to read.

In short, the duration of fixations and the number of regressions are not reliable guides for distinguishing between good and poor readers. What does distinguish the fluent from the less-skilled reader is the number of letters or words—or the amount of meaning—that can be identified in a single fixation. As a result, a more meaningful way to evaluate the eye movements of a poor reader and a skilled one is to count the number of fixations required to read a hundred words. Skilled readers need far fewer than the beginners because they are able to pick up more information on every fixation. A skilled college graduate reader might pick up enough information to identify words at an average rate of over one per fixation (including regressions) or about 90 fixations per 100 words. The beginner might have to look twice for every word, or 200 fixations per 100 words. The beginner tends to have tunnel vision.

IMPLICATIONS FOR READING

I said at the beginning of this chapter that discussion of the visual system would lead to three important implications for reading and for learning to read—that reading must be fast, that it must be selective, and that it depends on nonvisual information. By now the basic arguments underlying these implications may have become self-evident, but for emphasis they should be elaborated upon briefly.

Reading Must Be Fast

What is meant, of course, is that the brain must always move ahead quickly, to avoid becoming bogged down in the visual detail of the text to the extent that tunnel vision might result. This is not to suggest that the eyes should be speeded up. As I said earlier, reading can't be improved by accelerating the eyeballs. There's a limit to the rate at which the brain can make sense of visual information from the eyes, and simply increasing the rate at which fixations are made would have the consequence of further overwhelming the brain rather than facilitating its decisions.

In fact, the customary reading rate of three or four fixations a second would appear to be an optimum. At a slower rate the contents of sensory store may begin to fade, putting the reader in the position of staring at nothing. At a faster rate than four fixations a second, masking can intrude so that the reader loses information before it is properly analyzed.

The "slow reading" that must be avoided is the overattention to detail that keeps the reader on the brink of tunnel vision. Trying to read text a few letters or a single word at a time keeps a reader functioning at the level of nonsense and precludes any hope of comprehension. Classroom advice to slow down in case of difficulty, to be careful and examine every word closely, can easily lead to bewilderment.

Both word-perfect reading aloud and extensive deliberate memorization may require that a passage should be read more than once. A reader is unlikely to comprehend while reading *more slowly* than 200 words a minute, because a lesser rate would imply that words were being read as isolated units rather than as meaningful sentences. As we see in the next chapter, limitations of memory also prevent sense being built up from isolated words. Comprehension demands relatively fast reading but memorization slows the reader down. Therefore, heavy memory burdens should be avoided when one is learning to read or unfamiliar with the language or subject matter.

Reading Must Be Selective

The brain just doesn't have the time to attend to all the visual information available in most texts and can be easily inundated. Nor is memory able to cope with all the information that might be available from the page. The secret of reading efficiently is not to read indiscriminately but to *sample* the text. The brain must be parsimonious, making maximum use of what is already known and analyzing the minimum of visual information required to verify or modify what can be predicted about the text. All this may sound very complicated, but in fact it is something that every experienced reader can do automatically, and almost certainly what you are doing now if you can make sense of what you read. It is no different from what you do when you look around a room or at a picture.

But like many other aspects of fluent reading, selectivity in picking up and analyzing samples of the available visual information in text comes with experience. Once again the initiative for how the eyes function rests with the brain. When the brain has got all the visual information it requires from a fixation, it directs the eyes very precisely where to move next. The saccade will be either a progressive or regressive movement, depending on whether the next information that the brain requires is further ahead or further back in the page. The brain is able to direct the eyes appropriately, in reading as in other aspects of vision, provided it "understands" what it needs to find out. The brain must always be in charge. Trying to control eye movements in reading can be like trying to steer a horse by the tail. If the eyes don't go to an appropriate place in reading, it is probably because the brain doesn't know where to put them, not because the reader has insufficient visual ability to switch gaze to the right place at the right time.

Reading Depends on Nonvisual Information

Everything I have said so far should underline this final point. The brain—with its purposes, expectations, and prior knowledge—has to be in control of the eyes in reading. To assert that reading should be fast doesn't mean recklessly so. A reader must be able to use nonvisual information to avoid being swamped by visual information from the eyes. To say that a reader should only sample the visual information doesn't imply that the eyes can go randomly from one part of the page to another. Rather, the reader should attend to just those parts of the text that contain the most important information for the reader's purpose, whether every word, selected words, or selected portions of words. And this again is a matter of making maximum use of what is already known.

The experienced reader employs no more visual information to comprehend four words in a single glance than the beginning reader who requires two fixations to identify a single word. All the additional information that skilled readers require is contributed by what they know already. When fluent readers encounter a passage that is difficult to read—because it is poorly written or crammed with new information—the number of fixations (including regressions) they make increases, and reading speed goes down. Because of the additional uncertainty in the situation, they are forced to use more visual information to try to comprehend what they read.

The relative ability to use prior knowledge has consequences in all aspects of vision. Experts—whether in reading, art, sports, or engineering—may be able to comprehend an entire situation at a single glance, but the greater uncertainty of novices handicaps them with tunnel vision. When readers in a tachistoscopic experiment are presented with words in a language they don't comprehend, they are able to identify only a few letters. The fact that the words make sense to someone who knows the language is irrelevant; to the uninformed reader the letters are essentially random, and inability to see very much will result. The implication for anyone involved in teaching reading should be obvious. Whenever readers cannot make sense of what they are expected to read—because the material bears no relevance to any prior knowledge they might have—then reading will become more difficult and learning to read impossible.

ON SEEING BACKWARD

One thing the eyes and the brain can't do is see backward. I mention this fact because a belief exists that a visual handicap of this kind causes some children problems in learning to read. The basis of the myth is the indisputable evidence that many children at some point in their reading careers confuse reversible letters like *b* and *d*, *p* and *q*, and even words like *was* and *saw*, or *much* and *chum*. But seeing backward is both a physical and a logical impossibility, and a much simpler explanation is available.

It is physically impossible to see *part* of the visual field in a different orientation from the rest—to see one dog facing one way and one the other when they are both looking in the same direction. And it is logically impossible to see *everything* reversed because everything would still be seen in the same relationship to everything else and therefore nothing would be different; everything would still be seen the right way round. Of course, it is possible to make a mistake, to think a dog is facing east when it is facing west, especially if we are not familiar with the particular kind of dog, but that must be attributed to lack of adequate information or knowledge, not to a visual defect.

And indeed, the simple explanation of why so many children confuse *b* and *d* is lack of appropriate experience. The discrimination is not an easy one and can confuse adults whose information is limited, just as fluent readers of English become confused with the identification of similar letters in unfamiliar alphabets. The difference between *b* and *d* is minimal—a matter of whether the upright stroke is on the left or the right of the circle—and is not a difference that is significant or even relevant in most aspects of children's experience. A dog is a dog whichever way it faces. Those more general discriminations that do require distinctions of actual or relative direction, such as "left" and "right" or telling the time from the hands of a clock, are notoriously difficult for most children to learn.

Fluent readers don't usually mistake *b* and *d* when they read, but that is primarily because they have so many other clues and need not be concerned with individual letters. But to distinguish *b* from *d* when they occur in isolation, one at a time, is much harder, and the fact that we can normally do so with facility must be attributed to the years of experience we have had and the amount of time we are given, relatively speaking, to inspect the evidence. Being able to distinguish *b* from *d* doesn't make a reader, but being a reader makes the discrimination easier.

Because the difference between *b* and *d* is both unusual and difficult to perceive, it is relatively difficult for children to learn, especially if they don't understand the significance of the difference in the first place. That is why the appropriate experience for such children is not more drill on isolated letters, which are meaningless, but more meaningful reading. Children who have difficulty, perhaps confusing words like *big* and *dig*, must be reading words or sentences that are essentially meaningless (or as if they are meaningless). No one who is reading for sense could confuse words like *big* and *dig*, or *was* and *saw*, in a meaningful context. Unfortunately, children with a "reversals problem" are often given concentrated exercises on distinguishing word pairs like *big* and *dig* in isolation, increasing their apprehension and bewilderment. And if they show no progress with words in isolation they may be restricted to drills with *b* and *d* alone. But letters in isolation are considerably more difficult than letters in words because an important relational clue has been removed. The difference between *b* and *d* at the beginning of a word is that the upright stroke is on the outside for *b* (as in *big*) but on the inside for *d* (as in *dig*). But "outside" and "inside" are meaningless for letters in isolation. There is only one possible way of making learning to distinguish *b* from *d* even more difficult, and that is to show them one at a time. This removes every relational clue, and puts the learner into situations likely to confound even experienced readers.

It is sometimes argued that children see letters backward because they *write* them that way. But writing requires quite different kinds of skill. We all recognize faces and figures that we couldn't possibly draw. If my drawing of a face looks like a potato, that doesn't mean that I see a face as a potato, it means that I'm a poor artist. A child may draw a human figure as a circular head with matchstick arms and legs, but show them their own distorted efforts and an artist's representation, and they will readily indicate which looks most like what they see. Children don't and can't draw what they see, and the fact that they might write a few or many letters backward says nothing about their vision, simply that they haven't yet learned the difficult task of writing letters conventionally.

A LITTLE MORE PHYSIOLOGY

Anatomically, the brain is not all of a piece. In particular it is deeply split along a center line from the back of the head to behind the nose into two roughly symmetrical hemispheres, the left and the right. These two hemispheres are relatively tenuously connected to each other, at least near the surface areas of the brain, including areas that seem to be particularly involved with the organization of cognitive and motor functions. An old psychological and physiological puzzle, still not resolved, is how we piece together a coherent visual image of the scene in front of our eyes when the left half of the visual field (from both eyes) goes to one hemisphere and the right half goes to the other and there are no direct hemispheric connections between the two. Physiologically the picture is split down the middle, but subjectively the seams don't show.

It has long been known that the left hemisphere of the brain is usually largely responsible for motor and sensory control of the right side of the body and the right hemisphere for the left. Because of this general *cross-laterality*, people who suffer strokes or other forms of injury to the left side of their brain tend to lose motor control and possibly sensation in areas on the right side of their body, and damage to the right side of the brain affects the left side of the body. And it has also been known for over a century that for the majority of people, especially the right-handed, areas of the left side of the brain tend to be particularly involved with language. For such people, strokes or other injuries to the right side of the brain may leave language abilities largely unimpaired, and accidents to the left side of the brain are more likely to be associated with language loss. However, this hemispheric specialization is by no means universal or necessary. About 10 percent of the population has the right hemisphere primarily involved with language functions, and children who are born with or who early in life suffer damage to the left side of the brain can develop language relatively fluently with the right, although it becomes much harder to transfer language or to relearn it with the opposite hemisphere as they get older.

Many ingenious studies have been made of the general modes of functioning of the two sides of the brain, particularly with the living brains of people unfortunate enough to have had the surface connections between their two hemispheres severed by accident or unavoidable surgery. Such studies have shown that the two sides of the brain have quite different styles of operation. The left hemisphere (in most people) seems to be particularly involved in activities that are analytic and sequential (like language), for intellectual calculations and planning. In such people, the right hemisphere's characteristic responsibilities and mode of operation are more holistic and spatial; it is concerned with global, subjective, and emotional matters. The left side may be busier when we write a letter or plan an excursion, the right side when we listen to music or imagine a scene.

All this is fascinating and indeed a significant step forward toward understanding the mechanisms of the brain. However, it can also be misleading and conducive to spurious and even damaging conclusions if interpreted too literally. For the great majority of people the brain functions as a whole. We draw on the resources of both hemispheres to produce and understand language, just as we use all of our brain in the rest of our experience. It is a mistake to regard the two hemispheres as separate entities that function independently and even in opposition. Unfortunately, some educators and psychologists who know little about physiology (and some physiologists and neuroanatomists who know little about language and learning) talk as if we have two brains rather than two sides of a single brain. The hemispheres are sometimes referred to as the left and right brains, although this is literally (and only approximately) true for just a handful of people whose brains have been surgically or accidentally sectioned.

One danger of such reasoning is that it confuses a structural arrangement relevant only to the internal working of the brain with the way in which a person functions as a whole. There are no people who think only with the left or the right side of their brains, even if personalities and behavior reflect proclivities for more analytic or reflective approaches to life and learning. It is appropriate to say that a particular kind of activity or preference is dominant in a person, but not that the hemisphere is dominant. It makes sense to say a person has a good spatial orientation and tends to the contemplative; this gives a way of understanding the person and perhaps adapting to idiosyncratic learning preferences. It adds nothing to say that the person is right-brain dominant, and may indeed reduce understanding by switching attention from perceptible characteristics to an assumed and probably mythical cause.

Anyone capable of learning to produce and understand the language of a familiar environment has the ability to use both sides of the brain and to do all those things the two hemispheres are supposed to specialize in. No child comes to school with only half a brain, and hemispheric specialization or "asymmetry" should not be proposed as an explanation of difficulty in learning to read, especially when there are, as we shall see, so many alternative possibilities. In particular, it is wrong to work backward and to assume that because a child is slow or reluctant in learning to read there must be an imbalance or inadequacy of hemispheric function. There is no reading center in the brain. Many areas of the brain are active when we read, but none is involved in reading to the exclusion of anything else. Illness, injury, or very occasionally an inherent defect may affect the working of the brain so that ability to read is disturbed, but there is nothing physiologically or intellectually unique about reading. Advances in mapping the architecture of the brain help us mostly to understand the brain (or to further respect its complexity), not to understand language or learning.

It is important to know the possibilities and limitations of the brain, which is the reason we have already been so concerned with the mechanisms of perception and memory, but the actual manner in which the brain internally organizes its own affairs doesn't have a great relevance to education. At least, that is my view. I don't believe it would or should make the slightest difference to how reading should be taught if it were discovered tomorrow that we all have a critical neural center for reading in the foot (the left foot, for most people). Instruction should always be adapted to the circumstances in which an individual learns and understands best, but this is not promoted by speculation about hypothetical brain structures.

I stress this because there continues to be in education what I and some other researchers believe is a readiness little short of tragic to attribute learning and teaching failures to pseudomedical or pseudoscientific causes. Failures are blamed on perceptual or cognitive handicaps with evidence no more specific than the fact that the failure occurs and a convenient medical or scientific theory happens to be around. If a plausible explanation can't be found in terms of visual, acoustic, memory, or intellectual inadequacy, then an even vaguer "minimal learning disability" may be blamed. And the current excuse, the most popular explanation, always seems to follow the area of scientific research that is generating the most interest and receiving the most popular attention. Failure to learn is explained in terms of fad rather than fact. The association of subtle differences in learning, behavior, attitude, and personality with presumed differences in the architecture of the brain should not become a new phrenology, as unscientific as making judgments about people's character from the bumps on their skulls.

ISSUES

The mountain of experimental data on eye movements grows with every technological development. Basic "facts" about how the eyes move are rarely in dispute, but their interpretations are, especially when researchers feel themselves compelled to pronounce on "the nature of reading" and "instructional implications." At issue are such matters as whether the tendency of readers (in experimental situations) to direct fixations to every word in front of their eyes means that they are actually "reading" every word, identifying one word (or letter) at a time and comprehending one word at a time, or reading the way they normally would when they, not the experimenters, control the purpose, selectivity, anticipation, and comprehension of the reading.

SUMMARY

Reading is not just a visual activity. Both visual information and nonvisual information are essential for reading, and there can be a trade-off between the two. Reading is not instantaneous; the brain cannot immediately make sense of the visual information in a page of print. The eyes move in *saccades*, pausing at *fixations* to select visual information, usually progressing in a forward direction but, when needed, in *regressions*. Slow reading interferes with comprehension. Reading is accelerated not by increasing the fixation rate but by reducing dependency on visual information, mainly through making use of meaning.

Notes to chapter 5 begin on page 262 covering:

Vision and information

The rate of visual decision making

Eye movements in reading

On seeing backward

Hemispheric specialization

6 Bottlenecks of Memory

In chapter 2 I wrote of the diverse and massive amounts of knowledge that together comprise every individual's theory of the world. But I didn't discuss how we manage to deposit and maintain all of this knowledge in the vaults of memory nor how we draw on it when we need to.

Two chapters at the end of this book are concerned with the general topic of *learning*—with the *circumstances* in which our theory of the world develops and grows. But there are some specific issues related to *how much* can get into memory at any one time that are more appropriately considered at this point. These issues are related to the bottlenecks in *perception* that I discussed in the previous chapter—for example, the fact that beginning readers (or any reader confronted by an unfamiliar text) can see only a small amount at any one time, even as little as four or five letters. Now I must turn to some additional constraints that confront all readers, but especially those in difficulty. These are constraints on how quickly specific things can be taken into or out of memory.

Why should tunnel vision, the temporary inability to see what is contained in more than a small area in front of the eyes, be such a crippling handicap for readers, whatever their experience and ability? If a beginning reader can see only a few letters at a time—say, the first half of a word such as *ELEP* … —why can't these letters be remembered for the fraction of a second that the child requires to make a new fixation and see the rest of the word ... *HANT*? Unfortunately, memory has its own limitations and can't be called on to exceed its capacity when the visual system is overworked. Fluent reading demands not only parsimony in the use of visual information but also restraint in the burdens placed on memory. In both cases there are limits to how much the brain can handle. Overloading memory doesn't make reading easier and can contribute to making reading impossible.

There are a number of paradoxes about the role of memory in reading. The more we try to memorize, the less we are likely to recall. The more we try to memorize, the less we are likely to comprehend, which not only makes recall more difficult—it makes recall pointless. Who wants to remember nonsense? On the other hand, the more we comprehend, the more memory will take care of itself.

An implication of these paradoxes is that the prior knowledge already in memory is far more important in reading than efforts to memorize everything in a text. To repeat a theme that by now should be familiar, nonvisual information is critical.

THREE ASPECTS OF MEMORY

To begin, terms need to be clarified a little. We can use the word *memory* in a variety of ways, sometimes to refer to how well we can put something away for future use, sometimes to how long we can retain it, and sometimes to how well we can get to it. In this chapter, we consider four specific aspects or operating characteristics of memory: *input* (how material goes in), *capacity* (how much can be held), *persistence* (how long it can be held), and *retrieval* (getting it out again). We also consider what would appear to be several kinds of memory, because memory doesn't always look the same when examined in different ways.

Psychologists often distinguish three kinds or aspects of memory, depending on the time that elapses between the original presentation of something to be remembered and the test to see what can be retrieved. The first aspect, termed *sensory store*, we met in the previous chapter. It is related to information from its arrival at a receptor organ, such as the eye, until a perceptual decision is made, for example, the identification of letters or words. The second aspect, usually called *short-term memory*, involves the brief time we can maintain attention to something immediately after its identification, for example, remembering an unfamiliar telephone number as we dial it. Finally, there is *long-term memory*, which is everything we know about the world, our total stock of nonvisual information.

These three aspects of memory are often depicted in textbook "flow diagrams" as if they are separate locations in the brain or successive stages in the process of memorization, as indicated in Fig. 6.1. But such a diagram should not be taken too literally. I'm not sure that it is most appropriate to refer to different "kinds" of memory, so I use the more neutral term *aspects*.

There is no evidence that different memories exist in different places in the brain, nor that one memory starts functioning when the other leaves off, as the diagram might suggest. It is definitely misleading to imply that there is movement in just one direction from short-term to long-term memory, and to ignore the fact that there is always *selectivity* about how much is remembered and the manner in which remembering takes place.

However, a discussion must begin somewhere and proceed in some kind of sequence, so for convenience the three aspects of memory are dealt with in the left-to-right order. Later an alternative representation of memory is offered.

Sensory Store

The first aspect of memory can be quickly disposed of, because it is a theoretical necessity rather than a known part of the brain. Sensory store is a metaphor, hypothesized to account for the persistence of visual information after it is received by the eye, at the beginning of each fixation, while the brain is working on it. The operating characteristics of sensory store are quickly stated—input is very fast (the first few milliseconds of a fixation), capacity is at least large enough to hold visual information equivalent to 25 letters (although the brain may not be fast enough to identify anywhere near that number), persistence is very brief (about a second under optimal conditions, but normally erased before that time by another fixation), and retrieval depends on how fast sense can be made of the information.

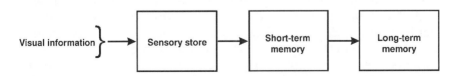

FIG. 6.1.   A typical flow diagram for memory.

Sensory store has little significance for reading instruction because there is nothing that can or need be done about it. Sensory store cannot be overloaded, nor can its capacity be increased by exercise. There is no evidence that children's sensory stores are less adequate than adults'. What needs to be remembered is that sense must be made of the contents of sensory store and that the contents don't persist very long. As a result, there is little point in speeding up fixations (which will simply erase sensory store faster) nor in slowing them down (which will result in blank stares). What makes the difference in reading is the effectiveness of the brain in using what is already known (nonvisual information) to make sense of incoming information (visual information) briefly held in sensory store.

Short-Term Memory

Can you repeat the sentence you are reading at this moment, without taking a second look at it? Whatever you can do to repeat what you have just read is a demonstration of the function of *short-term memory*. Short-term memory is—metaphorically speaking—a "working memory" or "buffer memory," where you retain in the forefront of your mind whatever you are attending to at a particular moment. As far as language is concerned, the contents of short-term memory are usually the last few words you have read or listened to or whatever thoughts you had in your mind instead. Sometimes short-term memory is occupied by what you are about to say or write, by an address you are looking for, or by a telephone number you want to call. Short-term memory is whatever is holding your attention. And short-term memory is of central importance in reading. It is where you lodge the traces of what you have just read while you go on to make sense of the next few words. It is where you try to retain facts that you want to commit to rote memorization.

Short-term memory would appear to have both strengths and weaknesses, just by virtue of the way it functions. On the credit side, there doesn't appear to be any undue delay in getting something into short-term memory. In fact if someone asks you to call a certain telephone number, your best strategy is to get on your way to dial the number, not to stand around trying to commit the number to memory. Similarly, there doesn't appear to be any particular problem about retrieving items from short-term memory. If something is in short-term memory you can get it out again at once. Indeed, if you can't immediately retrieve what you want—say, the telephone number—then you might just as well go back and ask for it again. Either you have retained the number in short-term memory, in which case it is accessible without delay, or it is gone for good. Short-term memory is what we happen to be attending to at the moment, and if our attention is diverted to something else, the original content is lost.

But if short-term memory seems a reasonably efficient device as far as input and output operations are concerned, in other respects it has its limitations. Short-term memory can't contain very much at any one time—little more than half a dozen items. A sequence of seven unrelated digits is about as much as anyone can retain. It is as if a benevolent providence had provided humanity with sufficient short-term memory capacity to make telephone calls and then had failed to anticipate area codes. If we try to hold more than six or seven items in short-term memory, then something will be lost. If someone distracts us when we are on our way to make that telephone call, perhaps by asking us the time of day or the location of a room, then some or all of the telephone number will be forgotten and there will be absolutely no point in cudgeling our brains for the number to come back. We shall just have to ascertain the number once again. For as much as we try to overload short-term memory, that much of its contents will be lost.

This is the reason why short-term memory can't be used to overcome tunnel vision. The child who has seen only *ELEP* ... just can't hold those letters in short-term memory, read another four or five letters, and get them all organized in a way that makes sense. As the fragments of one fixation go into short-term memory, the fragments from the previous fixation will be pushed out. This is not the same as the masking or erasure of sensory store—it is possible to hold a few items in short-term memory over a number of fixations. But holding such items in the forefront of our attention simply prevents very much more going in and has the obvious result of making reading much more difficult. Not much reading can be done if half your attention is preoccupied with earlier bits of letters and words that you are still trying to make sense of.

The second limitation of short-term memory involves its persistence. Nothing stays around very long in short-term memory. It is impossible to state an exact amount of time for the persistence of something in short-term memory, for the simple reason that its longevity depends on what you do with it. Ignore something in short-term memory for less than a second, and it will be gone. To retain it, you must keep giving it your attention. *Rehearsal* is the technical term often employed. To keep that telephone number in your head you must keep repeating it; it can't be allowed to elude your attention. Theoretically, material can be kept in short-term memory indefinitely, but only if constantly rehearsed, a procedure that is generally impractical because it prevents you from thinking about anything else. Material in short-term memory must be dealt with as expeditiously as possible. Retaining something for longer than a fixation or two, for example, preempts attention that is required for the task on hand in reading and promotes a further loss of comprehension. The more a reader fills short-term memory with unrelated letters, bits of words, and other meaningless items, the more the letters and bits of words that the reader is currently trying to understand are likely to be nonsense.

Long-Term Memory

Of course, memory is far more than whatever we happen to be thinking about at the moment. There is a vast amount that we know all the time, ranging from names and telephone numbers to all the complex interrelationships that we can perceive and predict among objects and events in the world around us, and only a small part of all of this knowledge can be the focus of our attention at any one time. Anything that persists in our minds quite independently of rehearsal or conscious knowledge is long-term memory, our continuous knowledge of the world. Long-term memory has some distinct advantages over short-term memory, especially with regard to its capacity. Nevertheless, long-term memory can't be used as a dump for any overflow of information from short-term memory, for long-term memory also has limitations.

Let's begin with the positive side. Where short-term memory is restricted in capacity to barely half a dozen items, the capacity of long-term memory would appear to be infinite. No limit has been discovered to how much can be lodged in long-term memory. We never have to erase an old friend's name to make room for the name of a new acquaintance.

Similarly, there is no apparent limit to the persistence of long-term memory. No question of rehearsal here. Memories we may not even be aware that we had, recollections of a childhood incident, for example, can quite unexpectedly revivify themselves, triggered perhaps by a few nostalgic bars of music, an old photograph, or even a certain taste or aroma.

But as everyone knows, the fact that there seems to be no theoretical limit to the capacity or persistence of long-term memory doesn't mean that its contents are constantly accessible. It is here that some failings of long-term memory become apparent. Retrieval from long-term memory is by no means as immediate and effortless as retrieval from short-term memory.

Indeed, retention and retrieval seem quite different in long- and short-term memory. Short-term memory is like a set of half a dozen small boxes, each of which can contain one separate item, by definition immediately accessible to attention because it is attention that holds them in short-term memory in the first place. But long-term memory is more like a network of knowledge, an organized system in which each item is related in some way or another to everything else. The organization and operation of long-term memory—our theory of the world—were discussed in chapter 2. Whether or not we can retrieve something from long-term memory depends on how it is organized. The secret of recall from long-term memory is to tap into the interrelationships.

Sometimes the effort to get hold of something in long-term memory can be frustrating. We know something is there but can't find a way to get to it. An illustration is the "tip-of-the-tongue" phenomenon (Brown & McNeill, 1966). We know someone's name begins with an S and has three syllables—and we are sure it is not Sanderson or Somerset or Sylvester. Suddenly the name appears in the set of alternatives that our mind is running through, or perhaps when someone else mentions the name, and then we recognize it at once. It was in long-term memory all the time, but not immediately accessible.

Success at retrieving something from long-term memory depends on the clues we can find to gain access to it and on how well it was organized in long-term memory in the first place. Basically, everything depends on the sense that we made of the material when we originally put it into memory. It is pointless to try to put an overflow of unrelated fragments from short-term memory into long-term memory—that is why rote learning is so often unproductive. It is not just that nonsense that goes in will be nonsense when it comes out; it is extremely difficult to get nonsense out at all.

There is another reason why it is not feasible to accommodate an overflow from short-term memory in long-term memory, concerned with the rate at which long-term memory can accept something new. In contrast to the practically immediate input of half a dozen items into short-term memory, committing something to long-term memory is extremely and surprisingly slow. To put one item into long-term memory takes 5 seconds—and in that 5 seconds there is little attention left over for anything else. The telephone number that will tax short-term memory to its capacity is at least accepted as quickly as it is read or heard, but to hold the same number in long-term memory so that it can be dialed the next day will require a good half minute of concentration, 5 seconds for each digit.

Committing fragments of text to long-term memory is not something that can be resorted to in reading to overcome limitations of the visual system or of short-term memory. Quite the contrary. Efforts to cram long-term memory will have the effect of interfering with comprehension. Beginning readers with tunnel vision, who cannot hold in short-term memory more than the few letters they see in a single fixation, are even more confounded if they try to put isolated letters or bits of words into long-term memory.

Fluent readers can find reading impossible if they overburden long-term memory, even if they are trying to read material that they would find completely comprehensible if they relaxed and were content to enjoy it. This problem can be acute for students trying to read a novel or Shakespearean play and at the same time trying to commit to memory the unfamiliar names of all the characters and every trivial detail or event. Memorization interferes with comprehension by monopolizing attention and reducing intelligibility. Most readers have encountered the perverse textbook that is incomprehensible the day before the examination—when we are trying to retain every fact—yet transparently obvious the day after—when we are reading to discover what we missed. If you are having difficulty comprehending what you are reading right now, it may be because you are trying too hard to memorize. On the other hand—as I shall demonstrate in a number of ways—comprehension takes care of memorization. If you comprehend what you read or hear, then long-term memory will reorganize itself so efficiently and effortlessly that you will not be aware that you are learning at all.

Long-term memory is extremely efficient, but only if the acquisition and organization of new material are directed by what we know already. Once again we find that what we know already tips the balance, making reading possible. It is time now to look at how prior knowledge helps to overcome the limitations of both short-term and long-term memory.

OVERCOMING MEMORY LIMITATIONS

There are some paradoxes to be resolved. The experimental evidence is that we can hold no more than half a dozen random letters in short-term memory, yet it is usually not difficult to repeat a sentence of a dozen words or more that we have just read or heard for the first time. It appears that no more than one letter or digit goes into long-term memory every 5 seconds, yet we can commonly recall many of the larger themes and significant details that we have read in a novel or seen in a film.

To explain these discrepancies I must clarify some rather loose language that I've been using. I've been talking about retaining "material," or half a dozen "things" or "items," in short-term memory and putting just one "item" into long-term memory. What are these "things" or "items"? The answer depends on the sense you are making of what you are reading or listening to. These "things" or "items" are units that exist in long-term memory already.

If you are looking for letters—or if you can only find letters in what you are looking at—then you can hold half a dozen letters in short-term memory. But if you are looking for words, then short-term memory will hold half a dozen words, the equivalent of four or five times as many letters.

It is a question of what you already know. Short-term memory is filled by a seven-digit telephone number, which also requires half a minute to put into long-term memory. But not if the number happens to be 123-4567 because that is a sequence that you already know. The number 1234567 will occupy just one part of short-term memory and will enter long-term memory within a few seconds because, in a sense, it is there already. Can you hold the letters *THEELEPELTJE* in short-term memory? Only if you recognize them as a word, which you will do if you can read Dutch. To put the same sequence of letters into long-term memory would require a good minute of concentration—and even then it is unlikely that you would be able to recall them all tomorrow—unless you already know the word, in which case you will commit it to memory as rapidly as the English word *teaspoon*, which the Dutch word happens to mean.

Psychologists refer to this process of storing the largest meaningful unit in short-term memory as *chunking*, which is a conveniently picturesque term but also a bit misleading. The term suggests that at the beginning we first attend to the small fragments (individual letters or digits), which we subsequently organize into larger units for efficiency in memory. But we are looking for the larger units all the time. When we move on to consider reading more specifically, it will be seen that written words can be identified without any reference to letters, and meaning without reference to specific words. It is not that we perceive letters, which we then—if we can—chunk into words, but that we can perceive words or meaning in the first place and never bother the visual system or memory with letters. The "items" that we commit to memory are the largest meaningful units we can find. In other words, what we put into short-term memory is determined by the largest units that we have available in long-term memory. It is what we know and are looking for that determines the content of short-term memory, which is the reason I present an alternative diagram of memory to that of Fig. 6.1. In Fig. 6.2, short-term memory is shown as part of long-term memory—the part concerned with what we happen to be attending to at the time. Short-term memory is not an antechamber of long-term memory but that part of long-term memory that we use to attend to, and make sense of, a current situation.

The arrow between short-term memory and sensory store is double-ended to acknowledge that the brain is *selective* about the visual information that it attends to, and the arrows between short-term and long-term memory are double-ended to represent their continual interaction.

One final qualification must be made. We can hold in short-term memory a few letters or a few words. But we can also put into short-term memory something far more mysterious—we can hold there large rich chunks of *meaning*. It is impossible to put a number to this—units of meaning can't be counted the way we count letters or words. But just as we can hold the letters contained in words in memory far more efficiently than letters that are unrelated to each other, so we can hold meaningful sequences of words in memory far more efficiently than we can hold individual unrelated words. The same applies to long-term memory; we can put an entire "meaning" away in just a few seconds—without any conscious awareness that we are doing so—even though that meaning might have been embedded in a dozen words or more. And by definition, any "meaning" that we put into long-term memory is going to be far easier to retain and retrieve because mean-

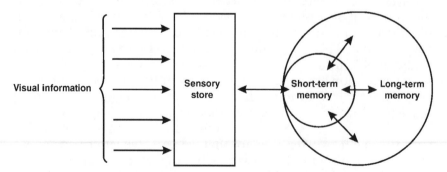

FIG. 6.2.   An alternative representation of memory.

ingfulness implies that the input is related to what we already know and makes sense to us.

We must get used to the notion that meaning is not dependent on specific words. This crucial point is elaborated many times in this book. When we retain a meaningful sequence of words in memory—either short-term or long-term—we are not primarily storing the words at all but rather the meaning that we attribute to them. "Meaning" is the largest and most efficient unit of analysis that we can bring to bear from what we know already to what we are trying to read (or hear) and understand. For the moment, I offer just one illustration of the fact that not only do we look for meaning, rather than specific words, when we comprehend speech or print but also that this is the most natural thing to do.

I have said that we can hold a dozen or more words in short-term memory if they are in a meaningful sequence, but that six or seven is the limit for words that make no collective sense, like the same sequence of words in reverse. Try memorizing: *memory term short in words more or dozen a hold can we*. We don't hold a sequence of a dozen or so words in short-term memory, but their meaning. If you ask a person to repeat a sentence, you will often get back the right meaning but not exactly the same words. The person who remembers is not so much recalling words as reconstructing a sentence from the meaning that was remembered. We don't attend to words; we attend to meanings. So a substantial "mistake" might be made in repeating exact words—the word *automobile* might be recalled as the word *car*, for example—but there is rarely the substitution of a tiny word that makes a big difference to meaning, such as *not*. We shall see, incidentally, that "errors" of this kind, that preserve meaning, are committed by experienced readers and also by children learning to read who are in the process of becoming good readers. Reading involves looking for meaning, not specific words.

Memory Without Bottlenecks

Much of what we have considered so far might be called *contrived* memory—whether by researchers, teachers, or ourselves—when remembering is in effect put under external control. In memory research, subjects are usually told what they must remember and recall. When we make a deliberate effort to commit a particular thing to memory or to get a particular thing out, we usually encounter the frustrating bottlenecks I have been describing.

But most of the time no particular effort is involved in remembering—and memory seems to be much more efficient. I have talked about how easily something goes into long-term memory provided we can make sense of it, provided it is relevant to what we are doing at the time. These are the occasions when memory could be said to be controlled "from the inside," by a brain naturally operating on the world and making sense of it. It is sometimes surprising to discover how much has gone into memory without our awareness. I have more to say about this in the chapters on learning, in which I stress that efficient and effortless memorizing depends on how well it is integrated with our current knowledge, purposes, and predictions.

I have also talked in the present chapter about how easily things can be retrieved from long-term memory, provided they are organized in relationships with relevant parts of our current theory of the world. The most relevant kind of relationship is when what we need to remember is part of what we are actually involved in at the time.

I am referring to an aspect of memory that we rely on just about every moment of the day, one that is incredibly efficient and rarely lets us down. It is memory that is not contrived in any way; it functions spontaneously, without effort or conscious management. Ironically, because of their predilection for studying aspects of memory that can be brought under *control* in the laboratory, experimental psychologists have largely ignored this aspect of remembering, which takes place without the conscious manipulation of the experimenters or their subjects. Because of their rather narrow viewpoint, such researchers have even persuaded themselves and many educators that remembering is normally difficult, effortful, and frequently unsuccessful.

But most of the time we remember automatically and without strain, even without awareness that we are making demands on memory. We don't usually have difficulty remembering our own name, where we live, or our telephone number. We remember our birthday and that of a few other people as well, and we remember holidays. We remember our friends' names, and how they look, and where they live, and even some of their telephone numbers. We remember everything about the world that is familiar to us. We remember that trees are called "trees" and birds "birds," even though we may not remember the names of particular kinds. We remember the meanings of just about every word we know, how these words are pronounced, and how many of them are spelled as well. We not only remember facts, we remember scenes, procedures, scenarios, scripts—all of the cognitive *schemes* discussed in chapter 2. We remember innumerable things. We don't remember these things all the time, of course. Our heads would be continually cluttered if we did. They come to mind just when it is appropriate for us to remember them, when they help us to make sense of the world we are in at the moment.

Psychologist George Mandler (1985) termed this everyday aspect of memory *reminding*, although he didn't want to say that it is different from any other facet of memory. In fact, Mandler suggested that apparent differences in kinds of memory are really only differences in the forms of tests, in the way memory is examined. If we look at the recall of something soon after it has come to our attention, then we talk about "short-term memory." If we consider something over a longer period, then we refer to "long-term memory." And instead of looking at particular things that we (or researchers) happen quite arbitrarily to be concerned with, if we consider what we continually remember for our own purposes, then we have this phenomenon of "reminding."

And as with comprehension and with putting things into memory, the conditions that make reminding fluent and effortless are meaningfulness, relevance, and personal involvement. We remember most easily when what we need to recall is most relevant to what we are engaged in doing and when we have no anxiety about not remembering. This is all part of the continually ongoing activity of "thinking." Memory is not a special faculty of the brain that functions independently of everything else. Thinking and the "reminding" aspect of memory are inseparable.

When we are able to read with comprehension, we are being reminded all the time. The events of the story (or the steps in the argument) carry us along as if we were experiencing them at first hand, and we rarely have to struggle to exercise our memory. We remember the meaning of particular words when we are reading those words; we recall what we have already read (and other aspects of nonvisual information) when it is appropriate to do so. And we are reminded of all manner of things that happen to be relevant to our understanding, and to our purposes in reading, at that particular time.

As a simple example, we are reminded of the appropriate meaning of the words (or we predict those meanings) in a sentence like *He wiped the tear from the child's eye*, but quite a different meaning in *He repaired the tear in the child's jacket*. Normally we would not even notice the word *tear* could have a different pronunciation and meaning than those that are appropriate for the context the word is in.

Of course, memory lets us down sometimes. We fail to remind ourselves to buy something at the store on the way home or to make a telephone call that we had planned. Often there is an explanation of why we forget—we are distracted, or confused, or possibly we may not even want to remember. If we fail to recall something, it is usually not because we have suffered a permanent loss of memory. We just cannot get access for the moment. And sometimes memory is frustratingly difficult. Remembering becomes difficult when it is conscious, when we *contrive* deliberately to remember something that has not sprung to mind at once.

Children don't need to be taught to use memory efficiently—to avoid overloading short-term memory and to refrain from forcing pointless detail into long-term memory. They naturally do these things. But reading instruction may make these natural efficiencies impossible. Anxiety while learning to read can force children into inefficient uses of memory. Reading, and therefore learning to read, depend on what you already know, on what you can make sense of. Reading teachers help to avoid overloading pupils' memories when they ensure that the material the children are expected to read makes sense to them, so that they are not required—either by the material or by the instruction—to engage in extensive and pointless memorization.

ISSUES

There is little dispute about the characteristics of memory I have outlined (although there is much technical debate about physiological aspects). Problems arise when the limitations of memory are ignored, for example, in expecting large amounts of detailed memorization to take place during reading or learning, or on requiring the memorization of material that is not meaningful to the learner.

SUMMARY

Short-term memory and *long-term memory* both have their limitations, but these are handicaps only to the readers who can make little sense of what they are doing in the first place. The differing characteristics of memory are summarized in Fig. 6.3. When a reader can make sense of text and doesn't strain to memorize, there is no awareness of the bottlenecks of memory. Fluent readers are immediately reminded of what is relevant for their current situation and purposes.

	Short-term memory (*working memory*)	Long-term memory (*permanent memory*)
Capacity	limited	practically unlimited
Persistence	very brief	practically unlimited
Retrieval	immediate	depends on organization
Input	very fast	relatively slow

FIG. 6.3.   Characteristics of short-term and long-term memory.

Notes to chapter 6 begin on page 269 covering:
Theories of memory
Chunking
Imagery
Children's memory

7 Letter Identification

After all the preliminaries, here is the first of four chapters specifically on the topic of reading. The point I'm heading for is that fluent reading doesn't normally require the identification of individual letters or words. But the most convenient route to that destination begins with a discussion of *letter identification*, focusing on an aspect of reading where the issue can be concisely stated: How is it that anyone who knows the alphabet is able to distinguish and name any of the 26 alternatives on sight? I'm talking about separate letters, not letters in sequences of any kind.

Unlike the reading of words, the question doesn't arise of whether isolated letters are read a bit at a time or all at once. Individual letters can't be "sounded out"; their appearance has a purely arbitrary relationship to the way they are pronounced. And there can be little question about their meaning; we "comprehend" a letter when we can say its name, and that is that.

Yet despite this simplification, letter and word identification are alike in one important aspect—both involve the discrimination and categorization of visual information. Later we'll see that the manner in which letters are identified is relevant to an understanding of the identification of words.

A brief digression may be in order to discuss the casual use of the terms *identification* and *recognition* as labels for how a letter or word (or meaning) is distinguished and named. They are not, strictly speaking, synonymous. *Identification* involves a decision that an object should be put into a particular category. There is no implication that the object being identified should have been met before. *Recognition*, on the other hand, literally means that the object has been seen before, although identification may not be involved. We *identify* people when we put a name to them, whether or not we have met them before (identification cards aren't recognition cards). We *recognize* people when we know we have seen them before, whether or not we can put a name to them (police identification parades should be called recognition parades).

Experimental psychologists and reading specialists usually talk about letter and word recognition, but the use of the term is doubly inappropriate. First, they would hardly consider a word to be recognized unless its name could be given; they wouldn't consider that a child recognized a word if all the child could say was "That's the same squiggle I saw yesterday." Second, skilled readers can very often attach a name to visual information that they have never met before. As a rather extreme case, do you "recognize" or "identify" the visual information *rEaDiNg* as the word *reading*? You almost certainly have never seen the word written that way before. The weight of evidence would seem to favor identification, and the term is therefore used in this book for formal purposes, such as chapter headings. But having made the distinction, we need not be dogmatic about it; "identify," "recognize," "categorize," "name," and even "read" will, in general, continue to be used as conventional usage and the context suggest.

It is also not strictly correct to refer to the characters that we strive to identify on particular occasions as "letters"; this implies that the perceptual decision has already been made. Whether a particular mark on the page should be characterized as a letter depends on the perspective of the viewer (whether the reader or the writer). As we have seen, *IO* may be identified as two letters or two numerals. Prior to an identification decision, the visual information that is *IO* is merely a pattern of contrasting ink marks on paper, more precisely referred to as a *visual configuration*, a *visual array*, or even a *visual stimulus*.

THEORIES OF PATTERN RECOGNITION

Letter identification is a special problem within the broader theoretical area of *pattern recognition*—the manner in which any two visual configurations are "cognized" to be the same. Recognition is of classical philosophical concern because it has been realized for over 2,000 years that no two events are ever exactly the same; the world is always in flux, and we never see an object twice in precisely the same form, from the same angle, in the same light, or with the same eye. A topic of general interest to psychology is what exactly determines whether two objects or events shall be considered to be equivalent. The equivalence decision clearly rests with the viewer and not in any property of the visual array. Are *J* and *j* the same? A printer would say no, although *JOY* and *joy* are the same word. Are two automobiles of the same year, model, and color identical? Possibly to everyone except their owners. It is the viewer, not the object, that determines equivalence.

We organize our lives and our knowledge by deciding that some things should be treated as equivalent—these are the things that we put into the same category—and some as different. Those differences between objects or events that help us to place them in category systems may be called by a variety of names, such as *defining attributes* or *central attributes* or *distinctive features*; in essence, they are the differences that we choose to make *significant*. The differences that we choose to ignore, the ones that don't influence our decision, are often not noticed at all. Obviously it is more efficient to pay attention only to significant differences, particularly in view of the limited information-processing capacity of the human brain. It is, therefore, hardly surprising that we may overlook differences that we are not looking for in the first place, like the sudden absence of our friend's beard, or the pattern of his tie, or the misspelling in the newspaper headline. Human beings owe their preeminent position in the intellectual hierarchy of living organisms to their capacity to perceive things as the same according to criteria that they themselves establish, selectively ignoring what might be termed *differences that don't make a difference*.

The manner in which particular letters or words are treated as equivalent has become a focus of theoretical attention because of its particular application to computer technology. There is an obvious economic as well as theoretical interest in designing computers that might be able to read. The construction of a computer with any fluent degree of reading ability has proved difficult for a number of reasons, one of which is that language can be understood only if there is an underlying understanding of the topic to which the language refers and the ability of computers to "understand" any topic is very limited indeed. It has not proved feasible to provide a computer with rules for identifying all the printed and handwritten letters that people are able to identify, let alone words or meanings, with anything like the facility with which humans can identify them. But if we consider the problems of pattern recognition from the computer point of view, we get some insights into what must be involved in the human skill (even though people aren't computers).

There are two basic ways in which a computer might be constructed to recognize patterns, whether numbers, letters, words, texts, photographs, fingerprints, voiceprints, signatures, diagrams, maps, or real objects, like faces. The two ways are essentially those that appear to be open theoretically to account for the recognition of patterns by humans. The alternatives may be called *template matching* and *feature analysis*, and the best way to describe them is to imagine trying to construct a computer capable of identifying the 26 letters of the alphabet in their various forms.

For both the template-matching and the feature-analytic devices, the ground rules are the same. At the input end is an optical scanner or "eye" to examine various patterns of visual information for each letter of the alphabet, and at the output end there is a set of 26 alternative responses, the names or representations of each of the letters. The aim is to construct a system between the input and output mechanisms to ensure that given an input of G, the computer will say or print out "g."

Template Matching

For a template-matching device, a series of internal representations must be constructed to be, in effect, a reference library for the letters that the device is required to identify. We might start with one internal representation, or *template*, for each letter of the alphabet. Each template is directly connected with an appropriate response, and between the optical detector (the "eye") and the templates we shall put a device capable of comparing any input letter with all of the set of templates. Any letter that comes into the computer's field of view will be internalized and compared with each of the templates, at least until a match is made. Upon matching the input with a template, the computer will perform the response associated with that particular template and the identification will be complete.

There are obvious limitations to such a system. If the computer is given a template for the representation A, what will it do if confronted with A or A, not to mention A or A? Of course, some flexibility can be built into the system. Inputs can be normalized to iron out some of the variability; they can be scaled down to a standard size, adjusted into a particular orientation, have crooked lines straightened, small gaps filled, and minor excrescences removed; in short, a number of things can be done to increase the probability that the computer will not respond "I don't know" but will instead match an input to a template. But, unfortunately, the greater the likelihood that the computer will make a match, the greater is the probability that it will make a mistake. This is the signal detection problem of chapter 4. A computer that can normalize A to make it look like the template A will be likely to do the same with 4 and H. The only remedy will be to keep adding templates to try to accommodate all the different styles and types of lettering the device might meet. Even then, such a computer will be unable to make use of all the supporting knowledge that human beings have.

Critical limitations of template-matching systems, for both computer and human, lie in their relative inefficiency and costliness. A single set of templates, one for each category, is highly restricted in the number of inputs that it can match, but every increase in the number of templates adds considerably to the size, expense, and complexity of the system, and also to the probability of false alarms. The template-matching model can work, but usually by cheating its way around the problem of the diversity of input representations. Instead of providing the computer with templates to meet many innumerable character styles, it makes sure the computer eye meets only a limited set of alternatives, like the numbers 5 2104 that are printed on our checks.

Feature Analysis

The alternative method of pattern recognition, *feature analysis*, dispenses with internal representations completely. There is no question of attempting to match the input with anything. Instead, a series of tests is made on the input. The results of each test eliminate a number of alternatives until, finally, all uncertainty is reduced and identification is achieved. The features are properties of the visual array that are subjected to tests to determine which alternative responses should be eliminated. Decisions about which alternatives each test will eliminate are made by the viewers (or computer programmers) themselves.

Let's again imagine constructing a device capable of identifying letters, this time using feature analysis. Remember, the problem is essentially one of using rules to decide into which of a limited number of categories might a very large number of alternative events be placed. In other words this is a matter of establishing equivalences.

At the input end of the system, where the computer has its optical scanner, we establish a set of "feature analyzers." A feature analyzer is a specialized kind of detector that looks for—is sensitive to—just one kind of feature in the visual information and that passes just one kind of report back. We might imagine that each analyzer looks for a particular distinctive feature by asking a question: One asks, "Is the configuration curved?" (like *C* or *O*); another asks, "Is it closed?" (like *O* or *P*); a third asks, "Is it symmetrical?" (like *A* or *W*); and a fourth asks, "Is there an intersection?" (as in *T* or *K*). Every analyzer is in effect a test and the message it sends back is binary—either "yes" or "no." Without looking too closely at the question of what constitutes a distinctive feature, we can say it is a property of visual information that can be used to differentiate some visual configurations from others—a "significant difference." A distinctive feature must be common to more than one object or event; otherwise, it could not be used to put more than one into the same category, it would be all one needs to know. But on the other hand, if the feature were present in all objects or events, then we could not use it to segregate objects into different categories; it would not be "distinctive." In other words, a feature permits the elimination of some of the alternative categories into which a stimulus might be allocated.

For example, a "no" answer to the test "Is the configuration curved?" would eliminate rounded letters such as *a, b, c, d* but not other letters such as *i, k, l, w, x, z.* A "yes" answer to "Is it closed?" would eliminate open letters such as *c, f, w* but not *b, d, o.* A question about symmetry would distinguish letters like *m, o, w, v* from *d, f, k, r.* Different questions eliminate different alternatives, and relatively few tests would be required to distinguish among 26 alternatives in an alphabet. In fact, if all tests eliminated about half of the alternatives, and there was no test that overlapped with any other, only five questions would be needed to identify any letter. (The logic of the previous statement is set out in the notes.) No one would actually suggest that as few as five tests are employed to distinguish among 26 letters, but it is reasonable to assume that there need be many fewer tests than categories—that is one of the great economic advantages of a feature-analytic system.

With an input bank of feature analyzers built into the letter-identification device, a link has to be provided to the 26 responses or output categories; "decision rules" must be devised so that the results of the individual tests are integrated and associated with the appropriate letter names. The most convenient way to set up the rules is to establish a feature list for each category, that is, for each of the 26 letters. The construction of the feature lists is the same for every category, namely, a listing of the analyzers that were set up to examine the visual configuration. The feature list for every category also indicates whether each particular analyzer should send back a "yes" or "no" signal for that category. For the category c, for example, the feature list should specify a "yes" for the "curved?" analyzer, a "no" for the "closed?" analyzer, a "no" for the "symmetrical?" analyzer, and so forth.

The actual wiring of the letter-identification device presents no problems—every feature analyzer is connected to every category that lists a "yes" signal from it, and we arrange that a categorizing decision (an "identification") is made only when "yes" signals are received for all the analyzers listed positively on a category's feature list. In a sense, a feature list is a *specification* of what the characteristics of a particular letter should be. *Descriptions* of a letter that is being looked at—the input—are compared with specifications of what the letter might be until a match is found.

And that, in schematic form, is a feature-analytic letter-identification device. The system is powerful, in the sense that it will do a lot of work with a minimum of effort. Unlike the template model, which to be versatile requires many templates for every decision that it might make together with complex normalizing devices, the feature-analytic device demands only a very small number of analyzers compared with the number of decisions it makes. Theoretically, such a device could decide among over a million alternatives with only 20 questions.

Functional Equivalence and Criterial Sets

A considerable advantage of the feature-analytic model over template matching is that the former has much less trouble adjusting to inputs that ought to be allocated to the same category but which vary in size or orientation or detail, for example, A, *A*, and *𝓐* The types of tests that feature analyzers apply are far better able to cope with distortion and noise than any device that requires an approximate match. But far more important, very little is added in the way of complexity or cost to provide one or more alternative feature lists for every category. With such a flexibility, the system can easily allocate not only the examples already given, but also forms as divergent as *Ꜳ*, a, *a*, and *𝓐* to the category "A." The only adjustment that need be made to the battery of analyzers is in wiring additional connections between them and the categories to which the analyzers are relevant, so that an identification will be made on any occasion when the specifications of any of the alternative lists are satisfied.

Call any set of features that meet the specifications of a particular category a *criterial set*. With the type of feature-analytic device being outlined, more than one criterial set of features may exist for any one category. Obviously, the more criterial sets that exist for a given device, the more efficient that device will be in making accurate identifications.

It is also useful to give a special name to the alternative criterial sets of features that specify the same category—we shall say that they are *functionally equivalent*. **A**, *a*, and *a* are functionally equivalent for our imagined device because they are all treated as being the same as far as the category "A" is concerned. Of course, the configurations are not functionally equivalent if they are to be distinguished on a basis other than their membership of the alphabet; a printer, for example, might want them categorized into different fonts or type styles. But as I pointed out earlier, it is the prerogative of the viewer, not a characteristic of the visual configuration, to decide which differences shall be significant—which sets of features shall be criterial—in the establishment of equivalences. All that is required to establish functional equivalence for quite disparate visual configurations is alternative feature lists for the same category.

Another powerful aspect of the feature-analytic model of pattern recognition is that it can work on a flexible and probabilistic basis. If a single feature list specifies the outcomes of ten analyzer tests for the categorical identification of a letter of the alphabet, a considerable amount of redundant information must be involved. Redundancy, as I noted in chapter 4, exists when more information is available than is required to reduce the actual amount of uncertainty. Ten analyzer tests could provide enough information to select from over a thousand equally probable alternatives, and if there are only 26 alternatives, information from five of those tests could be dispensed with and there might still be enough data to make the appropriate identification. Even if analyzer information were insufficient to enable an absolutely certain selection, it might still be possible to decide which alternatives are more likely, given the particular pattern of features that is discriminated. By not demanding that *all* the specifications of a particular feature list be satisfied before a category identification is made, the system can greatly increase its repertoire of functionally equivalent criterial sets of features. Such an increase significantly enhances the efficiency of the device at a cost of little extra complexity.

The fact that different criterial sets can be established within a single feature list provides an advantage that was alluded to in the previous paragraph—a feature-analytic system can make use of redundancy. Let's say that the system already "knows" from some other source of information that the configuration it is presented with is a vowel; it has perhaps already identified the letters *THR* ... and it has been programmed with some knowledge of the spelling patterns of English. The device can then exclude from consideration for the fourth letter all those feature lists that specify consonant categories, leaving considerably reduced criterial sets for selection among the remaining alternatives. (Three tests might easily distinguish among five or six vowels.)

A final powerful advantage of the feature-analytic model has also already been implied; it is a device that can easily *learn*. Every time a new feature list or criterial set is established there is an instance of learning. All that the device requires in order to learn is *feedback* from the environment. It establishes, or rejects, a new feature list for a particular category (or category for a particular feature list) by "hypothesizing" a relationship between a feature list and a category and testing whether that relationship is appropriate.

You may have noticed that the feature-analytic discussion develops easily into such topics as "learning" and "thinking." It is evident that the more efficient and sophisticated we make our hypothetical letter-identifying device, the more we are likely to talk about its realization in human rather than computer terms. It is time to discard the computer analogy and to direct a more specific focus on the human pattern recognizer.

The Human Letter Identifier

I'll use feature analysis as a model for the way in which letters are identified by readers. We learn to identify the letters of the alphabet by establishing feature lists for the required 26 categories, each of which is interrelated to a single name "A," "B," "C," and so forth. The visual system is equipped with analyzers that respond to those features in the visual environment that are distinctive for alphabetic discriminations (and many other visual discriminations as well). The results of the analyzer tests are integrated and directed to the appropriate feature lists so that letter identifications can occur. The human visual perceptual system is biologically competent to demonstrate all the most powerful aspects of the feature-analytic model outlined in the last section—to establish manifold criterial sets of features with functional equivalence, to function probabilistically, to make use of redundancy, and to learn by testing hypotheses and receiving feedback. Establishing feature lists, in other words, is natural.

Two aspects of letter identification must be distinguished. The first aspect is the establishment of cognitive categories themselves and especially the allocation of category names to them, such as "A," "B," "C." This might be termed "learning to *say* the letters of the alphabet." The second aspect of letter identification is the allocation of visual configurations to various cognitive categories—the discrimination of various configurations as different, as not functionally equivalent. This might be termed "learning to *recognize* (or *identify*) the letters of the alphabet." The greater part of perceptual learning involves finding out what exactly are the distinctive features by which various configurations should be categorized as different from each other and what are the sets of features that are criterial for particular categories. These are precisely the two aspects of object or concept learning involved in distinguishing one face from another, or cats from dogs. Categories must be established with unique names (like "cat" and "dog"), and rules must be devised for allocating particular instances to the appropriate categories.

The association of a name with a category is neither necessary nor primary in visual discrimination. It is quite possible to segregate visual configurations into different categories without having a name for them. We can see that *A* and & are different and know they should be treated differently, even though we may not have a category name, or even a specific category, for &. In fact, we can't allocate a name to & unless first we acquire some unconscious rules for discriminating it from *A* and from every other visual configuration with which it should not be given functional equivalence. The motivation for the establishment of a new category may come from either direction: Either a configuration such as & can't be related to any existing category, or a new name such as "ampersand" can't be related to an existing category. The intermediate steps that tie the entire system together are the establishment of the first feature lists and criterial sets for the category so that the appropriate feature tests and the category name can be related.

Not only is relating a name to a category not primary; it is not difficult. The complicated part of learning to make an identification is not in remembering the name of a particular category but in discovering the criterial sets of features for that category. Children at the age when they are often learning to read are also learning thousands of new names every year—names of friends and celebrities and automobiles and animals—as well as the names of letters and words. The person they learn from, the informal instructor, usually points to or refers to an object and says "That's an X," leaving the child to work out what the significant differences must be. The complicated part of learning is the establishment of functional equivalences for the categories with which names are associated.

The reason that "learning names" is frequently thought to be difficult is that all the intermediate steps are ignored and it is assumed that a name is applied directly to a particular visual configuration. Children may find it difficult to respond with the right name for the letters *b* or *d* (or for the words *house* and *mouse*, or for an actual dog or cat) but not because they can't put the name to the configuration. Their basic problem is to find out how two alternatives are significantly different. Once learners can make the discrimination, so that the appropriate functional equivalences are established, the allocation of the correct verbal label is a relatively easy problem because the label is related directly to the category.

The Letter Identifier in Action

Is there evidence to support the feature-analytic model of the human visual system? Some of the physiological evidence has already been indicated. There is no one-to-one correspondence between the visual information impinging on the eye and anything that goes on behind the eyeball. The eye doesn't send "images" back to the brain; the stammering pattern of neural impulses is a representation of discrete features detected by the eye, not the transfer of a "picture." In the brain itself, there is no possibility of storing templates or even acquiring them in the first place. The brain doesn't deal in veridical representations; it shunts abstractions through its complex neural networks. It is true that one aspect of the brain's output, our subjective experience of the world, is generated in the form of "percepts" that might be regarded as pictures, but this experience is a *consequence* of the brain's activity, not something the brain "stores" and compares with inputs. Our visual experience is the product of the perceptual system, not part of a visual process.

Now we can examine evidence for the feature-analytic model from two kinds of letter-identification experiments. (Details are given in the notes.) The basic assumption to be tested is that letters are actually conglomerates of features, of which there are perhaps a dozen different kinds. The only way in which letters differ visually from each other is in the presence or absence of these features.

Letters that have several features in common will be regarded as similar, and letters that are constructed of quite different feature combinations will be considered quite dissimilar in appearance. How does one assess similarity? Letters are similar—they are presumed to share many features—if they are frequently confused with each other. Letters that are rarely confused with each other are assumed to have very few features in common.

Of course, we don't confuse letters very often, and when we do the character of the error is usually influenced by nonvisual factors. We might, for example, think that the fourth letter in the sequence *REQW* ... is *U*, not because *W* and *U* are visually similar but because we normally expect a *U* to follow *Q*. However, large numbers of visual letter confusions can be generated by experimental techniques in which the letter to be identified is so "impoverished" that viewers can't see it clearly, although they are forced to make a guess about what the letter probably is. In other words, the experimental viewers must make letter-identification decisions on minimal visual information. The research assumption is that viewers who can't see the letter clearly must lack some vital information and thus be unable to make some feature tests. And if they are unable to make certain feature tests, then the tests they are able to make will not reduce all uncertainty about the 26 alternative responses. Viewers will still be left in doubt about a few possibilities that could be differentiated only by the tests that they have been unable to perform.

The actual method of visual degeneration is not important. The presentation may be a brief tachistoscopic presentation, or it may involve an image that is difficult to discriminate, projected at a low intensity or hidden behind a lot of visual noise. As soon as viewers start making errors, one can assume that they are not getting all the information that they need to make an identification. They are deciding on something less than a criterial set of features.

There are only two possibilities if viewers are forced to identify a letter on insufficient visual information: Either their guesses will be completely random, or they will respond in some systematic way. If guesses are *random* they could be to respond with any of the 26 letters of the alphabet. But if responses are *systematic*, the interesting possibility is that the viewers are selecting only from those alternative responses that remain after the features that can be discriminated have been taken into account. In such a circumstance, it is to be expected that the confusions will "cluster"; instead of 25 types of confusion, one for each possible erroneous response, there will be only a few types.

The evidence is that letter confusions fall into tightly packed clusters, and over two thirds of the confusions for most letters can be accounted for by three or four confusion types. If a mistake is made in the identification of a letter, the nature of the erroneous response is highly predictable. Typical confusion clusters can be very suggestive about the kind of information the eye must be looking for in discriminating letters. Some typical confusion clusters are (*a, e, n, o, u*), (*t, f, i*), and (*h, m, n*) (Dunn-Rankin, 1968).

The specific conclusion to be drawn from the kind of experiment just described is that letters are indeed composed of a relatively small number of features. Letters that are easily confused, like *a* and *e* or *t* and *f*, must have a number of features in common, and those that are rarely confused, like *o* and *w* or *d* and *y*, must have few if any features in common. The general conclusion that may be drawn is that the visual system is indeed feature analytic. Letter identification is accomplished by examination of the visual environment for featural information that will eliminate all alternatives except one, thus permitting an accurate identification to be made.

There is a second line of experimental evidence supporting the view that letters are arrangements of smaller elements, and this is related to the fact that recognition is faster or easier when there are fewer alternatives for what each letter might be. The classic example of such evidence has already been described in the tunnel vision demonstration of chapter 5, where it was shown that nonvisual information can be employed to reduce the amount of visual—or distinctive feature—information required to identify letters. There are other illustrations when the identification of words is considered in the next chapter.

WHAT IS A FEATURE?

The entire discussion of letter identification by feature analysis has been conducted without actually specifying what a feature is. The omission has been deliberate, because nobody knows what the distinctive features of letters are. Not enough is known about the human visual system to say exactly what is the featural information that the system looks for.

Of course, general statements about features can be made. There have been a number of attempts to do this, with reasoning like "The only difference between *c* and *o* is that the circle of *o* is 'closed'; therefore, being closed must be a distinctive feature," or "The only difference between *h* and *n* is the 'ascender' at the top of *h*; therefore, an ascender must be a distinctive feature." But we really don't know whether, or how, the eyes might look for "closed-ness" or for "ascenders." It can be argued that these hypothesized features are really properties of whole letters, and it is far from clear how a property of the whole could also be an element out of which the whole is constructed. It is obviously a reasonable proposal that the significant difference between *h* and *n* has something to do with the ascender, but it is an oversimplification to say that the ascender is the actual feature.

Fortunately, it is not necessary to know exactly what the features are in order to assist children in discriminating letters. We can trust children to locate the information required provided the appropriate informational environment is available. The appropriate informational environment is the opportunity to make comparisons and discover what the significant differences are. Remember, the primary problem of identification is to distinguish the presented configuration from all those to which it might be equivalent but is not; the configuration has to be subjected to feature analysis and put in the appropriate category. Presenting *h* to children 50 times and telling them it is "h" because it has an ascender will not help them to distinguish the letter. The presentation of *h* with *other* letters that are *not* functionally equivalent is the kind of information required for the brain to find out very quickly what the distinctive features are.

ISSUES

Whether physiological evidence—for example, from eye-movement or brain-function studies—should make any difference to how reading should be taught is a contentious question. Should learners be taught "feature recognition," for example, when the status of features is hypothetical and everyone who has learned to read in the past has coped without such specialized knowledge? This is part of a general issue that comes up constantly in this book, although frequently taken for granted elsewhere: whether *descriptions* of what readers do (or are hypothesized to do) should be the basis of what learners are *taught*.

SUMMARY

A feature identification model is proposed for letter identification. *Feature lists* permit the allocation of visual information to specific cognitive categories, in the present case for letters. Feature lists are *specifications* of what visual information has to be like in order to be allocated to a particular category. The names of letters are part of the interrelations among categories. To permit the identification of the same letter when it has different configurations, for example, $\mathcal{A}$ A, a, and **a**, *functionally equivalent* feature lists are established. For each feature list there will be a number of alternative *criterial sets* to permit identification decisions on a minimum of visual information, depending on the number and nature of the alternatives.

Notes to chapter 7 begin on page 274 covering:

Recognition versus identification

Theories of pattern recognition

8 Word Identification

The preceding chapter was devoted to letter identification. In this chapter, I show that the prior identification of letters is not required for the identification of entire words. This chapter is restricted to considering words in isolation, where there is no extrinsic clue to their identity. I am still not focusing on anything that might normally be regarded as *reading*, where a meaningful purpose and context are involved. But the chapter is another step toward a demonstration that procedures permitting the visual identification of words without the prior identification of letters also permit comprehension without the prior identification of words.

THREE THEORIES OF WORD IDENTIFICATION

There are three broad classes of theory about word identification: *whole-word identification, letter-by-letter identification*, and an intermediate position involving the identification of letter clusters, usually termed *spelling patterns*. In effect, these three views represent three attempts to describe the manner in which a skilled reader is able to identify words on sight. They are accounts of what a reader needs to know and do in order to be able to say what a word is. One or another of the three views is apparent in practically every approach to reading instruction.

The *whole-word* view is based on the premise that readers don't stop to identify individual letters (or groups of letters) in the identification of a word. Instead the word is identified on the basis of its shape, or its "structure." The view asserts that knowledge of the alphabet and of the "sounds of letters" is irrelevant to reading. One source of support for the whole-word view has already been alluded to—the fact that a viewer can report from a single tachistoscopic presentation either four or five random letters or a similar number of words. Surely if a word can be identified as easily as a letter, then it must be just as much of a unit as a letter; a word must be recognizable as a whole, rather than as a sequence of letters. Another piece of supporting evidence is that words may be identified when none of their component letters is clearly discriminable. For example, a name may be identifiable on a distant roadside sign, or in a dim light, under conditions that would make each individual letter of that name illegible if presented separately. If words can be read when letters are illegible, how can word recognition depend on letter identification? Finally, there is a good deal of evidence that words can be identified as quickly as letters. It has been shown that perception is far from instantaneous and that successively presented random letters—or random words—can't be identified faster than five or six per second (starting with Kolers & Katzman, 1966; Newman, 1966). And if entire words can be identified as quickly as letters, how can their identification involve spelling them out letter by letter?

A fundamental objection to the whole-word point of view is that it is not a theory at all; it merely rephrases the question it claims to answer. If words are recognized "as wholes," how are the wholes recognized? What exactly do readers know if they know what a word looks like? The qualification that words are identified "by their shapes" merely changes the name of the problem from "word identification" to "shape identification." Fluent readers are able to recognize at least 50,000 different words on sight (see Notes)—by what I call *immediate word identification*. Does that mean that readers have pictures of 50,000 different shapes stored in their minds and that for every word they encounter in reading they rummage through a pack of 50,000 templates in order to find a match? In what way would they sort through 50,000 alternatives? Surely not by starting at *aardvark* and examining each internal representation until they find a match. If we are looking for a book in a library, we don't start at the entrance and examine every volume until we come across the one with a title that matches the title we are looking for. Instead, we make use of the fact that books are categorized and shelved in a predictable way; there are shortcuts for getting to the book we want. It would appear reasonable that we make use of shortcuts to make our word identification decisions quickly. We can usually find some explanation for any error that we make. We may misread *said* as *sail* or *send* (or even as *reported* in circumstances where the substitution would make sense), but never as *elephant, plug,* or *predisposition.* In other words, we obviously don't select a word from 50,000 alternatives, but rather from a much smaller number. An unelaborated whole-word point of view can't account for this prior elimination of alternatives.

Besides, we have already discovered that 50,000 internal representations of shapes would be far from adequate to enable us to identify 50,000 different words. Even if we could identify *HAT* by looking up an internal representation, how could the same representation enable us to identify *hat* or *ḥat* or any of the many other ways in which the word may be written?

The letter-by-letter theory, which the whole-word view is supposed to demolish, itself appears to have substantial supportive evidence. Readers are frequently sensitive to individual letters in the identification of words. The whole-word point of view would suggest that if viewers were presented with the stimulus *fashixn* tachistoscopically, they would either identify "the whole word" without noticing the *x* or else fail to recognize the word at all because there would be no "match" with an internal representation. Instead, viewers typically identify the word but report that there is something wrong with it, not necessarily reporting that there is an *x* instead of an *o*, but offering such explanations as "There's a hair lying over the end of it"—an observation first made over a century ago (Pillsbury, 1897).

Furthermore, readers are very sensitive to the *predictability* of letter sequences. Letters don't occur haphazardly. In English, for example, combinations like *th, st, br,* and almost any consonant and vowel pair are more likely to occur than combinations like *tf, sr, bm, ae,* or *uo.* The knowledge that readers acquire about these differing probabilities of letter combinations is demonstrated when words containing common letter sequences are more easily identified than those with uncommon sequences. Readers can identify sequences of letters that are *not* English words just as easily as some English words, provided the sequences are "close approximations" to English—which means that they are highly probable letter combinations (Miller, Bruner, & Postman, 1954). The average reader, for example, hardly falters when presented with sequences like *vernalit* or *mossiant* or *ricaning*—yet how could these be identified "as wholes" when they have never been seen before?

A rather illogical argument is sometimes proposed to support the letter-by-letter theory. Because letters in some way spell out approximations to the sound of a word (the "phonics" point of view), word identification *must* be accomplished by identification of the individual letters. It would be about as compelling to suggest that we must recognize models of cars by reading the manufacturer's name on the back, simply because the name is always there to be read. Besides, the spelling of words is not a reliable guide to their sound. This question is so complex that phonics is given the next chapter to itself. For the moment we aren't concerned with whether knowledge of letters can be used to identify words, but rather with whether skilled readers normally and necessarily identify words "that they know" by a time- and attention-consuming letter-by-letter analysis.

The intermediate position—that words are identified through the recognition of *clusters of letters*—has the advantage of being able to account for the relatively easy identifiability of nonwords such as *vernalit*. It argues that readers become familiar with spelling patterns, such as *ve* and *rn* and even *vern*, which are recognized and put together to form words. The larger the spelling patterns we can recognize, the easier the word identification. The view is compatible with our normal experience that when a new word like *zygotic* or *Helsingfors* halts our reading temporarily we don't seem to break it down to individual letters before trying to put together what its meaning or sound must be. But many of the arguments that favor the whole-word position over letter analysis also work against the letter-cluster view. It may be useful, occasionally, to work out what a word is by analysis of letters or syllables, but normal reading doesn't appear to proceed on this basis; in fact, it would seem impossible. There isn't time to work out what words are by synthesizing possible letter or sound combinations. Besides, as the letter-cluster argument is pushed to its extreme it becomes a whole-word approach because the largest and most reliable spelling patterns are words themselves.

A Feature-Analytic Alternative

Any serious attempt to understand reading must be able to explain why it might sometimes appear that words are identified as wholes and at other times through the apparent identification of component letters or groups of letters. In the previous chapter, two models for letter identification were examined: feature analysis and template matching. The traditional whole-word theory that words are identified because of the familiarity of their "shape" is essentially a *template-matching* model, and arguments for its inadequacy have already been presented. The remainder of the present chapter considers the alternative, a *feature-analytic* model for the identification of individual words in isolation, or effectively so because context is ignored. The identification of words in meaningful sequences, which is of course far more representative of most reading situations, is considered in chapter 10.

Basically, the feature-analytic model proposes that the only difference between the manner in which individual letters and individual words are identified lies in the complexity of the categories and feature lists that the viewer employs in the analysis of visual information. The difference depends on whether the reader is looking for letters or for words; the process of looking and deciding is the same. If the reader's objective is to identify letters, then the analysis of the visual configuration is carried out with respect to the feature lists associated with the 26 letter categories, one for each letter of the alphabet. If the objective is to identify words, then there is a similar analysis of features in the visual configuration with respect to the feature lists, or specifications, of a larger number of word categories.

What are the features of words? They obviously include the features of letters, because words are made up of letters. The arrays of marks on the printed page that can be read as words can also be distinguished as sequences of letters, so the "distinctive features" that constitute significant differences between one letter and another must also be distinctive features of words. For example, whatever visual information permits us to distinguish between *h* and *n* must also permit us to distinguish between *hot* and *not*. At first glance, many more discriminations and analyses of distinctive features would appear to be required to distinguish among tens of thousands of alternative words compared with only 26 alternative letters, but we shall see that the difference is not so great. In fact, no more information—no more featural tests—may be required to identify a word in meaningful text than to identify a single letter in isolation.

If the distinctive features of the visual configurations of letters are the same as those for the visual configurations of written words, it might be expected that feature lists for letter and word categories would be similar. However, feature lists for word categories allow an additional dimension to those for letters—the analysis of word configurations involves the position of features within a sequence. The number of "positions" in a word feature list reflects the number of times a particular feature could occur in the sequence of letters that constitute the word and obviously corresponds to the number of letters. A feature test that will be applied only once for the identification of a letter may be employed several times in the identification of a word, with the maximum number of tests equaling the number of letters in the word. This congruence between "position" and "letter" occurs because the distinctive features of individual letters become the distributed distinctive features of words. But it doesn't follow that individual letters must be identified in order for words to be identified. I therefore use the term "position" rather than "letter" to avoid any implication that a word is identified from its letters, rather than by the distribution of features across its entire configuration.

There could be a few distinctive features of words that are not features of letters, for example, the total width of the word configuration and—if the word is in lower case—the relative heights of different parts. Many words in context can be identified by their contours (Haber & Haber, 1981; Haber, Haber, & Furlin, 1983). But as I have already noted, not enough is known of the visual system to assert what distinctive features might actually be.

The feature-analytic view of letter identification proposes that because there is redundancy in the structure of letters—because there is more than enough featural information to distinguish among 26 alternatives—not all features need be discriminated for a letter to be identified. Therefore, a number of alternative criterial sets of features may exist within each feature list, information about the features within any set being sufficient for an identification to be made. It would be expected that criterial sets could also exist for words to be identified, except that now they would extend over a second dimension and take into account feature combinations across the entire word. As I explained in chapter 7 and its notes, five or six features would be adequate to identify any letter, although there are doubtless more. That means that words, with an average length of about five letters, must consist of at least 25 distinctive features. The actual uncertainty of words in isolation (see page 264) requires only half that number (and only about a quarter for words in context).

Redundancy Among Distinctive Features of Words

Experienced readers acquire wide knowledge of the way in which letters are grouped into words, for example that *th* and *sp* are frequent combinations and that *tf* and *sr* are not. This knowledge of the way words are spelled, or *orthographic information*, is an alternative nonvisual source of information to the *featural* or *visual* information available to the eyes from the page. To the extent that both of these sources of information reduce the number of alternative ways in which a written or printed word might be constructed, there is redundancy. The duplication of information resulting from orthographic predictability is a form of *sequential redundancy*, because its source lies in the fact that the different parts of a word are not independent; the occurrence of particular alternatives in one part of the sequence of letters limits the range of alternatives that can occur anywhere else in the sequence.

The orthographic redundancy of English is enormous. If all 26 letters of the alphabet could occur without restriction in each position of a five-letter word, there could be nearly 12 million different five-letter words, compared with perhaps 10,000 that actually exist.

I have been referring to the sequential constraints that one letter places on the occurrence of other letters in a word. But precisely the same argument can apply to features. Obviously, if we can say that the occurrence of the letter T in the first position of a word restricts the possibilities for the second position to $H, R, A, E, I, O, U,$ and $Y,$ then we can also say that the occurrence of the features of the letter T restricts the possible features that can occur in the second position. In fact, we can avoid mentioning letters and specific positions altogether and say that when certain features occur in one part of a word, there are limits to the kinds of feature combinations in other parts of the word and to what the word as a whole might be. A reader implicitly knowledgeable about such limitations is able to make use of *sequential redundancy among features*, and as a result will be able to identify words with so little visual information that the identification of letters is completely bypassed. Similar arguments concerning featural redundancy are made by linguists to explain the pronunciation and recognition of spoken words (Pinker, 1999, pp. 93–94).

The visual identification of words becomes very fast and efficient. Fraisse (1984) observed that experienced readers could often name printed words like *house* and *tree* flashed on a screen quicker than they could name drawings of the referents of the same words, even though they had previously seen the full set of words and drawings they would be asked to identify.

To summarize, the difference between letter and word identification is simply the category system that is involved—the manner in which featural information is allocated. If the reader is examining an array of visual information in order to identify letters, the visual information will be tested and identifications made on the basis of the feature lists for the 26 categories. If the purpose is to identify words, the visual information will be tested with respect to the feature lists for words, and there will be no question of letter identification. It follows from this argument that it should be impossible to identify a word and its component letters simultaneously, because one can't use the same information to make two different kinds of decision.

Because letter identification and word identification involve the same featural information, it is not possible to identify a configuration both as a word and as a sequence of letters at the same time. We can see the configuration *cat* either as the letters *c, a, t* or as the word *cat*, but not as both simultaneously. Similarly, we can see the configuration *read* either as the word pronounced "reed" or as the word pronounced "red" but not as both at once; and *IO* can be seen either as numerals or as letters but not as both. We can't apply the same information to two categories simultaneously, just as we can't use the same contour as part of two figures simultaneously—we can't see the vase and the faces of Fig. 2.1 (page 18) simultaneously.

LEARNING TO IDENTIFY WORDS

Two aspects of learning to identify words are analogous to the two aspects of learning to identify letters outlined at the end of the last chapter. One aspect is establishing criterial sets of functionally equivalent distinctive features for each category, the specifications for qualifying configurations, and the other aspect is associating a name with a category. For letter identification, it was asserted that relating the name to the category was not a problem; children learn names for visual configurations all the time. In word identification, there may indeed be a problem in relating names to categories, because children may have difficulty not in remembering the name for a category once they have found out what it is, but in ascertaining the category name in the first place. When children are beginning to discover written language, helpful adults often act as mediators by saying what the printed words are, leaving to the child the more complex task of discovering how to distinguish one word from another. Someone says to them "That word is *cat*" or "This is how your name is written." Or they read a simple story with them.

Finding out the name of a category in the absence of outside help may be termed *mediated word identification* and is the topic of the next chapter. Word identification must be *mediated* when a word can't be identified on sight by allocation to a category through an existing feature list. By contrast, I refer to word identification as discussed in this chapter as *immediate word identification*. The term *immediate* is used not in the sense of instantaneous, which we know is not the case, but to mean not mediated, indicating that a word is identified directly from its features. The aspect of learning with which the remainder of this chapter is concerned is the establishment of appropriate visual feature lists for immediate word identification.

It will help if we imagine a specific instance. A child is about to learn to recognize a particular written word, say, *John*. The task confronting the child is to discover the rules for recognizing this event when it occurs again, which means finding out something about the configuration that will distinguish it from other configurations that should not be called "John." Assume that the child has already discovered that a reliable distinguishing characteristic for the configuration is not the color of the paper that it is printed on or the color of the ink, both of which may be reasonable cues for other types of identification but which will sooner or later prove to be inadequate for the allocation of visual information to word categories. Also assume that the child at this time is not confronted by *John* in a number of different type styles. The ability to name any or all of the letters of the alphabet has no direct relevance in immediate word identification, although there will be an obvious (although by no means essential) advantage for children if they have learned to distinguish even a few letters, without necessarily being able to name them, because they will have begun to acquire cues about the features that distinguish words.

The problem for the child is to discover cues that will distinguish *John* from other configurations. The child may decide that a good cue lies in the length of the word, or the two upright strokes, or the shape of the "fish hook" at the beginning. In selecting a cue that will be the basis for recognition of the word, a child will establish the first tentative distinctive features to be looked for in the future when testing whether to allocate a configuration to the category "John."

Exactly what the first distinctive feature will be depends on the other words from which the child tries to distinguish the configuration *John*. Until the child comes across another word that is not *John*, there is no problem; the child applies the single test and calls every configuration that passes the test *John*. But until the child comes across another word that is not *John*, there can be no learning. What brings a child to the development of feature lists that will serve for reading is having to distinguish *John* from all the other configurations with which it is not functionally equivalent. The child will only really be able to identify *John* after learning not to apply that name to every other word configuration that is met. It is when the child is confronted by a configuration that should go into a different category that the soundness of the tentative discrimination is tested, and, of course, it is soon found to be wanting. If the hypothesized distinctive features were related to the length of the word, then the child would respond *John* to the configuration *Fred*. If the hypothesis involved the initial fishhook, the child would say "John" to *Jack*, or *June*, or *Jeremiah*. The more non-equivalent configurations—the more different words—children have to discriminate among, the more they will come to select as distinctive features those that will be appropriate to the eventual task of fluent reading. But until children can understand what they have to distinguish *John* from, they will never acquire an appropriate set of distinctive features for identifying that word.

The preceding statement doesn't mean that children must be able to *name* every other word they meet; not at all. All they have to do is see a representative sample of words that are not *John*, so that they can find out in what respects *John* is different. It doesn't matter if they can't discriminate among all the other words (although in learning to identify *John* they will learn something about all other words); the beginning can be the establishment of only two categories: configurations that are *John* and configurations that aren't *John*. Attempting to teach "one word at a time," repeatedly insisting "This is *John*; this is *John*," won't help children to learn the word because they will never learn how *John* may be distinguished from any other word. The notion that a child can learn to identify a word by repetition (or "practice") is a template theory. But there is no way for a child to transfer a picture of what is presented to the eyes into a storehouse in the brain. Children don't need to be told interminably what a word *is*; they have to be able to *see what it is not*.

Acquaintance with a wide variety of nonequivalent alternatives is everything. Through growing familiarity with the written form of language, children learn not only to discriminate distinctive features, to establish feature lists, and to recognize functional equivalences, but they also learn about redundancy. And by acquiring a pool of knowledge about the redundancy of words, they learn to identify words economically, on minimal quantities of visual information; they establish large numbers of alternative criterial sets. At no stage is there any need to belabor the presence of particular letters, or to make reference to their putative "sounds."

It is perhaps a sobering thought that just about everything that a child must learn, as described in the preceding paragraph, is never explicitly taught. Among the many positive things reading teachers can do—providing relevant demonstrations, collaboration, and encouragement—they can't include the provision of rules by which words are to be differentiated and recognized. That part of learning must be left to children themselves. They must be given the opportunity, and if necessary the assistance, to gain experience in reading so that they can achieve all the learning that is necessary.

A POSTSCRIPT ABOUT WORDS

One of the inevitable consequences of examining closely a subject like reading, about which so much is taken for granted, is that it turns out to be more complicated and less well understood than we thought it to be. An obvious first step in my discussion of word identification might have been to state clearly and precisely how many words the average fluent reader knows. This would give some useful knowledge about the dimensions of the problem. But the trouble with a simple request for a count of the words that a person knows is that the answer depends on what is meant by "word," and that in any case there is no way to compute a reliable answer.

Consider first the matter of deciding what we want to call a word. Should *cat* and *cats* (or *walk* and *walked*) be regarded as two different words or as two forms of the same word? Dictionaries usually provide entries only for the base or root form of words, refusing to count as different words such variations as plurals, comparatives, adjectival forms, and various verb tenses. If we want to call *cat* and *cats* (or *walk* and *walked*) different words (and certainly we would not regard them as functionally equivalent visually), the number of words we know on sight might turn out to be three or four times greater than the number of words the dictionary maker would credit us with. Furthermore, common words have many meanings as in "You can *bank* on the *bank* by the river *bank*." But if the same spelling is to be regarded as (at least) three different words because *bank* has several meanings, should a preposition like *by*, which has so many different senses, be counted as 40 words or more?

The next problem is to count. Obviously, it is not good enough simply to count the number of words that a person reads or hears or produces during the course of a day, for many words will be used more than once and others will occur not at all. To count the number of *different* words a person produces, we have to examine a torrent of very familiar words. But in how big a torrent shall we look? How can we ever be certain that we have given sufficient opportunity for all the words a person knows? Without a doubt, we shall find some new words in every additional sample of a thousand that we record, but surely a law of decreasing returns would apply. After analyzing, say, 100,000 words from one person, it would seem unlikely that many new ones would be produced. But such is not the case. Very many words with which we are quite familiar occur less than once in every million, and it may take anywhere from 2 months to 2 years for a person to produce that number of words. One very extensive analysis of nearly 5 million word occurrences in popular magazines (Thorndike & Lorge, 1944) found over 3,000 words that occurred an average of less than once in every million, and almost all of these words would fall under our category of known. Here are some of the words that occurred only once in every 5 million words: *earthiness, echelon, eclair, effluence, egotistic.* One or two may be a little unusual, but by and large they are words that we can recognize.

Obviously, it is not possible to count how many different words an individual might know, so an estimate is necessary. And many estimates have been offered, varying from 50,000 to over 800,000, depending on the definitions used and assumptions made. This gives one good answer to the question of how many words a person might know—it is impossible to say.

When Is a Word Not a Word?

Researchers who use experimental procedures in what they call reading studies frequently claim that their test materials are meaningful because they consist of words that appear in dictionaries, in contrast to nonword sequences of letters like *ricaning, vernalit, msk,* or *wbc.* It may be difficult to see why strings of letters that have no relevance to readers should be regarded as meaningful, even if the letters do happen to be in sequences that appear in dictionaries. A spoken word produced without expressive or communicative intent is simply noise, and there is little reason to regard a similarly produced written word as anything different.

ISSUES

There is lively technical speculation about the neurological processes assumed to underlie the identification of written words, presumably no different from the processes underlying our remarkably efficient facility for recognizing faces, places, dogs, cats, and innumerable other objects, and no better understood. The study of word identification is often confounded by the question of whether it is necessary to say a written word to oneself—to "decode" (or "recode") it—in order to understand it. Obviously we don't need to say to ourselves that an animal that suddenly confronts us is a dog in order to understand that it is a dog; rather, the wordless identification of "dogness" must precede the naming. Why then should we have to say that the written word *dog* is pronounced "dog" in order to understand it in a story? The relationship between the sounds of speech and the visual representations of written words is one of the most contentious issues in reading theory and research.

SUMMARY

Words, like letters, can be identified directly from the distinctive features that are the visual information of print. Immediate word identification takes place when feature analysis allocates a visual configuration to the feature list of a word category in cognitive structure, without the intermediate step of letter identification. Criterial sets of features within functionally equivalent feature lists permit the identification of words on minimal information, for example, when the reader can employ prior knowledge of the orthographic redundancy within words.

Notes to chapter 8 begin on page 277 covering:
Template and feature-analytic theories
Letter identification in words
Use of redundancy by children
Distributional redundancy among words

9 Phonics and Mediated Word Identification

The preceding chapter was concerned with *immediate* word identification, and the manner in which visual feature lists may be established and used so that words can be recognized on sight, without "decoding to sound" or any other means of *mediated* word identification. In fact, the chapter argued that letter-by-letter identification is unnecessary and even impossible for word identification in normal reading, thus leaving no room for decoding to sound. Immediate word identification is illustrated in Fig. 9.1.

In the preceding chapter, I was talking about the identification of words where the "name" of the word—its pronunciation when read aloud—is either known to the reader or otherwise available to the learner. The learner doesn't need to figure out what the visual configuration "says," but only how it should be recognized on future occasions. The situation is identical to that of a child who is told that a particular animal is a cat and then left to discover how to recognize cats on other occasions.

Suppose, however, that the name of a word is not immediately available to the learner—that there is no one to identify an unfamiliar word, and there are no context cues, perhaps because the word is seen in isolation or as part of a list of unrelated words. Now the

138

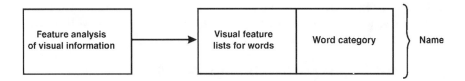

FIG. 9.1.   Immediate word identification.

learner has a double problem, not only to discover how to recognize the word in the future but to find out what the word is in the first place. This is like trying to discover how to distinguish cats and dogs without being told whether particular animals are cats or dogs. In such a situation in reading, a word obviously cannot be identified *immediately*; its identification must be *mediated* by some other means of discovering what it is. The present chapter is about the use of *phonics*—a set of relationships between letters and sounds—and other methods of mediated word identification. The use of phonic rules to mediate word identification is illustrated in Fig. 9.2.

In particular, this chapter examines the extent to which knowledge of the sounds associated with letters of the alphabet helps in the identification of words. For many, this process of decoding the spelling of words to their sounds is the basis of reading, a view that I don't think is tenable. It is not necessary and sometimes it is impossible to "say" what a written word is before we can comprehend its meaning; the naming of a word normally occurs after the identification of its meaning.

This chapter is still not the whole story of reading, even as far as words are concerned. In both the preceding and the present chapters, the assumption is made that the word a reader is trying to identify already exists in the reader's spoken language vocabulary; its meaning is known. The reader's problem is to identify the word, to discover or recognize its "name," not to learn its mean-

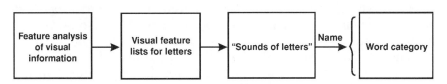

FIG. 9.2.   Mediated word identification: the phonic model.

ing. The next chapter deals with the situation of words that are truly new, where the meaning must be discovered as well as the name or pronunciation.

THE COMPLEXITY AND LIMITATIONS OF PHONICS

Mediated word identification is not the most critical part of reading, and phonics is not the only strategy available for mediated word identification. Nor is phonics the best strategy. Nevertheless, phonics frequently plays a central role in reading instruction, and it will clear the air if we examine the efficacy of phonics first.

Rules and Exceptions

The aim of phonics instruction is to provide readers with rules that will enable them to predict how a written word will sound from the way it is spelled. The value of teaching phonics depends on how many correspondences there are between the letters and sounds of English. A correspondence exists whenever a particular letter (or sometimes a group of letters) represents a particular sound (or absence of sound). Thus, *c* is involved in at least four correspondences—with the sound /s/ as in *city*, with /k/ as in *medical*, as part of /ch/ as in *much*, and with no sound at all as in *scientist*. Alternatively, a correspondence exists whenever a particular sound is represented by a particular letter or letters, as /f/ can be represented by *f*, *ph*, and *gh*. Thus, the total number of "spelling–sound" correspondences must be the same as the total number of "sound–spelling" correspondences. But by now it is probably no surprise that any question related to language involving a simple "how many" leads to a very complicated and unsatisfactory approximation to an answer. Phonics is no exception.

The first problem concerns our expectations about rules. If we expect a rule to mean a correspondence that has no exceptions, then we will have a difficult task finding any rules in phonics at all. Here is a phonic rule that would appear to have impeccable credentials: Final *e* following a single consonant indicates that the preceding vowel should be long, as in *hat* and *hate*, or *hop* and *hope*. And here are two instant exceptions: *axe* has a single consonant but a short /a/, while *ache* has a double consonant but a long /a/. We have the choice of admitting that a familiar rule is not impervious to exceptions, or else we have to make a rule for the exceptions. One explanation that might be offered is that *x* is really a double consonant, *ks*, and that *ch* is really a single consonant, *k*. But then we are in the rather peculiar position of changing the notion of what constitutes a single letter simply because we have a rule that doesn't fit all cases. And if we have to say that the definition of what constitutes a letter depends on the pronunciation of a word, how can we say the pronunciation of a word can be predicted from its letters? Besides, what can we say about the silent *e* at the end of *have* or *love*, which is put there only because there is a convention that English words may not end with a *v*? Or the *e* at the end of *house*, which is to indicate that the word is not a plural? Or the *o* in *money* and *women*, which is there because early printers felt that a succession of up-and-down strokes, like *mun* and *wim*, would be too difficult to decipher?

Having made the point that phonic rules will have exceptions, the next problem is to decide what constitutes an exception. Some exceptions occur so frequently and regularly that they would appear to be rules in their own right. It is quite arbitrary how anyone decides to draw the line between rules and exceptions. We have a choice of saying that the sounds of written English can be predicted by relatively few rules, although there will be quite a lot of exceptions, or by a large number of rules with relatively few exceptions. Indeed, if we care to say that some rules have only one application, for example, that *acht* is pronounced /ot/ as in "yacht," then we can describe English completely in terms of rules simply because we have legislated exceptions out of existence.

If the concept of a rule seems arbitrary, the notion of what constitutes a letter is even more idiosyncratic. It is true that in one sense there can be no doubt about what a letter is—it is one of the 26 characters in the alphabet—but any attempt to construct rules of spelling-sound correspondence is doomed if we restrict our terms of reference to individual letters. To start with, there are only 26 letters, compared with about 40 or more different sounds of speech, so many letters at least must do double duty. We find, of course, that many letters stand for more than one sound, while many sounds are represented by more than one letter. However, many sounds are not represented by single letters at all—*th*, *ch*, *ou* and *ue*, for example—so that we have to consider some combinations of letters as quite distinct *spelling units*—rather as if *th* were a letter in its own right (as it is in Greek, in two different forms for two different pronunciations). It has been asserted, with the help of a computer analysis of over 20,000 words (Venezky, 1967, 1970), that there are 52 "major spelling units" in English, 32 for consonants and 20 for vowels, effectively doubling the size of the alphabet.

The addition of all these extra spelling units, however, doesn't seem to make the structure of the English writing system very much more orderly. Some of the original letters of the alphabet are superfluous. There is nothing that *c* or *q* or *x* can do that couldn't be done by the other consonants. And many of the additional spelling units that are recognized simply duplicate the work of single letters, such as *ph* for *f* and *dg* for *j*. There are also compound vowels whose effect duplicates the silent final *e*, like *ea* in *meat* compared with *mete*. Some combinations of letters have a special value only when they occur in particular parts of a word—*gh* may be pronounced as *f* (or as nothing) at the end of a word (*rough*, *through*) but is pronounced just like a single *g* at the beginning (*ghost*, *ghastly*). Often letters have only a relational function, sacrificing any sound of their own in order to indicate how another letter should be sounded. An obvious example is the silent *e*; another is the *u* that distinguishes the *g* in *guest* from the *g* in *gem*.

So for our basic question of phonics, what we are really asking is, how many arbitrarily defined rules can account for an indeterminate number of correspondences between an indefinite set of spelling units and an uncertain number of sounds (the total and quality of which may vary from dialect to dialect)?

Some aspects of spelling are simply unpredictable, certainly to a reader with a limited knowledge of word derivations, no matter how one tries to define a spelling unit. An example of a completely unpredictable spelling–sound correspondence is *th*, which is pronounced in one way at the beginning of words like *this*, *than*, *those*, *them*, *then*, and *these*, but in another way at the beginning of *think*, *thank*, *thatch*, *thong*, *theme*, and so on. There is only one way for a learner to tell whether *th* should be pronounced as in /this/ or as in /think/, and that is to identify the word first. On the other hand, in many dialects there is no difference between the sounds represented by *w* and *wh*, as in *witch* and *which*, so that in some cases it can be the spelling that is not predictable, not the sound. Almost all common words are exceptions—*of* requires a rule of its own for the pronunciation of *f*, and *was* for the pronunciation of *as*.

The game of finding exceptions is too easy to play. I give only one more example to illustrate the kind of difficulty one must encounter in trying to construct—or to teach—reliable rules of phonic correspondence. How are the letters *ho* pronounced, when they occur at the beginning of a word? Here are 11 possible answers (all, you will notice, quite common words): *hope*, *hot*, *hoot*, *hook*, *hour*, *honest*, *house*, *honey*, *hoist*, *horse*, *horizon*.

Of course, there are rules (or are some of them exceptions?) that can account for many of the pronunciations of *ho*. But there is one very significant implication in all these examples that applies to almost all English words—in order to apply phonic rules, *words must be read from right to left*. The way in which the reader pronounces *ho* depends on what comes after it, and the same applies to the *p* in *ph*, the *a* in *ate*, the *k* in *knot*, the *t* in *tion*. The exceptions are very few, like *asp* and *ash*, which are pronounced differently if preceded by a *w*. The fact that sound "dependencies" in words run from right to left is an obvious difficulty for a beginning reader trying to sound out a word from left to right, or for a theorist who wants to maintain that words are identified on a left-to-right basis.

In summary, English is far from predictable as far as its spelling–sound relationships are concerned. Just how much can be done to predict the pronunciation of a relatively small number of common words with a finite number of rules we see later. But before this catalog of complications and exceptions is concluded, two points should be reiterated. The first point is that phonic rules at best can only be considered as probabilistic, as guides to the way words might be pronounced, and that there is rarely any indication of when a rule does or does not apply. The rule that specifies how to pronounce *ph* in *telephone* falls down in the face of *haphazard* or *shepherd*. The rule for *oe* in *doe* and *woe* will not work for *shoe*. The only way to distinguish the pronunciation of *sh* in *bishop* and *mishap*, or *th* in *father* and *fathead*, is to know the entire word in advance. The probability of being wrong if you don't know a word at all is very high. Even if individual rules were likely to be right three times out of four, there would still be only one chance in three of avoiding error in a four-letter word.

The second point is that *phonic rules look simple if you already know what a word is*. I don't intend to be facetious. Teachers often feel convinced that phonic rules work because letter–sound correspondences appear obvious when a word is known in advance; the alternatives are not considered. And children may appear to apply phonic rules when they can recognize a word in any case—or because the teacher also suggests what the word is—thereby enabling them to identify or recite the phonic correspondences that happen to be appropriate.

The Efficiency of Phonics

A classic attempt to construct a workable set of phonic rules for English was made by Berdiansky, Cronnell, and Koehler (1969).

The effort had modest aims—to see how far one could go in establishing a set of correspondence rules for the 6,092 one- and two-syllable words among 9,000 different words in the comprehension vocabularies of 6- to 9-year-old children. (The remaining words, nearly one third of the children's vocabularies, were all three or more syllables, adding too much complexity to the phonic analysis.) The words were all taken from books to which the children were normally exposed—they were the words that the children knew and ought to be able to identify if they were to be able to read the material with which they were confronted at school.

The researchers who analyzed the 6,092 words found rather more than the 52 "major spelling units" to which I have already referred—they identified 69 "grapheme units" that had to be separately distinguished in their rules. A group of letters was called a *grapheme unit*, just like a single letter, whenever its relationship to a sound could not be accounted for by any rules for single letters. Grapheme units included pairs of consonants such as *ch, th*; pairs of vowels such as *ea, oy*; and letters that commonly function together, such as *ck* and *qu*, as well as double consonants like *bb* and *tt*, all of which require some separate phonic explanation. The number of grapheme units should not surprise us. The previously mentioned 52 major units were not intended to represent the only spelling units that could occur but only the most frequent ones.

An arbitrary decision was made about what would constitute a rule: It would have to account for a spelling–sound correspondence occurring in at least 10 different words. Any distinctive spelling–sound correspondence and any grapheme unit that did not occur in at least 10 words was considered an "exception." Actually, the researchers made several exceptions among the exceptions. They wanted their rules to account for as many of their words as possible, so they let several cases through the net when it seemed to them more appropriate to account for a grapheme unit with a rule rather than to stigmatize it as an exception.

The researchers discovered that their 6,092 words involved 211 distinct spelling–sound correspondences. This doesn't mean that 211 different sounds were represented, any more than there were 211 different grapheme units, but rather that the 69 grapheme units were related to 38 sounds in a total of 211 different ways. The results are summarized in Table 9.1.

Eighty-three of the correspondences involved consonant grapheme units, and 128 involved vowel grapheme units, including no fewer than 79 that were associated with the six "primary" single-letter vowels, *a, e, i, o, u, y*. In other words, there was a total

TABLE 9.1

Spelling–Sound Correspondences Among 6,092 One- and Two-Syllable Words in the Vocabularies of 9-Year-Old Children

	Consonants	Primary Vowels	Secondary Vowels	Total
Spelling–sound correspondences	83	79	49	211
"Rules"	60	73	33	166
"Exceptions"	23	6	16	45
Grapheme units in rules	41	6	19	69

of 79 different ways in which single vowels could be pronounced. Of the 211 correspondences, 45 were classified as exceptions, about half involving vowels and half consonants. The exclusion of 45 correspondences meant that about 10% of the 6,092 words had to be set aside as "exceptions."

The pronunciation of the remaining words was accounted for by a total of 166 rules. Sixty of these rules were concerned with the pronunciation of consonants (which are generally thought to have fairly "regular" pronunciations) and 106 with single or complex vowels.

Conclusions that can be drawn from this research are far-reaching in their implications. The first is that phonics is complicated. Without saying anything at all about whether it is desirable to teach children a knowledge of phonics, we have an idea of the magnitude of the endeavor. We know that if we really expect to give children a mastery of phonics, then we are not talking about a dozen or so rules. We are talking about 166 rules, which will still not account for hundreds of words children might expect to meet in their early reading.

It is obvious that the most that can be expected from a knowledge of phonic rules is that they may provide a *clue* to the sound (or "name") of a configuration being examined. Phonics can provide only approximations. Even if readers do happen to know the 73 rules for the pronunciation of the six vowels, they would still have no sure way of telling which rule applies—or even that they are not dealing with an exception. And in any case, the sounds that letters are supposed to represent don't actually exist as separate units in speech—they are part of a continuous flow of sounds that overlap and constantly change. The sophisticated trick of being able to isolate the supposed individual sounds of speech is called *phonological* (or *phonemic*) *awareness*, which has nothing to do with reading (except that it is easier for readers) but is regarded as being of supreme importance in some quarters. There is more about phonemic awareness in the notes to this chapter.

There is still one issue to be considered concerning the *effectiveness* of phonics. Is the limited degree of efficiency that might be attained worth acquiring? Other factors have to be taken into account related to the *cost* of trying to learn and use phonic rules. There is the possibility that reliance on phonics will involve readers in so much delay and confusion that short-term memory will be overloaded, and they lose the sense of what they are reading. A tendency—or requirement—to rely on phonic rules may create a handicap for beginning readers whose biggest problem is to find meaning and develop speed in reading. Working memories don't have an infinite capacity, and reading is not a task that can be accomplished at too leisurely a pace. Other sources of information exist for finding out what a word in context might be.

The Cost of "Reform"

The convoluted relation between the spelling of words and their sound has led to frequent suggestions for modifying the alphabet or for rationalizing the spelling system. These intentions share misconceptions and difficulties. A number of contemporary linguists would deny that there is anything wrong with the way most words are spelled; they argue that a good deal of information would be lost if spelling were changed (Chomsky & Halle, 1968; Pinker, 1999). Most of the apparent inconsistencies in spelling have some historical basis; spellings are not arbitrary—they have become what they are for quite systematic reasons. And because spelling is systematic and reflects something of the history of words, much more information is available to the reader than we normally realize. (The fact that we are not aware that this information is available doesn't mean that we don't use it; we have already seen a number of examples of the way in which we have and use a knowledge of the structure and redundancy of our language that we can't put into words.)

Spelling reform might seem to make words easier to pronounce, but only at the cost of information about the way words share meanings, so that rationalizing words at the phonemic level might make reading more difficult at syntactic and semantic levels. As just one example, consider the "silent *b*" in *bomb*, *bombing*, and *bombed*, which would be an almost certain candidate for extinction if spelling reformers had their way. But the *b* is something more than a pointless appendage; it relates the previous words to others like *bombard*, *bombardier*, and *bombardment* where the *b* is pronounced. And if you save yourself the trouble of a special rule about why *b* is silent in words like *bomb*, at another level there would be a new problem of explaining why *b* suddenly appears in words like *bombard*. Remove the *g* from *sign* and you must explain where it comes from in *signature*.

Another argument in favor of the present spelling system is that it is the most competent one to handle different dialects. Although there is almost universal acceptance of the idea that words should be spelled in the same way by everyone, we don't all pronounce words in the same way. If the spelling of words is to be changed so that they reflect the way they are pronounced, whose dialect will provide the standard? Is a different letter required for every different sound produced in any dialect of English we might encounter? Or should we have different spelling systems for different dialects? Phonics instruction becomes even more complicated when it is realized that in many classrooms teacher and students don't speak the same dialect and that both may speak a different dialect from the authorities who suggested the particular phonic rules they are trying to follow. The teacher who tries to make children understand a phonic difference between the pronunciation of *caught* and *cot* will have a communication problem if this distinction is not one that the children observe in their own speech. The teacher may not even pronounce the two words differently, so that although the teacher thinks the message to the child is "That word isn't *cot*; it's *caught*," the message coming across is "That word isn't *cot*; it's *cot*."

Spelling and Meaning

The manner in which words are spelled in English becomes a problem primarily if reading is regarded as decoding written words to sound, and if the primary function of spelling is seen as representing *sounds* of spoken words. But spelling also reflects meaning, and where there is a conflict between pronunciation and meaning it is usually meaning that prevails, as if even the spelling system of written language recognized the priority of meaning. For example, the plural represented by a simple *s* in written language may be pronounced in three different ways in speech—as the /s/ sound on the end of *cats*, the /z/ sound on the end of *dogs*, and the

/iz/ sound on the end of *judges*. Would print be easier to read if the past tense of verbs were not indicated by a consistent *-ed* but rather reflected the pronunciation, so that we had such variations as *walkt* and *landid*? The reason that *medicine* and *medical* are spelled as they are is not because *c* is sometimes arbitrarily pronounced /s/ and sometimes /k/ but because the two words have the same root meaning, represented by *medic*. This shared meaning would be lost if the two words were spelled *medisin* and *medikal*. It should be noted, incidentally, that the consistent representation of the various pronunciations of the plural meaning by *s* or the past-tense meaning by *-ed* rarely causes difficulty to readers, even beginners, provided they are reading for sense. It is not necessary for teachers to instruct children that *-ed* is often pronounced /t/ (among other things). If a child understands a word, the pronunciation will take care of itself, but the effort to produce pronunciation as a prerequisite for meaning is likely to result in neither being achieved.

Of course, spelling can be a problem, both in school and out, but it is a problem of *writing*, not of reading. Knowing how to spell doesn't make a good reader because reading is not accomplished by decoding spelling. And good readers aren't necessarily good spellers; we can all read words that we can't spell. I'm not saying that knowledge of spelling is unimportant, only that it has a minimal role in reading, and that undue concern with the way in which words are spelled can only interfere with a child's learning to read.

There is a frequent argument that if spelling and decoding to sound are as irrelevant to reading as the preceding analyses indicate, why should we have an alphabetic written language at all? My view, set out in chapter 1 (p. 5), is that the alphabetic system is more of a help to the writer than to the reader, and more of a convenience to the printer (or scribe) than to the author. For a variety of reasons, writing may be harder to learn and to practice than reading, at least if the writer aspires to be conventionally "correct" with respect to such matters as spelling, grammar, punctuation, neatness, layout, and so forth. But as we shall see in chapter 10, although writing may not do much to facilitate one's ability as a reader, extensive reading can take care of most of the learning problems of writers.

The alphabet exacts its own price from readers. The Chinese ideographic system can be read by people from all over China, although they might speak languages that are mutually unintelligible. If a Cantonese speaker cannot understand what a Mandarin speaker says, they can write their conversation in the nonalphabetic writing system they share and be mutually comprehensible. This is something English speakers can't do with speakers of other languages unless they employ the small part of their own writing systems that is not alphabetic, such as arithmetic symbols like 2 + 3 = 5. Imagine the immense savings if all the spoken languages used in the United Nations shared the same meaning-based writing system.

When we can't remember or don't know how a word should be *written*, we have little recourse to anything but what we know about spelling. It doesn't help much in writing to look at the words before and after the one that is giving difficulty. But in reading we have more effective alternatives before we need call on phonics for clues to identifying a word, and it is to these alternatives that we now turn.

STRATEGIES OF MEDIATED WORD IDENTIFICATION

To repeat, the problem we are concerned with is that of a reader who encounters a word that cannot be recognized on sight, for which a visual feature list must be established. The reader will know the meaning of the word once it is identified; the problem is to identify the word by some kind of mediation.

Phonics, as we have seen, is one such strategy, but a most inadequate and time-consuming one. Fortunately other strategies are often available. An obvious alternative is simply being told what the word is. Before most children come to school, well-intentioned adults say to them "That word is *John*," or "That word is *cereal*," just as on other occasions they say, "That animal is a cat," in all cases leaving it to the child to solve the more complex problem of working out exactly how to recognize the word or animal on future occasions. But when the children get to school this support is frequently taken away from them, at least as far as reading is concerned. Another well-intentioned adult is likely to say to them, "Good news and bad news today, children. The bad news is that no one is ever likely to tell you what a word is again. The good news is that we are going to give you 166 rules and 45 exceptions so that you can work it out for yourselves."

Alternative Identification Strategies

Ask experienced readers what they do when they come across a word they don't recognize, and the most probable answer will be that they skip it, coming back to the word later if necessary. Passing over a word is a reasonable first strategy because it is unnecessary to understand every word to understand a passage of text, and lingering to try to decipher a word may be more disruptive to comprehension than missing the word completely. The second preferred strategy is to predict, which doesn't mean a reckless stab in the dark but making use of context to eliminate unlikely alternatives for what the unfamiliar word might be. The final strategy may be trying to work out what the word is from its spelling, not so much by decoding the word to sound with phonics as by making use of what is already known about other words. The final strategy might be called *identification by analogy*, because all or part of the unknown word is compared with all or part of words that are already known.

Examine the same question with a child who is gaining experience in reading and again you are likely to get the same sequence of strategies. The best learners tend to skip occasional unknown words (unless constrained to "read carefully" and figure out every word). The second preference, especially if there is no helpful adult around to provide assistance, is to hypothesize what a word might be based on the meaning of the text, and the final choice is to use what is known about similar-looking words. Trying to sound out words without reference to meaning is a characteristic strategy of poor readers; it is not one that leads to fluency in reading. The act of reading, on the other hand, usually helps with learning unfamiliar words, as we shall see.

What is the best method of mediated word identification? The answer depends on the situation a reader is in. Sometimes the best strategy will indeed be to ignore the unfamiliar word, because sufficient meaning may be carried by the surrounding text, not only to compensate for lack of understanding of the unknown word but also to provide critical cues to what the unknown word might be on future occasions. For a child beginning to learn to read, or confronted by text where many words are unfamiliar, the best situation is probably to have a more competent reader to turn to, if necessary by reading the entire passage to the child. But if the reader can understand enough of the passage to follow its sense, then a most effective strategy may be identification by analogy, making use of what is already known about reading.

Phonics in itself is almost useless for sounding out words letter by letter, because every letter can represent too many sounds. But uncertainty about the sound of a particular letter diminishes as letters are considered not in isolation but as part of letter clusters or "spelling patterns." This has led a number of theorists to argue that the basic unit for word recognition should be regarded as the syllable rather than the individual letter, particularly syllables that rhyme with known words. And indeed it is true; the pronunciation of syllables is far less variable than the pronunciation of the individual letters that make up syllables. The trouble is that it would be impossible for a beginner to learn to read by memorizing the pronunciation of hundreds of syllables, because syllables in themselves tend to be meaningless—there are relatively few one-syllable words—and the human brain has great difficulty in memorizing, and particularly in recalling, nonsense. What a reader can turn to for a ready-made store of syllabic information is *words* that have already been learned. It is far easier for a reader to remember the unique appearance and pronunciation of a whole word like *photograph*, for example, than to remember the alternative pronunciations of meaningless syllables or spelling units like *ph*, *to*, *gr* or *gra*, and *ph*. A single word, in other words, can provide the basis for remembering different rules of phonics, as well as the exceptions, because not only do words provide a meaningful way to organize different phonic rules in memory, they also illustrate the phonic rules at work.

Identification by Analogy

The mediated word identification strategy of identification by analogy means looking for cues to the pronunciation and meaning of an unfamiliar word from words that look similar. We don't learn to sound out words on the basis of individual letters or letter clusters whose sounds have been learned in isolation but rather by recognizing sequences of letters that occur in words that are already known. Such a strategy offers an additional advantage to the reader because it does more than indicate possible pronunciations for all or part of unknown words; it can offer suggestions about *meaning*. As I pointed out earlier, English spelling in general respects meaning more than sound—words that look alike tend to share the same sense. And as I have reiterated throughout this book, the basis of reading and of learning to read is meaning. The advantage of trying to identify unknown words by analogy with words that are known already is not simply that known words would provide an immediately accessible stock of pronunciations for relatively long sequences of letters but that all or part of known words can provide clues to meaning, which is always a far better clue to pronunciation than just the way an unknown word is spelled.

This is not to suggest that the existence of spelling–sound correspondences should be concealed from children learning to read, but the correspondences will be learned as they are encountered in meaningful reading, not as a result of being drilled into beginners. There remain the three fundamental problems with spelling–sound correspondences: the total number of rules and exceptions, the time it takes to apply them in practice, and their general unreliability. The problem of the number of rules is solved if they are not taught in the abstract, outside of meaningful reading. The easiest way to learn a phonic generalization is to learn a few words that exemplify it, which means—another point that will bear some reiteration—that *children master phonics as a result of reading rather than as a prerequisite for reading*. The time problem is overcome by resorting to phonics in actual reading as infrequently as possible.

The problem of the unreliability of phonic generalizations is another matter. Phonic generalizations alone will not permit a reader to decode the majority of words likely to be met in normal reading, simply because there are always too many alternatives. This is the reason that producers of phonic workbooks prefer to work with strictly controlled vocabularies. There's not as much uncertainty of pronunciation with *The fat cat sat on the mat* as there is with *Two hungry pigeons flew behind the weary ploughman*, a sentence that makes more sense but defies phonic analysis. Text that conforms to phonic regularities is referred to as "decodable text," which is usually synonymous with "unnatural English."

Meaning Plus Phonics

Phonic generalizations may be of limited utility if all they are required to do is reduce alternatives, without being expected to identify words completely or to decode them to sounds. To give an example, the use of phonics will never succeed in decoding *horse* if the word appears in isolation or is one of thousands of possible alternatives. But if the reader knows that the word is either *horse*, *mule*, or *donkey*, then the strategy will work effectively. Not only is a minimal amount of phonic analysis required to know that *mule* and *donkey* could not begin with *h*, but not much more can be expected of phonic rules in any case. This is why I have asserted that phonics is easy—for the teacher and the child—if they know what a word is in the first place. And because of the allure of the alphabet, it can look as if phonics is doing all the work.

Phonic strategies can't be relied on to eliminate all uncertainty if the reader has no idea what the word might be. One way to reduce uncertainty in advance is to employ the mediating technique of making use of context. Understanding of the text, in general, will reduce the number of alternatives that an unknown word might be. The other way to reduce uncertainty in advance is to employ the alternative mediating technique of identification by analogy, comparing the unknown word with known words that provide hypotheses about possible meanings and pronunciations. The reason that we can so easily read nonwords like *vernalit, mossiant,* and *ricaning* is not because we have in our heads a store of pronunciations for meaningless letter sequences like *vern, iant,* or *ric* but because these close approximations to English are made up of parts of words or even entire words that are immediately recognizable, such as *govern, vernal, lit, moss,* and so forth.

To ignore alternative means of reducing uncertainty is to ignore the redundancy which is a central part of all aspects of language. The prior elimination of unlikely alternatives is, after all, the foundation on which reading takes place, according to the analysis of comprehension that was offered in chapter 4. By this analysis, readers are usually unaware of the strategies employed as words are tentatively identified and feature lists established. Phonic generalizations function almost as sentinels; they can't decipher unknown words on their own, but they will protect readers against making reckless hypotheses.

LEARNING MEDIATED WORD IDENTIFICATION STRATEGIES

The basis of all learning—and especially of language learning—is sense. It is pointless to expect a child to memorize lists of rules, definitions, examples, even names, if these have no apparent purpose or utility to the child. Not only will learning be difficult, but recall will be almost impossible. The mediated word identification strategies that have been discussed can fall into the category of meaningless learning for a child expected to acquire them outside a context of meaningful reading. A child should not be expected to memorize phonic rules, or the pronunciation of isolated syllables and letter clusters, prior to learning how to read. Identification by analogy can also only be fostered after a child has begun to read.

Learning is self-directing and self-reinforcing when children are in a situation that makes sense to them, that can be related to what they know already. Rules that can't be verbalized about many aspects of the physical world and of language are hypothesized and tested with little conscious awareness. Where children can understand a relationship they will learn the relationship, whether it is the relationship of a name to a word, of a meaning to a word, or of a spelling–sound correspondence.

What all this means is that *reading guarantees increasing returns*. The more experience that children have in reading, the more easily they will learn to read. The more they can recognize words, the more easily they will be able to understand phonic correspondences, to employ context cues, and to identify new words by analogy. The more that children are able to read—or are helped to read—the more they are likely to discover and extend these strategies for themselves.

By acquiring an extensive "sight vocabulary" of immediately identifiable words, children are able to understand, remember, and utilize phonic rules and other mediated identification strategies. But such a summary statement doesn't imply that the way to help children read is to give them plenty of experience with isolated words and word lists. The easy way to learn words is to experience lots of them in meaningful text. We are considering only a limited and secondary aspect of reading when we restrict our attention to individual words. As we turn our attention to reading sequences of words that are grammatical and make sense, we find that word identification and learning are more easily explained theoretically and more easily accomplished by the child.

The time has come to complete the picture of reading by acknowledging that words are rarely read or learned in meaningless isolation. Reading is easiest when it makes sense, and learning to read is also easiest when it makes sense. We are ready to view reading from a broader and more meaningful perspective.

ISSUES

The difficulty many children experience in learning phonics rules, or indeed in making sense of them, has led to the notion that such children lack "phonemic awareness," that is, the ability to deconstruct the *sounds* of spoken words. It is taken for granted that the tenuous relationship between letters and sounds must be of central importance to readers of alphabetic writing systems (compared with readers of nonalphabetic systems like Chinese)—why else have an alphabet? An alternative view is that phonics appeals particularly to researchers and program developers who like to break reading down into parts that are easily controlled in instructional systems and tests.

SUMMARY

Mediated word identification is a temporary expedient for identifying unfamiliar words while establishing feature lists to permit immediate identification. Alternative strategies for mediated word identification include asking someone, using contextual cues, analogy with known words, and a limited and controlled use of phonics (spelling–sound correspondences). Attempting to decode isolated words to sound is unlikely to succeed because of the number, complexity, and unreliability of phonic generalizations. Phonic rules will help to eliminate alternative possibilities only if uncertainty can first be reduced by other means, for example if the unfamiliar words occur in meaningful contexts. Spelling–sound correspondences are not easily or usefully learned before children acquire some familiarity with reading.

Notes to chapter 9 begin on page 280 covering:

A defining moment

The relevance of phonics

Phonological and phonemic awareness

Word identification by analogy

Spelling

10 The Identification of Meaning

Previous chapters showed how a system of feature analysis could be employed both for the identification of letters and for the direct identification of words. Word identification doesn't require the prior identification of letters, at least not when the word that readers are concerned with is familiar to them, a part of their "sight vocabulary." It is only when words can't be identified immediately that the prior identification of letters may become relevant at all, and then only to a limited extent depending on the amount of contextual and other information that the reader might have available. The alternatives are summed up in Fig. 10.1.

Now I want to show that comprehension, which in this chapter is referred to as the *identification (or apprehension) of meaning*, doesn't require the prior identification of words. The same feature-analytic procedure that underlies the identification of letters and words is also available for the immediate apprehension of meaning from print. Although mediated meaning identification may sometimes be necessary, if for some reason meaning can't immediately be assigned to text, attempting to make decisions about possible meaning by the prior identification of individual words is highly inefficient and unlikely to succeed.

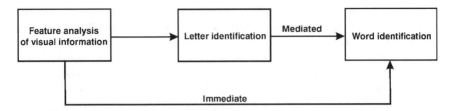

FIG. 10.1.   Immediate and mediated word identification.

In other words, immediate meaning identification is as independent of the identification of individual words as immediate word identification is independent of the identification of individual letters. The alternatives are represented in Fig. 10.2. The argument is presented in three steps:

1. Showing that immediate meaning identification *is* accomplished; that readers normally identify meaning without or before the identification of individual words.
2. Proposing how immediate meaning identification is accomplished.
3. Discussing how immediate meaning identification is learned.

In a final section, I briefly discuss the *mediated* identification of meaning, or what a reader might do when the direct apprehension of meaning is not possible.

USING MEANING IN READING

One demonstration has already been given that readers employ meaning (or sense) to assist in the identification of individual words rather than laboring to identify words in order to obtain

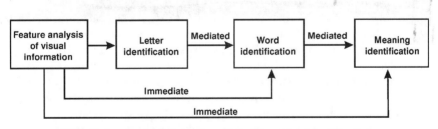

FIG. 10.2.   Immediate and mediated meaning identification.

meaning. I am referring to the research showing that from a single glance at a line of print—the equivalent of about 1 second of reading—a reader can identify four or five words if they are in a meaningful sequence but scarcely half that amount if the words are unrelated to each other. The explanation in chapter 5 was that with meaningful text a reader could recruit nonvisual information to reduce alternatives so that the amount of visual information that the brain can handle in a second would go twice as far, to identify four or five words instead of a couple. The nonvisual information that the reader already possesses can only be meaning, or prior knowledge of the way in which words go together in language that is not only grammatical but makes sense.

The Constant Search for Sense

It is important to understand that the reader in the situation just discussed is constantly making use of meaning; meaningfulness facilitates the identification of every word in the line. The reader doesn't first identify one or two words by a word identification strategy, as if they had nothing to do with the other words in the line, and then make an educated guess about the rest. Indeed, that same research shows that if two words had to be identified to give a clue about the others, then there would be no time left for the others to be identified. Two is the limit for words that have no meaningful relationships. Where a sequence of words does make sense, the identification of every word is facilitated, the first as well as the last, just as individual words can be identified in conditions in which none of their component letters would be individually discriminable. It is all a matter of the prior elimination of unlikely (and impossible) alternatives.

The research just discussed is historic; it was first conducted and reported a century ago. But in a sense, the fact that meaning facilitates the identification of individual words is demonstrated every time we read, because reading would be impossible if we labored along, blindly striving to identify one word after another with no prior insight into what the meaning of those words might be. Eye-movement studies may show that in some circumstances the eyes briefly come to rest on all or most words, but reading is not achieved saccadically. The eyes may "look at" words one at a time, but the brain deals with words in meaningful clusters. Slow reading is not efficient reading because it tends to create tunnel vision, overload short-term memory, and leave the reader floundering in the ambiguity of language. It's impossible to read normally text that doesn't make sense, as you can experience for yourself if you try to read the following passage:

> Be might words those of meaning the what into insight prior no with, another after word one identify to striving blindly, along labored we if impossible be would reading because, read we time every demonstrated is words individual of identification the facilitates meaning that fact the, sense a in but.

The words you have just tried to read are what I hope is a meaningful English sentence—because I used it myself in the previous paragraph—written backward. Any difference between the rate and ease with which you could read the backward and forward versions of that sentence can only be attributed to whether you were able to make sense of it. If you had read the backward passage aloud, incidentally, you probably would have sounded very much like many "problem readers" at school, who struggle to identify words one at a time in a dreary monotone, as if each word had nothing to do with any other. Such children seem to believe—and may well have been taught—that meaning should be their last concern; that sense will take care of itself provided they get the words right.

Professional readers, for example broadcasters, know the importance of prior understanding of what they are about to read, which is why they like to scan through a script in advance. Looking ahead also helps the silent reading of novels and technical books—we can get a general idea of what will transpire and then go back where necessary to study particular points. General comprehension comes out of fast reading, and the slow reading that might be necessary for memorization or for reflection on detail can only be accomplished if comprehension has already been taken care of. Conversely, meaning can interfere with some reading tasks. Proofreaders tend to overlook misprints if they attend to the sense of what they read; they see the spellings and words that should be on the page rather than those that actually are there. Sometimes proofreaders will deliberately read backward in order to give all their attention to spelling and individual words, but then of course they will overlook anomalies of meaning. Their dilemma highlights the fact that attention to individual words and attention to meaning are alternative and not concurrent aspects of reading.

The prior use of meaning ensures that when individual words must be identified, for example in order to read aloud, a minimum of visual information will be used. And as a consequence, mistakes will occasionally occur. If a reader already has a good idea of what a word might be, there is not much point in delaying to make extra certain what the word actually is. As a result, it is not unusual for even highly experienced readers to make misreadings that are radically different visually—like reading *said* when the word is *announced* or *reported*—but that make no significant difference to the meaning. Beginning readers often show exactly the same tendency, demonstrating that children will strive for sense even as they learn to read (provided the material they are expected to learn from has some possibility of making sense to them). The mistakes that are made are sometimes called *miscues* rather than *errors* to avoid the connotation that they are something bad (Goodman, 1969). The miscues show that these beginning readers are attempting to read in the way fluent readers do, with sense taking priority over individual word identification. Of course, reading with minimal attention to individual words will sometimes result in misreadings that do make a difference to meaning, but one of the great advantages of reading for meaning is that one becomes aware of mistakes that make a difference to meaning. An important difference between children who are doing well in reading and those who are not is not that good readers make fewer mistakes, but that they go back and correct the mistakes that make a difference. Children who are not reading for sense have no chance of becoming aware of even important errors.

The Priority of Meaning

A unique illustration of the manner in which meaning takes priority over the identification of individual words was provided by Kolers (1966), who asked bilinguals fluent in English and French to read aloud from passages of text that made sense but where the actual language changed from English to French every two or three words. For example:

> His horse, followed de deux bassets, faisait la terre résonner under its even tread. Des gouttes de verglas stuck to his manteau. Une violente brise was blowing. One side de l'horizon lighted up, and dans la blancheur of the early morning light, il aperçut rabbits hopping at the bord de leur terriers.

The subjects in this experiment could read and understand such passages perfectly well, but when they had finished they often could not remember whether particular sentences or words were in English or French. Most significantly, they frequently substituted for a word in one language an appropriate word in the other. They might read *porte* when the word was *door*, or *hand* when *main* was given, getting the meaning right but the language wrong. This doesn't mean that they weren't looking at individual words at all—the passage was not completely predictable—but they were looking at words and finding meanings, just as an English speaker might look at *2,000* and understand "two thousand" while a French speaker would look at the same print and understand "deux milles."

An important and perhaps difficult point to understand from the preceding discussion is that it is possible to make meaningful decisions about words without saying exactly what the words are. In other words, we can *see* that the written word *door* means door without having to say aloud or to ourselves that the word *is* "door." Written words convey meaning directly; they are not intermediaries for spoken language. An obvious example is provided for English by words that have different spellings for the same sound, like *their* and *there*. It is easy to detect the spelling error in *The children left there books behind* because *there* represents the wrong meaning. The difference between *their* and *there*, *read* and *reed*, and *so*, *sew*, and *sow* is evidently not that the different spellings represent different sounds, because they don't, but that the different appearances of the words indicate different meanings. The visual appearance of each word indicates meaning directly.

The fact that readers can, do, and must read directly for meaning is similarly apparent with a written language like Chinese, which doesn't correspond to any particular sound system. It would be pointless to argue whether a particular Chinese symbol represents the Mandarin or the Cantonese word for *house* because it simply represents a *meaning*. The fact that some written languages are based on letters that are more or less related to the sounds of a spoken language is quite coincidental as far as readers are concerned. There is no evidence that fluent readers need to identify letters in order to identify familiar words, and English spelling is an inadequate guide to the identification of words that are unfamiliar.

My final example that written language indicates meaning directly comes from studies of brain-injured patients. People unable to find the exact word have been reported, for example, as reading the isolated word *ill* as "sick," *city* as "town," and *ancient* as "historic" (Marshall & Newcombe, 1966) or *injure* as "hurt," *quiet* as "listen," and *fly* as "air" (Shallice & Warrington, 1975).

COMPREHENSION AND THE REDUCTION OF UNCERTAINTY

I have tried to show that meaning can take priority over the identification of individual words in two ways, both for experienced readers and for beginners. In the first case, the meaning of a sequence of words facilitates the identification of individual words with relatively less visual information. In the second case, written words can be understood without being identified precisely. Usually both aspects of meaning identification occur simultaneously; we comprehend text using far less visual information than would be required to identify the individual words and without the necessity of identifying individual words. Both aspects of meaning identification are, in fact, reflections of the same underlying procedure—the use of minimal visual information to make decisions specific to implicit questions (or predictions) about meaning on the part of the reader.

I'm using a rather awkward expression, "meaning identification," as a synonym for comprehension in this chapter to underline the fact that the way in which a reader makes sense of text is no different from that by which individual letters or words may be identified in the same text. I could also use the rather old-fashioned psychological term *apprehension* to refer to the way meaning must be captured, but that would cloud the similarities between comprehension and letter and word identification. What is different about comprehension is that readers bring to the text implicit questions about meaning rather than about letters or words. The term *meaning identification* also helps to emphasize that comprehension is active. Meaning doesn't reside in surface structure, waiting to be picked up. The meaning that readers comprehend from text is always relative to what they already know and to what they want to know. Put in another way, comprehension involves the reduction of a reader's uncertainty, asking questions and getting them answered, which is a point of view already employed in the discussion of letter and word identification. Readers must have *specifications* about meanings, specifications that constantly change as meanings develop.

A passage of text may be perceived in at least three ways: as a sequence of letters from an alphabet, as a sequence of words of a particular language, or as an expression of meaning in a certain domain of knowledge or understanding. But a passage of text is none of these things, or at least it is only these things potentially. Basically, written text is a conglomeration of marks on a page or screen, variously characterized as visual information, distinctive features, or surface structure. Whatever readers perceive in text—letters, words, or meanings—depends on the prior knowledge (nonvisual information) that they happen to bring and the implicit questions they happen to be asking. The actual information that readers find (or at least seek) in the text depends on their original uncertainty.

Consider the sentence that you are reading at this moment. The visual information in the sentence can be used to make decisions about letters, for example, to say that the first letter is *c*, the second *o*, the third *n*, and so forth. Alternatively, exactly the same visual information can be used to decide that the first word is *consider*, the second word *the*, the third word *sentence*, and so forth. The reader employs the same visual information, selects from among the same distinctive features, but this time sees words, not letters. What readers see depends on what they are looking for, on their implicit questions or uncertainty. Finally, exactly the same visual information can be employed to make decisions about meaning in the sentence, in which case neither letters nor words would be seen individually. It is not easy to say precisely what is being identified in the case of meaning, but that is due to the conceptual difficulty of saying what meaning is—using words to describe something beyond words—not because the reader is doing anything intrinsically different or difficult. The reader is using the same source of visual information to reduce uncertainty about meaning rather than about letters or words.

As we have already seen, the amount of visual information required to make a letter or word identification depends on the extent of the reader's prior uncertainty, on the number of alternatives specified in the reader's mind (and also the degree to which the reader wants to be confident in the decisions to be made). With *letters* it is easy to say what the maximum number of alternatives is—26 if we are considering just one particular letter in upper or lower case typeface in the English alphabet. It is similarly easy to show that the amount of visual information required to identify each letter goes down as the number of alternatives that the letter might be (the reader's uncertainty) is reduced. The fewer the alternatives, the more rapidly or easily a letter is identified, because fewer distinctive features need to be discriminated for a decision to be made.

It is not so easy to say what the maximum number of alternatives is for *words*, because that depends on the range of alternatives that the reader is considering, but again it is not difficult to show that the amount of visual information required to identify a word goes down as the reader's uncertainty is reduced. A word can be identified with fewer distinctive features when it comes from a couple of hundred alternatives than from many thousands.

Finally, it is quite impossible to say how many alternative meanings there might be for a passage of *text*, because that depends entirely on what an individual reader is looking for, but it is obvious that reading is easier and faster when the reader finds the material meaningful than when comprehension is a struggle. The less uncertainty readers have about the meaning of a passage, the less visual information is required to find what they are looking for in the passage.

The Use of Nonvisual Information

In each of the preceding cases, nonvisual information can be employed to reduce the reader's uncertainty in advance and to limit the amount of visual information that a reader must attend to. The more prior knowledge a reader can bring to bear about the way letters go together in words, the less visual information is required to identify individual letters. Prediction, based on prior knowledge, eliminates unlikely alternatives in advance. Similarly, the more a reader knows about the way words go together in grammatical and meaningful phrases—because of the reader's prior knowledge of the particular language and of the topic being discussed—the less visual information is required to identify individual words. In the latter case, meaning is used as part of nonvisual information to reduce the amount of visual information required to identify words.

Many people can follow the meaning of a novel or newspaper article at the rate of a thousand words a minute, which is four times faster than their probable speed if they were identifying every word, even with meaning to help them. There is a prevalent misconception that for this kind of fast reading the reader must be identifying only one word in every four and that this gives sufficient information at least for the gist of what is being read. But it is easy to demonstrate that identifying one word in four won't contribute very much toward the intelligibility of a passage. Here is every fourth word from a movie review: "Many * * * been * * * face * * * business * * * sour * * * If * * * to * * * ." The passage is even less easy to comprehend if the selected words are in groups, with correspondingly larger gaps between them. It is somewhat easier to comprehend what a passage is about if every fourth *letter* is provided rather than every fourth word, and, of course, my argument is that reading at a thousand words a minute is possible only if the omissions occur at the *featural* level.

It should not be thought that there is a special kind of distinctive feature for meaning in print, different from the distinctive features of letters and words. There is no "semantic feature," for example, that *house* and *residence* physically have in common that we should expect to find in print. What makes visual features distinctive as far as meaning is concerned is precisely what makes them distinctive for individual letters and words—the particular alternatives that already exist in the reader's uncertainty. The same features that can be used to distinguish the letter *m* from the letter *h* will also distinguish the word *mouse* from the word *house* and the meaning of *we went to the mill* from the meaning of *we went to the hill*. It is not possible to say what particular features a reader might employ to distinguish meanings; this would depend on what the reader is looking for, and, in any case it is not possible to describe the features of letters or words either. The situation is only additionally complicated by the fact that we can't say precisely what a meaning is.

Capturing "Meaning"

As I pointed out in chapter 3, in the discussion of the chasm between the surface structures and the deep structure of language, meaning lies beyond words. One can't *say* what meaning is in general, any more than one can say what the meaning of a particular word or group of words is, except by saying other words that are themselves surface structure. The meaning itself can never be exposed. This inability to pin down meaning is not a theoretical defect or scientific oversight. We should not expect that researchers will soon make a wondrous discovery that will enable us to say what meanings are. Meaning, to repeat myself, can't be captured in words.

A reader doesn't comprehend the written word *table* by saying the spoken word *table* either aloud or silently, any more than the spoken word *table* can itself be understood simply by repeating it to oneself. And neither the written nor the spoken word *table* is understood by saying silently to oneself "a four-legged flat-topped piece of furniture," or whatever other definition might come to mind, because the understanding of the definition would itself still have to be accounted for. There can be no understanding and no explanation unless the web of language is escaped. The actual *words*, written or spoken, are always secondary to meaning, to understanding.

We are normally unaware of *not* identifying individual words when we read because we are not thinking about words in any case. Written language (like speech) is *transparent*—we look through the actual words for the meaning beyond, and unless there are noticeable anomalies of meaning, or unless we have trouble comprehending, we are not aware of the words themselves. (When we deliberately attend to specific words, for example, in the subtle matter of reading poetry, this is a consequence of asking a different kind of question in the first place. The sounds that we can give to the words don't so much contribute to a literal interpretation as establish a different—a complementary or alternative—kind of mood or meaning.)

Reading Aloud and Silently

Of course, word identification is necessary for reading aloud, but as I have tried to show, the identification of words in this way depends on the prior identification of meaning. The voice lags behind the understanding and is always susceptible, to some extent, to diverging from the actual text. The substitution of words and even phrases with appropriate meanings is again not something a reader will be aware of; the reader's main concern, even in reading aloud, must be with the sense of the passage. Misreadings (miscues) would have to be pointed out by a listener following both the text and the reading. Misreadings of this kind are not normally made if the words to be read are isolated or in arbitrary lists, but then there is no way that meaning could be sought in such words. Besides, in such circumstances readers usually have the leisure to scrutinize sufficient visual information to identify individual words precisely (giving the words a label rather than a meaning) because nothing is lost by reading slowly. According to Huey (1908), instruction at the beginning of the 20th century placed oral reading long after silent. Currently the trend is the reverse. Huey was critical of any emphasis on reading aloud, which he considered much more difficult and unnatural than reading silently (p. 359). He considered "reading aloud" the opposite of "reading for thought."

Subvocalization (or reading silently to oneself) can't in itself contribute to meaning or understanding any more than reading aloud can. Indeed, like reading aloud, subvocalization can only be accomplished with anything like normal speed and intonation if it is preceded by comprehension. We don't listen to ourselves mumbling parts of words or fragments of phrases and then comprehend. If anything, subvocalization slows readers down and interferes with comprehension. The habit of subvocalization can be broken without loss of comprehension (Hardyck & Petrinovich, 1970).

Most people don't subvocalize as much as they think. If we "listen" to ascertain whether we are subvocalizing, subvocalization is bound to occur. We can never hear ourselves not subvocalizing, but that doesn't mean that we subvocalize all the time. Why do we subvocalize at all? The habit may simply be a holdover from our younger days, when we were expected to read aloud. A teacher knows that children are working if their fingers are moving steadily along the lines and their lips are moving in unison. Subvocalization may also have a useful function in providing "rehearsal" to help hold in short-term memory words that can't be immediately understood or otherwise dealt with. But in such cases subvocalization indicates lack of comprehension rather than its occurrence. There is a general tendency to subvocalize when reading becomes difficult, when we can predict less.

Prediction and Meaning

We don't normally read with our minds blank, with no prior purpose and no expectation of what we might find in the text. We don't look for meaning by considering all possibilities, nor do we make reckless guesses about just one; instead, we predict within the most likely range of alternatives. In this way we can overcome the information-processing limitations of the brain and also the inherent ambiguity of language. We can derive meaning directly from text because we bring expectations about meaning to text. The process is normally as natural, continuous, and effortless as the way we bring meaning to every other kind of experience in our life. Comprehension is not a matter of putting names to nonsense and struggling to make sense of the result, but of operating in the realm of meaningfulness all the time.

LEARNING TO IDENTIFY MEANING

There's no need for a special explanation about how children learn to apprehend meaning from print because no special process is involved. Children naturally try to bring sense to print, as they try to bring sense to all their encounters with the world around them. For them there is no point in language that is not meaningful, whether spoken or written. They perceive spoken language by looking for meaning, not by focusing on the sounds of words.

The Expectation of Sense

There is a classic illustration of the priority that meaning takes as children learn to talk. Even when children try to "imitate," it is meaning that they imitate, not meaningless sounds. McNeill (1967) reported an exchange between mother and child which went like this:

Child: Nobody don't like me.

Mother: No, say "Nobody likes me."

Child: Nobody don't like me.

(eight repetitions of this exchange)

Mother: No, now listen carefully, say *"Nobody likes me."*

Child: Oh! Nobody don't likes me.

Even when children are asked to perform a language exercise, they expect it to make sense. Like the child in the previous example, it takes them a long time to understand the task if they are required to attend to surface structure, not to meaning. Children don't need to be told the converse, to look for sense; that is their natural way of learning about language. Indeed, they won't willingly attend to any noise that doesn't make sense to them.

Just as children don't need to be told to look for meaning in either spoken or written language, so they also don't need to learn special procedures for finding meaning. Prediction is the basis of comprehension, and all children who can understand the spoken language of their own environment must be experts at prediction. Besides, the very constraints of reading—the constant possibility of ambiguity, tunnel vision, and memory overload—serve as reminders to learners that the basis of reading must be prediction.

Certainly there is no need for a special explanation of how comprehension should be *taught*. Comprehension is not a new kind of skill that has to be learned for reading but the basis of all learning. However, it may happen that children at school are taught the *reverse* of comprehension, being instructed instead to take care to "decode" correctly and not "guess" if they are uncertain. They may even be expected to learn to read with materials and exercises specifically designed to discourage or prevent the use of nonvisual information.

Of course, there are differences between the comprehension of written language and the comprehension of speech or of other kinds of events in the world, but these are not differences of process. The differences are simply that readers must use distinctive features of *print* to test predictions and reduce uncertainty. Children need to become familiar with these distinctive features of print and with how they are related to meaning. This familiarity and understanding can't be taught, any more than rules of spoken language can be taught, but formal instruction is similarly unnecessary and in fact impossible. The experience that children require to find meaning in print can only be acquired through meaningful reading, just as children develop their speech competence through using and hearing meaningful speech. And until children are able to do meaningful reading on their own account, they are clearly dependent on being read to, or at least on being assisted to read. Let me summarize everything I have just said: *Children learn to read by reading*.

The Right to Ignore

A final point. It is not necessary for any readers, and especially not for beginners, to understand the meaning of *everything* they attempt to read. Whether adults are reading novels, menus, or advertisements, they always have the liberty to skip passages and to ignore many small details, either because they are not comprehensible or because they are not relevant to their interest or needs. Children, when they are learning spoken language, seem able and willing to follow adult conversations and television programs without comprehending every word. A grasp of the theme, a general interest, and the ability to make sense on the basis of a few comprehensible parts can be more than sufficient to hold a child's attention. Such partially understood material is indeed the basis for learning; no one will pay attention to any aspect of language, spoken or written, unless it contains something that is new. For children, a good deal that is not comprehensible will be tolerated for the opportunity to explore something that is new and interesting. But children are rarely given credit for their ability to ignore what they can't understand and to attend only to that from which they will learn.

Unfortunately, the right of children to ignore what they can't understand may be the first of their freedoms to be taken away when they enter school. Instead, attention may be focused on what each child finds incomprehensible in order to "challenge" them to further learning. Anything a child understands may be set aside as "too easy." Paradoxically, many reading materials are made intentionally meaningless. In such cases there is no way in which children will be able to develop and profit from their ability to seek and identify meaning in text.

MEDIATED MEANING IDENTIFICATION

Reading normally involves bringing meaning *immediately* or directly to printed text, without awareness of individual words or their possible alternative meanings. There are occasions, however, when the meaning of the text or of particular words can't be immediately comprehended. On these occasions, mediated meaning identification may be attempted, involving the identification of individual words before comprehension of a meaningful sequence of words as a whole. There are two cases to be considered, the first concerned with the mediated meaning identification of entire sequences of words, such as phrases and sentences, and the second concerned with the mediated identification of the meaning of occasional individual words.

I have already argued that the first is rarely possible. The meaning of a sentence as a whole is not understood by putting together the meanings of individual words (chap. 3). Individual words have so much ambiguity—and usually alternative grammatical functions as well—that without some prior expectation of meaning there is little chance for comprehension even to begin. In addition, constraints of visual information processing and memory are difficult to overcome if the reader attempts to identify and understand every word as if it had nothing to do with its neighbors and came from many thousands of alternatives. So although some theories of reading and methods of reading instruction would appear to be based on the assumption that comprehension of written text is achieved one word at a time, the present analysis leaves little on this topic to be discussed. To attempt to build up comprehension in such a way must be regarded as highly inefficient and unlikely to succeed.

But the second sense of mediated meaning identification— where the passage as a whole is comprehensible and perhaps just one word is unfamiliar and not understood—is a more general characteristic of reading. In this case, the question is not one of trying to use the meanings of individual words to construct the meaning of the whole, but rather of using the meaning of the whole to provide a possible meaning for an individual word. And not only is this possible, it is the basis of much of the language learning that we do. The bulk of the vocabulary of most literate adults must come from reading (Nagy, Herman, & Anderson, 1985). It's not necessary to understand thousands upon thousands of words to begin to learn to read—basically, all that is required is a general familiarity with the words and constructions in the written material from which one is expected to learn, and then not all of those. And it seems highly unlikely that our understanding of many of the words that we have learned as a result of reading should be attributed to thousands of trips to the dictionary or to asking someone else what the word might be. We learn the meaning from the text itself.

Informal evidence that we quite coincidentally learn new words while reading comes from those words whose meaning or reference we know well but which we are not sure of pronouncing correctly, so there is no way we could have learned about them from speech. I am referring to words like *Penelope* (Penny-loap?), *Hermione* (Hermi-own?), *misled* (mizzled? myzeled?), and *gist* (like guest or jest?), and perhaps *slough* and *orgy*, not to mention innumerable foreign words, names, and places. There is what I like to call the *facky-tious* phenomenon (*tious* to rhyme with *pious*) after the occasion when the mother of a friend commented that one didn't often hear the word *facky-tious* these days. My friend confessed that he couldn't remember the last time he heard the word and asked what it meant. "A little sarcastic or supercilious," he was told. Something clicked. "You mean *facetious*," he said. "No," replied his mother thoughtfully, "though the two words do have a similar meaning. Come to think of it," she added, "I don't think I've ever seen the word *facetious* in print."

The question, of course, is where she got the correct meaning of *facky-tious*, which she had never heard in speech and had obviously never asked anyone about. And the answer must be that she learned it the way most of us learn the meaning of most of the words we know—by making sense of words from their context, using what is known to comprehend and learn the unfamiliar. Mediated meaning identification from context is something that experienced readers do frequently, without awareness, and is the basis not just of comprehension but of learning.

Learning new words without interference with the general comprehension of text is another example of the way that children—and all readers—continually learn to read by reading. The vocabulary that develops as a consequence of reading provides a permanent source of knowledge for determining the probable meaning and pronunciation of new words. If you know both the meaning and the pronunciation of *auditor* and *visual*, you will have little difficulty in comprehending and saying a new word like *audiovisual*. The larger your capital, the faster you can add to it—

whether with words or material wealth. The best way to acquire a large and useful sight vocabulary for reading is by meaningful reading. If the text makes sense, the mediation and the learning take care of themselves.

SO HOW *DO* YOU RECOGNIZE NEW WORDS? (A REPRISE)

This section is repetitious, but I think it has to be. My contention in this book is that reading is a direct relationship between print and meaning. When you look at a line of type, your immediate experience is a meaningful event. There is no "decoding" of written words to the sounds of words, or to speech. Reading is normally a silent affair, just as we normally recognize houses, cars, people, and other aspects of a street scene without having to say a name for everything we encounter. Our understanding of the situation is immediate. Actual names are usually irrelevant for our understanding (unless we are telling someone else about the experience, in which case we put words to our understanding). We don't have to say the words first in order to get the meanings, the understanding.

The same applies to reading. We don't have to say to ourselves, or to anyone else, what a word is in order to understand that word. The understanding has to come first. Saying the word is something extra you do in order to recite what you read to yourself, in an "inner voice," or aloud to someone else.

But the question inevitably arises, "What about words you've never met before? If you don't use phonics, how do you learn to recognize those words, and how do you learn to say them?" The question usually means, "How do I *teach* children to identify and say words they have never met before?" Teachers often feel they have to find things to *do*, to instruct children, rather than arrange situations where the desired learning will take care of itself.

I'll discuss the issue in three steps: (1) summarizing how text is understood when the words are familiar, in silent reading and in reading aloud, (2) explaining how unfamiliar words are understood, and (3) explaining how unfamiliar words are read aloud.

1. How Familiar Words Are Understood

In silent reading, which is the normal and natural way to read, the words in their sequence and setting are interpreted immediately. We move directly from the words to their combined meaning, with no analysis or transformation into any aspect of spoken language.

We understand the words *The dog jumped over the fence* the way we would understand a picture of a dog jumping over a fence, without having to say to ourselves "The dog jumped over the fence." The sounds of the words are irrelevant.

In reading aloud, for our own purposes or to other people, an extra step is required. First we have to understand what we are reading, then we have to say what we understand. We don't transform the uninterpreted words (or their component letters) into sound; we put sound to the words that we have interpreted. We do this in exactly the same way that we identify the dog that we see jumping the fence. We don't say "There's a dog," and then understand that it is a dog that we have seen. We recognize a dog, and then say the word that we have for animals that we recognize as dogs.

The problem in all of this, as I explained in chapter 1, is that it is so difficult to escape the lure of *letters*, to overcome the apparently self-evident fact that words are comprised of letters—just as buildings may be made of bricks—and therefore the sounds the letters represent must have something to do with reading (although individual bricks have nothing to do with our recognition of buildings.) Where possible I prefer to talk about the *structure* of written words, which happens to consist of letters, rather than talk about letters. No one expects structure to decode to sound.

2. How Unfamiliar Words Are Understood

I am talking now about *understanding*, not about reading aloud or about transposing written language into silent speech to ourselves. How do we get the meaning of an unfamiliar word before we even try to say it? The answer is that the meaning comes from the context in which the word occurs. Words we do know indicate the meaning of the word we don't know. Or rather, the entire grammatical and semantic structure of the meaningful sequence in which the unknown word is embedded, together often with cues within the structure of the unknown word itself (words that look alike tend to share similar meanings), enmeshes the unknown word in a network of understanding, so that the probable meaning is immediately apparent. And if we make a mistake, the later meaningful context usually tells us that our assumption was wrong, and probably suggests a more appropriate interpretation. In brief, we get the meaning of one small part from the meaning of the whole (just as you would have little difficulty inferring the meaning of the word *glerp* if I told you I left my glerp at home this morning and got soaked by rain later in the day).

There is substantial evidence that readers quickly become extremely proficient at attributing the correct meaning to unfamiliar words in the normal course of reading, not just experienced adult readers, but high school and even younger students. One encounter with an unfamiliar word in a meaningful context is enough to give an approximate meaning; half a dozen encounters are sufficient to draw an accurate conclusion. In this way teenaged readers can learn thousands of new words every year (see notes to chap. 12).

It is a perfectly natural thing to do. Children from the second year of their lives accurately infer the meaning of new spoken words about 20 times a day, with no allowance for forgetting—both from the language itself and the situation in which it occurs. Someone says "Like a drink of blunk?," holds out a beaker of orange juice, and the child knows what blunk is. Children do this without instruction from adults or frequent visits to a dictionary. This is the way vocabularies grow, in spoken and written language. But it applies only to words that occur in meaningful contexts, either spoken or written; it doesn't apply to words that are presented in lists or in any other contrived instructional context. As I frequently reiterate, we learn when we understand; learning is a by-product of understanding. In effect, children learn about language the way archaeologists decipher ancient texts, by bringing sense to them. It's all very natural.

If the meaning of the unfamiliar word that we have identified is already in our spoken language vocabulary, then we can associate the written word with the spoken word, the sight with the sound. The association is mediated by meaning. Our inner "lexicon" is not a list of the sounds of words with meanings attached; it is a list of meanings with sounds and written forms attached. When we become familiar with the meaning of written words, we employ our lexicon of meanings to establish a relationship between the written word and its spoken counterpart. The sequence is

     written word → meaning → spoken word

not

     written word → spoken word → meaning

If the written word has a meaning that we *can't* associate with a spoken word, then it remains one of those written words that we can recognize and understand without being able to put it into speech (or only with a very rough approximation of what the pronunciation of the word might be). It is precisely the situation we are often in when we encounter recognizable and comprehensible symbols that we haven't put a name to, such as perhaps ◐ *&* R$_X$ ▶ 𝄞 and ●.

3. How Unfamiliar Words Are Read Aloud

How can we put a sound (or a name) to an unfamiliar word? It depends on how many words we are familiar with. Words have many structural similarities—they begin with the same letters (one of the 26 alternative shapes), they end with certain patterns like *ed, ing, ance*, and so forth. From our experience with other words, we know how they are pronounced, and also how parts of them are pronounced. We can pronounce familiar structures in unfamiliar words the same way we pronounce the same structures in familiar words. If we know the pronunciation of *contain* and *persist*, we can make a good attempt at the pronunciation of *consist*, especially if we can take meaning and grammatical structure into account as well. This is not the use of phonics, which we have seen in chapter 9 could not possibly work, nor does it demand prior learning of the parts of words in isolated exercises. All it demands is experience in reading. The use of analogies to indicate both meaning and sound is natural and automatic (provided "guessing" has not been inhibited).

The system is not perfect, but no system for putting sounds to unfamiliar words could be perfect. Linguists recognize that the spelling of words doesn't even attempt to indicate aspects of speech that the reader/speaker might be expected to know already. For example, everyone knows—unconsciously—from their patterns of speech that the past-tense ending *ed* is pronounced /d/ at the end of words like *pulled*, but that it is pronounced /t/ at the end of words like *walked*, while in words like *handed* it is pronounced like /id/. Final *s* is pronounced /s/ at the end of words like *cups* but like /z/ at the end of words like *beds*. None of this has anything to do with phonics, which doesn't acknowledge these distinctions. The difference comes from our knowledge (unconsciously acquired) of subtle and specialized rules of spoken language. The component letters of written words also tell us nothing about the intonation, whether for example that stress falls at the beginning, like *a*corn, or at the end, like a*bout*.

We recognize new and unfamiliar words because of what we already know of words that are familiar. We can put meanings and pronunciations to them because of what we know about spoken words that have a similar appearance.

All this is done very rapidly. Researchers have found that "fast mapping" of a tentative meaning takes place on the first encounter, and half a dozen more encounters suffice to fully round out the conventional meaning—with no "feedback" beyond the context in which the word occurs (see chap. 12 notes). For the sounds of written words the mapping is just as fast, if bothered with at all. The sounds are not always correct—we get the meaning but mispronounce the conventional sounds for words we haven't encountered in speech. Such words may then go into our spoken-language vocabulary with an inappropriate pronunciation, to be corrected fairly rapidly if we hear the word spoken, but otherwise to remain idiosyncratic.

How do we get the *correct* pronunciation? Phonics can't be depended on. Either someone tells us how the word is pronounced at a helpful time, or we subsequently hear the word spoken and make the connection to the word we have encountered in our reading. Nothing about finding meanings and pronunciations for new words is normally a *problem* for learners, only for people who think that writing is a visible form of speech, rather than that writing and speech are related but independent forms of language.

Neither the sounds of letters nor words themselves are represented in speech the way they are in writing. If we didn't have a writing system we wouldn't know what words are, and no one would try to break down the flowing intermingling sounds of speech into individual segments like letters. Only meaning can be common to spoken and written language, and meaning is not something that can be decomposed into segments in any form of language.

ISSUES

A persisting issue is whether individual words have to be specifically identified in normal reading, one at a time, before the meaning of a phrase, sentence, or passage can be comprehended. Such issues are difficult to resolve experimentally—evidence of where the eyes are focused doesn't necessarily indicate what the reader is thinking about. Meaning as a concept is difficult enough to contemplate in any case. To try to pinpoint meaning by studying where the eyes fixate can be like trying to study digestion by analyzing knife and fork movements. As we shall continue to see, driving many of the controversies about the nature of reading are deep-rooted beliefs about how children should be taught.

SUMMARY

Comprehension, the basic objective of reading, also facilitates the process of reading in two ways. *Immediate meaning identifica-*

tion makes unnecessary the prior identification of individual words, and comprehension of a passage as a whole facilitates the comprehension and, if necessary, the identification of individual words. *Mediated meaning identification* increases the probability of tunnel vision, memory overload, and ambiguity caused by over-dependence on visual information.

Notes to chapter 10 begin on page 289 covering:

Effects of meaningful context

Context and prediction

"Dual process"

11 Reading, Writing, and Thinking

So far we have been primarily concerned with topics much broader than reading—like language, comprehension, and memory—or with narrow aspects of reading—like letter or word identification. In this chapter, the spotlight can finally be directed on reading itself, on the specific act, when something meaningful is in front of a reader's eyes, and the reader is looking at it for a purpose. What does it mean to read? What can be said to be happening? And what do readers need to know?

Reading is never an abstract, meaningless activity, although it is frequently studied in that way by researchers and theorists and still taught in that way to many learners. Readers always read *something*, they read for a *purpose*, and reading and its recollection always involve *feelings* as well as knowledge and experience.

Reading can never be separated from the intentions and interests of readers, or from the consequences that it has on them. This chapter is mainly concerned with what reading means to readers. Reading also can never be separated from writing or thinking. Although this book is not specifically directed to either of these large topics, their relevance can't be ignored, and the chapter ends with brief comments on writing and thinking. Learning to read (which also will be found inseparable from the act of reading itself) is the specific concern of chapter 13.

On Definitions of Reading

Books on reading often attempt to define their terms with formal statements like "reading is extracting information from print." But such imposing declarations provide no insight into reading, and can lead to fruitless debates. A definition doesn't justify its author using a common word differently from anyone else. Formal definitions are useful only if there is a reason for using words in a specialized, narrow, or otherwise unpredictable way, and even then they can cause more trouble than they are worth because readers prefer to interpret familiar words in familiar ways. Philosopher Karl Popper (1976) pointed out that precision in language can only be increased at the cost of clarity. As I have already discussed, common, easily understood words tend to have a multiplicity of meanings, and what usually gives a word an unambiguous interpretation is neither prior agreement nor fiat but the particular context in which it happens to be used. As Popper also said, it is better to *describe* how a word is used than to *define* it.

Take the question of whether reading necessarily involves comprehension, an issue sometimes discussed at great length. Such a question asks nothing about the nature of reading, only about the way the word is used on particular occasions. And the only possible answer is that sometimes the word reading implies comprehension, and sometimes it doesn't. When we suggest that someone should read a particular book, we obviously include comprehension in our recommendation—it would be redundant if not rude to say "I think you ought to read and comprehend this book." But on the other hand, our friend might reply, "I've already read it, but I didn't understand it," now obviously excluding comprehension from the meaning of the word *reading*. Everything depends on the general sense in which words are used, even in the same conversation, in two successive sentences. If there is doubt, it is better to provide a more complete description of how the word is being used than to attempt a general definition.

Consider, for example, the differences between reading a novel, a poem, a social studies text, a mathematical formula, a telephone directory, a recipe, the formalized description of some opening moves in chess, or an advertisement in a newspaper. Novels are usually read for the *experience*, for involvement in a situation, not unlike watching a play or movie or participating in actual events, where we are caught up with the characters and motivations of individual people and with how circumstances will deal with them. To read a novel is to participate in life. A poem may evoke a much more intense experience, especially emotionally, involving a particular mental attitude and a sensitivity to the sounds as well as to the meanings of words, akin in many ways to listening to music. The social studies text may lack the direct emotional and aesthetic connection of a novel or poem, but generate more detailed analytic thought—thinking that is more "off the page" and general than the details directly presented in the print. The mathematical formula is a tool, to be lifted (with understanding) from its position in the text and used elsewhere, and the telephone directory is like a collection of keys, each of which will unlock a particular connection. A recipe is a description of actions for the reader to follow, chess notation involves participation in a game, and a newspaper advertisement is a device for persuading readers to act in particular ways.

These descriptions are clearly inadequate for the richness that is reading. My aim in attempting a list was to illustrate the richness by demonstrating the inadequacy. And even then, I oversimplified. There isn't one kind of novel or one kind of advertisement, and the same texts can be read in different ways. A novel can be read like a social studies text, and a social studies text like a novel. A newspaper advertisement may be read like a poem. Moreover, each of these different ways of reading texts is more like other forms of behavior or experience that don't involve reading than they are like other forms of reading. I equated reading a novel with watching a play, not with reading a play, and reading a recipe is obviously more like cooking than like reading about any other kind of activity. There is no one activity that can be summed up as *reading*; no description that can be summarized as the "process" that is involved.

The meaning of the word reading in all these senses depends on everything that is going on—not just on what is being read, but on why a particular reader is reading. It might be said that in all of the examples I have given, answers are sought to questions that vary with the person asking them. And the only thing that makes all of these different activities reading is that the answers are being sought in print.

Asking Questions, Finding Answers

Because of the limitations on the amount of visual information from a text that the brain can deal with, the location and nature of the answers must to some extent be predictable. Thus the reader must have relevant expectations about the text. All questions must be couched within a prediction, a range of possible alternatives. This leads to a very broad description that I have already offered—that comprehension of text is a matter of having relevant questions to ask (that the text can answer) and of being able to find answers to at least some of those questions. To use a term I introduced earlier and will shortly elaborate more fully—reading depends on the reader's *specification of the text*.

The particular questions a reader might ask can range from the implications of a single word to matters related to the style, symbolism, and worldview of the author. I have avoided any attempt to list and characterize all these different questions because of their very specific—and sometimes specialized—nature. Instead, I have focused on three kinds of question that all fluent readers seem able to ask and answer in most reading situations, related to the identification of letters, words, and meanings. These three kinds of question are alternatives, all three can't be asked simultaneously, and it is unnecessary for the reader to attempt to ask them in sequence.

From this perspective, it doesn't make sense to ask whether print basically consists of letters, words, or meanings. Print is discriminable visual contrasts, marks on paper or a monitor screen, that have the potential of answering certain questions—usually implicit—that readers might ask. Readers find letters in print when they ask one kind of question and select relevant visual information; they find words in print when they ask another kind of question and use the same visual information in a different way; and they find meaning in print, in the same visual information, when they ask a different kind of question again. It should be rare for a reader to ask questions about specific letters (except when letters themselves have a particular relevance, for example, as a person's initials or as a compass direction *N*, *S*, *E*, or *W*). It should also be rare for a reader to attend specifically to words, unless again there is a particular reason to identify a word, for example, a name.

Comprehension, as I have said, is relative; it depends on getting answers to the questions being asked. A particular meaning is the answer a reader gets to a particular question. Meaning therefore also depends on the questions that are asked. A reader "gets the meaning" of a book or poem from the writer's (or a teacher's) point of view only when the reader asks questions that the writer (or teacher) implicitly expects to be asked. Disputes over the meaning of text, or the "correct" way to comprehend text, are usually disputes over the questions that should be asked. A particular skill of accomplished writers (and of accomplished teachers) is to lead readers to ask the questions that they consider appropriate. Thus, the basis of fluent reading is the ability to find answers in the visual information of written language to the particular questions that are being asked. Written language makes sense when readers can relate it to what they know already (including those occasions when learning takes place, when there is a comprehensible modification of what readers know already). And reading is interesting and relevant when it can be related to what the reader *wants* to know.

READERS, WRITERS, AND TEXT

Readers must bring meaning to texts; they must have a developing and constantly modifiable set of expectations about what they will find. This is their *specification of the text*. But obviously writers make a contribution too. They must have their own specifications. And there must be a point at which readers and writers intersect. That point is the text, and the next section is about the interconnections of readers, writers, and texts.

Global and Focal Predictions

So far throughout this book I have talked as if predictions are made and dealt with one at a time. But predictions are usually multiplex, varying widely in range and significance. Some predictions are overriding; they carry us across large expanses of time and space. Other predictions occurring concurrently are far more transient, arising and being disposed of relatively rapidly. Our predictions are layered and interleaved.

Consider the analogy of driving a car. We have a general expectation that we will reach a certain destination at a certain time, leading to a number of relatively long-range predictions about landmarks that will be met along the route. Call these predictions *global*, because they tend to influence large parts of the journey. No matter how much our exact path might have to be varied because of exigencies that arise on the way, swerving to avoid a pedestrian or diverting down a side street because of a traffic holdup, these overriding global predictions tend to bring us always toward our intended goal.

But although global predictions influence every decision until our intended goal is reached, we simultaneously make more detailed predictions related to specific events during the course of the journey. Call predictions of this nature *focal*, because they concern us for short periods of time only and have no lasting consequence for the journey as a whole. Focal predictions must be made, often quite suddenly, with respect to the oncoming truck or the pedestrian or as a consequence of a minor diversion. In contrast to global predictions, we can't be specific about focal predictions before the journey begins. It would be useless to try to predict before starting the specific location of incidents that are likely to occur on the way. The occasion for a focal prediction may arise out of particular sets of local circumstances, but the prediction itself will still be influenced by our global expectations about the journey as a whole. For example, the modified focal predictions that will result if we have to make an unexpected detour will still be influenced by our overriding intention of eventually reaching a particular destination.

We make similar global and focal predictions when we read. While reading a novel, for example, we may be concerned with a number of quite different predictions simultaneously, some global that can persist through the entire length of the book, others more focal that can rise and be disposed of in a single fixation.

We begin a book with extremely global predictions about its content from its title and from what perhaps we have heard about it in advance. Sometimes even global predictions may fail—we discover that a book is not on the topic we anticipated. But usually global predictions about content, theme, and treatment persist throughout the book. At a slightly more detailed level, there are likely to be still quite global expectations that arise and are elaborated within every chapter. At the beginning of the book we may have such predictions about the first chapter only, but in the course of reading the first chapter expectations about the second arise, the second leads to expectations about the third, and so on to the end. Within each chapter there will be rather more focal predictions about paragraphs, with each paragraph being a major source of predictions about the next. Within each paragraph there will be predictions about sentences and within each sentence predictions about words.

Lower level predictions arise more suddenly; we will rarely make focal predictions about words more than a sentence ahead of where we are reading, nor predictions about sentences more than a paragraph ahead, nor predictions about paragraphs more than a chapter ahead. The more focal the prediction, the sooner it arises (because it is based on more immediate antecedents) and the sooner it is disposed of (because it has fewer long-range consequences). In general, the more focal a prediction, the less it can be specifically formulated in advance. You would be unlikely to predict the content of the present sentence before you had read the previous sentence, although the content of the paragraph as a whole was probably predictable from the previous paragraph. On the other hand, predictions at the various levels inform each other. The entire process is at once extremely complex and highly dynamic; Fig. 11.1 is an attempt to illustrate it in a simplified and static diagram.

In general, the expectations of Fig. 11.1 should be regarded as developing from left to right; the past influences our expectations for the future. But it can occasionally help at all levels of prediction in reading to glance ahead. The sequence of reading doesn't have to follow the page numbering of the book. Similarly, there should perhaps be diagonal lines all over the diagram as the outcomes of local predictions have their effect on global predictions and the global expectations exert their constant influence on specific focal predictions. At any moment, the character of our existing expectations about the book, chapter, paragraph, sentence, and word is our ever-changing specification of the text.

Don't interpret the diagram too rigidly. It isn't necessary to predict at every level all of the time. We may become unsure of what a book as a whole is about and, for a while, hold our most global predictions to the chapter or even to a lower level while we try to grasp where the book might be going. Sometimes we may have so much trouble with a paragraph that we find it impossible to maintain predictions at the chapter level. At the other extreme, we may find a chapter or paragraph so predictable, or so irrelevant, that

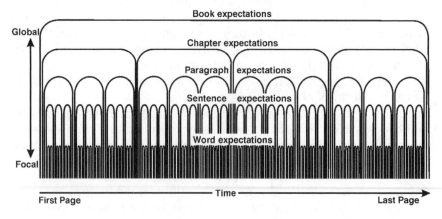

FIG. 11.1.   Layers of prediction in reading a book.

we omit predictions at lower levels altogether. In plain language, we skip. It is only when we can make no predictions at all that a book will be completely incomprehensible. It should also not be thought that there are clearly defined boundaries between the different levels of prediction; the global–focal distinction doesn't describe alternatives but rather the extreme ends of a continuous range of possibilities.

The Writer's Point of View

We may consider now the *intentions* of writers, using the framework of Fig. 11.1 that represented the predictions of readers. To some extent, the patterns of predictions and intentions can be seen as reflections of each other.

Writers of books often begin with only global intentions of what the book as a whole will be about and of the way the subject will be treated. These global intentions, in due course, determine lower level intentions for every chapter. Within each chapter more focal intentions arise about every paragraph, and within each paragraph quite detailed focal intentions arise regarding sentences and words. And just as the more focal predictions of the reader tend to arise at shorter notice and to be dispensed with more quickly, so the more focal intentions of the writer extend over a shorter range in both directions. What I want to say in the present sentence is most specifically determined by what I wrote in the previous one and will, in turn, place a considerable constraint on how I compose the following sentence. But these focal constraints are at the detailed level. My intention in every sentence that I write is also influenced by the more global intentions for the paragraph as a whole, and of course my intention in every paragraph reflects the topic I have selected for the chapter and more generally for the book.

The intentions of writers can be represented by exactly the same framework that I have used to represent the predictions of readers in Fig. 11.1. The only difference would be that now the diagram should be captioned "Layers of intention in writing a book," with the word *intentions* replacing *expectations* at every level from global to focal. The same qualification would also apply about not taking the diagram too literally. Authors may at times be fairly sure about their global intentions at book, chapter, and even paragraph levels but be lost for focal intentions concerning particular sentences and individual words. At other times the words may flow without any clear indication of where they are going, with the paragraph and other more global intentions remaining obscure.

Global and Focal Conventions

The cascading diagram of Fig. 11.1 can be used for a third time, to represent the basic relationship between writers and readers. First I used Fig. 11.1 to represent the reader's point of view, the texture of *predictions*. Then with a slight modification of labeling it was used from the writer's point of view, as a network of *intentions*. Finally it can be employed as a representation of the text itself, the meeting ground of writer intentions and reader expectations.

In what way do writers manifest their various intentions, and what is it that readers predict at the various global and focal levels? As I outlined in chapter 3, the answer is *conventions*. Conventions exist in every aspect of language; they correspond to every kind and level of intention and expectation. In considering the written language of books, Fig. 11.1 needs simply to be relabeled "Layers of convention in a book," with the word *convention* replacing expectations (or intentions) at every level. There are global conventions for books as a whole—these are *genre schemes, story grammars*, and the conventions of *register*. There are conventions for the way paragraphs are arranged into chapters and chapters into books—these are the *discourse structures*. There are conventions for the way sentences are organized into paragraphs—these are the conventions of *cohesion*. There are the conventions for the organization of words in sentences, the conventions of *grammar* and of *idiom*. And there are conventions for the words themselves, the conventions of *semantics*, and for the physical representation of those words, the conventions of *spelling*. Complete sets of conventions exist for traditional texts—and for the hypertexts of the Internet.

When labeled for conventions, Fig. 11.1 is, I think, a reasonably appropriate way to characterize an entire text. Texts are static—they don't change their structure from moment to moment (unless someone is working on them). But the figure offers only a way of *thinking* about readers and writers; I wouldn't want to suggest that such a structure ever exists in its entirety or in a stable form in anyone's head. We can inquire into particular global and focal intentions or predictions in writers' and readers' minds at particular times, but we should never expect to find a complete or unchanging set of them the way the diagram might suggest. Instead we would find that writers and readers, each in their own way, have in their minds a *specification* of a text, a specification of global and focal elements far less complete and detailed than Fig. 11.1, but far more dynamic and flexible.

The Specification of a Text

Consider the matter first from the writer's point of view. What does a writer have in mind (a) before a text is begun to direct the writing that will be done, (b) while the text is being written to ensure that it follows the writer's developing intentions, and (c) when the text is done, when the writer can say "That's what I intended to write"? My answer each time is a *specification*.

The specification of a text is similar in many ways to the specification of a house. Such a specification is not the house itself, nor is it the plans for a house. It is a cluster of intentions and expectations, of constraints and guidelines, which determine what the plans and ultimately the house will be like. Specifications are never complete—we wouldn't say to the architect, "This is *exactly* how we want the house," because in that case we wouldn't need the architect. Specifications will have gaps, they may even be internally inconsistent, and during the designing of the plans we or the architect may find a need for the specifications to be changed. Indeed, specifications should be expected to change as the execution of the plans develops, so that eventually there is a match between the plans (and house) and the specifications, between the aim and its fulfilment, partly because the house was designed around the constraints of the specifications but also because the specifications were changed and developed to meet the contingencies of actually designing and building the house. A different architect might have designed a different house, but we would still say "That is what we wanted" if the design is in accordance with our final specifications.

So it is with the writer. The book (or any other kind of text) that the author plans will initially develop in conformity with certain specifications that don't contain all the details of the text. And as the text develops the specifications will change, partly as the demands of the text change but also as a consequence of what has already been written. And at the end, if the final text is compatible with the final specification, the author will say, "That's what I wanted to write," even though the constantly changing specification at no time spelled out exactly what the book would contain at all of its global and focal levels, and even though a different book might have been written to the same initial specifications on a different occasion.

So it is too with readers. We begin with a sketchy specification of the text ("This is a book about reading"), which develops in the course of our reading, consolidating in terms of what we have read so far and elaborating when necessary for the prediction of what is to come. Focal aspects of the specification are developed to make sense of detail as we come to it but then discarded as we move on to the next detail. Apart from the occasional quotation or specific idea that might lodge in our mind, we shall in general be far more concerned with the persisting global aspects of our specification than with the transient focal ones. And at the end we will have a specification that is still not the book itself but that is our ultimate comprehension of the book (just as the specification we can put together a week or a month later is our memory of the book at that time).

How we comprehend when we read is a matter of the richness and congruence of the specification that we bring to the text and of the extent to which we can modify the specification in the course of reading the text. What we comprehend and what we are left with in memory as a consequence of the reading depend on how our experience with the text modifies our specification. Subsequent reflection may change the specification even more, of course, which is the reason that we often can't distinguish in memory what we read *in* a text from what we read *into* it.

FLUENT READING AND DIFFICULT READING

A distinction is often drawn between *fluent reading* and *beginning reading* to contrast the virtuoso manner in which experienced readers are supposed to read with the stumbling, less proficient behavior of learners. But the distinction isn't valid. It's usually possible to find something that any beginning reader can read easily, even if only one word. And it's always possible to find something an experienced reader can't read without difficulty. The advantage of an experienced reader over a neophyte lies in *familiarity* with a range of different kinds of text, not in the possession of *skills* that facilitate every kind of reading.

For beginners and experienced readers alike, there is always the possibility of *fluent reading* and the possibility of *difficult reading*. There is no sudden transition from beginning reading, when nothing can be read without difficulty, to fluent reading, when all reading is easy. The more we read, the more we are able to read. Learning to read begins with one word and one kind of text, continues a word and a text at a time, and the learning never stops. Every time a reader meets a new word, something new is likely to be learned about the identification and meaning of words. Every time a new text is read, something new is likely to be learned about reading different kinds of text. Learning to read is not a process of building up a repertoire of specific skills, which make all kinds of reading possible. Instead, experience increases the ability to read different kinds of text.

Even experienced readers have difficulty in reading some texts—because of the way the texts are written, or because of inadequate nonvisual information on the reader's part, and sometimes because of pressures or anxieties involved in the particular act of reading. And when otherwise competent readers experience difficulty in reading, they tend to read like beginners. By the same token, when beginners find easy material to read, they tend to read like experienced readers.

In other words, the critical difference is not between experienced and beginning reading, or even between "good reading" and "poor reading," but between fluent reading, which even beginners can do in the right circumstances, and difficult reading, a situation in which even experienced readers can sometimes find themselves. The problem for children learning to read is that everything they might attempt to read is likely to be difficult.

Fluent reading involves pursuing a complex and ever-changing set of objectives in order to make sense out of print in ways that are relevant to the purposes of the reader. Neither individual letter identification nor individual word identification are involved unless they are relevant to the particular requirements of the reader. Nor is every potential "meaning" on a page examined unless it has some bearing on the reader's purposes. Fluent reading is based on a flexible specification of intentions and expectations, which change and develop as a consequence of the reader's progression through a text. Thus, fluent reading demands knowledge of the conventions of the text, from vocabulary and grammar to the narrative devices employed. How much conventional knowledge is required depends on the purposes of the reader and the demands of the situation. Knowledge need not be complete; in fact, provided there is sufficient comprehension to maintain the reader's attention, learning is likely to take place wherever specific knowledge is lacking.

The Consequences of Reading

Reading is more than just a pleasant, interesting, and informative experience. It has consequences, some of which are typical of any kind of experience we might have. Other consequences are uniquely particular to reading.

General consequences of experience are an increase in specific memories and knowledge. I haven't found any studies of how much individuals normally remember from what they read (outside of artificial experimental situations looking at how much can be recalled of specific items determined by the researcher). But common observation would suggest that individuals remember as much about books that they find interesting and readable as they do about "real life" experiences in which they are involved. Many anecdotal reports indicate remarkable memories on the part of readers for the appearance, titles, authors, characters, settings, plots, and illustrations of books that were important to them, often extending back to childhood. With books, as with every other kind of experience, we remember what we understand and what is significant to us.

There are also specific consequences. Experience always results in learning. Experience in reading leads to more knowledge about reading itself. Not surprisingly, students who read a lot tend to read better (Anderson, Hiebert, Scott, & Wilkinson, 1985). They don't need to read better in order to read a lot, but the more they read, the more they learn about reading. The same researchers reported that students who read more also tended to have larger vocabularies, better comprehension, and generally did better on a range of academic subjects. In other words, reading makes people smarter.

Other things are learned through reading. I've argued at length (Smith, 1983b, 1994) that it is only through reading that anyone can learn to write. The only way to learn all the conventions of spelling, punctuation, capitalization, paragraphing, grammar, and style is through reading. Authors teach readers about writing.

In the next two chapters, I describe learning in metaphorical terms as the *membership of clubs*. By joining the club of readers, even as beginners, individuals can learn to become readers and writers. But reading also opens the doors to any club that can be the topic of a book, which probably means most of the clubs in the world and certainly many clubs that could not exist in the world as we know it. Reading is the club of clubs, the only possibility for many experiences of learning.

And finally, there are emotional concomitants and consequences of reading. Reading, like everything else, inevitably involves feelings. On the positive side, reading can provide interest and excitement, stimulate and alleviate curiosity, console, encourage, rouse passions, relieve loneliness, assuage tedium or anxiety, palliate sadness, and on occasion induce sleep. On the negative side, reading can bore, confuse, and generate resentment. The emotional response to reading is treated insufficiently in most books about literacy (not excluding the present volume), although it is the primary reason most readers read, and probably the primary reason most nonreaders don't read.

Because of the range and depth of feelings involved, attitudes toward reading become habitual. Reading can become a desired activity or an undesirable one. People can become inveterate readers. They can also become inveterate nonreaders, even when they are capable of reading. One of the great tragedies of contemporary education is not so much that many students leave school unable to read and to write, but that many graduate with an antipathy to reading and writing, despite the abilities they might have. Nothing about reading or its instruction is inconsequential.

READING AND THINKING

The heading may be a trifle misleading. Reading *is* thinking, as I hope I have demonstrated throughout this chapter. And the thinking we do when we read, in order to read, is no different from the thinking we do on other occasions. Just as we can't talk without thinking, or understand what someone is saying without thinking, or make any sense of the world without thinking, so it is impossible to read and not think. (If we sometimes say that we have spoken without thinking, we mean that we didn't consider all the implications of what we said.) Reading is thinking that is partly focused on the visual information of print; it's thinking that is stimulated and directed by written language. The only time we might attempt to read without thinking is when the text we are trying to read is meaningless to us, a situation unlikely to persist in normal circumstances.

It is true that we may read a story or magazine to relax, in order not to think about particular things—but we obviously have to think enough about whatever we are reading in order to be distracted from other thoughts. If we fail to read every story with the intensity and acumen of a literary critic, it is probably not because we can't think, but because we aren't interested in reading like a literary critic.

The thought in which we engage while reading is like the thought we engage in while involved in any kind of experience. Fulfilling intentions, making choices, anticipating outcomes, and making sense of situations are not aspects of thinking exclusive to fluent reading. We must draw inferences, make decisions, and solve problems in order to understand what is going on in situations that involve reading and situations that don't. Reading demands no unique forms or "skills" of thought.

An enormous advantage of reading over thinking in other circumstances is the *control* that it offers over events. Readers can stop the action, and pause in the middle of an experience for reflection. Readers can relive reading experiences, as often as they wish, and examine them from many points of view. Readers can even skip over experiences they are not interested in having or that would disrupt their flow of thought. Readers have *power*.

Reading is no different in essence from any other manifestation of thoughtful activity—but it may be the most natural and satisfying form of thinking available to us. The human brain runs on stories. Our theory of the world is largely in the form of stories. Stories are far more easily remembered and recalled than sequences of unrelated facts. The most trivial small episodes and vignettes are intrinsically more interesting than data. We can't see random patterns or dots (or clouds or stars) without putting faces or figures to them. We can't even observe small points of light moving randomly against a dark background without seeing them "interact" with each other in a narrative fashion (Michotte, 1946).

Thinking thrives on stories, on the construction and exploration of patterns of events and ideas, and reading often offers greater scope for engaging in stories than any other kind of activity.

ISSUES

The rift between the "experience" and "information" approaches to teaching reading is less an unresolved problem than a gulf between totally antithetical points of view, making a tremendous difference to how research is interpreted, theories developed, and teaching and learning perceived. The nature of reading itself is at issue: whether it is a process of acquiring information from print that may be turned on in any circumstances, or a creative experiential interaction in an environment of print. When teachers and learners are evaluated on "performance indicators" or on the "product" or "output" of reading instruction, it is almost invariably acquisition of information rather than quality of experience that is assessed.

SUMMARY

Reading—like writing and all other forms of thinking—can never be separated from the purposes, prior knowledge, and feelings of the person engaged in the activity nor from the nature of the text being read. The *conventions* of texts permit the *expectations* of readers and the *intentions* of writers to intersect. *Global* and *focal expectations* and intentions form a personal *specification* that readers and writers develop and modify as they proceed through a text. The fluency of reading depends as much on characteristics of the text and reader as on reading ability. Experienced readers who find a text difficult may read like beginners.

Notes to chapter 11 begin on page 294 covering:

Comprehension and thinking

Reading speed

Comprehension and context

Benefits of reading

12 Learning About the World

This chapter introduces the topic of learning. It is not specifically concerned with learning to read, a matter postponed to the next and final chapter. But this chapter is relevant to the *manner* in which children learn to read, because this is the same as the manner in which children achieve mastery of spoken language and, even earlier, begin learning about the world in general through their first elaborations of a theory of the world.

The chapter is linked with many of the preceding chapters, with their emphasis on meaning and comprehension in reading, because it shows that the basis of all learning, including learning to read, is comprehension. Children learn by relating their understanding of the new to what they know already, modifying or elaborating their prior knowledge. Learning is continuous and completely natural, and it is not necessary to propose separate "processes" of motivation and reinforcement to sustain and consolidate learning (nor should it be necessary for teachers to regard incentives and rewards as separate concerns that can be grafted onto reading instruction). Children may not always find it easy or even necessary to learn what we try to teach them, but they find the state of not learning anything intolerable.

CONSTRUCTING A THEORY OF THE WORLD

Chapter 2 discussed the complex yet precise and accurate theory of the world that we all possess. Obviously, we were not born with such a theory. The ability to construct a theory of the world and to predict from it may be innate, but the actual content of the theory, the specific detail underlying the order and structure that we come to perceive in the world, is not part of our birthright. But equally obviously, very little of our theory can be attributed to instruction. Only a small part of what we know is actually *taught* to us.

The Cat and Dog Problem

Consider again what we know that enables us to tell the difference between cats and dogs. What were we taught that has given us this ability? It is impossible to say. Just try to write a description of cats and dogs that would enable a being from outer space—or a child who has never seen cats and dogs before—to tell the difference. Anything you might want to say about the appearance of some dogs, that they have long tails or pointed ears or furry coats, will apply to some cats and not to other dogs. The difference between cats and dogs is *implicit* knowledge that we can't put into words. Nor can we communicate this knowledge by pointing to a particular part of cats and dogs and saying "That's where the difference lies."

Differences obviously exist between cats and dogs, but you can't find and don't need language to distinguish them. Children without language can tell the difference between cats and dogs. Cats and dogs can tell the difference between cats and dogs. But if we can't say what this difference is, how can we teach it to children? What we do, of course, is point out to children examples of the two kinds of animal. We say "That's a cat" or "There goes a dog." But pointing out examples doesn't teach children anything; it merely confronts them with the problem. In effect, we say, "There is something I call a cat. Now you find out why." The "teacher" poses the problem and leaves the child to discover the solution.

The same argument applies to just about everything we can distinguish in the world, to the letters of the alphabet, to numbers, chairs and tables, houses, foodstuffs, flowers, trees, utensils, and toys, to every kind of animal, bird, and fish, to every face, every car and plane and ship, thousands upon thousands of objects that we can recognize not only by sight but by other senses as well. And when did anyone tell us the rules? No one has ever told us, "Chairs can be recognized because they have four legs and a seat and possibly a back and arms." (You can see how inadequate a description would be.) Instead, somebody once said in passing, "There's a chair," and left us to decide not only how to recognize chairs on other occasions but also to discover what exactly the word *chair* means, how chairs are related to everything else in the world.

With reading we don't even need someone to pose the problem in the first place. Reading at the same time presents both the problem and the possibility of its solution. Just by virtue of being a reader, every one of us has acquired a sight vocabulary of at least 50,000 words, words that we can identify on sight the way we recognize familiar faces and houses and trees. How did we acquire this enormous talent? Fifty thousand flashcards? Fifty thousand times a teacher wrote a word on a board and told us what it was? Fifty thousand times we blended together the sound of a word through phonics? We have learned to recognize words by reading.

Not only can we recognize 50,000 words on sight—and also, of course, by sound—we can usually make sense of all these words. Where have all the meanings come from? Fifty thousand trips to the dictionary? Fifty thousand vocabulary lessons? We have learned all the conventions of language by making sense of it. What we know about language is largely implicit, just like our knowledge of cats and dogs. So little of our knowledge of language is actually taught; we underestimate how much of language we have learned.

Most of our theory of the world, including most of our knowledge of language, whether spoken or written, is not the kind of knowledge that can be put into words; it is more like the implicit cat-and-dog kind of knowledge. Knowledge that no one can put into words is not knowledge that can be communicated by direct instruction.

How, then, do we acquire and develop the theory of the world we have in our heads? How does it become so complex and precise and efficient? There seems to be only one answer: *by testing hypotheses*.

Learning by Hypothesis Testing

Children learn by testing hypotheses. For example, a child might hypothesize that the difference between cats and dogs is that cats have pointed ears. The child can then test this hypothesis by saying "There's a cat" or "What a nice cat" when any animal with pointed ears passes by, and "There's a dog" (or "That's not a cat") for any animal without pointed ears. Any reaction tells the child whether the hypothesis is justified or not. If someone says, "Yes, there's a pretty cat," or accepts the child's statement by making no overt response, then the child has learned that the hypothesis has worked, on this occasion at least. The child's theory can be tentatively modified to include a rule that cats are animals with pointed ears. But if someone says to the child, "No, that's a dog," then the child knows that the hypothesis has failed. Another hypothesis must be selected and tested. Clearly, more than one test will be required; it will take experience with cats and dogs before a child can be reasonably certain of having uncovered dependable differences between them (whatever the differences may be). But the principle is always the same: Stay with your theory for as long as it works; modify your theory—look for another hypothesis—whenever it fails.

Note that it is essential for the child to understand the problem in the first place. Children won't learn to recognize cats simply by being shown cats; they will not know what to look for. Both cats and dogs must be seen in order for the hypothesis about their relevant differences to arise. Children learn each letter of the alphabet by seeing them all; they must see what the alternatives are.

There is an intimate connection between comprehension and learning. Children's tests never go beyond their theories; they must comprehend what they are doing all the time they are learning. Anything that bewilders a child will be ignored; there is nothing to be learned there. It isn't nonsense that stimulates children to learn, but the possibility of making sense; that's why children grow up speaking language and not imitating the noise of the air conditioner. Children don't learn by being denied access to problems. A child learning to talk must be immersed in spoken language, and it is far better that a beginning reader having difficulties should be helped to read than be deprived of reading.

This process of hypothesis testing goes on instinctively, below the level of awareness. If we were aware of the hypotheses we test, then we could say what it is that enables us to tell the difference between cats and dogs. We are no more conscious of the hypotheses that underlie learning than we are of the predictions that underlie comprehension, or of the theory of the world itself. Indeed, there is basically no difference between comprehension and learning; *hypotheses are simply tentative predictions*.

LEARNING ABOUT LANGUAGE

When does all this testing take place? I think that for young children there is only one answer: They are testing hypotheses all the time. Their predictions are always tentative. This assertion is best illustrated with respect to the topic with which we are most concerned, namely, language.

Bringing Meaning to Speech

Children who have just begun to talk frequently make statements that are completely obvious. A child looking out of a window with you will say something like "See big plane" although you may even have pointed out the plane in the first place. Why then should the child bother to make the statement? The answer is, because the child is testing hypotheses. In fact, a child could be conducting no fewer than three different tests at the same time in that one simple situation.

The child could be testing the hypothesis that the object you can both clearly see in the sky *is* a plane, that it is not a bird or some other unidentified flying object. When you say "Yes, I see it," you are confirming that the object is a plane. Even silence is helpful, because the child would expect you to make a correction if the hypothesis were in error. The second hypothesis that the child might be testing concerns the sounds of the language, that "plane" is the right name for the object, rather than "pwane," "prane," or whatever else the child might say. Once again the child can assume that if you don't take the opportunity to make a correction, then there is nothing to be corrected. A test has been successfully conducted. The third hypothesis that the child may be testing is linguistic, whether "See big plane" is a grammatically acceptable and meaningful sentence in adult language. The feedback comes when the adult says "Yes, I can see the big plane." The child learns to produce sentences in your language by using tentative sentences for which you both already know the meaning, *in a situation that you both comprehend.*

The same principle of making sense of language by understanding the situation in which it is used applies in the other direction as children learn to comprehend adult speech. At the beginning of language learning, infants must be able to understand what adults say before they can understand adult language. Does that statement sound paradoxical? What I mean is that children don't come to understand sentences like "Would you like a drink of juice?" or even the meaning of a single word like *juice* by figuring out the language or by having someone tell them the rules. Children learn because initially they can hypothesize the meaning of a statement from the situation in which it is uttered. An adult saying "Would you like a drink of juice?" is usually carrying or indicating a drink of juice. This language is situation-dependent speech. From such situations a child can hypothesize what might happen the next time someone mentions *juice*. The situation provides the meaning and the utterance provides the evidence; that is all a child needs to construct hypotheses that can be tested on future occasions. Children don't learn language to make sense of words and sentences; they make sense of words and sentences in understanding how language is used (Macnamara, 1972). Adults help children to do this through "caretaker talk"—sometimes called "motherese" (and "fatherese")—engaging infants in language use, making language easy and useful. We shall see a similar phenomenon in the way adults (or other experienced readers) support children in their learning to read by reading to them and for them.

There is an interesting role for the eyes to play in these first experiences with language. Newson and Newson (1975) noted that the sharing of meaning is facilitated by a convergence of gaze. When a parent offers an infant a drink of juice, they are probably looking not at each other but at the juice that the adult is offering. When a parent says "There's a big dog" to a baby who doesn't understand the word, the gaze of parent and baby is likely to converge on the dog. By bringing a possible meaning to the utterance, the infant can hypothesize a relationship between the two, and thus test, confirm, or modify provisional rules about this relationship—a highly efficient procedure that will work only if the infant can make sense of the purpose of adult language.

I know of no research on how much spoken language children might learn simply by observation. But if a baby can hypothesize and test a potential meaning when offered juice, there is no reason why the child could not test a similar hypothesis by overhearing one adult offer another a cup of coffee, provided the situation is visible. The child could again compare probable meaning with utterance. There are obvious limits to the number of language interchanges in which infants are directly involved. It might at least seem possible that most infants overhear far more language than is actually addressed to them, although again there is no research on the issue. And by and large much of this overheard domestic language would be situationally meaningful; it would have purposes and outcomes that are both predictable and testable.

It is in fact the purposes of language, the uses to which it is put, that are the key to infant language learning. As the linguist Halliday (1973) pointed out, children learn language and its uses simultaneously. They don't learn language, either spoken or written, which they then use for various purposes. The learning comes with the use of language and with the understanding of its uses. Language learning is incidental. Children don't learn about language as an abstraction, as an end in itself, but as a means of achieving other ends, like getting another drink of juice, learning to distinguish cats from dogs, or enjoying a story from a book. The basic insight that must enable a child to make sense of speech is that its sounds are not random; they are not arbitrarily substitutable. By this I mean that the sounds of speech make a difference—they are there for a purpose. An adult can't produce the sounds "There's a truck" when the intended meaning is "Let's go for a walk."

THREE ASPECTS OF LEARNING

Learning is the modification or elaboration of what is already known, of cognitive structure, our theory of the world. What exactly is modified or elaborated? It can be any of the three components of the theory: the category system, the rules for relating objects or events to categories (sets of distinctive features), or the complex network of interrelations among categories.

Children are constantly required to establish new categories in their cognitive structure and to discover the rules that limit the allocation of events to a new category. They have to learn that not all animals are cats and dogs but that some animals are. Children learning to sight-recognize the printed word *cat* have to establish a visual category for that word, just as they must have a category for actual cats, distinguished from other categories for dogs, and so forth. Skilled readers develop categories for every letter of the alphabet and also for every word that can be identified on sight, together, possibly, with categories for frequently occurring syllabic groups of letters, for rhymes, and for meaningful segments like plurals and tense markers. This process of learning to establish categories involves hypothesizing what are the significant differences—the only reason to establish a new category is to make a new differentiation in our experience, and the learning problem is to find the significant differences that should define the category.

Each category that we distinguish must be specified by at least one set of distinctive features. Every time children succeed in learning to recognize something new, they must have established a new set of distinctive features. But usually they go further and establish *alternative* sets of features for specifying the same categories. They learn that an a̲, *a*, or even an *A* should be categorized as the letter "a" just as many different-looking animals must be categorized as a cat. Any set of features that will serve to categorize an object is a *criterial set*, and alternative sets for the same category are *functionally equivalent*. As children learn, they discover more and more ways in which to make the decision that a particular object or event should be categorized in a certain way. The number of functionally equivalent criterial sets gets larger. Learning is also involved in the ability to make use of less and less featural information to comprehend text. We ran into many examples of the use of functionally equivalent criterial sets of features in our discussions of letter and word identification. Most skilled readers can identify words that have had large parts (many features) obliterated and can make sense of text that has even more features obliterated. All this is possible because we have learned to make optimal use of the information that is available, both visually and from our acquired knowledge of the language.

Finally, children constantly learn new interrelationships among categories, developing their ability to make sense of language and the world. Understanding how words go together in meaningful language makes prediction possible, and therefore comprehension. These interrelationships are also not taught. But a child can learn them by the same process of hypothesis testing. Comprehension is the basis of a child's learning to read, but reading, in turn, contributes to a child's growing ability to comprehend by permitting elaboration of the complex structure of categories, feature lists, and interrelationships that constitute every child's theory of the world.

LEARNING ALL THE TIME

Learning is continual and effortless, as natural as breathing. A child doesn't have to be especially motivated or rewarded for learning. Children will strive to avoid situations where there is nothing to learn, just as they will struggle to escape situations where breathing is difficult. Inability to learn can be suffocating.

There's no need to worry that children who are not constantly driven and cajoled will "take the easy way out" and not learn. Young children who read the same book twenty times, even though they know the words by heart, are not avoiding more "challenging" material in order to avoid learning; they are still learning. It may not be until they know just about every word in a book that they can get on with some of the more complex aspects of reading, such as testing hypotheses about meaning and learning to use as little visual information as possible.

Underestimating Learning

It is because children learn continuously and effortlessly that adults generally fail to give them credit for the amount of learning that they do. It is a common adult belief that learning is a difficult and even painful activity, that it involves grappling with something that you don't understand, and therefore necessarily leaves marks of effort and strain. But in fact, the sight of a child struggling to learn is a clear sign that learning is *not* taking place, that the child is confronted by something incomprehensible. When learning does occur, it is inconspicuous.

Because of this myth that learning is effortful, many adults believe that they themselves don't learn often or without strain. They regard learning as a struggle to make sense of a textbook or set of exercises, not as something that takes place whenever they relax to read a magazine or enjoy a movie. But the next day they can relate a large part of what interested them in the magazine and recall a surprising amount of detail from the movie, detail that may stay with them for months or years afterward. If we can remember, we must have learned, and it is pointless to argue that this wasn't learning because there was no conscious effort to remember.

Children are equipped with a very efficient device that prevents their wasting time in situations where there is nothing to learn. That device is called *boredom*, and boredom is something all children want to avoid. A child who is bored in class is not demonstrating ill will, inability, or obstinacy; boredom should convey just one very clear message for the teacher. There is nothing in the particular situation for the child to learn.

There are two reasons why there might be nothing for a child to learn in a particular situation, and hence two reasons for boredom, that arise from quite different sources. One reason why children might have nothing to learn is very simple—they know it already. Children won't attend to anything they already know. But children will also suffer and exhibit the same symptoms of boredom because they can't make sense of what they are expected to learn. Teachers might believe that a certain exercise will improve useful knowledge or skills, but unless the learner can see sense in the exercise, the instruction is a waste of time. (I know this is hard on teachers who are obliged to follow a set curriculum, but learning is natural and administrative edicts often aren't.)

The Risk and Rewards of Learning

There is one other reason why children might turn their faces against learning, and that is its risk. In order to learn you must take a chance. When you test a hypothesis, there must be a possibility of being wrong. If you are certain of being right, there can be nothing to learn because you know it already. And provided there is a possibility of being wrong, you learn whether you are right or not. If you have a hypothesis about what constitutes a cat, it makes no difference whether you say "cat" and are right or say "dog" and are wrong. In fact, you often get the most useful information when you are wrong because you may be right for the wrong reason, but when you are wrong you know you have made a mistake.

Many children become reluctant to learn because they are afraid of making a mistake—consider the relative credit children are given in and out of school for being "correct" and for being "wrong."

There's no need for learning to be extrinsically rewarded. The final exquisite virtue of learning is that it provides its own reward. Learning is satisfying, as everyone knows. It is part of the totally fulfilling and absorbing state of *flow* described by Csikszentmihalyi (1990), which we achieve only by losing ourselves in what we are doing. Deprivation of learning opportunities is boring, and failure to learn is frustrating. If a child needs reward or special recognition for learning, then there is only one conclusion to be drawn: that the child doesn't see any sense in the activity in the first place.

THE CONDITIONS OF LEARNING

I want to elaborate upon what I have said about learning in a rather different way. Learning is continuous, a natural state of the brain, and children therefore are likely to be learning all the time. There can be no other explanation for the enormous amount of unsuspected learning of the conventions of language that takes place. What then are the conditions under which these ever-learning brains succeed in learning as much as they do? And why is it that learning sometimes fails, as it sometimes does for all of us, so that something that even the learner wants to master remains unlearned? Three constituents seem to determine what is learned, when it is learned, and whether indeed learning will take place at all. These may be termed *demonstrations*, which are learning conditions existing in the world around us; *engagement*, which is the interaction of the learner with a demonstration; and *sensitivity*, the learner's learning condition (Smith, 1981).

Demonstrations

The first essential constituent of learning is the opportunity to see what can be done and how. Such opportunities may be termed *demonstrations* because they literally show a potential learner "This is how something is done." The world continually provides demonstrations, through people and through their products, by acts and by artifacts.

Every act is a cluster of demonstrations. Saying to a child "Here's your juice" demonstrates the meaning of the word juice and the language with which juice is presented. Saying "There's a big dog" demonstrates that there is a category of objects called dogs, that "dog" is the name of that category, and that the animal being referred to is a member of that category with all the appropriate distinctive features. A teacher who stands before a class demonstrates how a teacher stands before a class, how a teacher talks, how a teacher dresses, how a teacher feels about what is being taught and about the people being taught. A tired teacher demonstrates how a tired teacher behaves; a disinterested teacher demonstrates disinterest. Enthusiasm demonstrates enthusiasm. The fact that children are learning all the time is a ticking bomb in every classroom. What kind of reading do children see teachers doing? What do teachers demonstrate about their interest in reading?

Every artifact is a cluster of demonstrations. Every book demonstrates how pages are put together, how print and illustrations are organized on pages, how words are set out in sentences, and how sentences are punctuated. A book demonstrates the appearance and meaning of every word in that book. It demonstrates a particular genre scheme, discourse structure, and perhaps a story grammar too. What do our artifacts in the classroom demonstrate? Is it possible that children, and older students, are exposed to demonstrations that books can be incomprehensible, that they can be nonsense?

An important category of demonstrations is self-generated, like those we can perform in our imagination. We can try things out in the mind—in the world inside rather than in the world around us—and explore possible consequences without anyone actually knowing what we are doing. How much opportunity do children have for such private demonstrations?

Engagement

I chose the term *engagement* deliberately for the productive interaction of a learner with a demonstration, because my image is of the meshing of gears. Learning occurs when the learner *engages* with a demonstration, so that it becomes, in effect, the learner's demonstration.

Most people are familiar with the experience of reading a book or magazine and stopping suddenly, not because of something they didn't understand, but because their attention was engaged by a spelling they didn't know. They didn't start to read to have a spelling lesson, nor could they have predicted the unfamiliar spelling that they actually met, but when they encountered it—perhaps a name that they had only previously heard on radio or television—they stopped and in effect said, "Ah, so that's the way that word is spelled." At such a moment we can catch ourselves in the act of learning; we have not simply responded to a spelling, we have made it a part of what we know. Sometimes it is not a spelling that stops us, but a particularly interesting fact or the answer to a question that has been puzzling us for some time.

The second example is similar. Once again we find ourselves pausing while we read, this time not because of a spelling or some other piece of information, and certainly not for lack of under-standing, but simply because we have just read something that is *particularly well put*, an interesting idea appropriately expressed. This time we have engaged not with a spelling or an interesting new item of information, but with a style, a tone, a register. We are learn-ing about language from the way someone else is using it.

The two examples given were necessarily of situations in which we might actually be consciously aware of a learning moment. But such moments are rare. Perhaps we catch ourselves engaging with a new spelling or idea because it is a relatively infrequent event in our lives, because we have learned most of the things we want or expect to learn by now. New information or experiences can be surprising. But children learning the sounds, meanings, and written appearance of scores of new words every day of their lives are hardly likely to be stopped, like an adult, by the novelty of actually meeting something new. Instead, most of their learning must be so constant and casual that it doesn't intrude into con-sciousness.

Learning by engaging in the demonstrations of others is a par-ticularly efficient and economical way for children to learn, be-cause it limits the possibility of mistake and uncertainty. You are not likely to be in error if you let the demonstrator do your learn-ing trials for you. This is learning by conducting experiments, where the other person (who can do it) conducts the experiment. It is hypothesis testing where the appropriate hypothesis is easily available in the skilled performance of the demonstrator. The act of learning becomes *vicarious*.

Sensitivity

What makes the difference between whether we learn or don't learn from any particular demonstration? The answer can't be motivation, a grossly overrated factor, especially in schools where it is sometimes used to cover a multitude of other possibilities. For a start, learning of the kind described in this chapter usually occurs in the absence of motivation, certainly in the sense of a deliberate, conscious intention. It makes no sense to say an infant is motivated to learn to talk or that we are motivated to remember what is in the newspaper, unless the meaning of motivation is made so general that it can't be separated from learning.

On the other hand, motivation doesn't ensure learning. No matter how much they are motivated to spell, or to write fluently, or to learn a foreign language, many people still fail to learn these things. Desire and effort don't necessarily produce learning. Indeed, the only relevance of motivation to learning that I can see is that it puts us in situations where appropriate demonstrations are particularly likely to occur, and that learning will certainly not take place if there is motivation *not* to learn.

Closer to the truth is that we learn when we expect to learn, when learning is taken for granted. But a *conscious* expectation is not precisely what is required. Infants may take learning to talk for granted, but not in the sense of consciously expecting it. Rather, what seems to make the difference is *absence* of the expectation that learning will not take place.

This is how I propose to define *sensitivity*, the third constituent of every learning situation: the absence of expectation that learning will not take place, or that it will be difficult. Where does sensitivity come from? Every child is born with it. Children don't need to be taught that they can learn; they have this implicit expectation that they exhibit in their earliest learning about language and about the world—they believe they are omnipotent. Experience teaches children that they have limitations, and unfortunately, experience often teaches this unnecessarily.

Why is learning to walk usually so much easier than learning to swim? Walking must surely be the more difficult accomplishment. Infants have minimal motor coordination and on two tottering feet must struggle against gravity. Little wonder walking takes several months to master. Swimming, on the other hand, can be learned in a weekend—if it is learned at all. It is learned when the learner has much better motor coordination and is in a supportive element—water. And it must be as "natural" as walking. So why the difference? Could it be that difficulty and failure are so often anticipated with swimming and not with walking?

Why is learning to talk generally so easy while learning to read is sometimes so much harder? The answer can't be the intrinsic difficulty of reading. Infants learning to talk start with essentially nothing; they must make sense of it all for themselves. Despite the remarkable speed with which they are usually credited with learning about language, it still takes them several years to show anything approaching mastery. Reading should be learned more quickly, as it has so much language understanding to support it. And when children do learn to read, whether they learn at 3 years of age, or 6, or 10, they learn—in the observation of many teachers—in a matter of a few weeks. The instruction may last for years, but the learning is accomplished in weeks. What is the difference? I can only think that with reading an expectation of failure is frequently communicated to the child.

The apparent "difficulty" of some learning can't be explained away on the basis of age. Teenagers are expected to learn to drive cars—surely as complicated a matter as learning to swim, if not to read—and lo, they learn to drive cars. In fact, for anything that interests us, where the learning is taken for granted, we continue to learn throughout our lives. We don't even realize we are learning, as we keep up to date with our knowledge of language, music, astronomy, automotive engineering, spelling, world affairs, video games, the television world, or whatever—for the "kind of person" we happen to be.

Engagement takes place in the presence of appropriate demonstrations whenever we are sensitive to learning, and sensitivity is an absence of expectation that learning will not take place. Sensitivity is obviously related to two factors I mentioned earlier regarding willingness to engage in critical thinking, namely, disposition and authority. Individuals who don't feel competent to think critically on particular occasions, because of the way they perceive themselves or the way others perceive them, could be said to lack sensitivity for critical thinking. If they don't feel it is appropriate or possible for them to behave in a particular way, they will also feel that it is inappropriate (and probably impossible) for them to learn to behave in those ways. Lacking the disposition and authority to learn, they will decline opportunities for the necessary engagement.

Sensitivity doesn't need to be accounted for; its absence does. Expectation that learning will not take place is itself learned. The ultimate irony is that our constant propensity to learn may in fact defeat learning; we can learn that particular things are not worth learning or are unlikely to be learned. Children are indiscriminate in their learning—the ticking bomb in the classroom—and they can learn things that they would really do much better not learning at all. Learning that something is useless, unpleasant, difficult, or improbable may be devastatingly permanent in its effect.

LEARNING—A SOCIAL EVENT

So far, learning has been discussed as if it were the entire responsibility of the learner, a matter of individual effort. But this is not the case. Whether or not learning takes place usually depends more on people around learners than on the learners themselves. Personal effort doesn't guarantee learning, nor does conscious motivation. Learners often need do nothing in order to learn. Someone else does something, and the learner learns—the vicarious aspect of learning. Neither the learner nor the people around the learner need know that learning is taking place.

Family and friends are generally unaware of how much even the youngest children learn of spoken language, for example. Infants don't *practice* talking, they *say* something—and usually they are right first time. They occasionally make mistakes, of course, and when they do, grownups regard the mistakes as cute and tell their friends. But most of the time parents are unaware that learning is taking place, until they suddenly find themselves saying, "Where did junior learn to say that?" Then they stop having private conversations in front of the child. Learning inconspicuously and effortlessly continues into adulthood. How else would we all learn the meanings of the scores of thousands of words that we know, and to talk the way we do? Where does it all come from?

The typical absence of evident error might seem to provide problems for the hypothesis testing point of view adopted earlier in this chapter. If children test hypotheses in order to learn, they must get the hypotheses right most of the time. And right or wrong, where do the hypotheses come from?

The answer to all of these questions must be—from other people. Much of what children (and adults) learn, they learn when they are interested in something someone else is doing. They learn as if they were doing it themselves.

Learning From Other People

George Miller (1977) recognized the importance of other people in the title of his book *Spontaneous Apprentices: Children and Language*. He argued that infants learn to talk and to understand speech by apprenticing themselves to adults or to more competent children. And they learn to talk in exactly the same way as the people they apprentice themselves to. Children don't even learn to talk like the people they hear talking most. (Once they get to school, children hear their teachers talking more than anyone else, but they don't grow up talking like teachers—unless they are going to become teachers themselves.)

No *modeling* is involved. This is not a matter of infants saying, "I want to be like that person," and studying and practicing the other person's behavior. Instead, the child seems effortlessly to learn what the other person does. The other person is an unwitting surrogate for the child's learning. If this is trial-and-error learning, other people conduct the trial, and because they can already do what they are doing, there are very few errors.

A baby babbles, someone else puts the utterance into conventional language—"You want a drink of juice?"—and the child has learned something about drinks of juice, without practice, without error. One adult says to another, "Pass the salt"—it could be babble as far as the infant is concerned—but the adult behavior allows the infant to hypothesize the meaning of the utterance. If the salt is passed, the child has learned by hypothesis testing, without error and without anyone knowing that learning has taken place.

We learn when we comprehend. (A struggle to learn is always a struggle to comprehend.) Other people help us to learn by helping us to understand. That is essentially the social nature of learning, even when we are learning from books, when it is the author's responsibility to facilitate the reader's comprehension.

Joining the Spoken Language Club

An alternative metaphor for explaining how infants learn about language (and everything else) is that they join a club (Smith, 1988). Infants join communities of people they see themselves as being like, who accept the infants as being like them, and the infants learn to be exactly like other members of the club. They learn not to be like members of the clubs they don't belong to.

A spoken-language club is probably the first club most infants join, but it has exactly the same advantages as any other club they might join later in life. First, more experienced members disclose the nature of the club's activities. These are the demonstrations I have referred to in this chapter. In the spoken language club, members demonstrate to the child what spoken language can be used for, how it helps to fulfill intentions in a variety of ways.

Second, when new members of the club themselves want to engage in club activities—when they want to use spoken language to fulfill their own intentions—more experienced members of the club help. They don't give newcomers *instruction* from which learning is supposed to take place, they provide *collaboration*. To be specific, other members help the infant to say what the infant is trying to say, and they help the infant to understand what the infant is trying to understand. The learner is totally involved because everything centers on the learner's intentions and interest—this is the engagement to which I referred earlier.

Children finish up talking exactly like their friends, the other members of the spoken language club they eventually affiliate with. They learn to dress and ornament themselves exactly like their friends—like the kind of person they see themselves as being. They learn the other club members' ways of perceiving the world, their attitudes, their values, their dislikes, their imperatives. They learn a *culture*—not by practice or by trial and error, but by imperceptibly yet inevitably coming to be exactly like the kind of person they see themselves as being. In other words, the clubs they join become their identity.

If we see ourselves as members of a club, and the club members don't exclude us, then we can't help becoming like the other members because of the demonstrations and collaboration we receive. But if we are rejected by a club, or if we decide to exclude ourselves, then we not only fail to become like the club members, we often become as different from them as we can be. We lose our sensitivity—and it is usually almost impossible to get it back. It is as if we don't want to be mistaken for members of the club—except that none of the learning or failure to learn is under conscious control. Everyone fails, in one way or another, to become members of clubs of people who have mastered things like statistics, automobile engines, computer programming, algebra, identifying constellations—or reading or writing. This has nothing to do with motivation or effort—the most conspicuous things most of us have failed to learn are often things we have been most motivated to learn, and that we have spent the most "time on task" trying to learn.

ISSUES

Despite all the everyday evidence to the contrary, it is still commonly taken for granted that learning is the result of frequency and intensity of effort. Many politicians and media authorities—and even some self-styled researchers—appear convinced that failure to learn indicates a lack of trying on the part of students and their teachers. I don't know where they learned this.

SUMMARY

Most of what individuals know about language and the world is not formally taught. Instead, children develop their theory of the world and competence in language by testing *hypotheses*, experimenting in meaningful and purposeful ways with tentative modifications of what they know already. Thus the basis of *learning* is *comprehension*. Children learn continuously, through *engagement* in *demonstrations* that make sense to them, whenever their natural *sensitivity* for learning is undamaged. Learning is a social activity. Children learn from what other people do and help them to do.

Notes to chapter 12 begin on page 299 covering:
Language learning
Vocabulary
Motivation

13 Learning About Written Language

The implication of this present chapter can be summed up in very few words. The primary role of reading teachers is to ensure that children have adequate demonstrations of written language being used for meaningful purposes and to help children to fulfill such purposes themselves. Where children see little relevance in reading, then teachers must show that reading is worthwhile. Where children find little interest in reading, then teachers must create interesting situations. No one ever taught reading to a child who wasn't interested in reading, and interest can't be demanded. Teachers must themselves be conspicuous users of written language. What applies to children applies also to older students, and to adults.

This book is primarily about reading, and this chapter is primarily about learning to read. But nothing a child learns about reading—whether about letters, words, or meaning—will make any sense unless the child has an understanding of what can be done with written language. Hence the title of this chapter. Every learner must know—and be able to trust—that written language can be used for worthwhile purposes, that it is not meaningless marks.

LEARNING TO READ BY READING

Learning to read doesn't require the memorization of letter names, or phonic generalizations, or a large vocabulary, all of which are taken care of in the course of learning to read, and little of which will make sense to a child without experience of reading. Nor is learning to read a matter of application to all manner of exercises and drills, which can only distract and even discourage a child from the business of learning to read. And finally, learning to read is not a matter of relying on instruction, because the underlying skills of reading—namely, the efficient uses of nonvisual information—can't be explicitly taught. But they can be learned from experience.

Learning to read is like the cat-and-dog problem. No one can teach explicitly the relevant categories, features, and interrelationships that are involved. Yet children are perfectly capable of solving the problems for themselves provided they have the opportunities to generate and test their own hypotheses. Learning to read is especially like learning spoken language. No one can even begin to explain to infants what essential features and conventions of speech should be learned, let alone construct a course of study for infants to follow; yet even this complex problem is solved by children, without any apparent strain or difficulty, provided again that they have the opportunity to exercise their innate learning ability and are *helped* to use and understand speech. All that children require to master spoken language, both to produce it themselves and more fundamentally to comprehend its use by others, is to experience language being used in meaningful settings. Children easily learn about spoken language when they are involved in its use, when it has the possibility of making sense to them. And in the same way children will try to understand written language by being involved in its use, in situations where it makes sense to them and they can generate and test hypotheses.

No infallible method of instruction will ever be found to direct a child's progress in learning to read. But it is not possible to chart the precise course of a child's learning spoken language either (or learning the difference between cats and dogs). It is possible to specify the *conditions* under which children will learn to read, and these are again the general conditions that are required for learning anything—the opportunity to generate and test hypotheses (naturally and unconsciously) in a meaningful context. And to reiterate the constant theme, the only way a child can do all this for reading is to read. If the question arises of how children can be expected to learn to read by reading before they have learned to read, the answer is very simple. At the beginning—and at any other time when it is necessary—the reading has to be done for them. Before children acquire competence in reading, everything will have to be read to them, but as their ability expands they will need only occasional help.

One of the beautiful things about written language that makes sense is that it increasingly provides crucial assistance to learners. Authors can take over teaching children to read. Meaningful written language, like meaningful speech, not only provides its own clues to meaning, so that children can generate appropriate learning hypotheses, but it also provides the opportunity for tests. If a beginning reader is not sure of a likely meaning, the context (before *and* after) can provide clues. And the subsequent context will indicate whether the child's hypotheses were right or wrong. Reading text that makes sense is like riding a bicycle; children don't need to be told when they are losing control.

Let me list the advantages a child gains from reading meaningful texts: building vocabulary, understanding the possibilities and limitations of letter–sound relationships, developing mediated word and meaning identification ability, acquiring speed, avoiding tunnel vision, preventing memory overload, relying on sense, acquiring familiarity with such conventions as the appropriate discourse structure, grammar, and register—in short, increasing relevant nonvisual information and gaining experience in using it more efficiently. And always the child will be the best guide for learning in the most efficient manner, because children will not willingly limit their vision, overload memory, or tolerate nonsense. Children also will not tolerate *not learning*, so there is no reason to expect that they will be satisfied with what has become simple and routine for them.

It is also easy to list the conditions required for children to take advantage of the learning opportunities that reading meaningful text provides. There are only four: plentiful access to comprehensible and interesting reading material, assistance where needed (and only to the extent that it is required), willingness to take the necessary risks (anxiety increases the proportion of visual information a reader needs), and freedom to make mistakes.

I have said little about motivation because it is not something that can be artificially promoted or maintained, certainly not by means of extrinsic "reinforcers" such as irrelevant material rewards, improved grades, or even extravagant praise. None of these is necessary for a child to learn spoken language. All the satisfaction that a child requires is in the learning itself, in the utility and understanding that result. And the impetus in the first place? Why do children set themselves the enormously time-consuming task of learning spoken language? Not, I think, in order to communicate; children can't understand this use of language until they have mastered some. And certainly not to get their material needs fulfilled or to control the behavior of others. Children are never so well looked after as before they can use language; afterward they can be told to wait, to do without, or to do it themselves. I think there can be only one reason why children apply themselves to learning spoken language—because it is *there*, an interesting and functioning part of the world around them. They learn when its sense, its utility, and its meaningfulness are demonstrated to them. And because language is meaningful, because it changes the world and is not arbitrary or capricious, not only do children succeed in learning it, but they *want* to learn it. Children will learn anything that is meaningful to them, unless the learning becomes too difficult or too costly for them, in which case the learning itself becomes meaningless. The child's sensitivity for reading is destroyed.

Children will endeavor to understand and engage in anything they see adults doing, provided the adults demonstrate enjoyment and satisfaction in doing it. If meaningful written language exists in the child's world and is conspicuously used with satisfaction, then the child will strive to join the club; that is in the nature of childhood. There is no need for special explanations about why children should want to learn to read, only for why they might come to the conclusion that reading is pointless or too costly.

TWO CRITICAL INSIGHTS

There are two special insights that children must have in order to learn to read. These insights are fundamental, in the sense that children who don't have them are bound to find reading instruction nonsensical and won't therefore succeed in learning to read. Yet not only are these insights not taught in school, but much of what constitutes formal reading instruction might be seen as contrary to these insights, and thus likely to inhibit them. The insights are, first, that print is meaningful, and second, that written language is not the same as speech.

Insight 1: Print Is Meaningful

There is no need to belabor why the insight that print is meaningful is an essential precondition for learning to read. Reading is a matter of making sense of print, and meaningfulness is the basis of learning. For as long as children see no sense in print, for as long as they regard it as arbitrary or nonsensical, they will find no reason to attend to print. They won't learn by trying to relate letters to sounds. Written language doesn't work in that way, and it is not something that can make any sense to children.

Research has offered abundant evidence that children may be as much immersed in written language as they are in speech, and they respond to it with similar intelligence. I am not referring to school nor to those overrated books that are supposed to surround and somehow inspire some privileged children to literacy. I refer instead to the wealth of situation-dependent print to be found on every product in the bathroom, on every jar and package in the kitchen, in the television guide (and in commercials on television and the web), in comics, catalogs, advertising fliers, telephone directories, on street signs, storefronts, gas stations, billboards, at fast-food outlets, supermarkets, and department stores. All of this print is meaningful; it makes a difference. We no more predict cereal in a package labeled *detergent* than we expect candy in a store advertising *dry cleaning* or a concert in a television program announced as *football*.

For those not blind to it (and experienced readers often are unseeing in this way) our visual world is an ocean of print, most of it (check your supermarket) literally in front of our eyes. Even children who can't yet read pay attention to this ambient print. I have told of a 3½-year-old boy who obviously couldn't read the words *luggage* and *footwear* on signs in a department store (because he got both of them wrong) but who nevertheless asserted that the first said "cases" and the second said "shoes" (Smith, 1976). Here was one child who could bring meaning to print long before he could read the actual print, and who therefore had acquired the insight that differences in print are meaningful.

There is only one way in which such an insight might be achieved, and that is when a child observes print being responded to in a meaningful way. At this point, I am not referring to the reading of books or stories, but to the occasions when a child is told, "That sign says, 'Stop,'" "The word on that door is 'Boys,'" or "This is the jar for cookies." Television commercials may do the same for a child—they not only announce the product's name, desirability, and uniqueness in spoken and written language, but they even demonstrate the product at work. And just as with the spoken language of the home, there is a great deal a child might learn from this situation-dependent written language by hypothesizing a likely meaning and seeing if the hypothesis is confirmed. Children can test hypotheses about the meaning of the printed word *toys* in a mall, not because anyone reads it to them, but by ascertaining whether the sign does in fact indicate the location of the toy store. There is a consistency between the print and its environment. The print that normally surrounds children is potentially meaningful, and thus provides an effective basis for learning.

There may be very little meaningful print in school, in the sense that it would not be possible to substitute one word for another. A teacher writes the words *table* or *chair* on the board but could just as well write *horse* or *cow*. The words in word lists, or the sentences in many "stories," could be changed without any child noticing anything out of place. Teachers may believe there are good reasons for a particular exercise or element of instruction, but if children can't see the sense of the enterprise, then it can reasonably be regarded as incomprehensible. A brief list of fundamentally incomprehensible aspects of reading instruction to which children may be exposed would include:

1. The decomposition of spoken words to "sounds." The spoken word *cat*, in some contexts, can make sense, but the sounds /kuh/, /a/, /tuh/ never do.

2. The decomposition of written words to letters. The printed word *cat*, in some contexts, can make sense—when it refers to a real or imaginary animal with which children can meaningfully interact. But the letters *c*, *a*, and *t* are arbitrary visual symbols that have nothing to do with anything else in the child's life.

3. The relating of letters to sounds. For a child who has no idea of reading to be told that some peculiar shapes called letters—which have no apparent function in the real world—are related to sounds that have no independent existence in the real world must be jabberwocky.

4. Meaningless drills and exercises. There are so many candidates for this category, ranging from deciding which of three ducks is facing the wrong way to underlining silent letters in words, that I won't attempt to make a list. Children may learn to score high on repetitive and nonsensical tasks (especially if they happen to be competent readers), but such a specialized ability won't *make* readers of them.

The preceding kinds of activity may, through their very incomprehensibility, make learning to read more complicated, arduous, and nonsensical than it need be. It is not until children have begun reading that they have a chance of making sense of such activities at all. Children who lack the insight that written language should make sense may never achieve it, and children who have the insight may be persuaded they are wrong.

Insight 2: Written Language Is Different From Speech

The first insight was concerned primarily with written language in the form of single words (or small groups of words) like labels and signs. These kinds of print function very much like the everyday *situation-dependent* spoken language outside school in that cues to meaning (and constraints on interpretation) are provided largely by the physical situation in which they occur. Now I want to consider *context-dependent* written language, where constraints on substitutability and interpretation are placed not by the physical environment but by the syntax and semantics of the text itself. As I discussed in chapter 3, the conventions of written and spoken language are evidently not the same, and probably for very good reason, including the fact that written language has become especially adapted for being read.

Children who expect written language to be exactly the same as speech are likely to have difficulty in predicting and comprehending its conventions and thus in learning to read. They must be familiar with how written language works. Immersion in functional language, the possibility of making sense, a plentiful experience, and the opportunity to test hypotheses would seem to be just as easily met with written language as with speech. In fact, written language might seem to have several advantages, because a number of tests can be conducted on the same piece of material, and a second hypothesis tried if the first fails. By virtue of its internal consistency, the text itself can provide relevant feedback about the correctness of hypotheses.

How might children who can't yet read acquire and develop the insight that speech and written language are not the same? Only by being read to, or at least by hearing written language read aloud. The kind of reading that would most familiarize children with written language is coherent *stories*, ranging from items in newspapers and magazines to traditional fairy tales, ghost and adventure stories, history, and myth. All of these types of story are truly written *language*—produced for a purpose in a conventional medium and distinguishable from most school texts by their length, sense, and semantic and syntactic richness. There is no evidence that it is any harder for children to understand complex texts (when they are read to them or when they can explore them for themselves) than it is difficult for children to understand the complex adult speech that they hear around them and on television.

Children at school may not be provided with complex written material as part of their reading instruction for the obvious reason that they couldn't be expected to read it by themselves. Because material in which children are likely to be interested—and from which they would be likely to learn—may be too difficult for them to read by themselves, less complex material is found or produced in the expectation that children will find it "simpler." And when these specially tailored-for-children texts also seem to confound beginners, the assumption may be made that the fault lies with the children or with their "language development."

And indeed, it may be the case that the language of such texts is unfamiliar to many children. But this inadequacy need not have its roots in the particular kind of spoken language with which the child is familiar nor even in the possibly limited experience of the child with print. The reason is more likely to be associated with the child's unfamiliarity with the artificial language of school books, whether of the truncated "Sam the cat sat on the mat" variety or the more florid "Down the hill, hand in hand, skipped Susie and her friend." This is also so different from any other form of language, spoken or written, that it is probably safest to put it into an exclusive category of "school language."

Such material tends naturally to be unpredictable for many children, who consequently have enormous difficulty understanding it and learning to read from it. And ironically, it may be concluded that written language is intrinsically difficult for children, who would be better off learning from "spoken language written down." The text is then based on the intuition of a textbook writer or classroom teacher about what constitutes spoken language—or more complex still, a dialect of that language or even children's language. All of these are problems that would confound a professional linguist. The result is quite unlike written language yet has none of the advantages of speech, because it will have to be comprehended out of context. Children may learn to recite such print, but there is no evidence that it will make them readers. Any insight they might have in advance about the nature of written language is likely to be undermined, and worse, they might become persuaded that the print that they first experience in school is a model for all the written language that they will meet throughout their lives—a conviction that would be as discouraging as it is misleading.

ON INSTRUCTIONAL METHODS

I have not said anything about the best (or the worst) programs, methods, or materials for teaching children to read. This was intentional, because the conclusion to which all my analysis, research, and experience with teachers and with children in schools has led is that children don't learn to read from programs. In particular, they can't learn from the more structured, systematic "reading skills" programs where every supposed learning step is predetermined for the child; they can't acquire or maintain the two basic insights just discussed. Only people—and written language itself—can demonstrate how written language is *used*. Programs can't anticipate what a child will want to do or know at a particular time. They can't provide opportunities for engagement. And anything a program teaches that is irrelevant to a child will be learned, if it is learned at all, as something that is irrelevant.

No "method" of teaching will take care of all the contingencies. Nor should the development of a foolproof method be expected, despite the billions of dollars that have been spent in its pursuit and exploitation. Although some methods of teaching reading are obviously worse than others (because they are based on very weak theories of the nature of reading), the belief that one perfect method might exist to teach all children is contrary to all the evidence about the multiplicity of individual differences that every child brings to reading.

Research is of little help in the selection of appropriate methods. Research tells us that all methods of teaching reading appear to work for some children in contrived circumstances but that none works for all. Some teachers seem to succeed whatever the method they are formally believed to employ. We must conclude that the instructional method is not the critical issue. (Researchers recognize this point and have to control in their studies for the "variability" introduced first by the differing experience of children and second by the varying influence of teachers.) It might not be particularly unfair to say that many children learn to read—and many teachers succeed in helping them—despite the instructional method used.

The analysis I have made can't be translated into a system for teaching, although it can indeed be translated into an environment for learning. In fact, the analysis explains environments in which children do learn to read, whether or not there is a program that is supposed to be teaching the child to read at the same time. These are environments in which at least some written language makes sense, and in which an autonomous teacher has a critical role.

Whatever the setting, books and other interesting reading materials must play a large part in it. Far more learners become readers in libraries than in experimental laboratories.

The Never-Ending Debate

Two basic theories of how children learn to read have been contrasted in these pages. One point of view is sometimes termed the "natural approach," "meaning approach," "psycholinguistic," "real books," or "whole language." The opposing point of view, which relies heavily on phonics and other exercises and drills, is generally called the "skills approach," "mastery," or "direct instruction." Between the two sides is a gulf.

Many reading theorists and researchers have taken strong positions on one side of this gulf or the other, perpetuating what Jeanne Chall (1967) nearly 40 years ago called "The Great Debate." The debate is still unresolved. In Smith (1992) I referred to it as "never-ending," and in the notes, beginning on page 316, I discuss why "the interminable controversy" is unlikely to end—and why it engenders such intense feeling.

The Role of Computers

For anyone who believes there are basic skills that children must master in order to become readers and writers, and that repetitious exercises, correction, tests, and grading are essential for learning those skills, computers constitute an ideal educational technology. With sophisticated graphics, tightly controlled instructional sequences and loops, constant testing, immediate feedback of results, and ability to document and compare every score, computer-based literacy programs offer systematic instruction in a form that can appeal to everyone. Children enjoy them because they make "fun" out of previously tedious ritual, like television cartoons. Parents like the computer programs, because the technology is labeled "educational." Teachers may like them because they plot a path for every student and keep them on track. And administrators can find the success and control that computer-assisted instruction promises irresistible.

Such computer programs must be questioned about what they demonstrate to learners about literacy. Yet major publishers of reading and writing programs, from kindergarten through high school, now invest in elaborate software programs. The worksheet activities and tests contained in their print materials are now presented on computer screens in endless profusion and variety. And the same claims of instructional efficacy are made. There is no evidence that such computer programs have succeeded in making children literate, and there are no convincing theories that they could succeed. Such programs could rapidly give children a totally false idea of the purposes and possibilities of literacy (Smith, 1986).

This doesn't mean that computers have no place in the literacy classroom. As word processors, computers have helped the youngest children to become writers, by assisting them in the physical act of writing and also in such writerly activities as drafting, editing, and preparing clean and legible copies of their texts. And when used in these and a variety of other practical ways—in simulations, games, design activities, communication links, drama, art, and music—computers seem able to stimulate children to talk more, plan more, think more, write more, and read more. The issue is not whether computers should be in classrooms, but how they should be used.

TEACHING READING

As I said at the beginning of this chapter, teachers must demonstrate to their students that reading is worthwhile, and create interesting reading opportunities. They must themselves be conspicuous users of written language.

Where children have difficulty in reading, teachers must see that they are helped to read what they would like to read. In part, this assistance can be given by developing the confidence of children to read for themselves, in their own way, taking the risk of making mistakes and being willing to ignore the completely incomprehensible. Even bizarre personal interpretations are better than none at all; children find out soon enough the mistakes that make a difference. But children will also from time to time look for help from others, either in answering specific questions or in assisting with reading generally. Such reading on behalf of the child can be provided by the teacher, an aide, or by other children.

The Learner's Point of View

Children themselves must judge whether materials and activities are too difficult or too dull. Anything children would not listen to or understand if it were read to them is unsuitable material for them to be expected to read. A child's preference is a far better yardstick than any readability formula, and grade levels have no reality in a child's mind. Teachers need not be afraid that children will engage in reading so easy that there is nothing to learn; that would be boring. Children learn about reading as long as they read, but they can never learn about reading by not reading.

There is no simple formula to ensure that reading will be comprehensible; no materials or procedures are guaranteed never to interfere with a child's progress. Instead, teachers must understand the factors that make reading difficult, whether induced by the child, the teacher, or the task. Examples include the concentration on visual detail that will cause tunnel vision; the overloading of short-term memory by attention to fragments of text that make little sense; logjams in long-term memory as a child strives to be ready to answer questions afterward or to write "reports"; attempts to sound out words at the expense of meaning; slow reading; anxiety not to make a mistake; lack of assistance when a child needs it for sense or even word identification; or too-insistent "correction" that may be irrelevant to the child and that may in the long run inhibit the self-correction that is an essential part of learning. All of these ways in which reading is made harder can be characterized as limitations on the extent to which children can use nonvisual information.

And conversely, what makes reading comprehensible for children is the teacher's facilitation of the use of nonvisual information. Not only should a child come into every reading situation with relevant nonvisual information—in plain English, with adequate prior understanding—but the child must also feel free to use it. A child's fund of knowledge and confidence should be constantly developed, but this will occur as a consequence of reading. Not only should the teacher try to avoid materials or activities that are nonsense to the child, there should be active encouragement for the child to predict, to understand, to enjoy. The worst habit for any learner is to treat text as if there were no sense to be found in it. Where there is a mismatch, where there is little likelihood that a child will comprehend the material, then the preference should be to change the material rather than to try to change the child.

For older students, teachers may be reluctant to change material because a certain content is expected to be learned, but they still have a choice. Students can't learn two things at the same time; they can't simultaneously learn to read and to master an unfamiliar subject matter like history or math. If the teacher's intention is to improve reading, then students must have material they can easily understand. If the intention is to extend subject matter knowledge—which will in turn make reading easier—then until the student can read it with some fluency the subject matter must be taught in some other way, by lecture, film, board work, or individual tuition. The two can be taught *concurrently*—the math need not wait for the reading competence any more than the reading need wait for the math skills—but they can't be learned simultaneously.

Teaching the Hard Way

Teachers sometimes try to resolve problems the hard way—for example, in expecting poor readers to improve while they are doing less reading than better readers. When children have trouble understanding text they may be given isolated word drills, while problems with word identification may provoke attention to letter identification and sound blends. Actual reading may be postponed in favor of phonemic awareness exercises. But letters (and their phonic interrelations) are recognized and learned best when they are parts of words, and words are recognized and learned more easily when they are in meaningful sequences. Good readers tend to be good at letter and word identification and at phonic drills, but these more specific skills are a consequence, not a cause, of good reading (Samuels, 1971). Good readers tend also to understand the technical jargon of reading such as *letter, word, verb, sentence, paragraph*, but this again is a result of being able to read. Practice with definitions doesn't make readers (Downing & Oliver, 1973/1974). Knowledge of specialized words is necessary only if they are made a focal part of the instruction, if it is necessary for children to understand the words in order to be allowed to get on with the business of learning to read and write. It is not an essential prerequisite for literacy.

Children may also be confounded by instruction that is as unnecessary as it is futile, often as a consequence of a theoretical vogue among specialists. When, for example, Noam Chomsky popularized transformational linguistics as a technical method of analyzing language, many people thought children would not learn to read unless they became miniature linguists themselves and children were made to spend a lot of time doing exercises in transformational grammar that made no apparent difference to their language ability. After psychologists became interested in the theoretical notion of distinctive features, there were several efforts to teach children the distinctive features of letters, although no one could convincingly demonstrate what these features might be.

Children who had difficulty with the alphabet or with these exercises were sometimes diagnosed as having poor feature discrimination, although they had no reported difficulty with knives and forks or dogs and cats. Phonic-based reading programs and materials have flourished whenever linguists have become particularly interested in the spelling–sound correspondences of language, and there have been moves toward teaching "prediction" as if it were something foreign to most children's experience. "Phonological awareness" is urged as a necessity for learning to read, with the result that children may spend more time attempting to deconstruct speech than exploring written language. In all of these cases, concepts that scientists have found useful as hypothetical constructs in their attempts to understand their discipline have become something a child must learn as a prerequisite for learning to read. (How children learned to read before these concepts were devised is not explained.) There is a growing acknowledgment today of the importance of comprehension as the basis of learning, but at the same time there is a feeling that comprehension itself must be taught, that it can be broken down into a series of "comprehension skills" that presumably can be learned without comprehension.

I am not saying that it is not useful for children to know the alphabet, to build up sight vocabularies, or even to understand the relationships between the spelling of words and their sounds and (more importantly) their meaning. *But all of these are by-products of reading that make more sense as reading itself is mastered and understood.* It is pointless for teacher and child to labor over activities that won't facilitate learning to read and that will become easy once reading experience develops.

It is certainly not the case that teachers should never correct or make suggestions. But correction or advice may be offered too soon. A child pauses while reading aloud and half the class shouts out the next word, although the reader may be thinking about something else six words behind or ahead. Problems arise when corrections and explanations sap children's confidence or stop them in their tracks for what might be quite extraneous reasons. The teacher should always ask, "What is causing the confusion here?" Children afraid of being corrected may become afraid of speaking, reading, and writing.

The First Steps

Children begin to read with the first written word they are able to recognize. Nonvisual information is so important that reading potential is enhanced with every expansion of a child's knowledge of the world or of spoken language. (But there is no particular need for extensive prior knowledge of the world or of spoken language for a child to begin to read, just enough to make sense of the first print that will be read. Much of the knowledge and language skills of fluent readers is again a consequence of literacy rather than its cause.)

There is no "best age" for learning to read. Many children have learned to read, often spontaneously, as young as 3 years of age (Clark, 1976), and it is equally well documented that adult illiterates can learn in a few months provided their sensitivity has not been blunted by years of failure with formal reading instruction (Freire, 1972). Many of the early readers who have been studied did not have above-average intellect or any particular social or cultural privileges; they simply found reading something that was useful and straightforward to learn, usually without any particular consciousness of what they were doing. Whether a child will learn to read is not something that can be determined with reference to a calendar or the learner's "mental age."

Similarly, there is no unique mental condition of "reading readiness." Children are ready to learn to read whenever they have a purpose and intelligible opportunity for reading, not in terms of settling down to a concentrated period of systematic instruction but in an explorer's interest in signs and labels, in telephone directories and catalogs, and in stories. In educational contexts, reading readiness is often related more to the form and demands of instruction than to reading itself. Obviously, if instruction emphasizes knowledge of letter names, then a child who can't grasp the nature of the alphabet is not ready. If instruction requires detailed attention to the sound patterns of a particular dialect, then a child who can't do this is not ready. But none of this has anything to do with reading itself. It is difficult to see what kind of special physical, emotional, intellectual, or cultural status is required for learning to read, except the two basic insights I have already discussed.

Reading should blend smoothly into all the other visual and linguistic and intellectual enterprises of a learner's life. There is no magical day when a "pre-reader" suddenly becomes a "learner," just as there is no landmark day when learning is completed and a reader graduates. No one is a perfect reader, and we all continue to learn every time we read.

None of this is to say that all children will easily learn to read; there has always been evidence that such is unlikely to be the case. But failure need not be attributed to *dyslexia*, a disease that only strikes children who can't read, and that is invariably cured when they can read. I have argued that there is nothing unique about reading, either visually or as far as language is concerned. There are no evident visual defects that are specific to reading, but this doesn't mean that there are no general visual anomalies that will interfere with learning to read. The few children who have difficulty learning to understand speech, or learning anything, may also find learning to read difficult.

But there is no convincing evidence that children who can see normally, with or without spectacles, and who have acquired a working competence in the language spoken around them, might be physically or congenitally incapable of learning to read. It can't be denied that some children who seem able and even bright in all other respects may fail to learn to read. But there can be other reasons for this failure that don't presuppose any physical dysfunction on the part of the child. Children don't learn to read who don't want to, or who see no point in doing so, or who are hostile to the teacher, or to the school, or to the social or cultural group to which they perceive the teacher and the school as belonging. Children don't learn to read who expect to fail, or who believe that learning to read will demand too much effort or stress, or whose image of themselves, for whatever reason, is that of a nonreader. Children don't learn to read if they have the wrong idea of the nature of reading, if they have learned—or have been taught—that reading doesn't make sense.

TESTS AND STANDARDS

It is in the context of failure that brief reference should be made to the effects on young readers of the current mania for constant testing and evaluation, and especially on those having difficulty in making sense of the way reading is taught.

Tests are primarily a bureaucratic tool. They are devised and dispensed for a variety of administrative and political reasons to categorize children and to evaluate teachers. But no reading test ever helped a child learn to read. And there is nothing in tests themselves to indicate why a child might not be succeeding in learning to read.

Problems arise in two ways. The first is that it is widely believed that the content of reading tests (or of comprehension or readiness tests) indicates what a child needs to know in order to learn to read. This is a fallacy. Tests may provide indicators of what children are able to do as a consequence of learning to read, so that children who are good readers tend to do well on tests (although not invariably) and children who are poor readers don't. But trying to teach a child to score well on individual items on a test won't teach a child how to read. Counting the number of times a child voluntarily visits the library might be a relatively sensible test indicator of reading ability, but training the child to visit the library more often would not in itself improve reading ability, although it would raise the test score. If anything, tests measure how well children have been able to make sense of formal reading instruction, to work their way through programs.

The reason for the close affinity of tests and programs is that they both treat reading in the same arbitrary and unnatural way. Because someone outside the classroom must determine what is appropriate for children to do and know (and that can be measured), and because for reasons of control and standardization it is necessary to break reading down into fragmented and predetermined sequences, tests and instructional programs both tend to become concerned with the same superficial and isolated aspects that are supposed to be "components" of reading.

Thus the first problem with tests is that they give teachers and children a distorted idea of the nature of reading and of what must be done to teach a child to read (or to satisfy some outside authority that the child is being taught to read). This is perhaps not too much of a handicap for a child who is indeed learning to read, who does reasonably well on the tests, and whose exposure to meaningful reading is not limited as a consequence. But tests can be devastating for children who don't do well, partly because they may then have opportunities to read meaningfully withdrawn from them (in favor of exercises and drills that they have already demonstrated they don't understand) and also because of the inevitable consequence for their self-esteem. The second major problem with tests is that they do nothing positive for the sensitivity of children who do badly on them.

Teachers don't need "off-the-shelf" tests to discover if their students are learning or if they are confused. Every teacher can tell (or should be able to tell) if a child has made progress in reading, just by talking with the child and looking at what the child is voluntarily reading. Learning to read doesn't inch along one item of information after another; there should be no difficulty in determining whether a child has progressed in ability and interest over a period of a few weeks. If the method of instruction is such that neither teacher nor child can tell whether progress is being made without recourse to a standardized test, then the instruction itself is essentially meaningless.

The best tests are "homemade," constructed on the spot to reassure the teacher that whatever a particular child is supposed to be learning at a particular time is making sense. Good teachers do this intuitively, and because such tests are a natural part of whatever activity the child is engaged in, they are both relevant and inconspicuous.

The situations that I have characterized as making reading more difficult, and thus likely to interfere with children's learning to read, are so much a fact of life in many classrooms that many teachers feel they can do little about them. Tests must be administered; instruction must be directed toward the tests; the language arts are arbitrarily and artificially fragmented; children are categorized and streamed; teachers are held accountable; certain curricula must be followed; concerns of parents and trustees must be assuaged; work must be graded; competition and anxiety are unavoidable. Much of a teacher's time is necessarily directed to classroom management, many activities are engaged in to satisfy "standards" or other demands laid down by external sources, and few teachers can find the time or the resources to provide an ideal learning environment for children all the time.

A theory of reading won't change all this (although it might provide ammunition for anyone who tries to resist). The kind of change that will make a difference in schools won't come with better theories or with better materials or even with better informed teachers, but only with individuals taking action toward change. The problem of improving reading instruction, in the long run, is a political question. But whether teachers can change their world or not, they will still be better off to the extent that they understand about reading and about how children learn to read. Teachers who can't relieve children of the disruptions of irrelevant demands and activities may at least protect them by pointing out that the activities have little to do with reading or with the child's learning ability. Children understand that meaningless tasks are often given to them simply to keep them occupied and quiet, but they are not helped by being led to believe that such tasks are an important part of learning to read.

THE LITERACY CLUB

There is substantial evidence that children know a great deal about literacy before they come to school (Ferreiro & Teberosky, 1982;

Goelman, Oberg, & Smith, 1984; Tolchinsky, 2003). They may not have learned to read and to write, but they know how literacy is used in the community to which they belong. If their family reads books and newspapers, they know about books and newspapers. If their family consults the television guide, they know about television guides. If they leave each other messages on the refrigerator door, they know about those too. If their friends read comics or consult catalogues, they know about comics and catalogues. If their friends use e-mail and the Internet, they probably know more about e-mail and the Internet than their parents do. Children know about signs, labels, lists, letters, greetings cards, telephone directories, and everything else that might be part of their personal written language environment. They also know roughly how written language works, that it consists of symbols written on lines, that it is laid out in various conventional ways. Before they can spell, they know there are rules of spelling. They have ideas of why people read, even before they can read themselves. They pretend to read and to write in their games.

There are no kits of materials or systematic exercises for teaching children how the world uses written language. They learn—usually without anyone being aware that they are learning—by participating in literate activities with people who use written language. It can all be summed up in a metaphor: Children learn about reading and writing by "joining the literacy club" (Smith, 1988). They are given demonstrations of what written language can be used for, and they receive collaboration when they become interested in using written language themselves. The assistance is usually completely casual, when someone points out that an approaching sign says "Stop" or "Burgers," the way one might say to a child "Look, there's a horse." Someone helps them to read what they are interested in reading and helps them to write what they would like to write.

Membership of the literacy club offers the same advantages as the spoken-language club that I discussed in chapter 12, and all the other clubs children might join. Children in the literacy club have opportunities to see what written language can do, they are encouraged and helped to do those things themselves, and they are not at risk of exclusion if they make mistakes or display a passing lack of interest. They learn to be like the other members of the club. (And if they learn from other demonstrations that reading and writing are boring activities or that they don't belong to the club, then they learn not to be like people who read and write.)

This doesn't mean that children are lost to literacy if they have not learned about reading and writing out of school. But it becomes all the more crucial for every child to have the opportunity to belong to the literacy club in school. For children who are not interested in reading and writing, it is even more important that activities in the classroom be made interesting and accessible for them. They need more demonstrations of worthwhile uses of literacy and more collaboration in engaging in those uses themselves. And in any case, children who have joined the club before they come to school should not then risk rejection because school definitions of literacy or perceptions of literate activities are different.

There is no need to fear that reading to learners, or writing for them, will make them passive and dependent. They won't always expect other people to do their reading and writing for them. No child has that much patience. The moment children feel they can read or write well enough to do what they want to do for themselves—often long before adults might think they are ready to do so—they reject the helping hand. It is no different when children learn to ride a bicycle. Children never want to be pushed when they can pedal away for themselves.

Margaret Meek (1988) described how the authors of children's books *teach* children how to read. These are the authors of the books that children love to read, time and time again. The children already know the stories before they open the books—or the stories are so predictable that they know what is on the next page before they turn to it. The children know the story, according to Meek, and the author shows them how to read it.

Spontaneous admission into the literacy club may even explain how children succeed in learning to read when subjected to intensive classroom regimes of phonics and worksheet activities (which then get the credit for the achievement).

Someone must do the learners' reading for them until they are able to read a few things for themselves, and they are ready to learn to read by reading. Reading for children need not take long—only until they can read enough for authors to take over. Very little actual reading ability is required for this to occur, if the right kinds of interesting and familiar materials are available (for details of such materials, ask a child). Indeed, for a child to know a story in advance by heart may be enough to turn the child over to the author. What matters is for the learner to be reading known or familiar texts like an experienced reader.

The role of the teacher is to support the reading and writing of all children until authors, and the children's own interest and self-perception, ensure their continued membership in the literacy club. For teachers who are themselves committed readers and writers, the opportunity to develop new club members should be a pleasure as well as a privilege.

ISSUES

Every controversy about reading instruction inevitably comes down to whether classroom practices should be determined by (1) what teachers know and can see of individual student interest, comprehension, and learning, or by (2) the prescriptions of intellectual and political authorities. Associated with the formalization of instruction is the question of whether learning can be guaranteed or even facilitated by assessment procedures that monitor and constrain the behavior of teachers and students, with inevitable discriminatory consequences.

SUMMARY

Learning to read depends on two basic insights—that written language is meaningful and that it is different from spoken language. Learners must rely on the visual information of print as little as possible. Teachers help children learn to read by stimulating interest and facilitating written language use to a degree that formal instructional programs, with their necessarily limited objectives, can't achieve. Teachers must ensure that all children receive the demonstrations and collaboration necessary to maintain membership in the literacy club.

Notes

Psycholinguistics and Cognitive Science

The term *psycholinguistics* as used in the subtitle and other places in this book refers to an area of overlap between specialized fields of psychology and linguistics, a common ground where psychologists (who study human behavior) and linguists (who study language) meet to explore the ways in which human language in its various forms is actually learned and used. In reading education, however, psycholinguistics became something of a battle cry (or term of opprobrium, depending on which side you were on). A heavily phonic approach to teaching reading has long been called "the linguistic method," and "psycholinguistic" became adopted in the early 1970s as the emblem of the opposing point of view (which has also been called the "meaning" and "whole language" approach to teaching reading).

There are two radically divergent points of view about the nature of reading. I have broadly characterized these theoretical perspectives as "inside-out" and "outside-in" (Smith, 1979), depending on whether the control in reading is presumed to originate with the reader or with the text. More generally, these

233

opposing positions have become known as "top-down" or "bottom-up." Top-down is roughly equivalent to my inside-out, implying that the reader determines how a text will be approached and interpreted. The bottom-up view is outside-in, putting the text in charge, with the letters on the page the first and final arbiters of the reader's responses.

Metaphors frequently betray their origins. Top-down and bottom-up are computer jargon, and are usually employed in discussions of reading by "cognitive scientists" (discussed later) who see the brain as some kind of computer. Inside-out and outside-in are terms reflecting a "constructivist" orientation (see chap. 2 notes), where knowledge is regarded as something generated inside the learner rather than imported or delivered from the outside. The present book, I should perhaps add, is strongly representative of the inside-out view. Naturally there have been attempts at compromise (or at carving out a third position), arguing for eclectic theories that are both top-down and bottom-up at the same time (discussed later). But no top-downer (or inside-outer) would want to claim that reading doesn't involve interaction with a text. Just because meaning has to be constructed by the reader doesn't mean that *any* meaning will do.

Labels can be promiscuous, and the word *psycholinguistic* has had a particularly wayward career. In the late 1960s and early 1970s the term primarily connoted academic studies into the nature of language and the manner in which infants learn to use it, focusing on the critical role of meaning and constructive thought. In education, the psycholinguistic perspective implied a similar focus on meaningfulness in literacy learning, opposed to packaged "skills-based" materials and activities. But publishers quickly produced "psycholinguistic materials" (or relabeled old materials as psycholinguistic). The principal successor to the psycholinguistic perspective in education became known as "whole language." Once again, this was originally a term connoting a philosophy of learning, opposed to artificial decontextualized exercises and drills. But as whole language gained influence and prominence in education, the perspective became distorted, the theory became a method, and publishers began to produce "whole language materials." A few proponents and almost all opponents of whole language regard it as a method rather than a philosophy. For many politicians, journalists, and producers of structured instructional schemes, whole language has become a derogatory expression.

The term *psycholinguistics* has also changed its connotations. Many researchers who originally called themselves psycholinguists employed "naturalistic" methods—they *observed* how children learned or used language in natural settings, rather than experimentally manipulating learning situations. Since the mid-1970s, however, numbers of language researchers have joined forces with computer and artificial intelligence specialists in a subdiscipline called *cognitive science*. This new breed of psycholinguists frequently has a distinctly experimental and prescriptive attitude to instruction. Attacks on whole language and other nonprescriptive approaches to reading instruction are usually made in the name of cognitive science, or just plain "science."

Cognitive science is primarily concerned with abstract theories related to the organization of knowledge, especially through language, in humans and in computers. Its influence in how reading should be taught is growing—not, I think, because cognitive science has anything significantly new to say about learning and education, but because it is intimately tied to the dominant technology of the day. It also claims to be authoritative because it asserts that its technological methodology is the only valid one. But because of its insistence on particular conceptualizations and procedures, cognitive science is also narrow. Cognitive science looks at reading, and also reading instruction, from a limited "knowledge and skills" perspective. For an excellent insider critique of the limitations of cognitive science, see Dodwell (2000).

Although I say that little of substance has changed in reading theory in recent decades, I don't mean that new concepts and theories don't make a difference. They do. New concepts are new ways of talking, and they encourage a focus on certain matters rather than on others. With the growth of cognitive science, for example, a profusion of new terms has been introduced for old concepts, such as "metacognition" (for "reflection" or "introspection") and "phonemic awareness" (for "listening to the sounds of language"). People who would have no trouble understanding the old terms can be overly impressed and even confused by the terms that supersede them. An unwarranted aura of infallibility may surround the "experts" who use the new terms with facility, especially if they claim special insight.

I have retained the word psycholinguistic in the subtitle of this book, partly because that was the way *Understanding Reading* was titled when it first came out in 1971, but also to indicate constraints I have continued to observe. The primary concern is with what readers need to know and do in order to make sense of written language. The book doesn't delve deeply into specific types of literate behavior, genre theory, literary criticism, semiotics, or social and cultural aspects of literacy.

Research

Research into the nature of reading and reading instruction boomed in the early 1970s with the support of enormous federal grants aimed at the eradication of illiteracy. The goal was never reached, largely because (I would argue) the research and instructional efforts were frequently predicated on fragmented and decontextualized outside-in theories of reading and instruction (Smith, 1986). There was a second massive infusion of funds around the beginning of the present century, not so much to extend the understanding of reading and learning to read as to promote and assert a particular point of view, namely, that phonics and phonemic awareness are the essential basis of instruction. It is difficult to find large-scale research coming from a more neutral point of view, but not difficult at all to find pronouncements and even legislation condemning such research, where it exists, as being "unscientific." All of this is discussed in chapter 13 and its notes.

I have obviously not attempted in this volume to summarize all of the research done in the name of reading. That would be impossible. Instead, I have drawn primarily from what helps me to construct a coherent picture of reading and of learning to read. People with an alternative point of view would be similarly selective in order to reject my conclusions. I make no attempt to be eclectic.

One aspect of eclecticism is the view that science is an incremental activity—that every bit of research is valid and worthwhile, adding a nugget of truth to an always-growing accumulation of knowledge and understanding. Such a view rests on a rosy belief that researchers never start from false assumptions and never finish with untenable conclusions. All reported findings are supposed to fit together like pieces of a jigsaw puzzle. Educational textbooks are frequently pastiches of this nature, covering immense amounts of ground without the provision of navigable pathways. The alternative point of view is that scientific research is based on conceptual *paradigms*, or ways of seeing the world, that frequently conflict. They are subjectively adopted and emotionally retained. A paradigm is rarely abandoned by its adherents unless they find it totally worthless and have another to replace it with (Kuhn, 1970). The research that is done, the evidence gathered, and the conclusions reached all depend on the researcher's beliefs and expectations.

Another common form of eclecticism, conspicuous in education, attempts to assimilate alternative points of view into established or "official" lines of thinking. Such conceptual dilution is frequently found in reviews of research produced by committees or by bureaucratic institutions that are not keen to call attention to positions different from their own. There are also eclectic approaches to teaching reading that entail using a little bit from every prominent theorist or instructional proponent, on the undiscriminating principle that every "authority" is probably a little bit right. Nonjudgmental approaches to instruction fail to recognize that inappropriate theories and methods can mislead the people most in need of a reliable and coherent understanding of the nature of reading, namely, children trying to learn and teachers trying to teach them. It is necessary to take a position. Some current views about reading and reading instruction must be wrong.

The "Issues" sections in this book acknowledge that there are deeply etched and keenly felt disputes over the nature of reading that may never be resolved, not to the extent that proponents of different points of view will be satisfied. Over the years I have come to the conclusion that the most critical need is for teachers and students to be able to make their own judgments and decisions rather than to trust authorities when there are conflicting points of view (the choice of authority is itself a decision, of course). To do this, one must recognize that profound differences exist. Indeed, if one wants to argue that other people are wrong, one has to admit the likelihood that one is wrong oneself (or at least that someone else might also be right) and find a reason why it is possible for two people living in the same world (if they can be said to be living in the same world) to have diametrically opposing theories about it.

Acknowledgment

All my books would be a hazy shadow of themselves without the educational insights and editorial acumen of Mary-Theresa Smith. I also acknowledge debts to innumerable authors, students, teachers, and friends. I would be delighted to put all their names in this book but mortified to leave any out. They know who they are.

NOTES TO CHAPTER 1,
THE ESSENCE OF READING, pp. 1–11

Matters of Interpretation

Walkerdine (1982) held that language, thinking, and "context" are not separate systems but are jointly related to a basic human need to interpret all kinds of signs. Urwin (1982) similarly argued that learning reflects social interaction, with a semiotic emphasis on the importance of "signs."

A forgotten German philosopher Hans Vaihinger (1852–1933) actually devised a "philosophy of as if" a century ago. He believed that in a frustrating and fundamentally unknowable world, people had to live by fictions—as if they had free will, as if ethical certainty were possible, as if a material world exists—disregarding uncertainties and logical contradictions (Vaihinger, 1952). But this pragmatic philosophy did not licence anyone to believe anything. Shifting from "as-if" to "this-is-how-it-must-be" was impermissible.

A contemporary French philosopher Clement Rosset (1989) said that certain words like "reality" and "actual" are "untheorizable," because they are the element in which we live. We can describe the content of a particular reality, but not explain the phenomenon of reality itself. It's as far back as definition goes. "Experience," "comprehension," and "learning"—and "reading"—are similarly untheorizable words. It makes no more sense to ask "What happens in the brain when you comprehend something?" than it would be to ask "What happens in the brain when you experience reality?"

On the point that everything is presumed to be natural until the opposite is taught, Fernandez-Armesto (2000), in his study of civilizations, relates stories (possibly apocryphal, but they make the point) of an early 18th century Huron Indian who believed that the stone streets of Paris were natural rock formations, and of an aboriginal visitor from St. Kilda of the same period who thought that the pillars and arches of a church in Glasgow were the most beautiful caves he had ever seen (p. 14).

Alphabets

The Chinese scholar Lin Yutang succeeded in compiling the first practical English–Chinese dictionary in the 1970s only by arbitrarily imposing an "alphabetical order" on 33 basic stroke formations in Chinese script. The alphabet is preeminently an instrument of control, from many points of view. One of the few times that public opinion in China was able to modify a national policy of Mao Tse-tung was when he tried to introduce an alphabet into Chinese writing based on European and Russian letters (Barlow, 1981). The peasants successfully resisted this purely administrative decree on the sound linguistic ground that the new script would prevent them from reading traditional ancient Chinese writings. Coulmas (1992) observed that no purely logographic writing system exists. Chinese is morpho-syllabic; each character represents a morpheme (meaning) and also a syllable. There are thousands of characters, many in disuse, with probably at least 5,000 in current use. Coulmas says that Chinese is no more difficult to read than English, and perhaps easier. For readers of classical Chinese it is certainly easier to read a Chinese text that is hundreds of years old than an alphabetic one because alphabetic writing systems are tied to pronunciation, which changes.

Writing Systems

Senner (1989) gave an accessible collection of essays on the origin of various writing systems, showing that writing was not the invention of one particular group of people and that it appears to have had its antecedents in drawing (pictographic) rather than in spoken language. Since the development of the alphabetic system, writing has often been modified to correspond more closely with spoken language, but at the same time, spoken language has always been influenced by the structure and use of written language. Written language tends to change less rapidly than speech and therefore has tended to put a brake on spoken language change (or to drift further apart from it). Even today, many people seem to feel that written language is a particularly pure form of language, a model for what spoken language should be like. The other origin of written language, pointed out by several of the contributors to Senner's volume, is not so much conventional speech as mathematics—from keeping track of the calendar and of astronomical (and astrological) phenomena to bureaucratic and commercial record keeping. See also Stevenson (1983), Sampson (1985), and Coulmas (1990). In a broad-ranging review of the evolution of civilizations all over the world, Fernandez-Armesto (2000) noted that "many societies are seen to have confided what was memorable, and therefore of lasting value, to oral transmission, and to have devised writing systems in order to record rubbish; fiscal ephemera, merchants' memoranda" (p. 29). He later concluded that writing systems all over the world developed "first as a commercial, priestly, and political tool, then as a medium for artistic expression … it was a mundane contrivance developed for potters' marks" (p. 217).

NOTES TO CHAPTER 2,
COMPREHENSION AND KNOWLEDGE, pp. 12–30

Knowledge and Constructivism

The view that comprehension is a constant state of mental activity corresponds to a philosophical and educational theory called *constructivism*, which holds that knowledge is *constructed* rather than passively received or delivered from the outside world. Jean Piaget in particular argued that individuals come to know the world through action rather than through their senses. Action in this sense means mental as well as physical, in the form of prediction and invention. The mental activity is sometimes referred to as *reflective abstraction*. One of Piaget's shorter and more accessible books is entitled *To Understand Is to Invent* (Piaget, 1976), a theme picked up by Constance Kamii (1985) in *Young Children Reinvent Arithmetic: Implications of Piaget's Theory*. There is another clear and concise outline of the contributions of Piaget to constructivist theory in Saxe (1991), an account of how poorly educated child candy-sellers on the streets of Recife, Brazil, invent their own complex mathematical and trading systems. For more general discussions of Piaget and constructivism, see Fosnot (1996).

Karl Popper proposed that the knowledge accumulated by every individual (and every culture) is a record of the problems they have had to solve. Popper tends to be fairly heavy going in his technical writing (e.g., Popper, 1973), but his views are expressed more concisely in an engaging autobiography (Popper, 1976) and even more clearly in a biography (Magee, 1973). Boulding (1981) argued from a behavioral scientist's point of view that human knowledge is a special system, unlike other information systems like libraries, computers, or the "real world." Human knowledge constitutes a world in itself and is not simply a combination of the "real world" and a brain. In other words—as I interpret it—we live in a world that we create, rather than in some concrete world that exists independently of us. I argue that reading can provide actual experiences in real worlds, not mere replicas of experiences in "representations" of the world. Our theory of the world is the basis of all our reality.

Yates (1985) analyzed the contents of momentary awareness—what we happen to be aware of at any particular instant—and found that although fragmentary it is always part of a complete world. Our thoughts and perceptions are never unrelated to the world as a whole. They are always capable of anticipating or simulating future events and thus provide a basis for the formulation of appropriate action. Such complex awareness, Yates argued, must reflect an underlying model of the world—a theory of the world. For thinking, see especially McPeck (1981), Bruner (1986), and Vygotsky (1978). Smith (1990) covered the same topic.

Paradoxically, the computer has provided a great impetus to many psychologists interested in comprehension, not necessarily because the brain is conceptualized as a kind of computer (although such a notion does underlie some theorizing) but because the computer has proved a convenient tool for simulating organizations of knowledge and memory. Some experimentalists believe that theories about human cognition "lack rigor" unless they can be simulated on a computer to prove that they are at least feasible, but others find such claims constricting if not misleading. I write more critically of these matters in the notes to chapter 4.

Prediction

Prediction as I have discussed it in this chapter is not a topic that has been widely examined, although there is an extensive psychological literature on the consequences of expectancy. Neisser (1977) explored the notion that perception is based on anticipated information from the environment and that our schemes (discussed later) are continually restructured through prediction and experience. Our cognitive structures are anticipations. Wildman and Kling (1978/1979) discussed "semantic, syntactic and spatial anticipation" in reading.

We don't know what we know unless we put it to use in some way, for example, by saying something or by imagining saying something (Polanyi, 1966). We similarly don't have direct access to thought. We can be aware of a decision that we have made, but attempts to reconstruct the "process" by which we came to that decision are inventions. Normally we are aware of thought only when we find it difficult to make a decision, just as the only time we are normally aware of comprehension is when we are confused. Most of the time the brain seems able to take care of our affairs very well, without our having to become consciously involved.

Templeton (1991) disputed that prediction plays a central role in reading, citing Perfetti (1991), Stanovich (1991), Vellutino (1991), and the "sophisticated eye-movement studies" of Rayner and Pollatsek (1989) "that show us precisely where beginning and mature readers look as they read connected text." But where readers look is not necessarily a reliable indicator of what they are thinking. Prediction is a frame of mind, an adjustment to a total situation (including one's own interests and purposes), not a specific way of threading through a text. People don't normally have periods of incomprehension and uncertainty before making sense of everything they do. There is more on this in chapter 5 and its notes.

Categories

There is considerable debate about the exact nature of the categorical organization of human knowledge. In particular, the hard-edged category boundaries implied by descriptions such as those given in this chapter have been challenged. It is not always the case that something either belongs in a category or it doesn't. Some things have a greater claim to being in a category—they are more "typical"—while others have only a tenuous membership, regardless of any distinctive features they might possess. Rosch (Rosch & Lloyd, 1978), for example, reported that robins are usually regarded as more typical birds than chickens, with eagles somewhere between. Penguins and emus are much closer to the boundaries between categories, which can be quite fuzzy. Rosch proposes that there are certain "natural" categories that form themselves around prototypical members, like carrots for vegetables and football for sports. The prototypical class members provide the main features of the category. Other possibilities achieve membership of the category to the extent that they share "family resemblances" with the prototypes. In a challenging and wide-ranging book taking off from Rosch's prototype theory, Lakoff (1987) rejected classical categorization theories (going back to Aristotle) and proposed instead what he called *experiential realism*. We perceive the world in terms of holistic "basic level" categories and bodily proportions, functions, and purposes, which provide metaphors for understanding the world. This is a compelling and scholarly book, technical in parts but reiterating insistently and persuasively the creative and imaginative nature of human thought.

Schemes

It is unusual for isolated cognitive categories to play a significant role in human thought or behavior. We normally function on the basis of much larger conceptual structures, the schemes or schemas that are constructed out of complex and often dynamic organizations of categories. The English word *schemes* is the standard term for the various kinds of abstract mental structure that enable us to make sense of the world and participate appropriately in it, but the area of study is still known as *schema theory*, perpetuating the Latin term introduced by Bartlett (1932).

One of the pioneers of schema research, Jean Mandler (1984), distinguished three broad categories of schemes: (a) *scenes*, or spatially organized knowledge, (b) *events*, like the scripts and scenarios I have mentioned in this chapter, and (c) *stories*, which have their own "grammars" of plots, characters, settings, episodes, motives, goals, and outcomes. Some theorists—myself included—would go further to argue that stories are the primary basis of all our perception and understanding of the world. The way we perceive, comprehend, and remember events is in the form of story structures that we impose on them, even though events may not present themselves to us in such ways. Rumelhart (1980) saw schemes as the building blocks of cognition, comparing them with the scripts of plays that can be performed by different groups of actors in different settings. Comprehension, according to Rumelhart and Ortony (1977), is the confirmation of tentative hypotheses about what schemes are relevant by finding the "slots" into which the details of events fit.

A more general point of view is provided by Katherine Nelson (1986) and her colleagues in many research papers and in a book entitled *Event Knowledge*. They show that children are skilled at expressing ideas in "generic," abstract representations rather than as descriptions of concrete events. Asked to describe a birthday party, for example, they talk about cakes, games and gifts, about expected behavior and events, rather than about specific occurrences on a particular occasion. They speak impersonally—"you" get presents—about events with no specific location in time and place. They tell a *story*. For arguments and evidence that perception is much too fast, rich, and subtle to be constructed from the discrimination and analysis of parts, see McCabe and Balzano (1986).

The Narrative Basis of Thought

Continuously and inevitably, we create stories to explain and understand the world and our role in it, to remember and to anticipate events, and to create worlds that might not otherwise exist. This urge to create narratives is so compelling that we impose them on otherwise meaningless situations. We strain to find objects in blurred patterns of color and shade (Potter, 1975), we detect faces and figures in clouds and other amorphous forms, and we impose structure on random sequences of letters or numbers (Klahr, Chase, & Lovelace, 1983; Restle, 1970). When people are shown randomly flashing points of light in a dark room, they see dramas, with objects moving to meet or to avoid each other (Michotte, 1946). When thought flows freely, in narrative form, comprehension, memory, and learning all seem to take care of themselves, as I try to show throughout this book. When the flow is broken, when comprehension, memory, and learning are manipulated from the outside, they may seem to be very difficult indeed. Often in these contrived situations, there is only boredom and bewilderment. The narrative nature of children's thought has been demonstrated by van Dongen (1987).

Rosen (1986) argued consistently that thought has a narrative basis. If he is correct, then reading and writing must be very fundamental human activities. In a chapter entitled "Stories of Stories: Footnotes on Sly Gossipy Practices" (Rosen, 1988), he looked at how readers creatively change stories in the retelling, in what he called "memory as art." In a study of how children make sense of the world through the construction of stories, at home and at school, Wells (1985) referred to "the guided reinvention of knowledge." Bruner (1986) claims we all employ two modes of thought that are complementary but irreconcilable—logical and intuitive (or the day view and the night view, truth-seeking versus meaning-making, well-formed arguments versus a good story). He proposes that the "self" develops through "autobiographical attitudes toward oneself," seen as talking to oneself about oneself, which doesn't come naturally, but requires knowledge of story conventions and genres (Bruner & Weisser, 1991). Salmon (1985) proposed three common metaphors for life—a card game (we're all dealt different hands to play as best we can), a natural cycle (birth, growth, death, regeneration), and a story (which provides everyone with an identity). Sadoski (1983) demonstrated that imagery improves both comprehension and recall of stories, and Black, Freeman, and Johnson-Laird (1986) showed that the more plausible we find a tale, the more we are likely to understand and remember it. In other words, we understand and remember best when we can engage our imagination. Other research would no doubt show that drama, excitement, personal relevance, and familiar settings and characters are conducive to increased comprehension and recall (unless they are so familiar that they are boring).

Thinking

An intriguing book stressing the creative and constructive nature of thought and also the brain's narrative mode of functioning is Jerome Bruner's (1986) *Actual Minds, Possible Worlds*. In *Mind in Society*, Lev Vygotsky (1978) underlined the social nature of thought, which he sees as internalized action. (Bruner would be more likely to see action as externalized thought.)

In a review article on research into metacognition, Bransford, Stein, and Vye (1982) observed that less successful students fail to activate knowledge that can help them to understand and re-member new information. One might argue whether being unable to "activate knowledge" (which in less exotic language means to make sense) is a cause of failure or simply a description of the condition such students find themselves in. The researchers also say that less successful students are less able to assess their own level of comprehension. But one can hardly be unaware of whether one is comprehending or confused—that is like asserting that we might be unaware of whether or not we feel hungry. Of course, we can believe we understand something when we are in error, just as we might feel hungry without needing food. But to make a mistake is not a failure of metacognition, of being out of touch with our own thought processes. It is simply a matter of be-ing wrong.

NOTES TO CHAPTER 3,
SPOKEN AND WRITTEN LANGUAGE, pp. 31–54

Surface Structure and Deep Structure

There is one notable exception to the statement that surface struc-ture is the part of language that exists physically and can be mea-sured in the world around us. That exception is the private *subvocal speech* that we "hear in our heads" when we talk to ourselves or "listen to ourselves" reading silently. It would be a mistake to believe that such an inner voice is deep structure, or that it is some special and (to ourselves) observable kind of raw thought. Subvocal speech is just as much a product of thought as overt speech, with the only difference being that it is uttered for our own benefit rather than anyone else's. Subvocal speech could be uttered aloud, just as the voice we hear in "silent" reading could be made audible to others. The inner voice is surface structure, with all the surface structure characteristics of vocabulary and grammar (albeit a little telegraphic at times). There must still be a deep structure underlying the utterances of the inner voice, a deep structure of meaning, which doesn't consist of sequences of words and sentences but of intangible concepts, interrelationships, and propositions. (There is more on subvocalization in chap. 9 and its notes.)

McNeill (1985), reflecting on the nature and origins of language, saw parallels between speech and gesture in function, development, use, and even loss with different kinds of aphasia. In a long and rather abstruse article entitled "Against Definitions," Fodor, Garrett, Walker, and Parkes (1980) argued that sentences are not understood by recovering definitions of words. We don't understand the statement that someone is a bachelor by understanding that he is an unmarried man. "Bachelor" and "unmarried man" are not representations of each other but rather alternative representations of the same underlying meaning. Anderson and Ortony (1975) also show that the interpretation of a sentence, its "mental representation," is always much richer than the words in the text literally entail.

Gibbs (1984) argued against the notion that sentences usually have "literal meanings" in the context in which they occur (a view that he said dominates theories of language). He cited experimental evidence that listeners don't necessarily "compute" the literal meaning of an utterance before understanding it. Golden and Guthrie (1986) showed that ninth graders respond quite differently to the same short story, in the way in which they empathize with particular characters or react to events in the text, depending on their prior beliefs about what is right and natural. It is, of course, unlikely that any two people could ever experience any complex series of events, written or "real," in the same way or come away with the same understanding of what took place.

My very general use of the terms *surface structure* and *deep structure* should not be taken to relate explicitly to any particular linguistic theory, although the distinction between physical manifestations of language and meaning is a prevailing view. Chomsky (1957), for example, in his original generative transformational grammar, employed the term *surface structure* to refer not to sound itself, and certainly not to writing, but rather as the abstract level at which "input to the phonological system" was realized. Similarly, Chomsky's deep structure was never meaning, but rather "input to an underlying semantic system" that itself required transformation and interpretation. Obviously, sound (or writing) and meaning are much further apart than even the surface structures and deep structures that Chomsky talked about. Furthermore, there are a great many controversies between Chomsky and other linguists and philosophers about the connotations of these terms, and use of them has changed radically over the years. Chomsky's thoughts on language are always significant and—when accessible to the layperson—interesting. Chomsky's clearest exposition is still his classic (1959) attack on the behaviorist theorizing of B. F. Skinner. For a fascinating debate between Piaget and Chomsky see Piattelli-Palmarini (1980).

Semiotics

Relatively comprehensible introductions to semiotics generally are provided by Davis (1991), Suhor (1992) and Fosnot (1996). The educator who has tried the most to make semiotics relevant to an understanding of reading and writing is Jerome Harste (see Harste, Woodward, & Burke, 1984). One aspect of semiotics to which Deely (1982) and Harste drew attention is concerned with major forms of logic and their relevance to thinking and learning generally. Two of the three forms are widely known, if not always well understood. The first is *deduction*, when conclusions about specific instances are drawn from general principles and procedures. Mathematics and formal logic are examples of deductive reasoning. The second category, *induction*, relates to the inferring of general principles from specific instances, for example through the "scientific method" of hypothesis testing. (The "deduction" done by detectives is usually induction.) Less well known yet possibly more interesting is the third category, *abduction*, when a new rule or explanation is hypothesized from a particular result or state of affairs. Such creative thinking is not normally considered part of either logic or science, but it may better characterize much of human thought, including that involved in reading and writing.

Discourse and Genre

Stein (1992) provided a useful but technical volume on reading and writing from a discourse analysis point of view. It contains a significant paper by Chafe (1992) noting the central role of "displaced consciousness" in reading, with the reader taking different roles and viewpoints. Critical discourse theory combines discourse analysis with social theory, examining, for example, why children from poorer homes and families often fail to do well at school. For an example, and an outline of critical discourse theory, see Rogers (2002) and Cadeiro-Kaplan (2002). The latter is a special issue of the journal *Language Arts* devoted to critical analyses of the literary curriculum and the language used to talk about literacy. The classic work on language in different socioeconomic contexts remains *Ways with Words* (Heath, 1983).

Halliday and his students in Australia have focused attention on the role of genre in writing, which they believe should be explicitly taught, leading to a considerable educational controversy in that country (Cairney, 1992); there is a summary in Smith (1994). The term *genre* originally referred to different types of writing, such as comedy, tragedy, epic. More recently the term came to refer to different kinds of media—newspapers, periodicals, novels, nonfiction—all of which have their own conventions. Current emphasis is on complete settings, including such matters as conversations, interrogations, and classroom procedures. The core is always structure or organization—of the text alone or of the situation. Littlefair (1991) found British students' knowledge of genre after three or four years of study was directly related to the amount and breadth of the reading they did. There are some interesting discussions of genre and related topics in Cazden (1992).

Text Organization and Comprehension

Texts that are difficult to understand because of the way they are written have been referred to as "inconsiderate" (Armbruster & Anderson, 1984). There is no doubt that texts can often be improved. Beck, McKeown, Omanson, and Pople (1984) revised two basal reader stories to make them more coherent without altering their plots, enhancing the comprehension of both skilled and less skilled readers. The length of the two stories was increased from 782 and 811 words to 900 and 957 words, but comprehension went up by a grade level for both second- and third-grade readers. Readability formulas based on word counts and sentence length have been generally discredited (e.g., MacGinitie, 1984; Krashen, 2002c). "Simplifying" reading material by fragmenting it into short sentences can greatly interfere with comprehension and recall. See also Slater (1985).

Many studies have demonstrated that texts are better understood and remembered if readers (of all ages and ability) are familiar with the relevant story grammars. McGee (1982) showed that third- and fifth-grade readers were aware of text structures and used them in recall, even the poor readers (although they did so less well than better readers, who might reasonably be expected to have had greater familiarity with stories). Mandler and Goodman (1982) found that reading speed dropped when story structures weren't congruent with readers' expectations and also that second sentences were read faster than the first sentences in chapters, when readers had gained an idea of what the chapter was about. Anderson and Pearson (1984) theorized about the relevance of schemes in reading comprehension. See also Grimes (1975) and Applebee (1977).

Piper (1987) suggested cautions about teaching students the explicit structures of story grammar, which he saw as no different from more traditional modes of analysis which have not fared well in education. Consciousness of structure doesn't necessarily promote understanding, he argued. In a careful review, Taylor (1992) observed that concern with text structure has required students to write "hierarchical summaries" and draw diagrams and "maps" of texts—"a whole new skill to learn." Beers (1987) argued that schema theory—and cognitive science generally—are inappropriate approaches to reading because of their underlying "machine metaphor." Johnson-Laird, Byrne, and Schaeken (1992) asserted that the brain is not a logic machine but a sense-making device.

Durkin (1981) looked critically at the significance of the "new interest" in comprehension for education. Efforts to systematize instruction have led to a widespread view that comprehension is a process, the opposite of which is ignorance. Comprehension, like thinking, is seen as a set of skills or procedures which can and must be taught. A typical example is the analysis of Pearson, Roehler, Dole, and Duffy (1992), which breaks comprehension down into a set of seven *strategies* based on schema theory (Anderson & Pearson, 1984). These strategies—supposedly "used differentially" by "expert" and "novice" readers—include: searching for connections between what they know and new information in text; "monitoring the adequacy of their models of text meaning"; taking steps to "repair faulty comprehension" when there is failure to understand;

distinguishing important from less important ideas in text; synthe-sizing information in and between texts; drawing inferences during and after reading for a "full, integrated understanding"; and asking conscious and unconscious questions of themselves, authors, and texts. Garner (1992) discussed "metacognition and self-monitoring strategies" as ways of getting students to ask themselves the ques-tions that teachers would ask them.

It might be argued that comprehension is the basis rather than a consequence of the previous strategies and that they all depend on prior knowledge (including knowledge of the kinds of things that can be done with texts). There is an enormous amount of research to show the importance of prior knowledge in reading, which ought, perhaps, to be considered self-evident. No one, as far as I know, has ever proposed an opposing point of view, although some instructional methodologies pay little attention to what learners may not comprehend or already know—what they may find either confusing or boring.

Robinson, Faraone, Hittleman, and Unrah (1990) reviewed comprehension research and instruction since 1783—from the ex-pectation that comprehension occurs spontaneously to the sys-tematic teaching of strategies and self-monitoring techniques. Cairney (1990) criticized "traditional comprehension practices" in schools as mainly directive and question based. There is a growing recognition of the role of inference in comprehension, usually dis-cussed either in terms of skills or as internal representations—for example, Kintsch (1988) and McNamara, Miller, and Bransford (1991). There are substantial and largely nontechnical discus-sions of "models of the mind" from both "scientific" and "philo-sophical" points of view in Mohyeldin Said, Newton-Smith, Viale, and Wilkes (1990). Fodor, an erudite linguistic philosopher prolifi-cally involved in many controversies related to language and thought, combines densely technical writing with an engaging lightheartedness, for example, a chapter entitled "Fodor's Guide to Mental Representation: The Intelligent Auntie's Vade-Mecum" in Fodor (1990).

Recondite contemporary theories like deconstructionism and intertextuality (which tend to take all meaning out of the text and away from authors and readers) were critically discussed by Eagleton (1983) in a readably acerbic review of literary theories from phenomenology to poststructuralism. In an extended pas-sage on reading, Eagleton analyzed the immense amount of inter-pretation and prior knowledge that a reader, usually quite unconsciously, must bring to bear just to get started on a novel, arguing that "the text itself is really no more than a series of 'cues' to the reader" (p. 76). For more on deconstructionism, focusing particularly on Bahktin's theory of intertextuality—the idea that the meaning of any text is determined by the complex and shifting meanings of all other texts—see Lodge (1990). Bloome and Egan-Robertson (1993) endeavored to make such theorizing relevant to classrooms. Finally, there is growing interest in *interest* as a factor in reading. Hidi, Baird, and Hildyard (1982) showed that interest can interfere with comprehension because it diverts attention; children will not pay extended attention to "trivial information" in texts unless it is interesting, in which case they will remember it.

Some Technical Terms

One might think that there could not be too much complication about the fact that the basic elements of language are sounds. The word *bed*, for example, is made up of three distinctive sounds /b/, /e/, and /d/ (it is a useful convention that the sounds of language are printed between oblique // strokes). With a few perverse exceptions, each sound of the language is represented by a particular letter of the alphabet, so the number of alternative sounds in English must be about 26. Unfortunately, none of the preceding statements is correct.

English has rather more functionally different sounds than it has letters in the alphabet, about 45. These sounds have the special name *phonemes*. A variety of letters can represent a single phoneme, and a variety of phonemes can be represented by a single letter or letter combination. It is necessary to be tentative in making statements about the total number of phonemes because it depends on who is talking and when. All dialects have roughly the same number of phonemes, but not always the same ones, so that words that are individually distinguishable in some dialects, such as *guard* and *god*, may not be distinguishable in others unless in a meaningful context. We often think we make distinctions between words when in fact we don't—redundancy in context is usually sufficient to indicate which alternative we intend. Many literate speakers don't have phonemes to distinguish among *Mary*, *marry*, and *merry*, or *cot*, *caught*, and *court*. Say these words one at a time and ask a listener to spell what you have just said. You may find that the listener can't observe all the differences you think you are making. Phonemes often drop out of casual or colloquial speech.

A phoneme is not so much a single sound as a collection of sounds, all of which sound the same. If that description seems complicated, a more formal definition will not appear much better—a phoneme is a class of closely related sounds constituting the smallest unit of speech that will distinguish one utterance from another. For example, the /b/ at the beginning of the word *bed* distinguishes it from words like *fed* and *led* and *red*, the /e/ in the middle distinguishes *bed* from *bad*, *bide*, and *bowed*, and the /d/ distinguishes the word from such alternatives as *bet* and *beg*. So each of the three elements in bed will serve to distinguish the word from others, and each also is the smallest unit that can do this. Each is a *significant difference*. It doesn't matter if the /b/ pronounced at the beginning of *bed* is a little different from /b/ at the beginning of *bad*, or if the /b/ in *bed* is pronounced in different ways on different occasions. All the different sounds that I might make that are acceptable as the sound at the beginning of *bed* and *bad* qualify as being the same phoneme. A phoneme is not one sound, but a variety of sounds any of which is acceptable to listeners as making the same contrast. The actual sounds that are produced are called *phones*, and the sets of "closely related" phones that all serve as the same phoneme are called *allophones* of each other (or of the particular phoneme). Allophones are sounds that the listener learns to treat as equivalent and to hear as the same.

When electronic equipment is used to analyze sounds heard as the same, quite marked differences can be found, depending on the sound that follows them. For example, the /d/ in *dim* is basically a high-pitched rising sound, while its allophone at the beginning of *doom* is much lower pitched and falling (Liberman, Cooper, Shankweiler, & Studdert-Kennedy, 1957). A tape recorder will confirm that the two words have no /d/ sound in common. If they are recorded, it is impossible to cut the tape in order to separate the /im/ or /oom/ from the /d/. Either one is left with a distinct /di/ or /doo/ sound, or else the /d/ sound disappears altogether, leaving two quite different kinds of whistle. Other phonemes behave in equally bizarre ways. If the first part of the tape-recorded word *pit* is cut and spliced at the front of the final /at/ of a word such as *sat* or *fat*, the word that is heard is not *pat*, as we might expect, but *cat*. The /k/ from the beginning of *keep* makes *top* when joined to the /op/ from *cop* and makes *poop* when combined with the /oop/ from *coop*.

There is a simple way to demonstrate that the sounds that we normally hear as the same can be quite different. Say the word *pin* into the palm of your hand and you will feel a distinct puff of air on the /p/; however, the puff is absent when you say the word *spin*. In other words, the /p/ in *pin* is not the same as the /p/ in *spin*—and both are different from the /p/ in *limp*. If you now pay careful attention to the way you say the words, you can probably detect the difference. Usually the difference is ignored, because it is not significant. Other word pairs provide a similar demonstration— for example, *kin* and *skin* or *team* and *steam*. You may also be able to detect a difference between /k/ in *cool* and /k/ in *keen*, a difference that is allophonic in English and phonemic in Arabic, or in the /l/ at the beginning and end of *level*. Japanese listeners often have difficulty in distinguishing between English words such as *link* and *rink* because there is no contrast at all between /l/ and /r/ in their language. In short, a phoneme is not something present in the surface level of spoken language—it is something that the listener constructs. We don't hear different sounds when we are listening to speech, but instead we hear significant differences, phonemes instead of phones. It could be argued that all the discrete sounds that are supposed to be discriminable in the continuous flow of speech are false analogies created by a bias toward visibly discriminable elements of writing—the alphabet, in other words.

The preceding technical distinctions may be further illustrated by reference to writing, where a comparable situation holds. Just as the word *sound* is ambiguous in speech, because it can refer to a phone or a phoneme, so the word *letter* is ambiguous in writing. We call *a* one letter of the alphabet, as distinguished from *b, c, d*, and so forth, but we also talk about *a*, A, a, and so on as being letters, although they all in a way represent the same letter. In the first case, the letter of the alphabet *a* is really a category name for a variety of written symbols such as *a*, A, a. The 26 category names for the letters in the English alphabet may be called *graphemes*, the written symbols (which are innumerable in their various forms) may be called *graphs*, and the graphs that constitute alternatives for a single grapheme are known as *allographs*.

Linguists make several other distinctions along the same lines. A *morpheme* is the smallest meaningful part of a word. A word may consist of one or more morphemes, some "free" like *farm* or *like* because they can occur independently, and some "bound" like *-er* (meaning someone who does something) and *-s* (meaning plural) or *un-* (meaning negative), which have to be joined to a free morpheme. Thus *farmers* is three morphemes, one free and two bound, and so is *unlikely*. Different *morphs* may represent the same morpheme—thus for plurality we can have not only *-s* but *-es, -en*, and a lot of quite odd forms like the vowel change in *man–men* or even nothing at all, as in the singular and plural *sheep*. Morphs that constitute the same morpheme are called *allomorphs*. Meaning itself may be considered in the form of elements sometimes called *sememes*. *Bachelor*, for example, comprises sememes related to maleness, age, marriage, and negation. Words in a dictionary—sometimes referred to as "lexical entries"—may similarly be termed *lexemes*.

Speech, Writing, and "Language"

Confusion may be caused when reading is referred to as a "language process." Of course reading is a matter of language. The problem arises when the word *language* is used synonymously with the word *speech*, with reading regarded as some kind of ancillary or parasitical process rather than a language activity in its own right. When Perfetti (1985), for example, argued for the "language" basis of reading, he was asserting that reading alphabetic text depends on "phonological awareness" of sound patterns in speech.

The priority given to speech is clearly inappropriate (although not always recognized to be so) in the case of deaf language. Deaf signing is at least as rich, flexible, and expressive as spoken language—although its development may be handicapped by efforts to anchor deaf language in speech. For powerful as well as moving discussions of the language and thought of deaf people, see Sacks (1989) and the references in that volume. On the other hand, the word language is often used metaphorically, for example, in references to "computer language" and "body language."

More About Words

A number of my observations about the ambiguity of words are derived from the work of the linguist Fries (1945), who calculated that the 500 most common words of our language have an average of 28 distinct dictionary meanings each. Miller (1951) pointed out that the 50 most common English words constitute 60% of talk and 40% of writing. A mere seven words do 20% of the work of English—*the*, *of*, *and*, *a*, *to*, *in*, and *is*. The 10 most common French words—*à*, *de*, *dans*, *sur*, *et*, *ou*, *que*, *ne*, *pas*, and *y*—constitute 25% of that language.

NOTES TO CHAPTER 4,
INFORMATION AND EXPERIENCE, pp. 55–71

Measuring Information and Uncertainty

A brief introduction to a few elementary calculations employed in *information theory* will allow some numbers to be put to the rate at which readers are able to deal with visual information from the eyes (our "channel capacity"). The same techniques also permit quantification of the uncertainty or redundancy of letters and words of English (or any other language) in various circumstances.

It is necessary to be a little circumlocutionary in putting actual figures to information and uncertainty because although both are measured with respect to alternatives, the measure is not simply the number of alternatives. Instead, information is calculated in terms of a unit called a *bit*, which always reduces by half the uncertainty on a particular occasion. Thus the card player who discovers that an opponent's strongest suit is red (either diamonds or hearts) gets one bit of information, and so does a child trying to identify a letter who is told that it comes from the second half of the alphabet. In the first case two alternatives are eliminated (the two black suits), and in the second case 13 alternatives are removed (and 13 still remain). In both cases the proportion of uncertainty reduced is a half, and therefore the amount of information received is regarded as one bit. The uncertainty of a situation in bits is equal to the number of times a "yes or no" question would have to be asked and answered to eliminate all uncertainty if each answer reduced uncertainty by a half. Thus there are two bits of uncertainty in the card-playing example because two questions will remove all doubt, for example: Q1. Is it a black suit? Q2. If yes, is it clubs? (If no, is it hearts?), or Q1. Is it spades or diamonds? Q2. If yes, is it spades? (If no, is it hearts?)

You can see it doesn't matter how the questions are posed, provided they permit a yes-no answer that will eliminate half the alternatives. The final qualification is important. Obviously, a single question such as "Is it clubs?" will eliminate all alternatives if the answer is "yes," but will still leave at least one and possibly more questions to be asked if the answer is "no." The most efficient way of reducing uncertainty when the answer can only be "yes" or "no" is by a binary split, that is, by partitioning the alternatives into two equal sets. In fact the word *bit*, which may have sounded rather colloquial, is an abbreviation of the words *binary digit*, or a number representing a choice between two alternatives.

The uncertainty of the 26 letters of the alphabet lies somewhere between four and five bits. Four bits of information (four questions) will allow selection among 16 alternatives, not quite enough, with the first bit reducing this number to 8, the second to 4, the third to 2, and the fourth to 1. Five bits will select among 32 alternatives, slightly too many, with the first eliminating 16 and the other four removing the rest of the uncertainty. In brief, x bits of information will select among 2^x alternatives. Two bits will select among $2^2 = 4$, three bits among $2^3 = 8$, four bits among $2^4 = 16$, and so on. One question settles only $2^1 =$ two alternatives, and no questions at all are required if you have only one alternative to begin with ($2^0 = 1$). Twenty bits ("twenty questions") are theoretically sufficient to distinguish among $2^{20} = 1,048,576$ alternatives. There is a mathematical formula that shows that the theoretical uncertainty of 26 letters of the alphabet is almost precisely 4.7 bits, although, of course, it is not easy to see how one could ask just 4.7 questions. (The formula is that the uncertainty of x alternatives is $\log_2 x$, which can be looked up in a table of logarithms to the base 2: $\log_2 26 = 4.7$, since $26 = 2^{4.7}$.) Can you calculate the uncertainty in a deck of 52 playing cards? Since 52 is exactly twice 26, the uncertainty of the cards must be one bit more than that of the alphabet, or 5.7 bits.

Measuring Redundancy

It will be helpful to pursue the matter of redundancy a little more deeply, partly because of the importance of the concept of redundancy to reading, but also because the discussion of how *bits* of uncertainty or information are computed contained an oversimplification that can now be rectified. We consider two aspects of redundancy, termed *distributional* and *sequential*.

Distributional redundancy is associated with the relative probability that each of the alternatives in a particular situation can occur. There is less uncertainty when some alternatives are more probable than others. And because there is less uncertainty when alternatives are not equally probable, there is redundancy. The very fact that alternatives are not equally probable is an additional source of information that reduces the uncertainty of the set of alternatives as a whole. Redundancy that occurs because the probabilities of alternatives are not equally distributed is therefore called distributional redundancy.

Uncertainty is greatest when every alternative has an equal chance of occurring. Consider a coin-tossing game where there are only two alternatives, head or tail, and there are equal chances of a head or a tail turning up. The informativeness of knowing that a particular toss of the coin produced a head (or a tail) is one bit, because whatever the outcome, uncertainty is reduced by a half. But now suppose that the game is not fair, and that the coin will come down head 9 times out of 10. What is the uncertainty of the game now (to someone who knows the coin's bias)? The uncertainty is hardly as great as when the odds were 50–50, because then there was no reason to choose between head and tail, while with the loaded coin it would be foolish knowingly to bet tail. By the same token, there is likely to be far less information on being told the outcome of a particular toss of the loaded coin. Not much uncertainty is removed if one is told that the coin has come down head because that is what was expected all the time. In fact, the informativeness of a head can be computed to be about 0.015 bit, compared with 1 bit if the game were fair. It is true that there is much more information in the relatively unlikely event of being told that a toss produced a tail—a total of 3.32 bits of information compared with the one bit for a tail when heads and tails are equally probable—but we can expect a tail to occur only once in every 10 tosses. The *average* amount of information available from the loaded coin will be nine tenths of the 0.015 bit of information for head and one tenth of the 3.32 bits of information for tail, which when totaled is approximately 0.35 bit. The difference between the 1 bit of uncertainty (or information) for the 50–50 coin, and the 0.35 bit for the 90–10 loaded coin, is the distributional redundancy.

The statement that the uncertainty of letters of the English language is 4.7 bits is perfectly true for any situation involving 26 equally probable alternatives—for example, drawing a letter from a hat containing one instance only of each of the 26 letters of the alphabet. But the letters of English don't occur in the language with equal frequency; some of them, such as *e, t, a, o, i, n, s*, occur far more often than others. In fact, *e* occurs about 40 times more often than the least frequent letter, *z*. Because of this inequality, the average uncertainty of letters is somewhat less than the maximum of 4.7 bits that it would be if the letters all occurred equally often. The actual uncertainty of letters, considering their relative frequency, is 4.07 bits, with the difference of about 0.63 bit being the distributional redundancy of English letters, a measure of the prospective informativeness that is lost because letters don't occur equally often. If letters were used equally often, we could achieve the 4.07 bits of uncertainty that the 26 letters currently have with a little over 16 letters. We could save ourselves about 9 letters if we could find a way to use the remainder equally often.

Like letters, words also have a distributional redundancy in English. One of the oldest and still least understood findings in experimental psychology concerns the "word-frequency effect," that more common words of our language can be identified on less visual information than less frequent words (Broadbent, 1967; Broadbent & Broadbent, 1975; Howes & Solomon, 1951). Computations of the distributional redundancy of letters and words in English are contained in Shannon (1951).

Sequential redundancy exists when the probability of a letter or word is constrained by the presence of surrounding letters or words in the same sequence. For example, the probability that the letter *H* will follow *T* in English words is not 1 in 26 (which would be the case if all letters had an equal chance of occurring in any position) nor about 1 in 17 (taking distributional redundancy into account), but about 1 in 8 (because only eight alternatives are likely to occur following *T* in English, namely, *R*, *H*, or a vowel). Thus the uncertainty of any letter that follows *T* in an English word is just three bits ($2^3 = 8$). The average uncertainty of all letters in English words is about 2.5 bits (Shannon, 1951). The difference between this average uncertainty of 2.5 bits and a possible uncertainty of 4.07 bits (after allowing for distributional redundancy) is the sequential redundancy of letters in English words. An average of 2.5 bits of uncertainty means that letters in words have a probability of about 1 in 6 instead of 1 in 26. This figure, of course, is only an *average* computed over many readers, many words, and many letter positions. There is not a progressive decline in uncertainty from letter to letter, from left to right, in all words. An English word beginning with *q*, for example, has zero uncertainty about the next letter *u*, an uncertainty of about two bits for the four vowels that can follow the *u*, and then perhaps four bits of uncertainty for the next letter, which could be one of over a dozen alternatives. Other words have different uncertainty patterns, although in general the uncertainty of any letter goes down the more other letters in the word are known, irrespective of order. Because of constraints in the spelling patterns of English—due in part to the way words are pronounced—there is slightly more uncertainty at the beginning of a word than at the end, with slightly less in the middle (Bruner & O'Dowd, 1958).

The orthographic (spelling) redundancy of print to which I have referred comprises both distributional and sequential redundancy for letters *within* words, while syntactic (grammar) and semantic (meaning) redundancy are primarily sequential redundancy *between* words. "Predictive" software on computers makes use of the sequential redundancy of both letters and words, in combination with a "virtual keyboard" on the monitor screen where letters (or other symbols) need only be touched or otherwise indicated in order for choices to be made. In contrast to the fixed array of keys on a "real" keyboard, the characters on a virtual keyboard can be replaced almost instantly, from letter to letter, so that the writer is confronted only by those items most likely to be required. If a *k* has already been selected, for example, only those letters likely to come next will be presented (like *l, n, r* or a vowel), reducing clutter and the time required for a decision to be made. Once one or more words have been selected, the software may be able to suggest entire words that are likely to come next, so that the writer need make only one choice, out of very few alternatives, to select an entire word. Predictive software can do more than anticipate letters and words based on their frequency in language as a whole—it can reflect probabilities of words and sequences of words in particular subject areas and even be "trained" to anticipate the probable word choices of individual writers.

Limitations of Information Theory

The first practical application of information theory was in measuring the efficiency of communication systems like telephone lines and radio links. The measure was related to the proportion of words emitted by the "transmitter" at one end of a communication channel that the "receiver" at the other end could correctly identify. Information theory had a brief but spectacular decade of influence in psychology in the 1950s and 1960s, primarily due to the erudition of George Miller (1956) in an article that referred to limits on human "capacity for processing information." For many psychologists this was a new and seductive way of talking about the brain.

Information theory became influential at a time when reading was primarily considered to be a matter of identifying letters and words. The text could be regarded as a transmitter, the reader as a receiver, and the visual system as a communication channel. The efficiency or "capacity" of this channel could be computed from the proportion of letters and words that the reader correctly identified under various conditions. The perspective and techniques were useful theoretically and enabled all kinds of interesting comparisons to be made. They helped to demonstrate in a quantifiable way that the visual system has limitations—we can't see everything that is in front of our eyes. The theory also offered some useful concepts, notably that of redundancy.

However, information theory itself has severe limitations, with respect to texts and to readers. It can measure "information" in its own narrow terms of reducing uncertainty among known sets of alternatives, but it can't say how meaningful a text is, or how much understanding there might be. Outside the experimental laboratory, readers usually read for meaning rather than for information—or they get their information enveloped in meaning. And when readers do "receive information," it is usually not in the limited sense of information theory. Statements like "More than a thousand kinds of brown algae exist" may be informative, but there is no way of saying how much uncertainty they reduce. Redundancy in spelling patterns can be calculated, but not redundancy in short stories. Information theory loses its utility once we get inside the head.

Besides, information doesn't seem to be what the brain is primarily concerned with (Smith, 1983a). The brain deals with understanding rather than information. Either information becomes understanding as part of our interconnected theory of the world, or it remains an isolated fact, at best potential meaning, like an item in an encyclopedia. Information can be derived from experience in the same way that vitamins can be obtained from food, but information is no more experience than vitamins are food. The semantic complication is compounded by the fact that in contrast with the narrow sense in which the word information is employed in information theory, its general use these days is totally undiscriminating, and therefore meaningless. Everything is information—the content of every book, journal, and television program, the entire educational curriculum, anything on a computer, even junk mail.

Rosenblatt (1978), in her distinction between reading for information and reading for experience, didn't use the word *information* in either the narrow information theory sense or the catch-all general sense. To her, information meant "facts." Perhaps because the terms *information* and *experience* have such broad general uses, she actually employed quite uncommon terms for what she wanted to explain. Informational reading she described as *efferent*, meaning "carrying outward" from the text, and the alternative she termed *aesthetic*, implying involvement in the text through the senses.

Computers and People

In the jargon of cognitive science (see notes to Preface), information, whether in humans or computers, is always "processed" rather than "understood." Almost everything now is a process in the educational research literature—and in disquisitions on teaching as well. It is rare to read of unadulterated reading, writing, comprehension, learning, or teaching; instead there is the reading process, the writing process, the comprehension process, the learning process, and the teaching process. And according to my dictionary, the word *process* has broad mechanical connotations—it entails a succession of actions or operations in a specific or prescribed sequence (much like the manner in which a computer is programmed). Among cognitive scientists, reading and comprehension are now both "text processing." Writing is "word processing." Thinking is "ideas management" or "the organization of knowledge."

Perhaps to underline the growing influence of computer-based ways of thinking, the word information is being superseded by *data* (a plural word that, like *criteria* and *media*, is commonly used in the singular), and the word knowledge by *database*. *Process* may be losing ground to *procedures*, an artificial intelligence term, and even to *instructions*, which are what computers run on. Schemas and scenarios are seen as procedures rather than as narratives. "Procedural" knowledge is contrasted with "propositional" knowledge. Larsen (1986) even argued that there is a need for "procedural literacy," which is not the same thing as "computer literacy," but rather the ability to produce and understand sequences of instructions for the organization of knowledge.

It can be argued that cognitive science has become an elaborate behavioristic stimulus-response system, despite the fact that it calls itself cognitive. Individuals are perceived as totally under the control of an environment, which is the source of all data or information. There are no intentions, feelings, or values except for what something outside the system has put into it. This is not my argument, but that of the foremost exponent of behaviorism, B. F. Skinner (1985), who claimed that the only difference between cognitive science and his own theory is in the language that is used.

The discussion of cognitive science is inseparable from discussion of the relationship of computers and the brain, a complex philosophical topic. Computers don't do anything unless told what to do and how to do it, so they are not like the human brain unless you believe that is what humans are like. Computers may do things that we can't do—like calculate thousands of prime numbers, or scrutinize complex landscapes, or generate elaborate designs—but nevertheless they are following procedures that humans give them (or that the computers develop as a consequence of earlier procedures that humans have given them). And there is no guarantee that the procedures computers follow are those used when humans make mathematical calculations, study a landscape, or paint a picture; they almost certainly are not. A computer doesn't have plans and intentions, except those it is given. It doesn't have wishes or feelings or values. These characteristics may be simulated on computers, but this doesn't give them human characteristics. Computers don't have experiences. They don't understand sarcasm, irony, or affection. They don't understand *anything*. Programming a computer isn't the same thing as teaching a person, and learning certainly isn't the same thing as being programmed. Computers are said to have learned when they perform differently. Human beings don't necessarily behave differently as a consequence of learning and can change their behavior without learning anything.

NOTES TO CHAPTER 5,
BETWEEN EYE AND BRAIN, pp. 72–94

Vision and Information

It is difficult to avoid referring to bursts of neural energy in the optic nerve as "information" or "messages" that the eyes send to the brain about the world. But both terms can be misleading, with their implication that the eyes know something that they try to communicate to the brain. It might be more appropriate to refer to the neural impulses that travel between eye and brain as *clues* to a world forever concealed from direct inspection. No scientist or philosopher can say what the world is "really like," because everyone's perception of the world—even when mediated by microscopes or telescopes, by photographs or x-rays—still depends on the sense the brain can make of neural impulses that have come through the dark tunnel between eye and brain. We can no more see the image of the world that falls on the retina than we can see the nerve impulses that the retina sends to the brain. The only part of vision of which we can ever be aware is the final sensation of seeing, constructed within the brain.

That there is a limit to how much print can be identified at any one time, varying according to the use a reader can make of redundancy, is not exactly a recent discovery. The illustration in this chapter of how much can be identified from a single glance at a row of random letters, random words, and meaningful sequences of words is derived directly from the early researches of Cattell (1885, republished 1973), Erdmann and Dodge (1898), and Dodge (1900). Descriptions of many similar experimental studies were included in a remarkably insightful book by Huey (1908, republished in 1967), which remains the only classic in the psychology of reading. A good deal of recent research on perception in reading is basically replication of early studies with more sophisticated equipment; nothing has been demonstrated that controverts them. Yet the pioneer research was neglected by experimental psychologists for almost a century and is still widely unknown in education, partly because behaviorism inhibited psychologists from studying "mental phenomena" and partly because "systematic" or "scientific" piecemeal approaches to reading instruction have concentrated on decoding and word attack—the "tunnel vision" extreme—at the expense of comprehension.

An excellent historical survey of eye-movement research was provided by Paulson and Goodman (1999), who took pains to give credit to "valid, reliable and high-quality work" done in the first decades of the 20th century, and even earlier. Huey (1908), for example, established that the first fixation in a line of text was not necessarily on the first word, nor was the last fixation necessarily the last word. Individual words were frequently skipped (from 30% to 80% of the time, depending on the familiarity of the language, material and genre to the reader), and some of the fixations were regressions. Two of the most prolific researchers, Judd and Buswell (1922), showed that context was the prime factor in determining the meaning of words in normal reading. Paulson and Goodman noted that a contemporary habit of restricting research reviews to the most recent 5 years not only leads to ignorance of an important knowledge base, but also conceals current misunderstandings or misrepresentations of original work. Their review was published on the Internet, perhaps appropriate for a study that begins with pioneer research conducted with homemade devices on tabletops.

The mathematics of information theory (chap. 4 notes) shows that readers identifying just four or five random letters, a couple of random words, or a meaningful sequence of four or five words in one glance are analyzing the same amount of visual information each time. The differences among the three conditions must be attributed to the varying amounts of nonvisual information that readers are able to contribute, related to distributional and sequential redundancy within the print. The random letter condition suggests that the limit for a single glance (the equivalent of a second of processing time) is about 25 bits of information, based on a maximum of 5 letter identifications of about 5 bits of uncertainty each (5 bits = 32 alternatives). In random sequences of letters, of course, there is no distributional or sequential redundancy that a reader can utilize. That 25 bits per second is indeed a general limit on the rate of human information processing was concluded by Quastler (1956) from studies not only of letter and word identification but of the performance of piano players and "lightning calculators" as well.

How is it possible then to identify two random words, consisting on the average of 4.5 letters each, with just 25 bits of visual information? Nine or 10 letters at 5 bits each would seem to require closer to 50 bits. But as I pointed out in the chapter 4 notes, because of distributional and sequential redundancy the average uncertainty of letters in English *words* is about 2.5 bits each (Shannon, 1951), the total average uncertainty for letters in two random words would be something under 25 bits. From a different perspective, random words taken from a pool of 50,000 alternatives would have an uncertainty of between 15 and 16 bits each ($2^{15} = 32,768$, $2^{16} = 65,536$), but due to distributional redundancy among words—and because unusual words are unlikely to be employed in reading studies—we can probably again accept the estimate of Shannon that the average uncertainty of English words without syntactic or semantic constraints (sequential redundancy) is about 12 bits per word. So whether we look at the random word condition from the point of view of letter uncertainty in words (about 2.5 bits per letter) or of isolated word uncertainty (about 12 bits per word) the result is still that the reader is making the identification of about 9 or 10 letters or two words with roughly 25 bits of visual information. The fact that both the number of letters identified and the effective angle of vision double in the random word condition compared with the four or five letters that can be perceived in the random letter condition reflects the use that the reader can make of redundancy. In other words, the viewer in the isolated word condition contributes the equivalent of 25 bits of nonvisual information to enable twice as much to be seen in a single glance.

In meaningful passages of English, there is considerable sequential redundancy among the words themselves. Speakers and authors are not free to choose any word they like whenever they please, at least not if they expect to make any sense. From statistical analyses of long passages of text and also by a "guessing game" technique in which people were actually required to guess letters and words, Shannon calculated that the average uncertainty of *words* in meaningful sequences was about 7 bits (a reduction over words in isolation of about a half) and that the average uncertainty of *letters* in meaningful sequences was only slightly over 1 bit (again reducing by half the uncertainty of *letters* in isolated words). On this basis, one would expect viewers in the meaningful word sequences condition to see twice as much again compared with isolated words, which is of course the experimental result. A phrase or sentence of four or five words can be seen in one glance, a total of 20 letters or more. This is four times as much as can be seen in the random letter condition, but still on the basis of the same amount of visual information: 4 or 5 random letters at about 5 bits each, or 20 letters in a meaningful sequence at just over 1 bit each. Put in another way, when reading sequences of meaningful words in text the reader can contribute at least three parts nonvisual information (in the form of prior knowledge of redundancy) to one part visual information so that four times as much can be perceived.

Other analyses of uncertainty and redundancy in English are included in Garner (1962, 1974) and in Miller, Bruner, and Postman (1954), with the latter using carefully constructed "approximations to English." McNeill and Lindig (1973) demonstrated that how much listeners perceive in spoken language also depends on what they are attending to—individual sounds, syllables, or entire words.

The Rate of Visual Decision Making

Many years after the first demonstrations of what can be seen in a single glance, other tachistoscopic studies showed that the limits can't be attributed to the amount of visual information that the eye can gather from the page, nor to viewers' forgetting letters or words already identified before they can report them. Rather, the bottleneck occurs as the brain labors on what is transiently a considerable amount of raw visual information, organizing "seeing" after the eyes have done their work. Perceptual decision making takes time, and there is a limit to how long visual information sent back by the eyes remains available to the brain.

Viewers in the kind of tachistoscopic experiment that I have described often feel that they have potentially seen more than they are able to report. The brief presentation of visual information leaves a vaguely defined "image" that fades before they are fully able to attend to it. The validity of this observation was established by an experimental technique called *partial recall* (Sperling, 1960) in which viewers are required to report only 4 letters out of a presentation of perhaps 12 so that the required report is well within the limits of short-term memory (see chap. 6). However, the viewers don't know *which* 4 letters they must report until after the visual presentation, so they must work from visual information that remains available to the brain after its source has been removed from before the eyes. At one stroke the experimental technique avoids any complication of memory by keeping the required report to a small number of items, while at the same time testing whether in fact viewers have information about all 12 items for a brief time after the eyes' work is complete.

The experimental technique involves presenting the 12 letters in three rows of 4 letters each. Very soon after the 50-msec presentation is ended, a tone is sounded. The viewer already knows that a high tone indicates that the letters in the top row are to be reported, a low tone calls for the report of the bottom row, and an intermediate tone indicates the middle line. When this method of partial recall is employed, viewers can normally report back the 4 required letters, indicating that for a short while at least they have access to raw visual information about all 12 letters. The fact that viewers can report any 4 letters, however, doesn't indicate that they have identified all 12, but simply that they have time to identify 4 before the visual information fades. If the cue tone is delayed more than half a second after the end of the presentation the number of letters that can be reported falls off sharply. The "image" is raw visual information that decays by the time about 4 letters have been identified.

Other evidence that visual information remains available in a sensory store for about a second and that the entire second is required if a maximum of four or five letters is to be identified has come from the masking studies described in this chapter (e.g., Averbach & Coriell, 1961; Smith & Carey, 1966). If a second visual array is presented to the eye before the brain has finished identifying the maximum number of letters that it can from the first input of visual information, then the amount reported from the first presentation declines. The second input of visual information erases information from the first presentation. However, it can be as disruptive for reading if visual information reaches the eye too slowly as it is if too fast. Kolers and Katzman (1966), Newman (1966), and Pierce and Karlin (1957) showed an optimum rate of about six presentations a second for receiving visual information about individual letters or words; at faster rates the brain can't keep up and at slower speeds there tends to be a greater loss of earlier items through forgetting. These studies and the earlier calculations of Quastler (1956) all tend to support the view that the "normal reading rate" of between 200 and 300 words a minute is an optimum; slower reading disrupts comprehension.

Eye Movements in Reading

Rayner (1997) summarized decades of his own and other research into what can be seen as the eye moves from one fixation to another. He confirmed the strong influence of context on where the eye lands in each fixation, usually on content words. Words are often skipped, depending on their length, frequency, and predictability. Readers are very accurate at regressing to a point in the text where comprehension problems occurred. Rayner cited numerous studies showing that the perceptual span can extend to 15 letter spaces to the right of the fixation point and 4 to the left (the reverse in languages that are read from right to left). No useful information comes from the line below the line fixated on. The span is not fixed, but varies with the experience of the reader and the predictability of the text. There is a "preview benefit" for words not clearly seen around the focal area of gaze, mainly from beginning letters. McClelland and O'Regan (1981) showed that this benefit is increased if readers are able to make predictions about what they will see.

The generalizability of conclusions from eye movement studies is limited because under laboratory conditions viewers often have no control over where they fix their gaze or of how long fixations may last. The experimenter makes these decisions for them. In many tachistoscopic and eye-movement studies, viewers are not even free to move their heads, which are constrained by chin rests or even bite plates. Yet head movements are a conspicuous part of normal reading. To avoid head movement constraints, some reading researchers have gone to another extreme by providing helmets equipped with electronic technology for their viewers to wear while looking at a computer screen. Many computer-based experiments also involve bizarre reading conditions, such as words that may change during a saccade or the presence of irrelevant words or lines of x's just outside the foveal (sharp focus) area (Rayner & Pollatsek, 1987). Important areas of the text may be removed, for example, when the letter in the center of the reader's field of vision is automatically obscured on every fixation (Rayner, 1992). The consequence that reading speed may be slowed by 50% in such circumstances is cited as demonstrating that readers *need* the information in the obliterated letter, although it could be argued that it is the distraction itself that causes the disruption. For other representative eye-movement studies see Rayner and Pollatsek (1989) and Stanovich (1991).

Duckett (2002) also challenged claims that good readers look at each successive word in turn as they read. In a close study of six first-grade beginning readers, reading aloud from computer screens, he found that they did not fixate on every word of a simple illustrated story, they spoke words that they did not fixate on, and they did not always fixate serially left to right. Fixations were selected strategically where, when and for as long as needed for them to get the sense of the story. Paulson (2002) showed that prediction overrides evidence as readers strive to make sense of the content of their fixations. They change the text rather than change their mind, supporting the view that reading is a constructive activity, depending on what is "behind the eyes." Kucer and Tuten (2003) examined the miscues of 24 fluent adult readers and found that the majority of miscues were influenced by the sense, syntax, and style of the author. The miscues paralleled those of young developing readers.

It might be asked why the most general and most efficient fixation rate in reading seems to be about four fixations a second when the information from a single glance persists for a second or more and at least 1 second is required for analyzing all the information that can be acquired from a single fixation. Why do readers make so many fixations when they can see four or five words at a glance? There has not been a good research answer to this question, but my conjecture is that the brain is less concerned with squeezing the last bit of information from each fixation than with receiving a smooth inflow of selected visual information as it builds up a coherent understanding of the text. Successive words provide useful anchorages for the eyes as the brain does its work. Obviously, readers must already have a good idea of where to fixate if their gaze rests primarily on content words.

Interesting analogies may be drawn between eye movements and hand movements. The top speed of movement for eye and for hand are roughly similar, and, like the eye, the hand moves faster when it moves over a greater distance. The hand performs the same kind of activity as the eye. It moves precisely and selectively to the most useful position, and it starts "picking up" only when it has arrived. But although the hands and eyes of children may move almost as fast and accurately as those of adults, they can't always be used as efficiently. Children lack the experience of the adult and may not know so precisely what they are reaching for.

On Seeing Backward

Moyer and Newcomer (1977) demonstrated that reversals are caused by inexperience with directionality rather than by perceptual deficits. Stanovich (1982a, 1982b) noted that normal readers may also make orientation errors ("reading or writing backward") that are not a cause of reading difficulties.

Hemispheric Specialization

A basic article about functional differences in the cerebral hemispheres and about the occasionally bizarre consequences of their being superficially disconnected was provided by one of the earliest researchers in the area, Sperry (1968). Discussions of the relationship between the hemispheres and language are included in several chapters in Caplan (1980). Research leading to the conclusion that hemispheric specialization should not be considered an explanation of reading difficulties in children is reported in Naylor (1980), Young and Ellis (1981), and in the chapter by Bryden in Underwood (1978).

NOTES TO CHAPTER 6, BOTTLENECKS OF MEMORY, pp. 95–109

Theories of Memory

One of the earliest and most coherent attempts to distinguish short-term and long-term characteristics of memory was by Norman (1969), revised and expanded into a comprehensive analysis of the processes and contents of memory (Norman, 1976). There are useful reviews by Kintsch (1982), Baddeley (1992), and Schneider and Shiffrin (1977), who particularly emphasized the relationship between short-term memory and attention. Lewis (1979) critically reviewed the short-term and long-term memory distinction, proposing that most forgetting is retrieval failure rather than storage loss and suggesting instead an active and inactive memory distinction with active memory part of the greater inactive one (similar to my Fig. 6.2).

Tulving (1985a, 1985b) proposed that there are *three* different memory systems, which he termed *episodic, semantic,* and *procedural.* He associated each with a different kind of consciousness (or absence of consciousness). Tulving's basic memory system is *procedural;* it is also the most primitive, the only one that animals have. It is also the only one of the three systems that can be completely independent of the other two. Procedural memories require overt action to become established and are not accessible to consciousness. Tulving called this condition *anoetic* (literally, "without knowledge"). We can never be aware of what we know procedurally (except by actually doing something, possibly in the imagination). Such a memory system may be fundamental, but it is not trivial. It is probably the aspect of our memory containing the "rules" of language, which are not learned consciously (Krashen, 1985). Tulving's *semantic* memory is a subset within the procedural, and it makes possible representations of states of the world not perceptually present (i.e., which we can imagine). Semantic memory includes facts—but not in any particular order. Most people, for example, know that both John F. Kennedy and Charles de Gaulle are dead, but they can't immediately say who died first. Semantic memory "describes" events and situations for us—it brings them to consciousness. Tulving calls this *noetic.* Finally, *episodic* memory, which is nested within the semantic system, is "self-knowing," or *autonoetic.* It is our awareness of the order or sequence of events, the only conscious form of memory that includes temporal relationships. Tulving stressed what few cognitive psychologists would dispute these days, that the quality of a particular memory depends on the manner and circumstances in which it was originally learned.

Another distinction frequently drawn is between *recognition* and *reproduction* memory. It is usually (but not always) easier to recognize a face or a place (or an object or symbol) than it is to draw it. We recognize correct spellings easier than we can produce them. At any age we can understand more of language than we can produce ourselves. This should not be taken as implying that we have two entirely different kinds of memory—that we go to one "store" for recognition and another for reproduction. It is not that we have a collection of pictures (or "images") in the brain that we can refer to for recognition. Mental images themselves have to be constructed, and we can usually recognize faces and other things more easily than we can imagine them. There is probably a simple explanation—that we usually need to produce less detail for recognition than for reproduction. To recognize a face, or even a word, we may need to see only a part of it, but reproduction means that we have to generate it all, without omission or error. For factual matters, a similar distinction is frequently made between *recognition* and *recall* memory. We may be able to agree that a certain actor starred in a particular movie, yet be quite unable to think of the actor's name if asked who the star of the movie was. Once again, it is probably more complex cognitively to construct or to complete what we think is a true statement than simply to recognize the statement as true when it is produced by someone else (see Anderson, 1980). In an article entitled "Good Morning, Mr ... er," Burton (1992) examined how it might be that we can recognize a face without being able to recall anything else about a person and that we may remember almost everything else about someone—their occupation, nationality, where they live—but still not get their name.

The idea that memory is constructive, or reconstructive, rather than a simple recall of original information, also has a long history in psychology, with its own classic by Bartlett (1932). See Smith (1990) for an extended discussion of the role of imagination in learning, comprehension, and thinking as well as memory, and Morris (1988) for descriptions of our remarkable memory capacity for things we are interested in, like sport scores. Reber (1989) showed that there are massive amounts of implicit learning, without awareness, and Bahrick and Hall (1991) demonstrated that the longer the period something is studied or experienced, the longer it is remembered. We remember names of people we know for a few years better than names we have known for a few weeks. People who do math in college can remember for half a century what they would soon forget from high school. Foreign language vocabulary fades within 3 years of one college semester, but over 60% is retained 25 years later with 5 college semesters of study.

Chunking

The two apparent bottlenecks of memory—the limited capacity of short-term memory and the slow entry into long-term memory—can both be circumvented by the strategy known as *chunking*, or organization of information into the most compact (most meaningful) unit. For example, it is easier to retain and recall the sequence of digits *1491625364964* when they are recognized as the first eight square numbers, or the letters *JFMAMJJASOND* as the initials of the months of the year, than to try to remember either sequence as a dozen or so unrelated elements. But it is a mistake to think that we normally perceive first and chunk afterward; we no more read the letters *h, o, r, s,* and *e,* which we then chunk into the word *horse,* than we perceive a particular nose, ear, eye, and mouth, which we then chunk into a friend's face. Chunking research and instruction both tend to get things backward, starting with arrays of ostensibly unrelated elements that the individual is supposed to group together in some meaningful way. In practice, prior knowledge and expectation of the larger grouping lead to the perception of elements in a chunked manner—if we recognize a word, we don't see the individual letters. The size or character of a chunk is determined by what we are looking for in the first place. A remarkable report of how a college student increased his short-term memory span from 7 to 79 digits with 230 hours of chunking practice over 20 months is contained in Ericsson, Chase, and Falcon (1980).

Imagery

One important and common means of chunking is to employ imagery to remember; there is a substantial literature demonstrating the unsurprising fact that our recall of particularly graphic sentences that we have heard or read is more likely to be related to scenes that we imagine from descriptions provided by the words than to the words themselves (Barclay, 1973; Sachs, 1974). But although we remember some sequences of words in terms of the pictures they conjure up, we also often remember scenes or pictures in terms of their descriptions. We recall a scene of birds flying over a town but not whether they were seagulls or pigeons, nor how many there were. There is nothing remarkable about any of this: We naturally try to remember in the most efficient manner possible. If a scene is easiest to remember, or most efficiently remembered, in terms of a description, because perhaps we are interested in particular things rather than in the scene as a whole, then the memorization will proceed accordingly. Not only is our recall influenced by the way we learned or perceived in the first place, but the manner of memorization will tend to reflect the most probable way in which we shall want to recall or use the information in the future. Sadoski, Goetz, and Kansinger (1988) reported that readers spontaneously generate images as they read. Long, Winograd, and Bridge (1989) agreed, especially when the text is interesting and facilitates image creation, which improves comprehension, memory, thinking—and enjoyment. Wilson, Rinck, McNamara, Bower, and Morrow (1993) added that readers will—when the text permits it and especially if a task requires it—construct mental models (like the floor plans of buildings) as they read about them.

Children's Memory

There is no evidence that children have poorer or less well-developed memories than adults. Simon (1974) argued that children have the same memory capacity as adults but don't chunk as efficiently; however, there is probably an adult bias behind the notion of chunking "efficiently." We tend to chunk—or to perceive and remember in rich meaningful units—that which is most rich and meaningful to us. Recall of strings of unrelated letters and digits, which is the test by which children are usually judged to have memories inferior to those of adults, is not the most meaningful of tasks, for children especially. The number of digits a child can repeat after a single hearing increases from an average of 2 at the age of 2½ to 6 at the age of 10 (and 8 for college students). But rather than suppose that children's memory capacity grows with their height and weight, one can argue that the younger children have had little experience, and see little sense, in repeating sequences of numbers, especially before they have become accustomed to using the telephone. The memory span of adults can be magically increased by teaching them little tricks or strategies, for example, to remember strings of numbers not as single digits (2, 9, 4, 3, 7, 8 ...) but as two-digit pairs (29, 43, 78 ...). Practice improves performance on any memory task but doesn't seem to improve memory beyond the particular skill into unrelated areas or activities. The best aid to memory for anyone of any age is a general understanding of the structure and purpose behind the required memorization. If chess pieces are arranged as part of an actual game, skilled players can recall the layout of most or all of the pieces on a board after just a couple of glances although beginners can remember the positions of only a few pieces. But if the pieces are organized randomly, then the skilled player can remember no more than the beginner.

NOTES TO CHAPTER 7,
LETTER IDENTIFICATION, pp. 110–124

Recognition Versus Identification

G. Mandler (1980) made a similar distinction to that made in this chapter between *identification* (putting a name to something) and *recognition* (deciding that something is familiar). He proposed a general theory of word recognition relevant to chapter 9 of this book. Benton (1980) discussed the remarkable human ability to recognize patterns (in this case, faces) years after perhaps only a single partial glimpse.

Theories of Pattern Recognition

Pinker (1984) gave a basic but technical examination of contemporary theories of visual perception, including template, feature, and other more complex models, and also a discussion of the nature and role of imagery. Pinker pointed out that there are problems with all theories—a horse, for example, would seem to consist of too many lines and curves to be easily recognized by "features" alone, yet it is inadequate to say that a horse must therefore be recognized by body parts like hooves, because the parts themselves would have to be recognized by features. The current alternative is to rely on "massively parallel" models, which search concurrently for numbers of features and for interrelationships among them. On the other hand, perhaps to show that pattern recognition should not be complicated and mystified out of proportion, Blough (1982) showed that pigeons can easily be taught to distinguish the letters of the alphabet. When shown a particular letter on one side of a screen, they had to distinguish it from two incorrect alternatives elsewhere on the screen by pecking at the correct alternative. The pigeons, which were hungry, were rewarded with 3 seconds of eating mixed grain for every 4 successive correct answers they gave in 2,700 test trials over 4 days. When they made mistakes, the birds demonstrated the same confusions as humans, for example, C–G–S, M–N–W, and D–O–Q.

It is not suggested that we have visual analyzers that function solely to collect information about letters of the alphabet. Information used in letter identification is received from analyzers involved in many visual activities, of which those concerned with reading are only a small part. The same analyzers might contribute information in other circumstances to the identification of words, digits, geometric forms, faces, automobiles, or any other set of visual categories, as well as to the apprehension of meaning. The brain makes a variety of specialized uses of very general receptor systems; thus statements can be made about analyzers "looking for" alphabetic features without the implication that a benign providence has "prewired" us to read the alphabet. We all have a "biological inheritance" that enables us to talk and read, to ride a bicycle and play the piano, not because of some specific genetic design, but because spoken and written languages, bicycles and pianos, were progressively developed by and for human beings with precisely the biological equipment that humans are born with. For an early attempt to specify possible features of English letters, see Gibson (1965).

Incidentally, it is just as appropriate to talk about distinctive features of speech as it is to refer to distinctive features of written language. In fact, the feature model for letter identification that was developed in the 1960s was inspired by a feature theory of speech perception published in the 1950s (Jakobson & Halle, 1956). In both theories a physical representation, acoustic or visual, is scanned for distinctive features which are analyzed in terms of feature lists that determine a particular categorization and perceptual experience. The number of physical features requiring to be discriminated will depend on the percipient's uncertainty and other sources of information about the language (redundancy) that can be utilized.

Just as the basic elements of the written or printed marks on a page are regarded as distinctive features smaller than letters, so elements smaller than a single sound are conceptualized as distinctive features of speech. Distinctive features of sounds are usually regarded as components of the process by which a phoneme is articulated, such as whether or not a sound is *voiced* (whether the vocal chords vibrate as for /b/, /d/, /g/ compared with /p/, /t/, /k/), whether the sound is *nasal* (like /m/ and /n/), the sound's *duration*, and the *position* of the tongue. Each distinctive feature is a significant difference, and the discrimination of any one feature may eliminate many alternatives in the total number of possible sounds (the set of phonemes). Every feature cuts the set of alternatives in a different way, so that theoretically a total of only six distinctive features could be more than enough to distinguish among 40 alternative phonemes ($2^6 = 64$). There are many analogies between the distinctive features of print and those of speech. The total number of different features is presumed to be much smaller than the set of units that they differentiate (26 for letters, about 40 for sounds). The number of features suggested for phonemes is usually 12 or 13 (note again the redundancy). Phonemes can be confused in the same manner as letters, and the more likely two sounds are to be confused with each other, the more distinctive features they are assumed to share. Some sounds, such as /b/ and /d/, which probably differ in only one feature, are more likely to be confused than /b/ and /t/, which differ in perhaps two, and /t/ and /v/, which may differ in three features. Spoken words may also differ by only a single feature. *Ban* and *Dan*, which have only a single feature's difference, should be rather more likely to be confused than *ban* and *tan*, and much more likely than *tan* and *van*; experimental evidence suggests that assumptions of this kind are correct (Miller & Nicely, 1955).

The perception of speech is no less complex and time-consuming than that of reading; what we hear is the end product of a decision-making procedure that leads to the identification (the categorization) of a sound or word or meaning prior to the perceptual experience. We rarely "hear" words and then identify them; the identification must precede the hearing, otherwise we would just hear noise. And we don't hear distinctive features of sound any more than we see distinctive features of written language; the unit that we are aware of discriminating is determined by the sense that the brain is able to make, the kind of question it is asking. Usually we are aware only of meaning for both spoken and written language. Occasionally we may attend to particular words, but in special circumstances we may become aware of the surface structure phonemes or letters. The features themselves evade our awareness completely.

NOTES TO CHAPTER 8,
WORD IDENTIFICATION, pp. 125–137

Template and Feature-Analytic Theories

In a long and technical summary of template and feature analytic theories of shape recognition, Hummel and Biederman (1992) stressed the need for "structural descriptions" that include relationships among parts rather than just point-by-point comparisons. The authors say that enormous numbers of units and connections are required to "bind" all the parts of any figure together into possible wholes that can be recognized from different angles. Their solution for computer recognition of a simple figure (a cone on a rectangular block) involves a seven-layered network of activating or inhibiting cells, with the sensitivity of each varying according to experience. Obviously, any attempt to specify (or teach) distinctive features and their relationships among letters or words is bound to be an oversimplification.

Letter Identification in Words

It has long been known that readers can make use of redundancy among distinctive features in words. Smith (1969) projected letters or words at such a low intensity that there was barely any contrast with the background on which they were shown, and then increased the contrast slowly, gradually making more and more visual information available until observers were able to make identifications. Under this procedure, viewers are not constrained by time or memory limitations and may choose to make either word or letter identifications with the information available at any moment. They typically identify letters within words before they say what an entire word is, although the entire word may still be identified before any of its letters could be identified in isolation (see also Wheeler, 1970). This finding is not inconsistent with the classic evidence that words can be identified before any of their component letters in isolation, but it does make clear that words are not recognized all-or-none "as wholes" but by analysis of their parts. The sequential redundancy among features that exists within word configurations permits identification of letters on fewer features than would be required if they were presented in isolation. The letter *h*, for example, requires fewer features to identify if presented in the sequence *hat* than if presented alone, even if the reader identifies the *h* before the *at*. The additional information that enables the earlier letter identification to be made in words is based on orthographic redundancy in the spelling of words, reducing the uncertainty of letters from over 4 bits (26 alternatives) to less than 3 (about 7 alternatives), as discussed in the notes to chapter 4. Even if a reader has not discriminated sufficient features in the second and third positions of the configuration *hat* to identify the letters *at*, there is still some featural information available from those positions, which, when combined with nonvisual information about featural redundancy within words, permits identification of the letter in the first position on minimal visual information.

There is other evidence that although words are identified "as wholes," in the sense that featural information from all parts may be taken into account in their identification, they are by no means identified on the basis of the familiarity of their shape or contour. Examples were given earlier in this chapter of the ease with which quite unfamiliar configurations like *rEaDiNg* could be read. Entire passages printed in these peculiar configurations can be read about as fast as normal text (Smith, Lott, & Cronnell, 1969). In fact if the size of the capital letters is reduced slightly so that they don't interfere with the discriminability of the lower case letters, for example, *rEaDiNg*, then there is no difference at all in the rates at which such words and normal text are read. The facility with which we can read passages of handwriting when individual letters and even words would be indecipherable on their own is further evidence that reading doesn't depend on letter identification.

Graphic support for the assertion that we attend to features rather than letters in words is provided by a recent snippet on the Internet. I haven't been able to trace the original source, but the text itself illustrates the point that it makes. It reads, "Acocdrnig to an elgnsih unviesitry sutdy the oredr of letetrs in a word dosen't mttaer, the olny thnig thta's iopmrantt is that the frsit and lsat ltteer of eevry word is in the crrecot ptoision. The rset can be jmbueld and one is stlil able to raed the txet wiohtut dclftfuiiy."

It is obviously an oversimplification to talk about the relative "discriminability" of individual letters of the alphabet or to assume that letters difficult to identify when standing alone must be difficult to perceive when in words. This argument applies especially to the issue of "reversals" of letter pairs like *b* and *d*, which are particularly bothersome to some children, to adults when perception is difficult, and also, apparently, to pigeons (Blough, 1982). Reversals were specifically considered in chapter 5. The amount of visual information required to identify a letter has relatively little to do with the physical characteristics of the actual configuration but depends much more on the reader's experience and the context in which the letter occurs. And precisely the same kind of argument applies to words. Children learning to read can often identify words in context that they can't identify in isolation (Pearson & Studt, 1975). It is misleading to talk of children's word identification ability in terms of their "sight vocabulary" or word attack skills.

Use of Redundancy by Children

There is no evidence that children need to be trained to seek or use redundancy in any way; perception naturally involves the use of prior knowledge and the youngest children demonstrate ability to limit uncertainty by eliminating unlikely alternatives in advance. Studies with young readers have found ability to use sequential redundancy very early (Lott & Smith, 1970). First-grade children who had had a limited amount of reading instruction in kindergarten showed themselves able to identify letters in words on less visual information than when letters only were presented. For children in fourth grade the difference between the information on which letters were identified in words and that on which the same letters were identified in isolation was equal to that of skilled adult readers, indicating that for familiar three-letter words at least, fourth graders could make as much use of sequential featural redundancy as adults. Krueger, Keen, and Rublevich (1974) subsequently confirmed that fourth-grade children may be as good as adults in making use of redundancy among letter sequences in words and nonwords.

Distributional Redundancy Among Words

The *sequential* redundancy that exists among words in text—which has a critical role in making reading possible—is discussed in the notes to chapter 10. But there is also a *distributional* redundancy among words, reflecting the obvious fact that some words are used far more often than others. The distributional redundancy of English words has not been formally calculated but is probably related to the maximum theoretical uncertainty of between 15 and 16 bits for a set of about 50,000 alternatives and the actual 12-bit uncertainty of isolated words computed by Shannon (1951) and discussed in the notes to chapter 4. Distributional redundancy among words complicates experimental studies of word identification because more frequent words are usually identified faster, more accurately, and on less visual information than less frequent words (see p. 258).

NOTES TO CHAPTER 9,
PHONICS AND MEDIATED WORD IDENTIFICATION,
pp. 138–155

A Defining Moment

I'll begin by reviewing the meaning of some terms that are widely but not always consistently used by reading theorists and researchers: *phones*, *phonology*, *phonetics*, *phonemes*, and *phonics*.

The natural sounds of speech are as turbulent and intermingled as the waters of a rushing stream. Nevertheless linguists and other scientists attempt to isolate basic elements of spoken language. The smallest unit they isolate is called a *phone*, which is not anything that anyone can normally detect or reproduce. Phones are like atoms; they don't exist in isolation and are modeled more by caricatures than actual replicas. The specialized study of phones and their production is called *phonology* or *phonetics*, the concern of *phonologists* or *phoneticians*—pairs of terms that are usually synonymous. Some educators believe that foreign language students need to know something about phonology; a few even think beginning readers need knowledge of this kind (although generally they don't mean what they say—their belief is that beginning readers need to know something about phonemes).

Phonemes are perceptual rather than physical phenomena, abstract composites of phones. They are defined as the smallest units of sound that differentiate one spoken word from another. Thus the initial sounds of *tip* and *dip* are phonemes, and so are the final sounds of *see* and *say*. The /t/ phone at the beginning of *tip* is not the same as the /t/ phone at the beginning of *top* (the following sound makes a difference to both of them), but because these two different /t/ phones don't differentiate one word from another—perceptually they are the same—they are not regarded as different phonemes. The number of phones in most languages exceeds 100, but the number of phonemes is much fewer—about 45 in English, depending on the analyzer and the dialect. Neither phones nor phonemes exist in written language, nor do they correspond directly with the letters of alphabetic written languages. To refer as I have done to a phone or phoneme as /t/ is conventional but may be misleading. The *sound* represented by the symbol /t/ is a product of the vocal system; it is not a letter and should not be confused with one. Phonologists and phoneticians use an extended cast of characters to denote sounds, such as ɐ, ɖ, and ʒ, which at least don't look as if they have anything to do with reading.

Phonics is concerned with correspondences between phonemes and *graphemes*, which have nothing to do with speech but are characters in writing systems. *Phonics* is not a scientific study at all, but a method of instruction, specifically concerned with teaching children relationships between graphemes and phonemes (or between letters and sounds), the utility of which is discussed throughout chapter 9. Phonics is sometimes incorrectly referred to as phonetics, just as "phonemic awareness" may also be called "phonological awareness." It can all be very complicated.

The Relevance of Phonics

The analysis of the relationship between the spelling of written words and the sounds of speech is mainly derived from the work of a group of researchers (Berdiansky, Cronnell, & Koehler, 1969) associated with the Southwest Regional Laboratory (SWRL), a federally sponsored research and development center in California. Researchers at SWRL and many other federally funded institutions have continued to analyze the maze of spelling–sound correspondences in English, and to devise instructional programs to teach these correspondences to children in the expectation that it will make them better readers and spellers. The 58th in the series of SWRL technical reports (Rhode & Cronnell, 1977) provided an analysis of a 10,000-word lexicon that they consider to be the basis of a kindergarten through sixth-grade communication skills program. This time, words of three or more syllables are included, a total of 27% of the 10,000. Ninety-nine grapheme units are distinguished, 77 related to 225 spelling–sound correspondence "rules" and 22 to 32 "exceptions." Eighty of the rules are associated with 48 consonant grapheme units, 111 with the six primary vowels (a/e/i/o/u/y), and 34 with 23 secondary vowel units (ai/au/etc.). Computer programs that convert written to spoken language do so not by reliance on phonic rules (the last resort) but by storing the complete sounds of thousands of written words. And even then such devices have difficulty selecting the appropriate pronunciation of the 200 or more *homographs* in English—common words like *wind, tear, read,* and *live*—which require syntactic and semantic knowledge to disentangle them.

The supposed value of phonics as a useful method of instruction has long been challenged. Clymer (1963a) told of problems of trying to teach a student a list of phonic generalizations when the student kept pointing out exceptions. Clymer analyzed 45 generalizations and concluded that 18 might be useful—and they depended on local dialect. For the most common "rule"—that when two vowels go walking, the first does the talking—he found 309 conforming words (*bead*) and 377 nonconforming (*chief*), and politely concluded that many commonly taught generalizations were of limited value. Elsewhere in the same issue he commented that because children can learn to read under a particular set of materials doesn't mean they should (Clymer, 1963b). Johnston (2001) reanalyzed Clymer's results and claimed that some broad generalizations are more applicable when broken down into specific letters—but then they are more complex to learn. She concludes that words are recognized and remembered more on the basis of patterns than on rules about sounds. See also Johnston (2000/2001) and Krashen (2002).

The classic volume on the relevance of phonics instruction is the frequently cited *Learning to Read: The Great Debate* (Chall, 1967), although the discussion is more about how reading is taught than how it is learned, and the conclusions may not be thought to follow inevitably from the evidence presented. The controversy, often reduced to a question of "code emphasis" (phonics exercises) versus "whole language" (meaningful texts), is discussed in chapter 13 and its notes.

Phonological and Phonemic Awareness

The mediated identification of written words through the blending (aloud, silently, or subconsciously) of sounds supposedly represented by their letters is frequently referred to as *phonological recoding*, or sometimes *phonological decoding*. The fact that many children have difficulty learning phonics, and difficulty learning to read despite intensive instruction in phonics, has led many researchers favoring the phonological recoding view to assert that such children suffer a deficiency related to spoken language perception. (It is not uncommon for difficulties children might experience in learning to read to be attributed to "deficits" on their part, rather than to externally produced factors such as confusion, depressed interest, or learning the wrong thing.) According to a widespread view, generally attributed to Isabelle Liberman and her colleagues at the Haskins Laboratories (Liberman & Liberman, 1992), the problem with such children is that they are unable to identify in spoken words the discrete sounds—or "phonological segments"—represented in writing by the letters of the alphabet. This ability to analyze hypothetical sounds has nothing to do with the understanding of speech, but is necessary for reading, according to this point of view.

The term *phonemic awareness* has gradually taken over from phonological awareness in recognition of the fact that the concern is with the identification of abstract phonemes rather than actual phones in sound. A major problem with all these analyses of the phonemic structure of spoken words is that the "units" are completely arbitrary and hypothetical—they don't exist as distinct elements in spoken language, in either the perception or the production of speech (Liberman & Liberman, 1992). Children find it difficult to understand the statement that *bet* consists of three elements and almost impossible to understand that *best* has four (at least until they are readers). The separate sounds that letters are supposed to represent and that beginning readers are supposed to be "aware of" are fictions. Sounds are "coarticulated" in the production of speech—at any moment in saying the word *bet* the speaker might be physically producing part of the /b/, /e/ and /t/ simultaneously. It is impossible to separate the three sounds electronically—or by trying to snip independent sections out of a tape recording. The "internal structure" of speech can't be displayed.

So although children may in some sense be aware of the fact that pairs of words rhyme, or begin with the same sound, or are "the same" or "different" in some way, to expect them to isolate the sounds in speech is a purely artificial task, based solely on the conventions of written (alphabetic) language. The code emphasis becomes not so much a matter of finding speech structures in writing, but of writing structures in speech—not something that is likely to be very easy or meaningful for children before they can read, and of limited utility afterward. Phonemic awareness might be regarded as another skill, like phonics, that children may be required to learn as a separate subject from reading. It all falls apart if reading is perceived to be the interpretation of written language directly, rather than through speech.

Another prolific and influential proponent of the view that reading proceeds on the basis of continual grapheme–phoneme analysis, and that phonics and phonemic awareness skills should be taught directly, is Ehri (1997). Despite concessions that "sight word reading" might be necessary for "irregular" spellings like *none*, *calf*, *break*, and *prove*, and demonstrations that individual words are identified immediately even if the reader intends to ignore them (because the words are printed over pictures that the readers are instructed to focus on and identify), she maintained that grapheme–phoneme connections are made and used "automatically," which means subconsciously, without any observable indication (p. 167). All this is accomplished by a "connection-forming mechanism." Ehri also talked of the importance of "practicing reading" to meet unfamiliar words and add them to the lexicon (p. 179). Theorists with a skills orientation often talk of children "practicing reading" rather than simply "reading." When I first encountered the expression I was tempted to practice laughing.

More articles with a similar approach are included in Lehr and Osborn (1994), who entitle their volume *Reading, Language and Literacy: Instruction for the Twenty-First Century* (without explaining exactly why instruction had to change with the advent of the present century). A typical chapter in the volume is by Adams (1994), who wrote, "The value of phonics instruction has been demonstrated with sobering consistency across literally hundreds of studies" (p. 3), without citing most of these studies, and subsequently admitted, "The phonics advantage documented by this research is neither awesomely large nor comfortingly reliable" (p. 4). Only 38 of these "hundreds" of studies made the cut for the National Reading Panel report (discussed in the chapter 13 notes).

Wolf and Katzir-Cohen (2001) reported that research into "phonological processes" has been insufficient to explain fluent reading and why it breaks down. Their view was that explicit instruction is required "to link phonological, orthographic, semantic and morphological processes to sub-lexical and word-level subskills" (p. 229), all of which must become automatic. The view that phonetic recoding takes place "automatically," at a subconscious level, even in fluent reading, is an almost Freudian theory that observable behavior is determined by specific processes so deep in our unconscious that they are undetectable. It is like saying that in our unconscious we still put our feet on the ground when we cycle because we did so a few times when we were learning to ride.

In a footnote in their book on *Phonological Skills and Learning to Read*, Goswami and Bryant (1990) admitted coming to the "uncomfortable conclusion" that phonological awareness doesn't seem to be of much use to children learning to read (p. 46). An extensive review of research had demonstrated "that there is very little direct evidence that children who are learning to read do rely on letter-sound relationships to help them read words" (p. 46). On the other hand, they noted "a great deal of evidence that these young children take easily and naturally to reading words in other ways ... they either recognize the word as a pattern or remember it as a sequence of letters" (p. 46). Goswami and Bryant's findings have not deterred others from employing the concept of phonological awareness in their theories of reading and pronouncements about instruction, often while citing the work of Goswami and Bryant but disregarding their 1990 conclusion—see Rieben and Perfetti (1991), Brady and Shankweiler (1991), and Gough, Ehri, and Treiman (1992) for numerous examples. The latter volume even includes a chapter by Goswami and Bryant (1992) themselves, citing their 1990 publication but not their uncomfortable conclusion. They still advocate teaching phonological awareness because children attempting to identify new words by analogy make extensive use of rhyme (see later discussion). Even in Finnish, a language that is supposed to have almost perfect sound–symbol correspondence for its alphabetic writing system, teachers have found that a heavy emphasis on phonics instruction may confuse children about the nature of reading and cause comprehension problems later (Korkeamäki & Dreher, 1993).

Scholes and Willis (1991) found that phoneme deletion—answering questions like "What is left if you remove the /k/ sound from *cat*?"—can't be done by nonreaders; it requires *literate* knowledge of alphabetical writing. Read, Yun-Fei, Hong-Yin, and Bao-Qing (1986) deduced from studies with adult Chinese readers that ability to manipulate "speech sounds" depends on knowing alphabetic writing. Liberman and Liberman (1992) themselves estimated that perhaps as many as 75% of children will "discover the alphabetic principle ... no matter how unhelpful the instruction" (p. 345). It might be wondered whether the remaining children are simply the victims of unhelpful instruction.

As stated in the main text (p. 146), "phonemic awareness" refers to a supposed ability to divide spoken words (or artificial words) into discrete sounds, represented by letters of the alphabet, alone or in combination. This is the complex system of "sound–spelling relationships" analyzed in chapter 9. However, the flow of speech is not broken down into discrete words (see p. 34), and the sounds that constitute speech are complexly produced and interrelated by various parts of the entire vocal apparatus (vocal cord, throat, mouth, tongue, nasal passages) and can't be isolated into discrete units, either by people or by electronic equipment. In other words, phonemes are artifacts, invented to correspond with the letter patterns of written words. They can only be detected by people who can read, or who have been specially trained with a limited set of sounds for a limited array of letters, and have no conceivable role in reading.

Why does phonemic awareness survive as a concept? Because it sounds reasonable to anyone believing that reading is a matter of decoding print to speech (the fascination with the alphabet), because it seems to account for the failure of phonics instruction, and because contrived "research" into the impossible relationship can be claimed to be "scientific" (and other research "unscientific").

Krashen (1999b) reviewed 15 studies of phonemic awareness training and found it had greater effect on tests of phonemic awareness than on tests of real words and reading comprehension. He has also reported that many children and adults with low phonemic awareness learn to read, as a result of massive amounts of interesting and comprehensible reading (Krashen, 2001a, 2001b, 2001c). In a detailed and impassioned critique of what she called the "Spin Doctors of Science," Taylor (1998) condemned many aspects of studies claiming to support phonemic awareness and massive phonics, from the statistical and sampling techniques involved to conclusions drawn from data presented, not to mention use made of those conclusions in media sound bites, and by politicians and the publishing industry.

Finally, it might be fair to consider what children think about phonemic awareness training. Castiglioni-Spalten and Ehri (2003), in a routine report on the effects of various kinds of word-segmentation training with 5-year-old children, noted a marked reluctance on the part of the children to cooperate or to pay attention. In a pilot study the experimenter, who followed a "fully prescribed and clearly scripted" training procedure, recorded "several off-task and resistence behaviors committed by students: refusing to use the mirror [used in part of the training]; leaving their seats without permission; playing with the blocks by building a tower, house, or train; throwing the blocks on the floor; talking about extraneous topics; interacting with others in the room; and expressing reluctance to finish the instruction" (p. 36). During the actual study, "students rarely committed such behaviors more than twice because the experimenter discouraged them" (p. 43)—by reminding students that she would report back to their teacher about how well they did ... and also by using a screen to isolate the children from distractions in the room (p. 36.) It would be hard to find a better description of induced boredom.

Word Identification by Analogy

The argument in the chapter that unfamiliar words may often be identified by analogy doesn't entail that phonological recoding is necessary for analogies to be made. Analogies can be made on the basis of visual characteristics—the beginning of *medication* looks like the beginning of *medical*. Goswami and Bryant (1990; see also Goswami, 1986, 1990) held to the view that learners confronted by words they are unable to identify immediately frequently attempt to do so by piecing together the known sound of the initial consonant or consonant cluster (the "onset") with the rhyming sound of the rest of the syllable of a similarly spelled word. The unknown word *teak*, for example, is likely to rhyme with the known word *beak* and *fright* with *night*. The view is usually referred to as "onset and rime" (employing the archaic spelling to better exemplify the basic assertion that words that rhyme often share similar spelling patterns). The onset–rime unit is seen as intermediate in size between individual phones and syllables, more predictable from its spelling than a single phoneme. See also Treiman (1992) and Treiman, Goswami, and Bruck (1990) for reviews of studies of children's abilities to detect rhymes, alliteration, and other partial aspects of spoken words.

However, Savage (2001) reevaluated claims relating rhymed sounds and reading, and concluded that the issue must remain controversial; any apparent correlations may be due to orthographic analogies (i.e., the visual structure of words) rather than the sounds. Goswami responded in the same issue (Goswami, 2001). See also Macmillan (2002). Christensen (1997) reviewed studies of relationship of onset and rhyme and phonemes, and concluded that "Overall, the picture of learning to read that emerges from this study is one of diversity and complexity. Children appear to acquire a range of phonological skills and literacy-related knowledge in a variety of ways." (p. 357). Like many publications, this article talks about the identification of new words in the context of "learning to read," that is, effects attributable to different kinds of instruction, rather than with what children learn as a consequence of reading, independently of whatever instructional regime they may be put into.

Spelling

Goswami and Bryant (1990), whose uncomfortable conclusion that phonological awareness may not help children learn to read has been noted, nevertheless proposed that such instruction should be continued because it will help them to spell. Unfortunately, children who spell words the way they are pronounced, as most children do naturally at the beginning (Read, 1971), spell poorly. Spelling by rule is also not an efficient strategy for spelling most common words (Brown, 1970). Although clues may be obtained from known words with similar meanings, the main requirement for good spelling is to *remember* individual spellings (Smith, 1994), a requirement that is not relevant to helping children learn to read. Gillooly (1973) argued that there is no justification for attempts to change the current spelling of English, which he said increases reading speed and is nearly optimum for learning to read. Venezky (1999) gave a scholarly analysis of the complexity and history of American English spelling, skewed by his reiterated belief that some "rules" must be taught.

Spelling is conspicuous, and probably the only aspect of writing that most people feel competent to pass judgment on, so errors are treated almost as antisocial behavior. As a consequence of this sensitivity, there is a widespread perception that most people (including often ourselves) spell badly. But in a review article entitled "How Well Do People Spell?" Krashen (1993a) reported that in self-generated writing, college freshmen achieved an accuracy of from 97.9% to 99.8% of the words written, although society demands perfection. He commented that it is unlikely that such high levels of competence occur from formal instruction; ability to recite rules doesn't make students any better spellers, nor does having errors pointed out. He concluded that the ability can only come from reading.

In an earlier review, Krashen and White (1991) went back almost a century to reanalyze two classic studies (Rice, 1897; Cornman, 1902) of the relation between spelling instruction and proficiency between Grade 3 and Grade 8, both of which found little difference as a result of instruction. Research through the 20th century suggested nothing different. The analysis raised the same doubts in the contemporary researchers that prompted the original studies—whether the direct teaching of spelling is worth the trouble.

NOTES TO CHAPTER 10,
THE IDENTIFICATION OF MEANING, pp. 156–177

Effects of Meaningful Context

Meaningfulness clearly has a substantial role in facilitating the identification of words in reading, reducing their uncertainty from at least 12 bits (the equivalent of 4,096 equiprobable alternatives) for words in isolation to fewer than 8 bits (256 alternatives) for words in context (chap. 4 notes). It is really irrelevant to talk of letters at this stage—letters are not normally a concern when meaningful text is read. But as a yardstick, it is interesting to recall from the chapter 4 discussion that the uncertainty of letters falls from 4.7 bits to scarcely 1 bit when context is meaningful, enabling perception of four times as much of a line of print. Not only can twice as many words be identified in a single glance when they are in a meaningful context, thus overcoming bottlenecks of information processing and memory, but problems of ambiguity and the gulf between surface structure and meaning are removed by the prior elimination from consideration of unlikely alternatives. Context has its effect because it contributes information that reduces the uncertainty of individual words through *sequential redundancy*; it places constraints on what each individual word might be. Sequential redundancy is usable only if reflected in the prior knowledge, or nonvisual information, that the reader can bring to bear. That is why I stress that the context must be *meaningful*, with all the relative connotations of that word. If a particular context is not comprehensible to a reader, or if for one reason or another the reader is reluctant to take advantage of it, then the context might just as well be nonsense, a random arrangement of marks on the page.

Meaningful context as I have been using the term exercises its constraints on word occurrence in two ways, syntactic and semantic. These are two types of restriction on the particular words an author can select—or a reader predict—at any time. (There are other constraints on authors, such as the limited set of words a reader might be expected to understand.) Choice of words is always limited by what we want to say (semantics) and how we want to say it (syntax). I have not tried to separate the effects of syntax and semantics in this discussion for the simple reason that I have not found a good way to do so. The theoretical analysis of chapter 2 argued that the two are inseparable—that without meaning it is pointless to talk about grammar. (Also as outlined in chap. 2, words can also be constrained by more general *situational* contexts; for example, there is a very small and highly predictable set of alternative words likely to occur on a toothpaste tube.)

There is no shortage of research demonstrating the powerful facilitatory effect of meaningful context on word identification. Indeed, there is no evidence to the contrary. But I must reiterate that *reading doesn't usually involve or rely on word identification.* Meaningful context makes reading for meaning possible and word identification unnecessary. The fact that meaningful context makes individual words easier to identify is basically as irrelevant as the fact that individual letters are easier to identify in words; the research evidence is merely a demonstration of the effect of meaningful context. Even when reading aloud is involved, so that the accurate identification of words is required, the prior apprehension of meaning is an important prerequisite. Reading aloud is difficult if prior comprehension is limited, and if word identification is given priority there will be interference with comprehension (Howe & Singer, 1975). Sharkey and Mitchell (1985) showed that word recognition in meaningful contexts is frequently minimal and not very predictable, especially when the context is itself a predictable "script"—when it is a familiar narrative, in other words. Levy (1978) reported that changing the wording but not the sense of written language did not affect a short-term memory task—meanings, not specific words, are retained whenever possible, even for brief periods. Sometimes context leads us astray, evidence again for the potency of meaning and prediction. Carpenter and Daneman (1981) gave several examples of "garden path" texts where context misleads rather than facilitates, such as "Cinderella could not go to the ball. There were tears in her dress." Crowder and Wagner (1991) show that readers use meaning from other words to help identify specific words in text; see also Goldsmith-Phillips (1989).

Experienced readers read familiar text at the highest possible level of comprehension, phrases if possible, then words— this applies to Chinese and Japanese logographic readers as well as to English language alphabetic readers (Tao & Healy, 2002). Experienced readers of both systems make more small unit errors (like letters in English text) in familiar than unfamiliar larger units. We all attend to the broader picture rather than the unimportant detail. Masonheimer, Drum, and Ehri (1984) observed that children may identify labels correctly even when a letter has been changed (like "Xepsi" for "Pepsi"). They reported this with some concern, because unlike the children, they were looking for mastery of letters, not of entire words or sense.

Context and Prediction

Some theorists have argued that context and prediction play a smaller role in reading than proposed in this book. But they tend to use the terms more narrowly than I do. For example, Stanovich (1992) concluded from eye-movement studies that "context effects" are minimal because visual information rapidly blurs outside the foveal area in the center of the field of view. Earlier, Stanovich (1986) asserted that poor readers depend more on prediction than fluent readers. But I see context in terms of a reader's understanding at any given point in the text of what it is about, enhanced by what has already been seen behind and sometimes ahead of where the eyes happen to fall. Such advance knowledge, primarily nonvisual rather than visual, facilitates reading by reducing the reader's uncertainty. There is a tendency to equate prediction with "guessing," a term I would never use to describe what fluent readers do. My definition of prediction—the prior elimination of unlikely alternatives—is precisely what makes experienced readers so effective when reading texts whose language and subject matter are familiar to them. Once again, everything hinges on the purposes of the reader and on the reader's freedom to be flexible and selective.

Various studies have demonstrated the readiness of children to make use of context in early reading (if they are so permitted), for example, Klein, Klein, and Bertino (1974), Golinkoff (1975/1976), Doehring (1976), and McFarland and Rhodes (1978). Rosinski, Golinkoff, and Kukish (1975) concluded that meaning is irresistible to children; it can interfere with performance on a task because they can't ignore it. Such studies also tend to show that use of context and reading ability increase together. This correlation is often attributed to the fact that better readers can make more use of context; less often, the possibility is considered that use of context makes better readers. Studies of children's misreadings tend to highlight the important fact that many of the errors, especially those made by better readers, preserve the meaning of the context and also that errors that make a difference to meaning are often subsequently corrected by children who are reading for meaning (and therefore are not errors that need be a great cause for concern). Children who read more literally, perhaps because of an emphasis on "accuracy" during instruction, may, however, make nonsensical errors without being aware of them.

The paradigm example of a child learning to read by meaning alone, without any possibility of decoding to sound, must be that of Helen Keller. Henderson (1976) reported the case of a deaf child who learned to recognize 4,400 printed words in 9 months at the age of 6 by relating them to manual signs in a meaningful context, basically in response to the child's own spontaneous inquiries. Ewoldt (1981) demonstrated that deaf children read in the same meaningful way as hearing children.

"Dual Process"

The most popular assumption about comprehension in experimentally based research on reading is centered on the notion that there is an "internal lexicon" in the head—a kind of mental dictionary—where the meanings of words are stored. Comprehension is achieved when definitions of the words that we read are "looked up" in the internal lexicon. The concept is a metaphor, not an explanation. It fails to explain how the internal definitions are understood and doesn't allow for selectivity, prediction, and all the other things that readers normally do. The idea actually precludes certain explanations—for example, that comprehension might on occasion be a pictorial or sensory image or a physical response, that comprehension is a state rather than a process, or that meaning is brought to language. It papers over the profundity of understanding. Yet the notion that such a lexicon actually exists is often taken for granted, and it is simply assumed that words are understood by being identified and "routed" to the internal lexicon. This is a great theoretical convenience, as it permits discussion of hypothetical "routes" between eye and understanding without any consideration of the nature of the terminus. Understanding can be ignored simply as "lexical access." Among many discussions of the internal lexicon, see Rieben and Perfetti (1991). Miller and Fellbaum (1991) discussed the enormous problems of constructing an actual lexicon of English—their database of 46,000 entries includes 26 different hierarchical relationships for nouns, up to 10 levels deep with at least three different categories of distinguishing features—parts, attributes, and functions. Nevertheless such semantic decomposition is popular (see also Miller & Johnson-Laird, 1975). A notorious example is McCawley's (1968) "Kill = cause become not alive," ridiculed together with all theories of innate grammar by Robinson (1975), who decried what he calls "linguistic atomism." Fodor (1981) said most words are not decomposable. If people know 50,000 word meanings, there must be close to 50,000 "primitive concepts."

Dual process theorists see two ways of getting from visual information to the internal lexicon—direct (which means an unmediated loop between word and meaning, similar to the general point of view of the present book but not necessarily in the same direction) and by phonological recoding. The idea is that the lexicon contains not only meanings but also spellings and pronunciations, information about syntactic functions, and possibly featural descriptions of various kinds. All these are alternative ways in which the lexicon can be entered, both for recognition and for production (writing and spelling).

Most researchers say both routes are possible but put different emphasis on each. Some theorists, like Gough (e.g., Gough & Walsh, 1991), argue that only a phonological route to the lexicon exists: that reading is a process of decoding the "cipher" of English spelling. Ehri (1992) claimed that access is through the spelling patterns of words, without necessarily recoding into phonological form (which nonetheless usually becomes available with recognition of meaning). Ehri called this the *visual-phonological route*, which is used even for "direct access." She cited evidence that children "learning to read by sight" find *msk* easier to learn and remember as the word "mask" than an arbitrary spelling like *uhe*, though nonreaders don't. Some orthographic utilization in word identification is obvious, for example, in distinguishing homophones like *their* from *there*. The term *orthographic* structure (literally, visual structure) is usually taken to refer specifically to spelling, although it can also refer to the shape or featural detail of words as a whole and to arrangements of letters, individually or in clusters, seen as visual configurations, not as guides to pronunciation. Walters, Komoda, and Arbuckle (1985) offered experimental evidence that phonological recoding plays a very small part in skilled reading and that it is unnecessary unless there are detailed memory demands. It is often assumed that decoding (or recoding) written language into speech will automatically provide meaning for written words. But spoken words must themselves be interpreted and they can be even more ambiguous than written words. Including a phonological loop in reading constitutes an additional step, not a shortcut, for understanding.

NOTES TO CHAPTER 11,
READING, WRITING, AND THINKING, pp. 178–193

Comprehension and Thinking

Reading and thinking are fundamentally inseparable, especially when reading is discussed or researched under the heading of comprehension. Vygotsky (1978) defined thinking as "internalized action," and reading might be regarded as "internalized experience." In a special "literacy" issue of *Harvard Educational Review*, Scribner and Cole (1978) made the important point that literacy doesn't change the basic way in which people reason. In any aspect of thinking, what we know already—our "prior knowledge"—is obviously an important factor in what we can accomplish. Tierney and Cunningham (1984) discussed the importance of building up and "activating" background knowledge prior to reading. Basically this is common sense—the more we know about a topic before reading, the more we understand. But there is a decidedly mechanistic tone about theorizing that talks of the provision, utilization, and activation of any aspect of thought, which in practice can lead teachers to spend more time on preparation for reading than on reading itself, although reading is a major source of prior knowledge. Undergraduates given scenic photographs to look at and descriptive paragraphs to read remembered a number of pictures and paragraphs a week later, but also remembered (with a high degree of confidence) photographs they had not seen—the images they had created from paragraphs they had read (Intraub & Hoffman, 1992).

Kimmel and MacGinitie (1984) showed that children may perseverate with inappropriate hypotheses while reading (and presumably in other circumstances). This is not necessarily the fault of the readers, however. Children can often cope well with paragraphs or entire texts where the "main idea" is at the beginning. But many school texts are not written in this way. Kimmel and MacGinitie show that school texts often begin with examples, analogies, and even refutations, and make their point clear only at the end. Nicholson and Imlach (1981) found that prior knowledge and text could compete when children were required to answer questions about their reading. Eight-year-olds could incorrectly impose their own expectations on narrative, but on the other hand they could also "be assailed by every word in the paragraph"—a phrase first used in an important article by Thorndike (1977). Paradoxically, O'Brien and Myers (1985) demonstrated that comprehension difficulty could occasionally improve recall, because readers spent more time looking back.

Comprehension in reading doesn't necessarily take place immediately or all at once. Samuels (1979) and O'Shea, Sindelar, and O'Shea (1985) showed, not surprisingly, that reading the same text more than once improves fluency, comprehension, and memory, especially for "poor readers" or for difficult texts. The effect is particularly pronounced if readers are cued to read for comprehension rather than for accuracy. This research underlines an important general point: It is usually more effective to read a text *quickly*, more than once, than to plod through it slowly once only. Initial "skimming," and even browsing through an entire book by glancing at occasional pages, adds to prior knowledge and facilitates subsequent efforts to make sense of the entire text.

Reading Speed

Carver (1985) criticized studies that claim to demonstrate fast rates of reading. He asserted that "comprehension" is rarely adequately defined or measured in such studies and held that unless readers comprehend the author's thoughts on a sentence-by-sentence basis (a procedure to which he gives the special name of *rauding*), then "skimming" rather than reading is taking place. Demonstration of rauding under laboratory conditions involves tests of recall of detail that constitute great impositions on memory. Not surprisingly, Carver's experimental subjects fail to meet such a criterion at speeds of more than 600 words a minute. But it can be argued that no one reading in normal circumstances would ever try to remember the detail of every sentence of a novel or even of a business letter. Inability to remember detail doesn't mean that a book was not comprehended or even that every sentence in that book was not comprehended at the appropriate time. Carver's own studies showed that "speed readers" were able to write an adequate 100-word summary of a 6,000-word text after perusing it for 4 minutes. Carver (1992) subsequently reported that college students typically read to memorize at 138 words per minute (wpm), to study for a multiple-choice test at 299 wpm, to "comprehend complete thoughts in sentences" at 300 wpm, to skim at 450 wpm, and to scan for a target word at 600 wpm. He refers to these different reading rates as gears and says that "shifting" flexibility is needed.

Saenger (1991) discussed how silent reading facilitates rapid reading and the scanning of text, subordinating the constraints of the text to the aims and biases of the reader. The purpose of the spaces between words in alphabetic writing, Saenger argued, is to facilitate silent reading. British researchers Harding, Beech, and Sneddon (1985) found that the reason more proficient readers aged from 5 to 9 years old appeared to "process larger units of information" was that they read faster and therefore had less of a memory handicap. Potter (1984), using a technique that delivers individual words at a controlled rate to readers (Forster, 1970), found that college students preferred a rate of 360 words a minute. At 720 words a minute, almost all the words could be read but ideas "seem to pass through the mind without being adequately retained"—on a sentence-by-sentence basis, at least. At 960 to 1,680 words a minute, most viewers felt they could not see most of the words or understand individual sentences, although they could be shown to have acquired some understanding. Potter, Kroll, Yachzel, and Harris (1980) corroborated that it is memory that takes time in reading. Increasing the rate of reading from 180 to 600 words a minute left comprehension unaffected but reduced memory for detail.

Comprehension and Context

There is some research suggesting that "poor" readers use context more than fluent readers (Stanovich, 1980, 1981, 1986; Stanovich, Cunningham, & Feeman, 1984; Perfetti & Roth, 1981; Perfetti, Goldman, & Hogaboam, 1979), contrary to the position argued in this book that inexperienced readers use less nonvisual information. The resolution of this apparent paradox may be that when reading is difficult, all readers *need* context more, and as Thompson (1981) pointed out, "good and poor readers" reading the same text are not doing equivalent reading—one is reading easy material and the other difficult. In the experimental conditions, inexperienced readers are forced to rely on context and every other source of available help. But there is a related factor. Experimenters, especially those with a cognitive science orientation, typically define "context" as a few words on the page on either side of a "target word" in contrived situations that emphasize word identification or memory. There is much more to nonvisual information than adjacent words on a page. Nonvisual information includes all of a reader's relevant prior knowledge, plus understanding of the text *as a whole*. In fact, adjacent words on the page should be considered *visual information*—they are not "context" so much as additional features to be analyzed if individual word identification is emphasized and difficult. And the less nonvisual information a reader can bring to bear, the more visual information, in the form of distinctive features from the text, needs to be identified. In such circumstances, readers may need supplementary features outside the boundaries of target words in order to identify those words. The eyes may appear to focus on individual words during reading (Just & Carpenter, 1980), but they have to be focused somewhere. The particular focal point doesn't necessarily indicate that words are being identified one at a time.

Benefits of Reading

Krashen (1993a) provided an excellent and concise summary of the benefits of "free voluntary reading" with regard to reading ability, comprehension, vocabulary, grammar, spelling, writing, second language learning, attitude toward school, career choice, public esteem, and self-esteem. He discussed the significance and value of every kind of reading that learners will voluntarily engage in, including comic books and "romances." New Zealand researcher Warwick Elley (1989) showed that vocabulary increases with reading—or with listening to stories. Elley (1992) reviewed reading instruction and achievement in 32 countries—mostly from 1,500 to 3,000 students in each, tested by researchers in their own country on ability to understand narrative, expository text, and "documents" (like charts, maps, and lists of instructions). Factors that consistently differentiated high and low scoring countries were large school and classroom libraries, frequent silent reading, and story reading aloud by the teacher. Age of beginning instruction (up to age 7), and even instruction in a language unfamiliar to the learner (English in Singapore), did not make a difference. Torrance and Olson (1985) reported that good readers speak in more complex utterances and use a wider range of metalinguistic words related to thinking and language. For discussions of how literacy can make a difference to an individual's knowledge of "language as an object," see Olson and Torrance (1991), particularly the chapter by Scholes and Willis (1991) arguing that learning to read promotes ability to talk and an understanding of grammar. West, Stanovich, and Mitchell (1993) questioned individuals waiting alone in an airport waiting area—111 who were "reading recreationally" for 10 continuous minutes and 106 others who did not read at all for 10 continuous minutes (with almost equal numbers of females and males in each group). They found significant differences in vocabulary size and "cultural knowledge" in favor of the readers, who also tended to be somewhat older and to have had more educational experience. West, Stanovich, and Mitchell also discussed evidence that there are much greater opportunities for learning new words from reading than from conversation or watching television—popular magazines, for example, providing three times the number of opportunities. Reitsma (1983) reported that experienced beginning readers can learn the "graphemic structure" (spelling) of new words as well as their meaning with little practice.

Eckhoff (1983) showed how children's reading influences what they write. If their primers contained "stories" in which each short sentence was on a separate line, children wrote their own stories in the same way. If their reading was richer and more conventional, so was their writing. Calkins (1980) found that children learned more about punctuation from their reading than from instruction and used more punctuation as a consequence. The children also adopted stylistic features of the texts they read, such as beginning sentences with "And" or ending them with "too." For a general argument that children learn to write by reading, see Smith (1994). Conversely, Tierney and Shanahan (1991) noted that children who write more are more enthusiastic and competent readers.

For the richness and diversity of the roles literacy plays in individual lives (without detracting from the overriding significance of oral language and experience generally), see Heath (1986). Csikszentmihalyi (1990) originated a concept of "flow" to denote the uniquely satisfying experience of being deeply and effortlessly involved in an activity to the extent of forgetting oneself, time, and everything else. Reading, he said, is perhaps the most often mentioned flow activity in the world. Nell (1988) described the marked physiological effects that reading can have, both arousing and relaxing.

On the other hand, it can be also argued that literacy is often overrated (Pattanayak, 1991; Smith, 1989). Nonliterates should not be regarded as "problems" to be cured, eradicated, or declared war on, nor should they be held responsible for social and economic crises of society. Graff (1987a, 1987b) provided compendious discussions of the history of literacy, the misunderstandings that surround it, and its social roles and functions, including a critical review of the "crisis" approach to literacy and alarms about declining standards or abilities. He asserted that the efficacy of literacy in improving an individual's life is a myth; literacy is a technology, or set of techniques, not an agent of change for individuals or societies. The "oral world" (of which writing is an extension rather than a replacement) is of continuing importance. In a more concise presentation of his views, Graff (1986) concluded that as

far as the current state of the world is concerned, "Literacy is neither the major problem, nor is it the main solution."

NOTES TO CHAPTER 12,
LEARNING ABOUT THE WORLD, pp. 194–211

Language Learning

Clark and Hecht (1983) reviewed research showing how comprehension precedes the production of language. Bridges, Sinha,
and Walkerdine (1981) demonstrated how infants figure out the
intentions of their mothers, taking into account the circumstances in which their mothers are talking, in order to understand what they are saying. Nelson (1985) proposed that children
learn primarily through being involved in meaningful events with
adults. The reasoning for why learning and comprehension are
the same, the consequence of engagement, demonstrations, and
sensitivity, is in Smith (1998). Krashen (2003) has long maintained that learning (which he terms *acquisition*) is a subconscious process, effortless and involuntary; we are not usually
aware of the knowledge we acquire. His "comprehension hypothesis" proposes that language acquisition takes place when we "understand messages" (not necessarily messages addressed to us
personally). Brown and Palincsar (1989) demonstrated that
"comprehension-learning" is social; children learn how to understand texts through discussion with other readers. Gallistel
(1990) argued that children learn language by analogy rather than
by rules, relating language they don't know to language they do
know. See also Fosnot (1996).

Vocabulary

In extensive research, Anglin (1993) found that children knew
10,000 words by their sixth birthday, and learned 4,000 new roots
between Grade 1 and Grade 5, leading to a further 14,000 new
words. The bulk of this expansion was done by "morphological
problem solving"—breaking new words down into component
morphemes. See also Nagy and Scott (2000) and E. Clark (1993).
In an intensive study, Carey (1978) estimated that 6-year-olds have
mastered (to some degree) an average of 14,000 words, noting that

"this massive vocabulary growth seems to occur without much help from teachers." According to Carey (1978), there is first a "fast mapping" when a child hypothesizes a probable general meaning for a new word. A gradual process of refining and adding "partial knowledge" of meaning ensues on successive encounters, with from 4 to 10 encounters required for word learning to be "complete." Rice (1990) described "QUIL"—quick incidental learning—with fast mapping often occurring when the word is first encountered, followed by a long period of refinement. The initial partial comprehension of a new word includes both a meaning and a syntactic role; it doesn't require explicit assistance from adults. In one 12-minute exposure to an animated television program, 5-year-olds on average "picked up" the meanings of 5 test words such as *gramophone, nurturant, viola, makeshift, malicious*, and *artisan* that occurred seven times each. Three-year-olds picked up an average of 1.5 of these words. Mandler (1992) analyzed how babies move from preverbal perceptions of different kinds of object to conceptions that can become language. Markman (1992) examined the assumptions that 2-year-olds appear to make in learning words concerning "whole objects," taxonomic relations, and mutual exclusivity. The word *dog* is likely to mean the whole animal, not a part of it or its color; the word is likely to apply to similar objects (a cat might be a dog, but not an umbrella), and objects will not have more than one name.

Nagy and Herman (1987) recalibrated earlier research results and calculated an *annual* growth in vocabulary between Grade 3 and Grade 12 of from 2,000 to nearly 4,000 words, and a median of 3,500. Nagy, Osborn, Winsor, and O'Flahavan (1994) analyzed 10,000 new words an average fifth-grade reader might encounter in a year (an avid fifth-grade reader might encounter several times that number), finding that more than half were clearly related to words already known, but 1,000 were "truly new." Skilled readers deal with these new words on the basis of context, phonics, or *structural analysis*, meaning familiarity with parts of words, including grammatical and meaningful units like *s* and *ed*. Structural analysis also helps spelling, for example, with segments like *ceive*, which has no clear meaning on its own but is part of several words. The authors note that in comparison with phonics, very little attention has been paid to structural analysis, which they say begins in early childhood, both to understand and coin new words, obviously without instruction. Nevertheless, the authors propose including word analysis as part of reading instruction—without recognizing that when outsiders take charge of what readers are able to understand and learn for themselves, interventions intended to be helpful often become obstacles.

Children required to learn specific new words in contrived experimental contexts—typically artificial words embedded in half a dozen unrelated sentences—usually find the task difficult. McKeown (1985), for example, required 30 fifth graders to figure out the meaning of artificial words in short sentences like "Eating lunch is a narp thing to do," and found that good readers could accomplish the task, but not poor readers (who presumably had difficulty reading the sentences in the first place). She concluded that "the meaning-acquisition process" is complex and difficult, even for high-ability readers. But this may be a case of what might be called the Laboratory Fallacy, which asserts that children who have difficulty on artificially contrived learning (or comprehension or memory) tasks will have similar difficulty in all situations. Schatz and Baldwin (1986) showed that "context cues" are not usually reliable predictors of word meaning—not in experimental situations where texts are brief and assembled in a contrived manner. The more naturalistic approach of Nagy and his colleagues that I have just cited suggests a different conclusion, although the technique of embedding unfamiliar words in minimal context is common in laboratories and classrooms.

McKeown (1993) showed that conventional dictionary definitions hardly facilitate learning word meanings. Instruction often focuses on words and meanings that are either too common or too uncommon to require attention, and examples given are often misleading. McKeown suggested alternatives that focus on *describing* in familiar language the circumstances in which the word is usually ("prototypically") used. Thus instead of defining *morbid* as "not healthy or normal," she proposed "showing a great interest in horrible gruesome details, especially about death"; and for *transitory*, instead of "passing soon or quickly, lasting only a short time" (which led to student sentences like "the train was transitory"), she suggested "describes a mood or feeling that only lasts a short time." McKeown observed that such changes still don't make the traditional method of looking up a word and writing a sentence a good way of building vocabulary. Miller and Fellbaum (1991) offered a detailed discussion of complex problems of definitions and dictionaries, and Schwanenflugel (1991) provided an interesting edited volume on the psychology of word meanings.

Motivation

The role of motivation in learning should be clarified, especially because failure to learn is frequently attributed to lack of motivation. However, learning continually takes place in the absence of conscious motivation—for example, the effortless growth of vocabulary. And the presence of motivation doesn't guarantee learning. We have all failed to learn things we have been highly motivated to learn, on which we may have expended considerable effort and "time on task." Learning normally depends not on effort but on the demonstrations, collaboration, engagement, and sensitivity discussed in this chapter. Interest and expectation of learning are better predictors of learning than overt motivation. At best, motivation has the beneficial effect of putting learners into situations where demonstrations and collaboration are likely to be found. And of course, anyone motivated not to learn, or anticipating failure, is likely to find the expectation fulfilled.

NOTES TO CHAPTER 13,
LEARNING ABOUT WRITTEN LANGUAGE, pp. 212–232

Learning to Read

Some of the most significant research into children's developing understanding of literacy has been done not by educators or psychologists—who tend to look at individuals in isolation, or in a personal relationship to "knowledge"—but by sociologists and anthropologists. The edited volume of Goelman, Oberg, and Smith (1984) contains summaries and reviews of research into the social basis of preschool literacy by workers in a number of disciplines and also outlines the prevailing methodologies. The primary method of research is not experimental, but observational. *Ethnographic* is the technical term for such research, also called "naturalistic research," and (by Yetta Goodman, 1978, 1980) "kid watching." Two of the main findings of this research are that children in all cultures develop insights into the forms and functions of written language before school and that these insights are based on meaning and use. The research also shows that learning about reading can't be separated from learning about writing, and about how written language is used.

The research has also made clear that children don't need to be economically privileged or the recipients of special kinds of instructional support in order to learn about reading and writing. Ferreiro (1978, 1985), for example, who demonstrated how 3- and 4-year-olds gain insights about letters, words, and sentences, did much of her work in the slums of Mexico City with children whose parents were illiterate. The fact that early readers have not necessarily had advantages is also made by M. Clark (1976) in her classic book on *Young Fluent Readers*, many of whom came from large poor families and were not "good risks" for reading instruction in school. Research shows that children raised in middle-class homes with well-educated parents generally do well in school, while other children tend to be behind when they start school and stay behind. Individuals— students and parents—are usually held responsible for this. But Neuman and Celano (2001) claimed that ecological research, which looks at contexts larger than family settings, shows that the environment of lower income families in and around Los Angeles tends to be strikingly lacking in places for reading, reading material, labels, logos, and books at home, in preschool, in local libraries, and in public library branches. There is social isolation and there are unequal opportunities. Duke (2000) found the same imbalance in the Greater Boston area. Not only were there more books and other materials in richer classrooms, but a greater proportion were displayed and made available for use. In math, higher socioeconomic status children studied "architectural shapes" while lower did mindless workbook tasks. Unequal library opportunities are also stressed by Krashen (1995). There are innumerable studies showing differences between the schools and schooling of poor and better off children, from the streets around the schools and their hallways and classrooms to materials and learning opportunities made available. See especially *Savage Inequalities: Children in America's Schools* (Kozol, 1991).

In a poignant article entitled *Literacy at Calhoun Colored School 1892–1945*, Willis (2002) examined the philosophy behind the education of African American children at a private independent boarding school in Alabama, which tried sincerely to raise skills levels of students while avoiding the power that full literacy might bring. The author commented that it is fashionable today to look to science, medicine, and psychology for explanations when the literacy development of any group differs from the mainstream, and to look for methods that will work for all. When these methods fail, students, their families, their communities, and their language

are blamed. Willis called for recognition of the relationship between power and knowledge as a primary factor in the way all students are educated and their performance assessed.

Clay (1992/1993) reported from extensive experience that the
best preparation for literacy is opportunities for conversation. She
referred specifically to bilingual schools in New Zealand concerned with the survival of the Maori language, and gave several
other international examples where children read to in preschool
had improved reading and speaking abilities in later years. If no
books are available, competent storytellers can prepare children
for literacy learning. Clay noted that children under 5 years of age
are "amazingly good" at learning and losing languages, depending
on the opportunities they have to use them. The least complicated
entry into literacy learning is to begin to read and write in the language already spoken. For further discussion of language policies
and literacy learning in multilingual situations, see Elley and
Mangubhai (1983).

Proficiency in oral language is not a prerequisite for learning to
read. Rottenberg and Searfoss (1992) showed that hearing-impaired children in a mixed preschool class learn about literacy in
the same ways hearing children do—without direct instruction—
and also learn about the hearing world. Hartman and Kretschmer
(1992) reported that hearing-impaired teenage students also learn
about reading by talking and writing about what they read. For a
summary of research demonstrating that children with "special
needs" don't learn to read and to write differently from other learners and don't require special kinds of instruction (although they
may need more time), see Truax and Kretschmer (1993).

Routman (2003) asserted that teachers should gradually hand
over responsibility for literacy development to learners, and explained how this involves demonstrations by the teacher, demonstrations with students, guided practice, and independent practice.

Free Voluntary Reading

Krashen (1993a) is an energetic advocate of "free voluntary reading" and reading for pleasure, in any genre including comic books
and romances. He claimed that most people are able to read and
write—there is no "literacy crisis"—but many don't do so very well,
not for want of instruction but because of lack of experience. He de-
plored the fact that many public and school libraries are closed or
starved for funds that are relatively plentiful for more structured
kinds of reading instruction and tests. Krashen and another popu-

lar free reading crusader, Jim Trelease, are so anxious to see children have the maximum opportunity and encouragement to read that they proposed that school libraries follow the model of commercial bookstores and facilitate eating and drinking among the books (Trelease & Krashen, 1996). They preemptively responded to predictable objections.

Von Sprecken and Krashen (2002) found that contrary to popular stereotypes, there is little evidence of a decline in interest in recreational reading during adolescent years, or of negative attitudes to reading (although both occur with school-related reading). Reading is also a powerful incentive for reading. Following a suggestion by Trelease that one positive reading experience—one "home run" book—is enough to establish someone as a reader, Von Sprecken, Jiyong, and Krashen (2000) questioned 214 fourth-grade students in three elementary schools in the Los Angeles area. Over half the students said they became interested in reading after just one book, which they could name (including "scary books," comics, and popular series). Cho and Krashen (1994) found that three Korean and one Mexican female speakers, aged from 21 to 35, all studying English as a second language, became "addicted" to the easy reading of a romance series highly popular with high school female students, voluntarily reading up to 23 volumes in a month, with dramatic gains in vocabulary, ability, and confidence to converse in English.

Commenting on the fact that many studies have shown a strong relationship between poverty and reading scores, Krashen (2002) drew on research to show that children from low-income families have very little access to books, in school and out, compared with children from high-income families. He argued that "readability" systems that direct children to certain books limit their choices of books they might understand and enjoy. Elley and Mangubhai (1983) reported success in Third World countries with a "book flood" program—based on the assumption that children can overcome the disadvantages of inadequate exposure to reading and poor motivation if their classrooms are flooded with high-interest illustrated reading books and the teacher helps them to read together. An updated, expanded discussion of widespread adoption in Fiji, Niue, Singapore, and South Africa was presented in a paper by Elley (1996).

Reading to Children

Reading to children is frequently recommended, although it is not always made clear what exactly the practice is expected to achieve.

Obviously, reading to children may interest them in stories (or whatever else is read to them) and also may demonstrate the interest and utility that other people find in reading. But every occasion when a child is read to can also be a reading (and writing) lesson, an opportunity to learn more about the conventions and purposes of written language. Taylor and Strickland (1986) described many family story-reading sessions and their benefits to children. Durkin (1984) studied 23 children of "average intelligence" who had frequently transferred schools, who became "successful readers" (reading above "grade level" by Grade 5). She found that the children had supportive parents who liked stories and read to them. Dombey (1988) also discussed children's movement into the nature of stories and into reading from hearing a story read. Eldredge (1990) showed that children learn more when they are helped to read—and therefore can read material that would otherwise be too difficult for them.

Heath and Thomas (1984) provided a fascinating case study of a teenaged, unemployed high school dropout mother of two (coauthor Charlene Thomas) herself learning to read in the course of helping her children learn to read. Another of Shirley Brice Heath's many insightful contributions is an article entitled "What No Bedtime Story Means" (Heath, 1982d). For more on Vygotsky and education, see Moll (1990).

Literacy and Schooling

The fact that children often learn so much before school and that cultural influences are so important doesn't release schools from responsibility or provide convenient justification for failures of instruction. If children have not received adequate environmental support for embarking upon literacy, then schools must provide it. The ethnographic research shows clearly the collaborative conditions under which learning to read and write takes place. If parents fail to read to children, it is all the more important that teachers read to them.

Sulzby (1985) discussed how kindergarten children, some as young as 4½, begin to make sense of stories, from commenting on pictures to telling a story that gains more and more fidelity to the text. There was always a story behind the children's comments—and the children's versions of the story always made sense. For a general, research-based review of many aspects of literacy and school, see the edited volume by Raphael (1986).

Intelligence has never been found to be an important factor in learning to read, although reading appears to contribute significantly to intelligence. Stanovich, Cunningham, and Feeman (1984) found only a low relationship between intelligence and reading ability in first-grade children. The correlation was higher by fifth grade, and the researchers attributed the increase to "reciprocal causation." They also found that children who quickly learned to read continued to read well through life, indicating the importance of avoiding obstacles, irrelevancies, and confusions in a child's early experiences with literacy.

Unsuspected and incidental influence of instruction on children's behavior has been well documented. Research on how children learn to read rarely remains uncontaminated by the influence that unrelated instruction has already had on them. Barr (1972, 1974) wrote seminal papers on the effect of instruction on children's reading. Holdaway (1976) commented on the importance of self-correction for children learning to read and on the risk that some instructional techniques take this responsibility away from them. Eckhoff (1983) was cited in the previous chapter notes for demonstrating that what children read is revealed in their writing. Juel and Roper/Schneider (1985) reported that what children read also shows up in how they read. In particular, texts made up of "decodable" regular words produced children whose main strategy in reading was to sound out unfamiliar words. DeFord (1981) reached a similar conclusion.

MacGinitie and MacGinitie (1986) argued that an emphasis on "mechanics" in the primary grades teaches students *not* to read, and they noted a deemphasis on extended writing, literature, and "content-rich reading" in high school. When students have difficulties with a text, teachers respond (or ask other students to respond) rather than bringing students back to the text. In a book-length analysis of British practices, Hull (1985) showed how the written and spoken language used in reading instruction and in content areas at all grade levels is frequently incomprehensible to students. He is particularly scathing when textbook or examination questions include words and phrases that students don't understand (because of their ambiguity or vacuous definitions) and complaints are then made that the students can't read. Hull's book was published in Britain. His occasional use of Anglicisms like "lower school" (junior high) and "sixth form" (12th grade) will illustrate for North American teachers his point that one doesn't have to be ignorant or learning disabled to be confused by unfamiliar uses of common words. MacGinitie (1984), in an article entitled "Readability as a Solution Adds to the Problem," reported that attempting to "simplify" texts by making them conform to formulas restricting word and sentence length can make them more difficult to read. Furness and Graves (1980) demonstrated experimentally that emphasis on accuracy (in oral reading) can actually reduce comprehension, just as an emphasis on correct spelling will inhibit children's writing. Paradoxically, both emphases result in less learning of what is supposed to be the object of the correction. Children reluctant to make mistakes will rarely venture beyond what they know already. Hiebert (1983) took a critical look at ability grouping.

Salmon and Claire (1984) made a 2-year study of four comprehensive (secondary) schools in Britain and found that classroom collaboration, both socially and in "learning," between teachers and students and among students, resulted in better student understanding of the curriculum. Chambers, Jackson, and Rose (1993) conducted a careful analysis and evaluation of a large-scale collaborative reading project in five inner-city schools in Britain. They found that new abilities were developed by teachers as well as by students as a result of reflective reading, group work, and lots of talk and discussion. Significantly, although all students in the primarily 8- to 13-year age group gained in reading ability compared with similar students in other schools, by far the greatest gains were made by students identified as "low achievers"—an unusual and important consequence. The evaluation is discussed in more detail in Gorman, Hutchison, and Trimble (1993).

Willinsky (1990) distinguished a view of literacy as a set of skills taught piecemeal in educational institutions from literacy as a social process, "making something of the world." He described many attempts to "reshape the classroom" from a place of formal instruction to a place where literacy is learned through experience, and stressed the importance of both individual voice and collaborative effort—among students and among teachers—rather than the following of timetables and agendas of others. Even where researchers have recognized the importance of active participation in literacy by the learner, he said, it is adopted as an extension of technological models of instruction. Courts (1991) contained a bitter attack on the skills approach to the teaching and testing of literacy (and thinking). See also Edelsky (1991) and Myers (1992) for the importance of "contexts," in school and outside, for literacy.

Mikulecky (1982) compared reading in school that was supposed to prepare students for the workplace and reading in various occupations. He found that students read less often and less competently than most workers on the job, though the students read easier material to less depth.

Books are often overrated in research and practice. Books have no unique or essential properties for literacy learning, and they are not always the easiest texts to read. Newspapers and magazines often contain material that can attract the attention of the smallest children, depending upon their interests and mood. Krashen (1987) reviewed the research on comics, showing that they can be highly productive materials for developing reading interests and ability, and also that comics frequently have rich vocabularies and conceptual content.

Teachers and Programs

"Whole language" is the instructional philosophy that reflects most consistently the view that meaning and "natural language" are the basis of literacy learning. Kenneth and Yetta Goodman are the theorists most closely identified with the origin and development of the whole language approach. Many TAWL (Teachers Applying Whole Language) groups have been established, especially in the United States and Canada. K. Goodman (1986) summed up the whole language view: "Many school traditions seem to have actually hindered language development. In our zeal to make it easy, we've made it hard ... primarily by breaking whole (natural) language up into bite-size, but abstract little pieces. We took apart the language and turned it into words, syllables, and isolated sounds. Unfortunately, we also postponed its natural purpose—the communication of meaning—and turned it into a set of abstractions, unrelated to the needs and experiences of the children we sought to help" (p. 7).

In *Report Card on Basal Readers*, Goodman, Shannon, Freeman, and Murphy (1988) criticized from a whole language point of view unnatural language and behaviors in the production and use of basal readers. Basal readers, they said, demonstrate a lack of trust in teachers, who are consequently "deskilled." Basal author Baumann (1992) responded with a defense of the books and a denial that they deskill teachers. See also Shannon (1989, 1993). Huck (1992) described how concern with whole language has led to a growth of "literature-based" teaching, summarizing the approach and its advantages. McGee (1992) also provided a historical review of the "literature-based reading revolution" showing that younger readers are capable of quite sophisticated responses to stories. See also Morrow (1992), Meek (1988), and

McMahon (1992). The term "literature" in this context usually refers to books written especially for children.

"Reading Recovery" is an early intervention tutoring program devised by Clay (1985), in which children who have not "caught on" to reading after a year spend about 3 months getting extra help—reading entire books but also taking "temporary instructional detours" at relevant times—in "concentrated encounters" with specially trained teachers; see also Pinnell (1989) and a chapter by Clay and Cazden in Cazden (1992). Wasik and Slavin (1993) included a useful detailed description and review of Reading Recovery and three other tutoring programs.

For social aspects of literacy and learning, see Ong (1982), Levine (1986), and several chapters in Olson, Torrance, and Hildyard (1985). Meek (1982, 1984) was insightful on social aspects of literacy instruction. See also Meek, Armstrong, Austerfield, Graham, and Plackett (1983) regarding a not always encouraging and successful struggle to help adolescents to read. Atwell (1987) also examined teaching reading and writing to adolescents. An excellent compendium of research in reading and writing (termed "comprehension and composition") is Squire (1987). Hedley and Baratta (1985) included important articles on reading, learning, and thinking generally, including ethnographic research. Tuman (1987) examined social attitudes toward reading and reading instruction.

Krashen (1985) examined the evidence and arguments that both spoken and written language are learned only by comprehension. He also examined the emotional blocks that can stand in the way of such learning. In "Learning to Read at Forty-Eight," Yatvin (1982) shared insights gained in belated efforts to learn to read Hebrew.

In addition to their interests (what they like to read about), children have their preferences—to read alone or in groups, for long or short periods, at particular times of day, with or without supervision. The best way to find out is to ask them or to observe them. A formalized characterization of "reading styles" and "learning styles" has been constructed by Carbo, Dunn, and Dunn (1987). For a discussion of this, and of other matters concerning instruction and teacher behavior from a generally whole language point of view, see Weaver (1988).

In the introductory chapter to the book *What Research Has to Say About Reading Instruction*, in a paragraph entitled "Teachers, You Have a Lot to Learn," Otto (1992) discussed dilemmas facing teachers, including the fact that there is already more reading research than a practitioner could sort out in a lifetime (with more coming faster than anyone could read it). But much of the research and argumentation is repetitious; it is not so difficult for teachers to find out what the research—and the issues—are about. The real dilemma is having to come to a decision. Kutz (1992) offered brief notes and a helpful bibliography on research by teachers, finding their own answers to questions.

Metalinguistic Awareness

The notes to the previous chapter included references related to the general role of metacognition in learning—the awareness of one's own thought processes. *Metalinguistic* awareness is meta-cognition specifically related to linguistic matters, particularly (in the case of reading and writing) to the nature of written language. It is not clear that such awareness plays an important role in learning, or, indeed, that such awareness can take place until after learning has occurred. It is difficult to see how terms like "letter," "word," and "sentence" can have any meaning to anyone who can't read. Many people able to converse fluently can't say what the difference is between nouns and verbs, or active and passive sentences, not to mention verbalizing the complexities of transformational grammars and the conventions of cohesion. Nevertheless, some theorists not only feel that metalinguistic understanding is essential for learning to read, but they define learning to read in terms of such understanding.

Ehri (1985) emphasized spelling instruction as a way to make children aware of the relation between words they hear and words they see. Metacognitive and metalinguistic theorists typically emphasize relationships of sound and spelling in reading rather than meaning. They also stress the role of cognitive *strategies*. A. Brown (1982), for example, discussed "self-regulatory strategies" that contribute to "learning how to learn from reading," including predicting, planning, checking, and monitoring knowledge of one's own abilities. She cited extensive documentation that better readers are more efficient and effective at such tasks, although there is always the chicken-and-egg problem of whether the competence produces better readers or that experienced readers naturally gain more competence. She notes that teachers treat good and poor readers differently. Shannon (1984, 1985) reviewed a mass of research indicating that schoolchildren who are identified as poor readers, or likely to be poor readers, do less reading, less interesting reading, more difficult reading, more exercises, and receive less assistance than other children. Hiebert (1983) looked at the consequences of ability grouping and also found that more able readers get the most meaningful reading with an emphasis on meaning, while the others received a greater emphasis on accuracy (which of course makes reading more difficult). See also Stanovich (1986) on the "Matthew effect" (that the rich get richer) in reading. Stanovich acknowledged that the main reason good readers get better is the differential treatment they receive in school (but as a believer with Gough and Hillinger [1980] that reading is an "unnatural act," he favored "surgical strikes" of specific skill instruction for children with problems). Metacognitive instruction tends to become a matter of more questions in preset sequences, or more drills, before reading actually begins, according to Langer (1982a, 1982b).

Dyslexia and Learning Disabilities

Staller (1982) reviewed research on the relationship between neurological impairment and reading disability and concluded that it is not yet possible to relate dyslexic behavior to specific neurological correlates. Berninger and Colwell (1985) studied 241 children between ages 6 and 12 identified as having no problem, a possible problem, or a definite problem in reading—and could find no support for the use of neurodevelopmental and educational measures in the diagnosis of specific learning disabilities. Dorman (1985) criticized research that defines or diagnoses dyslexia, because there is no agreement on what would constitute neurological evidence of neurological dysfunction in relation to reading. He concluded that "insistence upon the inclusion of [central nervous system] dysfunction in the definition and diagnosis of dyslexia seems to be putting the cart before the horse, in the sense that the neurological basis of any or all developmental reading disorders remains hypothetical." Lipson and Wixson (1986) also reviewed reading disability research and concluded that it must "move away from the search for causative factors within the reader and toward the specification of the conditions under which different readers can and will learn." Rather than accepting deficit explanations for reading problems, Wong (1982) proposed metacognitive factors, such as inadequate self-monitoring and self-questioning (in other words, attention to the meaning of what is read). Calfee (1983) said that dyslexia ought to be viewed as a problem with the development of the mind (i.e., experience) rather than a disease of the brain. Vellutino (1987) found no evidence that dyslexia is due to a visual deficit, nor to support remediation based on exercises to improve visual perception. He added, "In any case, not enough is yet known about how the brain works to enable anyone to devise activities that would have a direct and positive effect on neurological functions responsible for such basic processes as visual perception, cross-modal transfer and serial memory." Instead he recommends lots of assisted reading.

Johnston (1985) examined three case studies of adult reading disability and found "overwhelming feelings of inadequacy and confusion," anxiety, rational and irrational use of self-defeating strategies, conflicting motives, and inappropriate attributions of cause and blame, all going back to the individual's earliest reading experiences. Clay (1979) suggested that children become reading failures by learning the wrong things. Downing (1977) argued that society creates reading disabilities, for example, by artificially establishing "critical periods" for learning and through inappropriate expectations and stereotypes. Graham (1980) showed that "learning disabled" readers may have the same word recognition skills as children who are succeeding. Individual differences always occur, of course. Some people will find it harder to learn to read than others, but not because they have special "problems." Bryant and Impey (1986) concluded that there is no essential difference between dyslexics and normal readers—dyslexics simply are at the lower end of the scale of readers. They do nothing different from normal readers except they have more difficulty. Medical researchers Shaywitz, Escobar, Shaywitz, Fletcher, and Makuch (1992) also proposed that dyslexia and "learning disabilities" may not be medical conditions but simply the lower end of a normal distribution of abilities. For a discussion of dyslexia from a phonological coding point of view, see Rack, Snowling, and Olson (1992). In a careful examination of 30 years of research into reading failure, Hamill and McNutt (1981) could find no relationship to intelligence, perceptual or motor abilities, reasoning, or even affective factors, and only a marginal correlation with spoken-language ability.

The consequences of reading failure are rarely adequately stressed. Reichardt (1977) talked of children "playing dead or running away" from reading situations, defensive reactions among "reading handicapped students" whose physiological responses to reading ranged from complete apathy to hypertension. More generally, Seligman (1975) discussed "learned depression" (due to lack of control over failures) and "learned laziness" (due to lack of control over rewards), both consequences of situations where the learner lacks control and understanding. Coles (1987) warned of the misuse, overuse, and dangers of the term "learning disabled." For descriptions of how "at-risk" students and their teachers can learn from each other in linguistically and culturally diverse classrooms, see Heath, Mangiola, Schachter, and Hull (1991) and Truax and Kretschmer (1993). See also Atwell (1991).

Despite all the conjectures, it should not be surprising that no one has actually succeeded in finding a specific reading center or system in the architecture of the brain. Literacy has not existed as a cultural phenomenon long enough for the brain to develop specialized reading processes. One might just as meaningfully suggest areas of the brain dedicated to cycling or sewing. It has been known for over 100 years that one side of the brain (9 times out of 10 the left) is essential for the production and comprehension of language (except in infants, whose brains are more labile). But this asymmetry doesn't mean that only one side of the brain is involved in language. All thinking activities involve the entire brain. Different people obviously have different preferences—some like listening to music and others would rather look at pictures—but this doesn't mean that they lack parts of their brains or are "dominated" by one side of them. Looking at pictures, listening to music, and reading and writing involve experience, knowledge, and feelings and can't be restricted to one area of the brain. It is a naive interpretation of neurological, language, and learning research to imagine that reading can be learned only with the left side of the brain or with the right.

Evaluation, Testing, and Standards

Testing, evaluation, and the setting of "standards" exercise great control over teachers in classrooms and can have lasting consequences on learners, driving the curriculum and emphasizing skills that can be taught and tested by prescription. Although many teachers express alarm over evaluation and standardization, especially when imposed on them (and when results are publicized), a number of prominent teachers and teacher organizations have become associated with such efforts. For example, the International Reading Association and the National Council for Teachers of English joined forces with the federally funded Center for the Study of Reading in October 1992 to develop national standards (in the United States) for reading, the language arts, and English. Although acknowledging diversity, it was expected that the standards would define "a common core of what is valuable in the teaching and learning of

English" and reduce the "contention in the discipline," for example, over the role of phonics and the value of recommended reading lists. It was not explained how such disagreements might be caused by an absence of standards among teachers.

Hiebert and Calfee (1992) discussed the assessment of literacy, from standardized tests to portfolios, noting the growing public demand for assessment to drive instruction and policy decisions. They referred to concern about the deprofessionalization of teachers and discouragement of students and concluded that teachers are the best judges concerning instructional decisions. In a book entitled *Learning Denied*, Taylor (1991) related a dramatic example of the disruption that can occur in a child's life—in addition to the anxieties and conflicts of the teacher and the parents—as a result of testing and "early diagnosis." Giroux (1992) discussed how the testing movement ignores successful local knowledge in favor of trained "leadership," marginalized teachers, and standardization.

Santa (1999/2000), then president of the International Reading Association (IRA), eloquently pointed out that teachers assess students daily as part of teaching, but not for passing judgments. The term "assessment" has become distorted and misused to make high-stakes decisions on the basis of a single standardized test score, although Santa doubted whether the tests are valid indicators of anything. She added that fear of flunking a test is a child's greatest fear next to the death of a member of the family. Her remarks follow a position statement by the IRA Board of Directors (1999) expressing the "central concern ... that testing has become a means of controlling instruction as opposed to a way of gathering information to help students become better readers." Problems of "teaching in a world focused on testing" was the concern of Buckner (2002) in a journal issue dedicated to the effects of high-stakes testing on learners, teachers, and the development of literacy. Shannon (1996) said (in his title) that he is "mad as hell" over the use of standards and tests. So also was Ohanian (1999).

Is There a Crisis?

In *The Manufactured Crisis: Myths, Fraud, and the Attack on America's Public Schools*, Berliner and Biddle (1995) reviewed years of criticism, official and unofficial, on "failures" of American education, based on "evidence" that they say was either unavailable or misleadingly overgeneralized. None of the charges could be supported, they claimed, and blamed, among other things, industrialists worried about overseas competition, a long-established tradition of "school-bashing," scapegoating of educators to divert attention from social problems, self-interest of some government officials, and irresponsible actions of the media (p. 7). In *The Literacy Crisis: False Claims and Real Solutions*, McQuillan (1998) also documented how an alleged "literacy crisis" is fabricated.

Looking Ahead

A discussion of the future of books, the future of literacy, and the future of education would fill any number of books. Interesting articles that happened to cross my desk on one day recently are Sutherland-Smith (2002) on changes in reading from page to screen, Miller, DeJean, and Miller (2002) comparing literacy by teachers with integrated [electronic] learning systems, and Trushell (2002) on the future of the book (warning that "prophecy is a mug's game"). Bolter (1991) said that readers will have to learn to read electronic texts and "hypertexts" (networks of subtexts) in different ways from linear print-reading, following routes that the writers might not even have imagined. The notion of what constitutes readers and writers will change, and also the idea of "autonomous texts" that exist independently of readers and writers, with clearly defined beginnings and ends. I would merely state that whatever opportunities, possibilities, and demands descend on readers in the future, the act of reading, as described and discussed, will continue to be the same. And although learning will inevitably take place in different circumstances, learning will also be the same. My advice to anyone wanting to anticipate and prepare for the future is to read extensively, evaluate objectively, and think all the time.

The Interminable Controversy

In the previous edition of *Understanding Reading* (Smith, 1994b), I contended that the "never-ending debate" between advocates of whole language and those of direct instruction (or "code emphasis") would never end because it is not something that research or experimentation will resolve, or indeed that partisans are ever likely to change their minds about. The disagreement is fundamentally a dispute over whether teachers can and should be trusted to teach and learners trusted to learn. Two of the original protagonists in the dispute, Jeanne Chall and Kenneth Goodman, were still vigorously contending with each other after 30 years until Chall died in 1999. Their many adherents on each side, with Goodman and his wife Yetta still active, continue the struggle even more strenuously today as the issues have become more political.

Chall, who launched the term "The Great Debate" in the subtitle of her classic 1967 book *Learning to Read*, was fully aware of the gulf between the two points of view. In Chall (1992/1993) she declared, "Whole language proponents tend to view learning to read as a natural process, developing in ways similar to language [she means *spoken* language]. Therefore, like language, most whole language proponents say it is not necessary to teach reading directly. Direct instruction models, on the other hand, view reading as needing to be taught, and taught systematically" (p. 8). She cites the existence of many illiterate individuals as evidence that reading is not "natural" and needs to be taught, adding: "Generally, direct instruction models favor the systematic teaching and learning of the relationships of sounds and symbols. This goes under many names—phonics, decoding, phonological awareness, word analysis, word attack, phonetic analysis, sound-symbol relations, etc." (p. 8).

In the same publication, Goodman (1992/1993) began by asserting that whole language is "a broad, fundamental revolution in education" and that opposition to it is politically based. He said that reducing whole language "to a method of reading which is simply the opposite of an approach that stresses phonics trivializes the broad nature of this revolution" (p. 8). Because he didn't regard phonics as the issue, Goodman declined to debate it and instead focused on "why Jeanne Chall and others choose to frame the revolution in education over whether to use whole language or phonics in teaching reading." He said that "her words and her name are used by those outside the research community—including the far right—who focus on reading as a simple means of attacking public education. They quote Chall to support their claim that whole language is a conspiracy to deprive children of literacy" (p. 9). Goodman provided examples of attacks on whole language, in the media and in Congress, that often mistakenly conflate it with "look–say" and other "methods" of teaching reading, blaming it for illiteracy, confusion in classrooms, and even a serious public health problem, and frequently citing Chall as the authority for the condemnation of whole language and the desirability of phonics.

Advocates of whole language tend to see phonics and direct instruction as rigid, mindless, authoritarian, unfeeling, and unnecessary procedures, and the whole language philosophy is seen by its opponents as unrealistic, unscientific, romantic, and anarchistic idealism, threatening to the maintenance of standards and teacher accountability. Goodman unwittingly provided a limitless supply of ammunition to his detractors in the title of one of his earliest publications when he characterized reading as "a psycholinguistic guessing game" (Goodman, 1967). It is frequently cited, always pejoratively. For a critical review of the rhetoric of whole language, see Moorman, Blanton, and McLaughlin (1992), and for a critical description of the ways in which the term "whole language" is misunderstood and misused in classrooms, see Dudley-Marling and Dippo (1991).

As an example, Perfetti (1985) characterized the whole language or "psycholinguistic approach" as a whole word approach, which is misleading if not incorrect because "whole word approach" typically refers to an instructional method of teaching words in isolation, in lists or on flashcards, which is far from the whole language position. Beck and Juel (1992) presented typical arguments for an early need to decode—as a "tool" of reading, which they saw as an alternative to "word attack" or "look–say" methods of learning by repetition. They called on "substantial research support" to assert that "letters correspond to the sounds in spoken language"—giving as examples *cat* and *fat*. Similar views by Ehri and her colleagues have already been cited on p. 284. Despite the fact that studies of this kind are usually labeled "reading," they normally don't extend beyond the identification of words in isolation. In a spirited attack on whole language from the phonological awareness point of view, Liberman and Liberman (1992) consistently (and not untypically) compared reading with talking, contending that the former is unnatural and difficult while the latter is natural and easy. Gill (1992) made similar arguments. But if any comparison between spoken and written language is to be made, it should be between the "receptive" or "understanding" behaviors of reading and listening or the "productive" behaviors of writing and speaking. The manner in which infants learn to understand print should be compared with the manner in which they learn to understand the spoken language that surrounds them—both are based on bringing sense to meaningful situations, and very little additional effort is required to use the eyes rather than the ears. Using the vocal apparatus is another matter, and whether it is easier to learn to reproduce the pronunciation of a word than its spelling is a moot point, but it has nothing to do with teaching reading. In another impassioned assault, Thompson (1992) claimed that whole language lacks evidence and has a philosophy of abandoning students. He objected to the enthusiasm that permeates whole language. Miller (1991) offered a friendly but pointed appraisal of the "whole language bandwagon," observing evangelism, polemics, exploitation, deification, and vagueness and noting the problem of finding a brief answer for people wondering what whole language is.

From the opposite point of view, Carbo (1988) criticized many of Chall's analyses of research findings in an article entitled "Debunking the Great Phonics Myth," noting that despite a 20-year emphasis on phonics in American classrooms, at the time of writing the United States rated 49th in literacy out of 159 members of the United Nations and that New Zealand, which taught reading through a whole language approach, was ranked first. Chall (1989) was a response.

Weaver (1994) provided a compendious text discussing whole language theory and practice, from the point of view of teachers and parents. She said that extensive phonics is worst for children in lower reading groups (or lower socioeconomic groups) and that most recommendations by researchers (like Chall, 1967) acknowledge that systematic phonics is not superior to other approaches and should always be part of more general meaning-based instruction. The hyperbole usually comes from "interpreters" of the research, with a crusading agenda or links to complex and expensive commercial programs. Like Weaver, Krashen (2002a) argued that whole language is misrepresented and underrated in comparisons. See also his *Three Arguments Against Whole Language and Why They Are Wrong* (Krashen, 1999a).

In an article entitled "Captives of the Script: Killing Us Softly with Phonics," Meyer (2002) described problems of a teacher required to teach reading as a series of episodes of non words and non sentences: "The mandated program is so oriented to preciseness that her students are less willing to take risks as readers and writers." Children wonder why they are taught to read such "words" as *supermand, shoolbun,* and *reced.* The word "script" also arose in an article by Dudley-Marling and Murphy (2001), discussing difficulties many teachers have in teaching the language arts in the way they think most fitting and productive. The authors, experienced researchers and editors, argued that the professional autonomy of teachers is threatened by overregulation and the deregulation of schooling. They listed and briefly critiqued the most popular commercial reading programs and the scripts they provide "to keep all teachers on the same page." Pressure to adopt "scripted programs" from university-based researchers and market-based developers inhibited the improvisational skills and experience of teachers.

Phonics as a remedial reading technique is being introduced to secondary students, reported *Los Angeles Times* staff writer Duke Helfand (2002). He said 35,000 middle and high school students in the Los Angeles Unified School District lacking second- or third-grade reading skills were being given 2 hours a day of mandated phonics instruction, normally taught to 6-year-olds, in place of music and art. Classics like *Romeo and Juliet* were being replaced by books with big pictures, large print, and sentences like "Dad had a sad lad." Most students disliked the program and the classes, feeling that they were being treated as being "dumb," "retarded," or "little kids." Meanwhile, administrators were enthusiastic. They regarded it as "the last chance" for many students. Success was claimed when students scored well on timed tasks reading a list of words like *at, bat, sat,* and *Sam.*

In view of the extensive and sometimes indiscriminate manner in which a few "classic" or "important" publications are repeatedly cited on both sides of the debate, it may be relevant to note Cronbach's (1992) comment that large numbers of citations don't imply that an intended message has been widely understood, and Fiske and Campbell's (1992) observation that citations don't solve problems. Vincente and Brewer (1993) remarked that theoretical bias leads to misrepresentations in the reading and citing of original research—a bias that is increased as secondary sources are used.

I conclude this section with a personal note. Many of the arguments in successive editions of this book have been generally supportive of the whole language philosophy, and I am frequently identified as a proponent of whole language. Nevertheless, I have never called myself a whole language person, nor have I ever offered a blanket testimonial for a whole language approach. I should perhaps explain my reluctance to embrace the label. (1) I dislike all labels and slogans, which I regard as open invitations to abandon reflective thought. Once someone says or does something that is identified as whole language, there is no need to question further, the person is pigeon-holed. (2) I dislike all "methods" of teaching reading, and whole language, despite the best intentions of many of its adherents, has become a method. Experts talk about how to "do" whole language, whole language materials are produced, both for instruction and for assessment, and teachers look for whole language hints that they can introduce into their classrooms. Whole language becomes something that is done, not a way of thinking about children and learning. (3) Labels get stolen. People can call themselves "whole language teachers" while doing things totally alien to the underlying whole language philosophy.

Worse, they can encourage or persuade other teachers to engage in certain practices without understanding what they are doing. My preference in every case is for demonstrations, observations, debate, and critical thought.

Federally Commissioned Studies

In the 1980s the unending debate focused on a federally commissioned report entitled *Becoming a Nation of Readers* (Anderson, Hiebert, Scott, & Wilkinson, 1985), whose conclusions favored heavy early phonics instruction. The report was castigated in the following manner by the editor of the International Reading Association's annual review of reading research (Weintraub, 1986): "There's no guarantee that the big name is synonymous with quality. Even when well-funded and headed by a blue ribbon committee, a supposedly comprehensive review may be narrowly based, considerably less than comprehensive, and biased in its election of what is included and what is excluded .... I happen to concur that a very selective body of literature was included and some rather critical research excluded" (p. vi).

The book *Beginning to Read*, by Marilyn Jager Adams (1990), was commissioned by the U.S. Department of Education following a request by Congress for an examination of the role of phonics in reading instruction. It is frequently referred to by both sides of the debate. Adams acknowledged the difficulty and unnaturalness of breaking down speech into separate sounds and relating these sounds to spellings, how difficult and laborious phonics and word recognition instruction is for children before they are experienced readers, and observed specifically that "spelling–sound relationships are not the basis of reading skills and knowledge" (p. 10)—but ended by "concluding" that the "symbol–sound system should be taught explicitly and early, together with phonemic awareness training." Dorothy Strickland and Bernice Cullinan, two members of a panel set up by the Center for the Study of Reading to advise the author, felt constrained to declare polite but firm disagreement in an Afterword published with the volume. They were particularly concerned by the emphasis on phonics, the references to children who have not yet begun to receive instruction as "pre-readers" rather than "emergent readers," the selection of studies, interpretation of research, and the amount of research that took place in decontextualized situations. A similar controversy followed another federally commissioned report by Snow, Burns, and Griffin (1998) entitled

Preventing Reading Difficulties in Young Children, which presented similar conclusions.

Possibly the mother of all educational conflicts was ignited by the report of the National Reading Panel (2000)—set up by the National Institute of Child Health and Human Development— whose main publication was entitled *Teaching Children to Read: An Evidence Based Assessment of the Scientific Research Literature on Reading and Its Implications for Reading Instruction.* The terms "evidence based" and "scientific research" in the title are significant. The report is voluminous, but there is a 35-page summary. The conclusions once again are a catalog of recommendations stressing direct instruction of phonics and phonemic awareness skills. Any attempt to examine the content of the report and of opposing arguments in detail would simply be a further repetition of the interminable debate. But two unique characteristics of the report have wider implications. The first was the panel's decision to partition all research on reading into two categories, *scientific*— which in practice means supportive of the phonics point of view— and *unscientific*—which means everything else. The distinction has extensive consequences ranging from the funding of literacy research to the professional status of individual teachers and professors of education. The distinction was used to justify the panel's own decision that of over 100,000 research reports that came before them, only 428 warranted close attention, and of these only 38 were used as a basis for their conclusions. The second unique characteristic was the panel's political stance. The recommendations were prescriptive, and quickly mandated by federal and many state administrations as the sole basis of instruction for students in school and teachers at faculties of education, as well as for participants in inservice training.

Vehement criticism of the report and its conclusions followed immediately, starting with the only experienced reading teacher on the panel, Joanne Yatvin. She wrote a minority report that was not published or referred to in the summary but subsequently appeared in an academic journal under the title *Babes in the Woods: The Wanderings of the National Reading Panel* (Yatvin, 2002). Yatvin believed the members of the panel "lost their integrity" because government agencies at all levels are using the "science" of a flawed report to support changes in school instruction and teacher education. The titles of some related publications succinctly indicate the tenor of their contents: *Misreading Reading: The Bad Science that Hurts Children* (Coles, 2000); *Literacy as Snake Oil: Beyond the Quick Fix* (Larson, 2001); *Resisting Reading Man-*

dates: *How to Triumph With the Truth* (Garan, 2002); *Reading Between the Lines* (Metcalf, 2002); and *The Politics of Phonics* (Paterson, 2002). Articles by Yatvin, Garan, Paterson, and others are printed or reprinted in *Big Brother and the National Reading Curriculum: How Ideology Trumped Evidence* (Allington, 2002).

My personal view of the panels is that they share two common but misguided characteristics: (1) a fixation on the alphabet and on letter–sound relationships, and (2) a conviction that children will only learn when given explicit instruction. Others might add strong elements of commercial, political, or fundamentalist bias. Do I have a better idea? I think this is a case where ultimate truth is unattainable. But anyone who objectively studies language and observes children can see that characteristics 1 and 2 are both wrong. It is not difficult to see error. On the other hand, I would not presume to speculate on "what really happens in the head." Scans of various kinds may show activity in different regions of the brain at different times, but they no more explain reading than they explain consciousness, attention, awareness, or any other mental state. Some scientists (real scientists) believe we may never resolve such issues because we don't (and perhaps can't) ask the right questions; our organized perceptions of gross events in the physical world don't relate to quantum events in the physical brain in any way that we can comprehend (see Cohen & Schooler, 1997; Dodwell, 2000). The brain can never understand itself. This doesn't mean that we are helpless victims of ignorance or that anything goes; it means that we should avoid the pursuit of fictions and respect what can be unambiguously observed about the behavior, capacities, and feelings of people. Such an attitude won't end the interminable controversy, but it could take us beyond it.

Glossary

This list doesn't define words as a dictionary does, but rather indicates the general way that certain terms are employed in this book. Figures in parentheses indicate the chapter (or chapter notes) in which a term was first used or primarily discussed. Terms in *italics* appear elsewhere in the glossary.

Aesthetic reading: Reading done primarily for experience; contrasted with *efferent reading* (4).

Artificial intelligence: The study of systems designed to emulate human language and thought with computer technology (Preface).

Basics: See *skills learning*.

Cat and dog problem: Example of the fact that *distinctive features* cannot be explicitly taught but must be learned by the testing of *hypotheses* (12).

Categories: See *cognitive categories*.

Category interrelationships: The various ways in which *cognitive categories* can be combined as a basis for *prediction* or action (2).

Channel capacity: Limit to the amount of *information* that can pass through any part of an information-processing system (4).

Cognition: A particular organization of knowledge in the brain, or the reorganization of such knowledge (2). See *cognitive structure*. Also called thinking.

Cognitive categories: Prior decisions to treat some aspects of experience as the same, yet as different from other aspects of experience; the constantly developing framework of *cognitive structure* (2).

Cognitive questions: The specific information sought by the brain to make a decision among alternatives; the range of a *prediction* (2).

Cognitive science: An area of common concern in psychology, linguistics, and the design of computer systems, related to the manner in which knowledge can be acquired, stored, retrieved, and utilized (Preface). See also *artificial intelligence*.

Cognitive structure: The totality of the brain's organization of knowledge; everything an individual knows (or believes) about the world. Comprises *cognitive categories, feature lists,* and *category interrelationships.* Also referred to as *long-term memory,* the *theory of the world,* and *prior knowledge* (2).

Comprehension: The interpretation of experience; relating new information to what is already known; asking *cognitive questions* and being able to find answers to them; a normal state, the absence of confusion (2).

Constraint: The exclusion or reduced probability of certain alternatives; the mechanism of *redundancy* (4).

Context: The setting, physical or linguistic, in which words occur and that places constraints on the range of alternatives that these words might be (3).

Context-dependent language: Spoken or written language coherent within itself and not related to the concurrent physical situation in which it occurs (3).

Conventions: Arbitrary or accidental forms of behavior made meaningful by mutual understanding of and respect for their use and implications (3).

Criterial set: A set of *distinctive features* within a *feature list* that permits an *identification* to be made on minimal *information* from a given set of alternatives (7).

Criterion level: The amount of *information* an individual requires to make a particular decision, varying with the perceived *uncertainty* of the situation and the perceived risk and cost of making a mistake (4).

Decoding to sound: The view that reading is accomplished by transforming print into actual or subvocalized (implicit) speech through the exercise of *spelling–sound correspondences.* See also *phonological recoding* (9).

Deep structure: The meaningful aspect of language; the interpretation of *surface structure* (3).

Demonstrations: Displays, by people or artifacts, of how something is done (12).

Direct instruction: An educational philosophy based on the belief that learning takes place most effectively when learners are told in specific detail what they should learn and are monitored closely to ensure that they do so (13). Frequently contrasted with *whole language.*

Discourse structure: Conventions concerning the organization of language, for example, turn-taking and interruption in speech, and paragraphing and repetition in texts (3).

Distinctive features: *Significant differences* among visual (or acoustic) patterns, that is, differences that make a difference. For reading, any aspect of *visual information* that permits distinctions to be made among alternative letters, words, or meanings (7). See also *feature list*.

Distributional redundancy: Reduction of *uncertainty* because alternatives are not equally probable (4). May exist in letters or words. See also *featural redundancy*.

Efferent reading: Reading done primarily for information; contrasted with *aesthetic reading* (4).

Engagement: The interaction of a brain with a *demonstration*; the act of learning (12).

Ethnographic research: Observation of behavior in natural contexts; nonintrusive research; also termed "naturalistic research"; contrasted with controlled experimentation (13).

Event knowledge: Hypothesized mental representations of patterns of behavior in specific events; clusters of related expectations. See *scheme* (2).

Expectations: See *prediction*.

Featural redundancy: In reading, *redundancy* among the *distinctive features* of print as a consequence of constraints on letter or word occurrence (7).

Feature analysis: A theory of pattern recognition proposing that visual configurations such as digits, letters, or words are identified by the analysis of *distinctive features* and their allocation to *feature lists*; in contrast to *template theory* (7).

Feature list: A cognitive specification or "set of rules" for particular combinations of *distinctive features* that will permit *identification* in reading (7).

Feedback: Information that permits a decision whether an *hypothesis* is right or wrong (7).

Fixation: The pause for the selection of *visual information* as the gaze rests at one place in the text between *saccades* (5).

Functional equivalence: Specification of the same *cognitive category* by two or more *feature lists* (7).

Genre: Schemes for conventional structures of written language (3).

Grammar: See *syntax*.

Grapheme: A letter of the alphabet, one of 26 alternatives (9).

Grapheme unit: Single graphemes, or combinations of two or more letters of the alphabet that function as single graphemes (9).

Hypothesis: A tentative modification of cognitive structure (*cognitive categories, feature lists,* or *category interrelationships*) that is tested as a basis for *learning* (12).

Identification: In reading, a cognitive decision among letter, word, or meaning alternatives based on the analysis of selected *visual information* in print (7).

Immediate meaning identification: The *comprehension* of language without the prior identification of words (10).

Immediate word identification: The *identification* of a word on sight, without *information* from another person and without the prior *identification* of letters or letter combinations within the word (8).

Information: Any property of the physical environment that reduces *uncertainty*, eliminating or reducing the probability of alternatives among which a perceiver must decide (4).

Learning: The modification or elaboration of *cognitive structure*, specifically the establishment of new or revised *cognitive categories, category interrelationships,* or *feature lists* (12).

Letter–sound correspondence: See *spelling–sound correspondence.*

Lexical access: Computer-derived metaphor for making sense of words in reading or speech through reference to an internal *lexicon* (3).

Lexicon: A hypothesized mental store of knowledge about words, including their sound, spelling, and meaning. See *lexical access* (3).

Long-term memory: The totality of an individual's knowledge and beliefs, including summaries of past experience and ways of interacting with the world (2).

Mastery learning: See *skills learning.*

Meaning: A relative term; the interpretation that a reader places on text (the answer to a *cognitive question*). Alternatively, the interpretation an author or third party expects a reader to place on text. The product of *comprehension* (2).

Meaningful(ness): In reading, a text that is relevant to a reader's purpose, *expectations,* and *understanding* (2).

Mediated meaning identification: An inferior alternative to *immediate meaning identification,* attempting to derive meaning by the prior identification of words (10).

Mediated word identification: A less efficient alternative to *immediate word identification,* requiring analysis of letters or letter combinations within the word (9).

Memory: See *sensory store, short-term memory,* and *long-term memory.*

Metacognition: Thought about one's own thinking, understanding, or learning (2).

Metalanguage: Language about language (3).

Metalinguistic awareness: Understanding of *metalanguage,* notably the way aspects of spoken and written language may be discussed in reading instruction (13).

Noise: A signal that reduces no *uncertainty* (4).

Nonvisual information: Prior knowledge "behind the eyes" that reduces *uncertainty* in advance and permits *identification* decisions with less *visual information* (5).

Orthography: Spelling; the arrangement of letters in words (9).

Perception: *Identification* decisions made by the brain; subjective awareness of these decisions (2).

Phoneme: One of about 45 discriminable categories of *significantly different* speech sounds in English. Other languages have different sets of roughly the same number of phonemes (3).

Phonetics: The scientific study of the sound structure of speech; has nothing to do with reading (9). See *phonics.*

Phonics: Reading instruction based on the assumption that reading is decoding to sound and requires learning *spelling–sound correspondences* (9). Sometimes erroneously referred to as *phonetics.*

Phonological awareness: Ability to detect sounds in speech that are supposed to be represented by the letters of the alphabet. Also termed *phonemic awareness* (9).

Phonological recoding: Transforming written words to sound in order to understand their meaning (as opposed to understanding written words directly) (9).

Prediction: The prior elimination of unlikely alternatives; (in reading) the remaining set of alternatives among which an *identification* decision will be made from selected *visual information* in print (2).

Prior knowledge: Relevant knowledge already possessed that reduces *uncertainty* in advance and facilitates *identification* decisions (2). Also referred to as *cognitive structure* and *nonvisual information.*

Procedural knowledge: Knowledge of integrated sequences of behavior; see also *propositional knowledge, event knowledge* (2).

Propositional knowledge: Knowledge in the form of internalized statements (such as facts, proverbs, formulas); also referred to as *declarative knowledge* (as opposed to *procedural knowledge*) (2).

Psycholinguistics: An area of common concern in psychology and linguistics studying how individuals learn and use language (Preface).

Redundancy: *Information* that is available from more than one source. In reading, may be present in the *visual information* of print, in the *orthography*, the *syntax*, the *meaning*, or in combinations of these sources. Redundancy may be *distributional* or *sequential*. Redundancy must always reflect *nonvisual information*; prior knowledge on the part of the reader permits redundancy to be used (4).

Regression: An eye movement (*saccade*) from right to left along a line or upward on a page (in English and similar writing systems) (5).

Saccade: Movement of the eyes as the gaze moves from one *fixation* to another in reading (5).

Scenario: A generalized mental representation of conventional patterns of behavior in specific situations. See also *scheme* (2).

Scheme: A generalized mental representation of complex patterns of behavior or events; also referred to as *schema*, plural *schemata*. See also *scenario, script, event knowledge* (2).

Script: A generalized mental representation of conventional behavior on specific occasions (2).

Semantics: The meaningful aspect of language; the study of this aspect (2).

Sensitivity: The prior learning state of the brain; readiness for *engagement;* absence of expectation that learning will not occur (12).

Sensory store: In vision, the very brief retention of *visual information* while *identification* decisions are made; also called the *visual image* (6).

Sequential redundancy: Reduction of *uncertainty* attributable to *constraints* on the number or relative probability of likely alternatives in *context* (8, 10); may exist among letters or words and as a consequence of a reader's or listener's expectations. See also *featural redundancy*.

Short-term memory: The limited and constantly changing content of what is attended to at any particular moment (6).

Significant difference: A difference in the physical properties of an event that forms the basis of an *identification* decision (7).

Situation-dependent language: Spoken or written language referring to and made meaningful by the concurrent physical situation in which it occurs (3).

Skills learning: The view that learning takes place most effectively when learners are systematically taught and rigorously tested in "the basics" of what is to be learned—in literacy, for example, the alphabet, *phonics*, and rules of spelling and punctuation (13). Known also as *direct instruction* and *mastery learning*.

Specification: A constantly changing outline in a reader's (or writer's) mind about the structure and content of a text; the basis of *prediction* in reading (2).

Spelling–sound correspondence: The co-occurrence of a particular letter or group of letters in a written word and the assumed sound of the same part of the word in speech (9).

Surface structure: The physical properties of language; for reading—*visual information* (3).

Syntax: The manner in which words are organized in meaningful language; also referred to as "grammar" (2).

Tachistoscope: A projector or other viewing device with a shutter or timer controlling the presentation of *visual information* for brief periods of time (5).

Template theory: A theory of pattern recognition that visual configurations such as digits, letters, or words can be identified by comparison with prestored representations or templates in the brain; in contrast to *featural analysis* (7).

Text: A meaningful (or potentially meaningful) instance of written language; can range from a word to an entire book.

Theory: In science, a summary of a scientist's past experience, the basis for interpreting new experience and for predicting future events (2).

Theory of the world: The brain's *theory*; also known as *cognitive structure* and *long-term memory* (2).

Transformational grammar: Part of the theory of the world of every language user; the bridge between *deep structure* and *surface structure* (3).

Uncertainty: The amount of *information* required to make an *identification* decision, determined by the number of alternative decisions that could be made, the perceived probability of each alternative, and the individual's *criterion level* for making the decision (4).

Understanding: Sec *comprehension*.

Visual image: See *sensory store*.

Visual information: In reading, *information* that is available to the brain through the eyes from the *surface structure* of print, for example, from the ink marks on a page (3).

Whole language: An educational movement based on the belief that language learning takes place most effectively when learners are engaged collaboratively in meaningful and purposeful uses of language, as opposed to exercises, drills, and tests (13). Sometimes referred to as the naturalistic approach or (misleadingly) as child-centered learning, and known in Britain as real books. Frequently contrasted with *direct instruction*.

References

Adams, Marilyn Jager (1990). *Beginning to Read: Learning and Thinking About Print*. Cambridge, MA: MIT Press.

Adams, Marilyn Jager (1994). Phonics and beginning reading instruction. In Fran Lehr and Jean Osborn (Eds.), *Reading, Language and Literacy: Instruction for the Twenty-First Century*. Hillsdale, NJ: Lawrence Erlbaum Associates.

Allington, Richard L. (Ed.) (2002). *Big Brother and the National Reading Curriculum: How Ideology Trumped Evidence*. Portsmouth, NH: Heinemann.

Anderson, John R. (1980). *Cognitive Psychology and Its Implications*. San Francisco: Freeman.

Anderson, Richard C., Elfrieda H. Hiebert, Judith A. Scott, and Ian A. G. Wilkinson (1985). *Becoming a Nation of Readers: The Report of the Commission on Reading*. Washington, DC: National Academy of Education.

Anderson, Richard C. and Andrew Ortony (1975). On putting apples into bottles: A problem in polysemy. *Cognitive Psychology*, 7, 167–180.

Anderson, Richard C. and P. David Pearson (1984). A schema–theoretic view of basic processes in reading comprehension. In Pearson, P. David, Rebecca Barr, Michael L. Kamil, and Peter Mosenthal (Eds.), *Handbook of Reading Research* (Vol. 1). New York: Longman.

Anglin, Jeremy M. (1993). Vocabulary development: A morphological analysis. *Monographs for the Society for Research in Child Development*, #238, 58(10).

Applebee, Arthur N. (1977). A sense of story. *Theory Into Practice*, 16, 342–347.

Armbruster, Bonnie B. and T. H. Anderson (1984). Content area text-books. In Anderson, Richard C., Jean Osborn, and Robert J. Tierney (Eds.), *Learning to Read in American Schools: Basal Readers and Content Texts*. Hillsdale, NJ: Lawrence Erlbaum Associates.

Atwell, Nancie (1987). *In the Middle: Reading, Writing and Learning with Adolescents*. Portsmouth, NH: Heinemann.

Atwell, Nancie (1991). *Side by Side: Essays on Teaching to Learn*. Portsmouth, NH: Heinemann.

Averbach, E. and A. S. Coriell (1961). Short-term memory in vision. *Bell Systems Technical Journal, 40*, 309–328.

Baddeley, Alan (1992). Working memory. *Science, 255*, 556–559.

Bahrick, Harry P. and Lynda K. Hall (1991). Lifetime maintenance of high school mathematics content. *Journal of Experimental Psychology: General, 120*(1), 20–33.

Barclay, J. R. (1973). The role of comprehension in remembering sentences. *Cognitive Psychology, 4*, 229–252.

Barlow, John A. (1981). Mass line leadership and thought reform in China. *American Psychologist, 36*(3), 300–309.

Barr, Rebecca C. (1972). The influence of instructional conditions on word recognition errors. *Reading Research Quarterly, 7*, 509–529.

Barr, Rebecca C. (1974). The effect of instruction on pupil reading strategies. *Reading Research Quarterly, 10*, 555–582.

Bartlett, Frederick C. (1932). *Remembering: A Study in Experimental and Social Psychology*. London: Cambridge University Press.

Baumann, James F. (1992). Basal reading programs and the deskilling of teachers: A critical examination of the argument. *Reading Research Quarterly, 27*(4), 390–398.

Beck, Isabel L. and Connie Juel (1992). The role of decoding in learning to read. In Samuels, S. Jay and Alan E. Farstrup (Eds.), *What Research Has to Say About Reading Instruction* (2nd ed.). Newark, DE: International Reading Association.

Beck, Isabel L., Margaret G. McKeown, Richard C. Omanson, and Martha T. Pople (1984). Improving the comprehensibility of stories: The effects of revisions that improve coherence. *Reading Research Quarterly, 19*(3), 263–277.

Beers, Terry (1987). Commentary: Schema-theoretic models of reading: Humanizing the machine. *Reading Research Quarterly, 22*(3), 369–377.

Benton, Arthur L. (1980). The neuropsychology of facial recognition. *American Psychologist, 35*(2), 176–186.

Berdiansky, Betty, Bruce Cronnell, and John A. Koehler (1969). *Spelling–Sound Relations and Primary Form-Class Descriptions for Speech-Comprehension Vocabularies of 6–9 Year-Olds*. Inglewood, CA: Southwest Regional Laboratory for Educational Research and Development, Technical Report No. 15.

Berliner, David C. and Bruce J. Biddle (1995). *The Manufactured Crisis: Myths, Fraud, and the Attack on America's Public Schools*. Reading, MA: Perseus.

Berninger, Virginia Wise and Sarah O. Colwell (1985). Relationships between neurodevelopmental and educational findings in children aged 6 to 12 years. *Pediatrics, 75,* 697–702.

Black, Alison, Paul Freeman, and Philip N. Johnson-Laird (1986). Plausibility and the comprehension of text. *British Journal of Psychology, 77*(1), 51–62.

Bloome, David and Ann Egan-Robertson (1993). The social construction of intertextuality in classroom reading and writing lessons. *Reading Research Quarterly, 28*(4), 304–333.

Blough, Donald S. (1982). Pigeon perception of letters of the alphabet. *Science, 218,* 397–398.

Bolter, Jay David (1991). *Writing Space: The Computer, Hypertext, and the History of Writing.* Hillsdale, NJ: Lawrence Erlbaum Associates.

Boulding, Kenneth E. (1981). Human knowledge as a special system. *Behavioral Science, 26,* 93–102.

Brady, Susan A. and Donald P. Shankweiler (1991). *Phonological Processes in Literacy: A Tribute to Isabelle Y. Liberman.* Hillsdale, NJ: Lawrence Erlbaum Associates.

Bransford, John D., Barry S. Stein, and Nancy J. Vye (1982). Helping students learn how to learn from written texts. In Singer, M. H. (Ed.), *Competent Reading, Disabled Reader: Research and Application.* Hillsdale, NJ: Lawrence Erlbaum Associates.

Bridges, Allayne, Chris Sinha, and Valerie Walkerdine (1981). The development of comprehension. In Wells, Gordon (Ed.), *Learning Through Interaction: The Study of Language Development.* Cambridge, UK: Cambridge University Press.

Broadbent, Donald E. (1967). The word-frequency effect and response bias. *Psychological Review, 74,* 1–15.

Broadbent, Donald E. and Margaret H. P. Broadbent (1975). Some further data concerning the word frequency effect. *Journal of Experimental Psychology: General, 104,* 297–308.

Brown, Ann L. (1982). Learning how to learn from reading. In Langer, Judith A. and M. Trika Smith-Burke (Eds.), *Reader Meets Author/Bridging the Gap.* Newark, DE: International Reading Association.

Brown, Ann L. and Annemarie S. Palincsar (1989). Guided, cooperative learning and individual knowledge acquisition. In Resnick, Lauren (Ed.), *Knowing, Learning, and Instruction: Essays in Honor of Robert Glaser.* Hillsdale, NJ: Lawrence Erlbaum Associates.

Brown, H. Douglas (1970). Categories of spelling difficulty in speakers of English as a first and second language. *Journal of Verbal Learning and Verbal Behavior, 9,* 232–236.

Brown, Roger and David McNeill (1966). The "tip of the tongue" phenomenon. *Journal of Verbal Learning and Verbal Behavior, 5*(4), 325–337.

Bruner, Jerome S. (1986). *Actual Minds, Possible Worlds.* Cambridge, MA: Harvard University Press.

Bruner, Jerome S. and D. O'Dowd (1958). A note on the informativeness of parts of words. *Language and Speech, 1,* 98–101.

Bruner, Jerome and Susan Weisser (1991). The invention of self: Autobiography and its forms. In Olson, David R. and Nancy Torrance (Eds.), *Literacy and Orality*. Cambridge, UK: Cambridge University Press.

Bryant, Peter and Lawrence Impey (1986). The similarities between normal readers and developmental and acquired dyslexics. *Cognition, 24*, 121–137.

Buckner, Aimee (2002). Teaching in a world focused on testing. *Language Arts, 79*(3), 212–215.

Burton, Mike (1992). Good morning, Mr ... er. *New Scientist, 133*(1806), 39–41.

Cadiero-Kaplan, Karen. (2002). Literacy ideologies: Critically engaging the language arts curriculum. *Language Arts, 78*(5), 372–381.

Cairney, Trevor H. (1990). *Teaching Reading Comprehension: Meaning Makers at Work*. Milton Keynes: Open University.

Cairney, Trevor (1992). Mountain or mole hill: The genre debate viewed from "down under." *Reading, 36*, 23–29.

Calfee, Robert C. (1983). The mind of the dyslexic. In Hartwig, Elinor Linn (Ed.), *Annals of Dyslexia*, Vol. 33. Baltimore: Orton Dyslexia Society.

Calkins, Lucy (1980). When children want to punctuate: Basic skills belong in context. *Language Arts, 57*, 567–573.

Caplan, David (Ed.) (1980). *Biological Studies of Mental Processes*. Cambridge, MA: MIT Press.

Carbo, Marie (1988). Debunking the great phonics myth. *Phi Delta Kappan, 70*(3), 226–240.

Carbo, Marie, Rita Dunn, and Kenneth Dunn (1987). *Teaching Students to Read Through Their Individualized Learning Styles*. Reston, VA: Prentice-Hall.

Carey, Susan (1978). The child as word learner. In Halle, Morris, J. Breslin, and George A. Miller (Eds.), *Linguistic Theory and Psychological Reality*. Cambridge, MA: MIT Press.

Carpenter, Patricia A. and Marcel A. Just (1975). Sentence comprehension: A psycholinguistic processing model of verification. *Psychological Review, 82*, 45–73.

Carpenter, Patricia A. and Meredyth Daneman (1981). Lexical retrieval and error recovery in reading: A model based on eye fixations. *Journal of Verbal Learning and Verbal Behavior, 20*, 137–160.

Carver, Ronald P. (1985). How good are some of the world's best readers? *Reading Research Quarterly, 20*(4), 389–419.

Carver, Ronald P. (1992). Reading rate: Theory, research and practical implications. *Journal of Reading, 36*(2), 84–95.

Castiglioni-Spalton, M. and Linnea C. Ehri (2003). Phonemic awareness instruction: Contribution of articulatory segmentation to novice beginners' reading and writing. *Scientific Studies of Reading, 7*(1), 25–52.

Cattell, James McKeen (1973). Ueber die Zeit der Erkennung und Benennung von Schriftzeichen, Bildern und Farben [On the time required for recognizing and naming letters and words, pictures and colors.] *Philosophische Studien* (1885), *2*, 635–650. Translated and reprinted in Poffenberger, A. T. (Ed.), *James McKeen Cattell, Man of Science, 1860–1944* (Vol. 1). New York: Arno Press.

Cazden, Courtney B. (1992). *Whole Language Plus: Essays on Literacy in the United States and New Zealand.* New York: Teachers College Press.

Chafe, Wallace (1992). Immediacy and displacement in consciousness and language. In Stein, Dieter (Ed.), *Cooperating with Written Texts: The Pragmatics and Comprehension of Written Texts.* Berlin: Mouton de Gruyter, pp. 231–255.

Chall, Jeanne S. (1967). *Learning to Read: The Great Debate.* New York: McGraw-Hill.

Chall, Jeanne S. (1989). Learning to read: The great debate 20 years later: A response to "Debunking the great phonics myth." *Phi Delta Kappan, 70*(7), 521–538.

Chall, Jeanne S. (1992/1993). Research supports direct instruction models. In Point/Counterpoint: Whole language versus direct instruction models. *Reading Today, 10*(3), 8–10.

Chambers, Maryl, Adrian Jackson, and Mary Rose (1993). *Children Developing as Readers: The Avon Collaborative Reading Project*: Bristol, UK: County of Avon.

Cho, Kyung-Sook and Stephen D. Krashen (1994). Acquisition of vocabulary from the Sweet Valley Kids series: Adult ESL acquisition. *Journal of Reading, 37*(8), 662–667.

Chomsky, Noam (1957). *Syntactic Structures.* The Hague: Mouton.

Chomsky, Noam (1959). Review of *Verbal Learning* (by B. F. Skinner). *Language, 35,* 26–58.

Chomsky, Noam and Morris Halle (1968). *Sound Pattern of English.* New York: Harper and Row.

Christensen, Carol A. (1997). Onset, rhymes, and phonemes in learning to read, *Scientific Studies of Reading, 1*(4), 341–358.

Clark, Eve V. (1993). *The Lexicon in Acquisition.* Cambridge, UK: Cambridge University Press.

Clark, Eve V. and Barbara Frant Hecht (1983). Comprehension, production, and language acquisition. *Annual Review of Psychology, 34,* 325–349.

Clark, Margaret M. (1976). *Young Fluent Readers.* London: Heinemann.

Clay, Marie (1985). *The Early Detection of Reading Difficulties.* Portsmouth, NH: Heinemann.

Clay, Marie (1992/1993). Language policy and literacy learning. *Reading Today, 10*(3), 3–4.

Clay, Marie M. (1979). Theoretical research and instructional change: A case study. In Resnick, Lauren B. and Phyllis A. Weaver (Eds.), *Theory and Practice of Early Reading.* Hillsdale, NJ: Lawrence Erlbaum Associates.

Clymer, Theodore (1963a). The utility of phonic generalizations in the primary grades. *The Reading Teacher, 16,* 252–258.

Clymer, Theodore (1963b). Does "can" mean "should"? *The Reading Teacher, 16,* 217.

Cohen, Jonathan D., and Schooler, Jonathan W. (Eds.) (1997). *Scientific Approaches to Consciousness.* Mahwah, NJ: Lawrence Erlbaum Associates.

Coles, Gerald (1987). *The Learning Mystique.* New York: Pantheon.

Coles, Gerald (2000). *Misreading Reading: The Bad Science That Hurts Children*. Portsmouth, NH: Heinemann.

Cornman, O. (1902). *Spelling in the Elementary School*. Boston, MA: Ginn.

Coulmas, Florian (1990). *The Writing Systems of the World*. Oxford: Blackwood.

Coulmas, Florian (1992). On the relationship between writing system, written language, and text processing. In Stein, Dieter (Ed.), *Cooperating with Written Texts: The Pragmatics and Comprehension of Written Texts*. Berlin: Mouton de Gruyter.

Courts, Patrick L. (1991). *Literacy and Empowerment: The Meaning Makers*. New York: Bergin and Garvey.

Cronbach, Lee J. (1992). Four *Psychological Bulletin* articles in perspective. *Psychological Bulletin, 112*(3), 389–392.

Crowder, Robert G. and Richard K. Wagner (1991). *The Psychology of Reading: An Introduction*. New York: Oxford University Press.

Csikszentmihalyi, Mihaly (1990). *Flow—The Psychology of Optimal Experience*. New York: Harper & Row.

Davis, Steven (Ed.) (1991). *Pragmatics: A Reader*. Oxford: Oxford University Press.

Deely, John (1982). *Introducing Semiotics*. Bloomington: Indiana University Press.

DeFord, Diane E. (1981). Literacy: Reading, writing and other essentials. *Language Arts, 58*(5), 652–658.

Dodge, R. (1900). Visual perceptions during eye movement. *Psychological Review, VII*, 454–465.

Dodwell, Peter (2000). *Brave New Mind: A Thoughtful Inquiry into the Nature and Meaning of Mental Life*. New York: Oxford University Press.

Doehring, Donald G. (1976). Acquisition of rapid reading responses. *Monographs of the Society for Research in Child Development, 41*(2), No. 165.

Dombey, Henrietta (1988). Stories at home and at school. In Lightfoot, Martin and Nancy Martin (Eds.), *The Word for Teaching is Learning: Essays for James Britton*. London: Heinemann.

Dorman, Casey (1985). Defining and diagnosing dyslexia: Are we putting the cart before the horse? *Reading Research Quarterly, 20*(4), 505–508.

Downing, John (1977). How society creates reading disability. *Elementary School Journal, 77*, 274–279.

Downing, John (1979). *Reading and Reasoning*. New York: Springer-Verlag.

Downing, John and Peter Oliver (1973/1974). The child's conception of "a word." *Reading Research Quarterly, 9*(4), 568–582.

Duckett, Peter (2002). New insights: Eye fixations and the reading process. *Talking Points, 13*(2), 16–21.

Dudley-Marling, Curt and Don Dippo (1991). The language of whole language. *Language Arts, 68*, 548–554.

Dudley-Marling, Curt and Sharon Murphy (2001). Changing the way we think about language arts. *Language Arts*, *78*(6), 574–578.

Duke, Nell K. (2000), For the rich it's richer: Print experiences and environments offered to children in very low- and very high-socioeconomic status first-grade classrooms. *American Educational Research Journal*, *37*(2), 441–478.

Dunn-Rankin, Peter (1968). The similarity of lower case letters of the English alphabet. *Journal of Verbal Learning and Verbal Behavior*, *7*, 990–995.

Durkin, Dolores (1981). What is the value of the new interest in reading comprehension? *Language Arts*, *58*(1), 23–43.

Durkin, Dolores (1984). Poor black children who are successful readers: An investigation. *Urban Education*, *19*, 53–76.

Eagleton, Terry (1983). *Literacy Theory: An Introduction*. Minneapolis: University of Minnesota Press.

Eckhoff, Barbara (1983). How reading affects children's writing. *Language Arts*, *60*(5), 607–616.

Edelsky, Carole (1991). *With Literacy and Justice for All: Rethinking the Social in Language and Education*. Bristol, PA: Falmer.

Ehri, Linnea C. (1985). How orthography alters spoken language competencies in children learning to read and spell. In Downing, John and Renate Valtin (Eds.), *Language Awareness and Learning to Read*. New York: Springer-Verlag.

Ehri, Linnea C. (1992). Reconceptualizing the development of sight word reading and its relationship to recoding. In Gough, Philip B., Linnea C. Ehri, and Rebecca Treiman (Eds.), *Reading Acquisition*. Hillsdale, NJ: Lawrence Erlbaum Associates.

Ehri, Linnea C. (1997). Sight word learning in normal readers and dyslexics. In Blachman, Benita (Ed.), *Foundations of Reading Acquisition and Dyslexia: Implications for Early Intervention*. Mahwah, NJ: Lawrence Erlbaum Associates.

Eldredge, J. Lloyd (1990). Increasing the performance of poor readers in the third grade with a group-assisted strategy. *Journal of Educational Research*, *84*(2), 69–77.

Elley, Warwick (1989). Vocabulary acquisition from listening to stories. *Reading Research Quarterly*, *24*, 174–187.

Elley, Warwick B. (1992). *How in the World Do Students Read?* The IEA Study of Reading Literacy. The Hague: International Association for the Evaluation of Educational Achievement.

Elley, Warwick B. (1996). *Raising literacy levels in third world countries: A method that works*. Paper presented at the World Conference on Literacy, Philadelphia, March 1996.

Elley, Warwick B. and Francis Mangubhai (1983). The impact of reading on second language learning. *Reading Research Quarterly*, *19*, 53–67.

Erdmann, B. and R. Dodge (1898). *Psychologische Untersuchungen ueber das Lesen auf Experimenteller Grundlage*. Halle: Niemeyer.

Ericsson, K. Anders, William G. Chase, and Steve Falcon (1980). Acquisition of a memory skill. *Science*, *208*, 1181–1182.

Ewoldt, Carolyn (1981). A psycholinguistic description of selected deaf children reading in sign language. *Reading Research Quarterly*, *17*(1), 58–89.

Fernandez-Armesto, Felipe (2000). *Civilizations: Culture, Ambition, and the Transformation of Nature*. New York: Free Press.

Ferreiro, Emilia (1978). What is written in a written sentence? A developmental answer. *Journal of Education*, *160*(4), 25–39.

Ferreiro, Emilia (1985). Literacy development: A psychogenetic perspective. In Olson, David R., Nancy Torrance, and Angela Hildyard (Eds.), *Literacy, Language and Learning: The Nature and Consequences of Reading and Writing*. Cambridge, UK: Cambridge University Press.

Ferreiro, Emelia and Ana Teberosky (1982). *Literacy Before Schooling*. Exeter, NH: Heinemann.

Fiske, Donald W. and Donald T. Campbell (1992). Citations do not solve problems. *Psychological Bulletin*, *112*(3), 393–395.

Fodor, Jerry A. (Ed.) (1981). *Representations*. Cambridge, MA: MIT Press.

Fodor, Jerry A. (1990). *A Theory of Content and Other Essays*. Cambridge, MA: MIT Press.

Fodor, Jerry A., Merrill F. Garrett, E. Walker, and C. H. Parkes (1980). Against definitions. *Cognition*, *8*, 263–367.

Forster, Kenneth I. (1970). Visual perception of rapidly-presented word sequences of varying complexity. *Perception and Psychophysics*, *8*, 215–221.

Fosnot, Catherine Twomey (Ed.) (1996). *Constructivism: Theory, Perspectives and Practice*. New York: Teachers College Press.

Fraisse, Paul (1984). Perceptual processing of words and drawings. In Sarris, Victor and Allen Parducci (Eds.), *Perspectives in Psychological Experimentation: Toward the Year 2000*. Hillsdale, NJ: Lawrence Erlbaum Associates.

Freire, Paulo (1972). *Pedagogy of the Oppressed*. New York: Herder and Herder.

Fries, Charles C. (1945). *Teaching and Learning English as a Foreign Language*. Ann Arbor: University of Michigan Press.

Furness, David W. and Michael F. Graves (1980). Effects of stressing oral reading accuracy on comprehension. *Reading Psychology*, *2*(1), 8–14.

Gallistel, Charles R. (1990). *The Organization of Learning*. Cambridge, MA: MIT Press.

Garan, Elaine M. (2002). *Resisting Reading Mandates: How to Triumph With the Truth*. Portsmouth, NH: Heinemann.

Garner, Ruth (1992). Metacognition and self-monitoring strategies. In Samuels, S. Jay and Alan E. Farstrup (Eds.), *What Research Has to Say About Reading Instruction* (Second edition). Newark, DE: International Reading Association.

Garner, Wendell R. (1962). *Uncertainty and Structure as Psychological Concepts*. New York: Wiley.

Garner, Wendell R. (1974). *The Processing of Information and Structure*. Hillsdale, NJ: Lawrence Erlbaum Associates.

Gibbs, Raymond W. (1984). Literal meaning and psychological theory. *Cognitive Science, 8*, 275–304.

Gibson, Eleanor J. (1965). Learning to read. *Science, 148*, 1066–1072.

Gill, J. Thomas (1992). Development of word knowledge as it relates to reading, spelling and instruction. *Language Arts, 69*, 444–453.

Gillooly, William B. (1973). The influence of writing system characteristics on learning to read. *Reading Research Quarterly, 8*(2), 167–199.

Giroux, Henry (1992). Educational leadership and the crisis of democratic government. *Educational Researcher, 21*(4), 4–11.

Goelman, Hillel, Antoinette A. Oberg, and Frank Smith (Eds.) (1984). *Awakening to Literacy.* Portsmouth, NH: Heinemann.

Golden, Joanne M. and John T. Guthrie (1986). Convergence and divergence in reader response to literature. *Reading Research Quarterly, 21*(4), 408–421.

Goldsmith-Phillips, J. (1989). Word and context in reading development: A test of the interactive-compensatory hypothesis. *Journal of Educational Psychology, 81*, 299–305.

Golinkoff, Roberta Michnick (1975/1976). A comparison of reading comprehension processes in good and poor readers. *Reading Research Quarterly, 11*, 623–659.

Goodman, Kenneth S. (1967). Reading: A psycholinguistic guessing game. *Journal of the Reading Specialist, 6*, 126–135.

Goodman, Kenneth S. (1969). Analysis of oral reading miscues: Applied psycholinguistics. *Reading Research Quarterly, 5*(1), 9–30.

Goodman, Kenneth S. (1986). *What's Whole in Whole Language?* Richmond Hill, ON: Scholastic.

Goodman, Kenneth S. (1992/1993). Gurus, professors, and the politics of phonics, in Point/Counterpoint, Whole language versus direct instruction models. *Reading Today, 10*(3), 8–10.

Goodman, Kenneth S., Patrick Shannon, Yvonne S. Freeman, and Sharon Murphy (1988). *Report Card on Basal Readers.* Katonah, NY: Richard C. Owen.

Goodman, Yetta M. (1978). Kid watching: An alternative to testing. *National Elementary Principal, 57*(4), 41–45.

Goodman, Yetta M. (1980). The roots of literacy. In Douglass, Malcolm P. (Ed.), *Proceedings: Claremont Reading Conference, 44th Annual Yearbook.* Claremont, CA.

Goody, Jack and Ian Watt (1972). The consequences of literacy. In Gigliolo, P. P. (Ed.), *Language and Social Context.* London: Penguin.

Gorman, Tom, Dougal Hutchison, and John Trimble (1993). *Reading in Reform: The Avon Collaborative Reading Project*: Slough, UK: National Foundation for Educational Research in England and Wales.

Goswami, Usha C. (1986). Children's use of analogy in learning to read: A developmental study. *Journal of Experimental Child Psychology, 42*, 73–83.

Goswami, Usha C. (1990). Phonological priming and orthographic analogies in reading. *Journal of Experimental Child Psychology, 49*, 323–340.

Goswami, Usha C. (2001). Rhymes are important: A comment on Savage. *Journal of Reading Research*, 24(1), 19–30.

Goswami, Usha C. and Peter Bryant (1990). *Phonological Skills and Learning to Read*. Hove, UK: Lawrence Erlbaum Associates.

Goswami, Usha C. and Peter Bryant (1992). Rhyme, analogy, and children's reading. In Gough, Philip B., Linnea C. Ehri, and Rebecca Treiman (Eds.) *Reading Acquisition*. Hillsdale, NJ: Lawrence Erlbaum Associates.

Gough, Philip B., Linnea C. Ehri, and Rebecca Treiman (Eds.) (1992). *Reading Acquisition*. Hillsdale, NJ: Lawrence Erlbaum Associates.

Gough, Philip B. and M. L. Hillinger (1980). Learning to read: An unnatural act. *Bulletin of the Orton Society*, 30, 180–196.

Gough, Philip B. and Margaret A. Walsh (1991). Chinese, Phoenicians, and the orthographic cipher of English. In Brady, Susan A. and Donald P. Shankweiler (Eds.), *Phonological Processes in Literacy: A Tribute to Isabelle Y. Liberman*. Hillsdale, NJ: Lawrence Erlbaum Associates.

Graff, Harvey J. (1986). The Legacies of Literacy: Continuities and Contradictions in Western Culture and Society. In de Castell, Suzanne, Allan Luke, and Kieran Egan (Eds.), *Literacy, Society and Schooling: A Reader*. New York: Cambridge University Press.

Graff, Harvey J. (1987a). *The Labyrinths of Literacy: Reflections on Literacy Past and Present*. Philadelphia: Falmer.

Graff, Harvey J. (1987b). *The Legacies of Literacy: Continuities and Contradictions in Western Culture and Society*. Bloomington: Indiana University Press.

Graham, Steven (1980). Word recognition skills of learning disabled children and average students. *Reading Psychology*, 2(1), 23–33.

Grimes, Joseph E. (1975). *The Thread of Discourse*. The Hague: Mouton.

Haber, Lyn R., Ralph N. Haber, and Karen R. Furlin (1983). Word length and word shape as sources of information in reading. *Reading Research Quarterly*, 18(2), 165–189.

Haber, Ralph N. and Lyn R. Haber (1981). The shape of a word can specify its meaning. *Reading Research Quarterly*, 16(3), 334–345.

Halliday, Michael A. K. (1973). *Explorations in the Functions of Language*. London: Arnold.

Hamill, Donald D. and Gaye McNutt (1981). *The Correlates of Reading*. Austin, TX: Pro-Ed.

Harding, Leonora M., John R. Beech, and William Sneddon (1985). The changing pattern of reading errors and reading style from 5 to 11 years of age. *British Journal of Educational Psychology*, 55, 45–52.

Hardyck, C. D. and L. F. Petrinovich (1970). Subvocal speech and comprehension level as a function of the difficulty level of reading material. *Journal of Verbal Learning and Verbal Behavior*, 9, 647–652.

Harste, Jerome C., Virginia A. Woodward, and Carolyn L. Burke (1984). *Language Stories and Literacy Lessons*. Portsmouth, NH: Heinemann.

Hartman, Maria and Robert E. Kretschmer (1992). Talking and writing: Deaf teenagers reading *Sarah, Plain and Tall*. *Journal of Reading*, 36(3), 174–180.

Havelock, Eric A. (1976). *Origins of Western Literacy*. Toronto: Ontario Institute for Studies in Education.

Heath, Shirley Brice (1982). What no bedtime story means: Narrative skills at home and at school. *Language in Society, 11*, 49–76.

Heath, Shirley Brice (1983). Research currents: A lot of talk about nothing. *Language Arts, 60*(4), 999–1007.

Heath, Shirley Brice (1986). The functions and uses of literacy. In de Castell, Suzanne, Allan Luke, and Kieran Egan (Eds.), *Literacy, Society and Schooling: A Reader*. New York: Cambridge University Press.

Heath, Shirley Brice, Leslie Mangiola, Sandra R. Schachter, and Glynda A. Hull (Eds.) (1991). *Children of Promise: Literate Activity in Linguistically and Culturally Diverse Classrooms*. Urbana, IL: National Council of Teachers of English.

Heath, Shirley Brice and Charlene Thomas (1984). The achievement of pre-school literacy for mother and child. In Goelman, Hillel, Antoinette A. Oberg, and Frank Smith (Eds.), *Awakening to Literacy*. Exeter, NH: Heinemann.

Heckenmueller, E. G. (1965). Stabilization of the retinal image: A review of method, effects and theory. *Psychological Review, 63*, 157–169.

Hedley, Carolyn and Anthony N. Baratta (Eds.) (1985). *Contexts of Reading*. Norwood, NJ: Ablex.

Helfand, Duke (2002). Teens Get a Second Chance at Literacy Education. *Los Angeles Times*, July 21, 2002.

Henderson, John M. (1976). Learning to read: A case study of a deaf child. *American Annals of the Deaf, 121*, 502–506.

Hidi, Suzanne, William Baird, and Angela Hildyard (1982). That's important but is it interesting? Two factors in text processing. In Flammer, August and Walter Kintsch (Eds.), *Discourse Processing*. Amsterdam: North Holland.

Hiebert, Elfrieda H. (1983). An examination of ability grouping for reading instruction. *Reading Research Quarterly, 18*(3), 231–255.

Hiebert, Elfrieda H. and Robert E. Calfee (1992). Assessing literacy: From standardized tests to portfolios and performances. In Samuels, S. Jay and Alan E. Farstrup (Eds.), *What Research Has to Say About Reading Instruction* (2nd ed.). Newark, DE: International Reading Association.

Holdaway, Don (1976). Self-evaluation and reading development. In Merritt, John (Ed.), *New Horizons in Reading*. Newark, DE: International Reading Association.

Howe, M. J. A. and Linda Singer (1975). Presentation variables and students' activities in meaningful learning. *British Journal of Educational Psychology, 45*, 52–61.

Howes, D. H. and R. L. Solomon (1951). Visual duration threshold as a function of word-probability. *Journal of Experimental Psychology, 41*, 401–410.

Huck, Charlotte S. (1992). Literacy and literature. *Language Arts, 69*, 520–526.

Huey, Edmund Burke (1908). *The Psychology and Pedagogy of Reading*. New York: Macmillan. Reprinted Cambridge, MA: MIT Press (1968).

Hull, Robert (1985). *The Language Gap: How Classroom Dialogue Fails*. London: Methuen.

Hummel, John E. and Irving Biederman (1992). Dynamic binding in a neural network for shape recognition. *Psychological Review, 99*(3), 480–517.

Hunt, Earl and Franca Agnoli (1991). The Whorfian hypothesis: A cognitive psychology perspective. *Psychological Review, 98*(3), 377–389.

International Reading Association Board of Directors (1999/2000). Position statement. *Reading Today*, December 1999/January 2000, 37.

Intraub, Helen and James E. Hoffman (1992). Reading and visual memory: Remembering scenes that were never seen. *American Journal of Psychology, 105*(1), 101–114.

Jakobson, Roman and Morris Halle (1956). *Fundamentals of Language*. The Hague: Mouton.

Johnson-Laird, Philip N., Ruth M. J. Byrne, and Walter Schaeken (1992). Propositional reasoning by model. *Psychological Review, 99*(3), 418–439.

Johnston, Francine R. (2000/2001). Spelling exceptions: Problems or possibilities? *The Reading Teacher, 54*(4), 372–373.

Johnston, Francine R. (2001). The utility of phonic generalizations: Let's take another look at Clymer's conclusions. *The Reading Teacher, 55*(2), 132–143.

Johnston, Peter H. (1985). Understanding reading disability: A case-study approach. *Harvard Educational Review, 55*(2), 153–177.

Judd, C. H., and G. T. Buswell (1922). *Silent Reading: A Study of the Various Types*. Chicago, IL: University of Chicago Press.

Juel, Connie and Diana Roper/Schneider (1985). The influence of basal readers on first grade reading. *Reading Research Quarterly, 20*(2), 134–152.

Just, Marcel A. and Patricia A. Carpenter (1980). A theory of reading, from eye fixations to comprehension. *Psychological Review, 87*(6), 329–354.

Kamii, Constance K. (1985). *Young Children Reinvent Arithmetic: Implications of Piaget's Theory*. New York: Teachers College Press.

Kimmel, Susan and Walter H. MacGinitie (1984). Identifying children who use a perseverative text processing strategy. *Reading Research Quarterly, 19*(2), 162–172.

Kintsch, Walter (1982). Memory for text. In Flammer, August and Walter Kintsch. *Discourse Processing*. Amsterdam: North Holland.

Kintsch, Walter (1988). The use of knowledge in discourse processing: A construction-integration model. *Psychological Review, 95*, 163–182.

Klahr, D., W. G. Chase, and E. A. Lovelace (1983). Structure and process in alphabetic retrieval. *Journal of Experimental Psychology: Learning, Memory and Cognition, 9*, 462–477.

Klein, Helen Altman, Gary A. Klein, and Mary Bertino (1974). Utilization of context for word identification in children. *Journal of Experimental Psychology, 17*, 79–86.

Kolers, Paul A. (1966). Reading and talking bilingually. *American Journal of Psychology, 79*, 357–376.

Kolers, Paul A. (1967). Reading is only incidentally visual. In Goodman, Kenneth S. and James T. Fleming (Eds.), *Psycholinguistics and the Teaching of Reading*. Newark, DE: International Reading Association.

Kolers, Paul A. and M. T. Katzman (1966). Naming sequentially presented letters and words. *Language and Speech, 9*(2), 84–95.

Korkeamäki, Riitta-Liisa, and Mariam Jean Dreher (1993). Finland, phonics, and whole language: Beginning reading in a regular letter–sound correspondence language. *Language Arts, 70*, 475–482.

Kozol, Jonathan (1991). *Savage Inequalities: Children in America's Schools*. New York: Harper Collins.

Krashen, Stephen D. (1985). *Inquiries and Insights*. Hayward, CA: Alemany Press.

Krashen, Stephen D. (1987). *Comic Book Reading and Language Development*. Victoria, BC: Abel Press.

Krashen, Stephen D. (1993a). How well do people spell? *Reading Improvement, 31*, 9–20.

Krashen, Stephen D. (1993b). *The Power of Reading: Insights from the Research*. Englewood, CO: Libraries Unlimited.

Krashen, Stephen D. (1995). School libraries, public libraries, and the NEAP reading scores. *School Library Media Quarterly, 23*, 235–238.

Krashen, Stephen D. (1999a): *Three Arguments Against Whole Language and Why They Are Wrong*. Portsmouth, NH: Heinemann.

Krashen, Stephen D. (1999b). Training in phonemic awareness: Greater on tests of phonemic awareness. *Perceptual and Motor Skills, 89*, 412–416.

Krashen, Stephen D. (2001a). The testing movement and delayed gratification. *Educators for Urban Minorities, 2*(1), 48–50.

Krashen, Stephen D. (2001b). Low P.A. can read O.K. *Practically Primary, 6*(2), 17–19.

Krashen, Stephen D. (2001c). Does "pure" phonemic awareness training affect reading comprehension? *Perceptual and Motor Skills, 93*, 356–358.

Krashen, Stephen D. (2002). The lexile framework: The controversy continues. *CSLA Journal, 25*(2), 29–31.

Krashen, Stephen D. (2003). *Explorations in Language Acquisition and Use*. Portsmouth, NH: Heinemann.

Krashen, Stephen D. and Howard White (1991). Is spelling acquired or learned? A re-analysis of Rice (1897) and Cornman (1902). *ITL Review of Applied Linguistics, 91–92*, 1–48.

Krueger, Lester E., Robert H. Keen, and Bella Rublevich (1974). Letter search through words and nonwords by adults and fourth-grade children. *Journal of Experimental Psychology, 102*(5), 845–849.

Kucer, Stephen B. and Jenny Tuten (2003). Revisiting and rethinking the reading process. *Language Arts, 80*(4), 284–290.

Kuhn, Thomas (1970). *The Structure of Scientific Revolutions*. Chicago: University of Chicago Press.

Kutz, Eleanor (1992). Teacher research: Myths and realities. *Language Arts, 69*, 193–197.

Lakoff, George (1987). *Women, Fire, and Dangerous Things: What Categories Reveal About the Mind.* Chicago: University of Chicago Press.

Langer, Judith A. (1982a). Facilitating text processing: The elaboration of prior knowledge. In Langer, Judith A. and M. Trika Smith-Burke (Eds.), *Reader meets author/Bridging the gap.* Newark, DE: International Reading Association.

Langer, Judith A. (1982b). Reading, thinking, writing ... and teaching. *Language Arts, 59*(4), 336–341.

Larsen, Steen F. (1986). Procedural thinking, programming and computer use. In Hollnagel, E., G. Mancini, and D. Woods (Eds.), *Intelligent Decision Aids in Process Environments.* Berlin: Springer-Verlag.

Larson, Joanne (Ed.) (2001). *Literacy as Snake Oil: Beyond the "Quick Fix."* New York: Lang.

Lehr, Fran and Jean Osborn (eds.) (1994). *Reading, Language and Literacy: Instruction for the Twenty-First Century.* Hillsdale, NJ: Erlbaum.

Levine, K. (1986). *The Social Context of Literacy.* London: Routledge and Kegan Paul.

Levy, Betty Ann (1978). Speech analysis during sentence processing: Reading and listening. *Visible Language, 12,* 81–102.

Lewis, Donald J. (1979). Psychobiology of active and inactive memory. *Psychological Bulletin, 86,* 1054–1083.

Liberman, Alvin M., Franklin S. Cooper, Donald P. Shankweiler, and M. Studdert-Kennedy (1957). Perception of the speech code. *Psychological Review, 54,* 358–368.

Liberman, Isabelle Y. and Alvin M. Liberman (1992). Whole language versus code emphasis: Underlying assumptions and their implications for reading instruction. In Gough, Philip B., Linnea C. Ehri and Rebecca Treiman (Eds.) *Reading Acquisition,* Hillsdale, NJ: Lawrence Erlbaum Associates.

Lipson, Marjorie Y. and Karen K. Wixson (1986). Reading disability research: An interactionist perspective. *Review of Educational Research, 56*(1), 111–136.

Littlefair, Alison B. (1991). *Reading All Types of Writing: The Importance of Genre and Register for Reading Development.* Milton Keynes: Open University.

Lodge, David (1990). *After Bakhtin: Essays on Fiction and Criticism.* London: Routledge.

Long, Shirley A., Peter N. Winograd, and Connie A. Bridge (1989). The effects of reader and text characteristics on imagery reported during and after reading. *Reading Research Quarterly, 24*(3), 353–372.

Lott, Deborah and Frank Smith (1970). Knowledge of intra-word redundancy by beginning readers. *Psychonomic Science, 19*(6), 343–344.

MacGinitie, Walter (1984). Readability as a solution adds to the problem. In Anderson, Richard C., Jean Osborn, and Robert J. Tierney (Eds.), *Learning to Read in American Schools: Basal Readers and Content Texts.* Hillsdale, NJ: Lawrence Erlbaum Associates.

MacGinitie, Walter and Ruth K. MacGinitie (1986). Teaching students not to read. In de Castell, Suzanne, A. Luke, and Kieran Egan (Eds.), *Literacy, Society and Schooling: A Reader.* New York: Cambridge University Press.

Mackworth, Norman H. (1965). Visual noise causes tunnel vision. *Psychonomic Science*, 3, 67–68.

Macmillan, Bonnie M. (2002). Rhyme and reading. A critical review of the research methodology. *Journal of Research in Reading*, 25(1), 4–42.

Macnamara, John (1972). Cognitive basis of language learning in infants. *Psychological Review*, 79(1), 1–13.

Magee, Bryan (1973). *Popper*. London: Fontana.

Mandler, George (1980). Recognizing: The judgment of previous occurrence. *Psychological Review*, 87(3), 252–271.

Mandler, George (1985). *Cognitive Psychology: An Essay in Cognitive Science*. Hillsdale, NJ: Lawrence Erlbaum Associates.

Mandler, Jean Matter (1984). *Stories, Script, and Scenes: Aspects of Schema Theory*. Hillsdale, NJ: Lawrence Erlbaum Associates.

Mandler, Jean Matter (1992). How to build a baby: II. Conceptual primitives. *Psychological Review*, 99(4), 587–604.

Mandler, Jean Matter and Marsha S. Goodman (1982). On the psychological validity of story structure. *Journal of Verbal Learning and Verbal Behavior*, 21, 507–523.

Markman, Ellen M. (1992). Constraints on word learning: Speculations about their nature, origins and domain specificity. In Gunnar, Megan R. and Michael Maratsos (Eds.), *Modularity and Constraints in Language and Cognition* (The Minnesota Symposia on Child Psychology, Vol. 25). Hillsdale, NJ: Lawrence Erlbaum Associates.

Marshall, John C. and F. Newcombe (1966). Syntactic and semantic errors in paralexia. *Neuropsychologia*, 4, 169–176.

Masonheimer, Patricia E., Priscilla A. Drum, and Linnea C. Ehri (1984). Does environmental print identification lead children into word reading? *Journal of Reading Behavior*, 16(4), 257–272.

Mathews, Mitford M. (1966). *Teaching to Read: Historically Considered*. Chicago: University of Chicago Press.

McCabe, Viki and Gerald J. Balzano (Eds.) (1986). *Event Cognition: An Ecological Perspective*. Hillsdale, NJ: Lawrence Erlbaum Associates.

McCawley, James D. (1968). The role of semantics in a grammar. In Eamon Bach and R. T. Harms (Eds.), *Universals in Linguistic Theory*. New York: Holt, Rinehart and Winston.

McClelland, J. L. and J. K. O'Regan (1981). Expectations increase the benefit derived from parafoveal visual information in reading words aloud. *Journal of Experimental Psychology: Human Perception and Performance*, 7(3), 634–644.

McFarland, Carl E. and Deborah H. Rhodes (1978). Memory for meaning in skilled and unskilled readers. *Journal of Experimental Child Psychology*, 25, 199–207.

McGee, Lea M. (1982). Awareness of text structure: Effects on children's recall of expository text. *Reading Research Quarterly*, 17(4), 581–590.

McGee, Lea M. (1992). Exploring the literature-based reading revolution. *Language Arts*, 69, 529–537.

McKeown, Margaret G. (1985). The acquisition of word meaning from context by children of high and low ability. *Reading Research Quarterly*, 20(4), 482–496.

McKeown, Margaret G. (1993). Creating effecting definitions for young word learners. *Reading Research Quarterly*, *28*(1), 16–31.

McMahon, Susan I. (1992). Book club: A case study of a group of fifth graders as they participate in a literature based reading program. (IRA Outstanding Dissertation Award for 1991–1992). *Reading Research Quarterly*, *27*(4), 292–293.

McNamara, Timothy P., Diane I. Miller, and John D. Bransford (1991). Mental models and reading comprehension. In Barr, Rebecca, Michael L. Kamil, Peter Mosenthal, and P. David Pearson (Eds.), *Handbook of Reading Research*. New York: Longman.

McNeill, Daniel (1998). *The Face: A Natural History*. Boston, MA: Little Brown.

McNeill, David (1967). Developmental psycholinguistics. In Smith, Frank and George A. Miller (Eds.), *The Genesis of Language*. Cambridge, MA: MIT Press.

McNeill, David (1985). So you think gestures are nonverbal? *Psychological Review*, *92*(3), 350–371.

McNeill, David and Karen Lindig (1973). The perceptual reality of phonemes, syllables, words and sentences. *Journal of Verbal Learning and Verbal Behavior*, *12*(4), 419–430.

McPeck, John E. (1981). *Critical Thinking and Education*. Oxford: Martin Robertson.

McQuillan, Jeff (1998). *The Literacy Crisis: False Claims and Real Solutions*. Portsmouth, NH: Heinemann.

Meek, Margaret (1982). *Learning to Read*. London: Bodley Head.

Meek, Margaret (1984). Speaking of shifters. In Meek, Margaret and Jane Miller (Eds.), *Changing English: Essays for Harold Rosen*. London: Heinemann.

Meek, Margaret (1988). How texts teach what readers learn. In Lightfoot, Martin and Nancy Martin (Eds.), *The Word for Teaching is Learning: Essays for James Britton*. London: Heinemann.

Meek, Margaret, Stephen Armstrong, Vicky Austerfield, Judith Graham, and Elizabeth Plackett (1983). *Achieving Literacy: Longitudinal Studies of Adolescents Learning to Read*. London: Routledge and Kegan Paul.

Metcalf, Stephen (2002). Reading Between the Lines. *The Nation*, 28 January.

Meyer, Richard J. (2002). Captives of the script: Killing us softly with phonics. *Language Arts*, *79*(6), 452–461.

Michotte, A. (1946). *La Perception de la Causalité*. Louvain: Institut Supérieur de Philosophie.

Mikulecky, Larry (1982). Job literacy: The relationship between school preparation and workplace actuality. *Reading Research Quarterly*, *17*(3), 400–419.

Miller, George A. (1951). *Language and Communication*. New York: McGraw-Hill.

Miller, George A. (1956). The magical number seven, plus or minus two: Some limits on our capacity for processing information. *Psychological Review*, *63*, 81–92.

Miller, George A. (1965). Some preliminaries to psycholinguistics. *American Psychologist*, *20*, 15–20.

Miller, George A. (1977). *Spontaneous Apprentices: Children and Language*. New York: Seabury.

Miller, George A., Jerome S. Bruner, and Leo Postman (1954). Familiarity of letter sequences and tachistoscopic identification. *Journal of Genetic Psychology*, *50*, 129–139.

Miller, George A. and Christine Fellbaum (1991). Semantic networks of English. *Cognition*, *41*, 197–229.

Miller, George A. and Philip N. Johnson-Laird (1976). *Language and Perception*. Cambridge, MA: Belknap Press.

Miller, George A. and Patricia E. Nicely (1955). An analysis of perceptual confusions among some English consonants. *Journal of the Acoustical Society of America*, *27*, 338–353.

Miller, Larry (1991). The whole language path: Postholes and signposts. *Reflections on Canadian Literacy*, *9*(2), 123–127.

Miller, Larry, Jillian DeJean, and Rebecca Miller (2002). The literacy curriculum and use of an integrated learning system. *Journal of Research in Reading*, *23*(2), 123–135.

Mohyeldin Said, K. A., W. H. Newton-Smith, R. Viale, and Kathleen V. Wilkes (Eds.) (1990). *Modelling the Mind*. Oxford: Clarendon.

Moll, Luis C. (Ed.) (1990). *Vygotsky and Education: Instructional Implications and Applications of Sociohistorical Psychology*. Cambridge, UK: Cambridge University Press.

Moorman, Gary B., William E. Blanton, and Thomas M. McLaughlin (1992). The rhetoric of whole language, Parts 1 and 2. *Reading Psychology*, *13*(2) iii–xiv and *13*(3) iii–xiv.

Morris, P. E. (1988). Expertise and everyday memory. In Gruneberg, M. M., P. E. Morris, and R. N. Sykes (Eds.), *Practical Aspects of Memory: Current Research and Issues, Vol. I: Memory in Everyday Life*. Chichester, UK: Wiley.

Morrow, Lesley Mandel (1992). The impact of a literature-based program on literacy achievement, use of literature, and attitudes of children from minority backgrounds. *Reading Research Quarterly*, *27*(3), 251–275.

Moyer, Sandra B. and Phillis L. Newcomer (1977). Reversals in reading diagnosis and remediation. *Exceptional Children*, *43*, 424–429.

Myers, Jamie (1992). The social contexts of school and personal literacy. *Reading Research Quarterly*, *27*(4), 296–333.

Nagy, William E. and Patricia A. Herman (1987). Breadth and depth of vocabulary knowledge: Implications for acquisition and instruction. In McKeown, Margaret G. and M. E. Curtis (Eds.), *The Nature of Vocabulary Acquisition*. Hillsdale, NJ: Lawrence Erlbaum Associates.

Nagy, William E., Patricia A. Herman, & Richard C. Anderson (1985). Learning words from context. *Reading Research Quarterly*, *20*(2), 233–253.

Nagy, William E., Jean Osborn, Pamela Winsor and John O'Flahavan (1994). Structural analysis: Some guidelines for instruction. In Fran Lehr and Jean Osborn (Eds.), *Reading, Language and Literacy: In-*

struction for the Twenty-First Century. Hillsdale, NJ: Lawrence Erlbaum Associates.

Nagy, William E. and Judith A. Scott (2000). Vocabulary processes. In Barr, Rebecca, M. Kamil, Peter Mosenthal, & P. David Pearson (Eds.), *Handbook of Reading Research: Vol. III* (pp. 269–284). Mahwah, NJ: Lawrence Erlbaum Associates.

National Reading Panel. (2000). *Teaching Children to Read: An Evidence Based Assessment of the Scientific Research Literature on Reading and Its Implications for Reading Instruction*. Washington, DC: National Institute of Child Health and Human Development.

Naylor, Hilary (1980). Reading disability and lateral asymmetry: An information-processing analysis. *Psychological Bulletin*, *87*(3), 531–545.

Neisser, Ulric (1977). *Cognition and Reality*. San Francisco: Freeman.

Nell, Victor (1988). The psychology of reading for pleasure: Needs and gratifications. *Reading Research Quarterly*, *23*(1), 6–50.

Nelson, Katherine (1985). *Making Sense: Development of Meaning in Early Childhood*. New York: Academic Press.

Nelson, Katherine (1986). *Event Knowledge*. Hillsdale, NJ: Lawrence Erlbaum Associates.

Neuman, Susan B. and Donna Celano (2001). Access to print in low-income and middle-income communities: An ecological study of four neighborhoods. *Reading Research Quarterly*, *36*(1), 8–26.

Newman, Edwin B. (1966). Speed of reading when the span of letters is restricted. *American Journal of Psychology*, *79*, 272–278.

Newson, John and Elizabeth Newson (1975). Intersubjectivity and the transmission of culture: On the social origins of symbolic functioning. *Bulletin of the British Psychological Society*, *28*, 437–446.

Nicholson, Tom and Robert Imlach (1981). Where do their answers come from? A study of the inferences which children make when answering questions about narrative stories. *Journal of Reading Behavior*, *13*(2), 111–129.

Norman, Donald A. (1969). *Memory and Attention: An Introduction to Human Information Processing*. New York: Wiley (2nd ed. 1976).

O'Brien, Edward J. and Jerome L. Myers (1985). When comprehension difficulty improves memory for text. *Journal of Experimental Psychology: Learning, Memory and Cognition*, *11*(1), 12–21.

Ohanian, Susan (1999). *One Size Fits Few: The Folly of Educational Standards*. Portsmouth, NH: Heinemann.

Olson, David R. (1977). From utterance to text: The bias of language in speech and writing. *Harvard Educational Review*, *47*(3), 257–281.

Olson, David R., Nancy Torrance, and Angela Hildyard (Eds.) (1985). *Literacy, Language and Learning: The Nature and Consequences of Reading and Writing*. Cambridge, UK: Cambridge University Press.

Ong, Walter J. (1982). *Orality and Literacy: The Technologizing of the Word*. London: Methuen.

O'Shea, Lawrence J., Paul T. Sindelar, and Dorothy J. O'Shea (1985). The effects of repeated readings and attentional cues on reading fluency and comprehension. *Journal of Reading Behavior*, *17*(2), 129–142.

Otto, Wayne (1992). The role of research in reading instruction. In Samuels, S. Jay and Alan E. Farstrup (Eds.), *What Research Has to Say About Reading Instruction* (2nd ed.). Newark, DE: International Reading Association.

Paterson, Frances A. (2002). The politics of phonics. *Journal of Curriculum and Supervision, 15*(3). Reprinted in Allington (2002).

Pattanayak, D. P. (1991). Literacy: An instrument of oppression. In Olson, David R. and Nancy Torrance (Eds.), *Literacy and Orality*. Cambridge, UK: Cambridge University Press.

Paulson, Eric J. (2002). Are oral reading word omissions and substitutions caused by careless eye movements? *Reading Psychology, 23*(1), 45–66.

Paulson, Eric J. and Kenneth S. Goodman (1999). Influential studies in eye-movement research. *Reading Online*, <http://www.readingonline.org/past/past_index.asp?HREF-/critical/ACT.html>. Posted January 1999.

Pearson, P. David, Laurel R. Roehler, Janice A. Dole, and Gerald G. Duffy (1992). Developing expertise in reading comprehension. In Samuels, S. Jay and Alan E. Farstrup (Eds.), *What Research Has to Say About Reading Instruction* (2nd ed.). Newark, DE: International Reading Association.

Pearson, P. David and Alice Studt (1975). Effects of word frequency and contextual richness on children's word identification abilities. *Journal of Educational Psychology, 67*(1), 89–95.

Perfetti, Charles A. (1985). *Reading Ability*. New York: Oxford University Press.

Perfetti, Charles A. (1991). The psychology, pedagogy, and politics of reading. *Psychological Review, 2*, 70–76.

Perfetti, Charles A., S. R. Goldman, and T. W. Hogaboam (1979). Reading skill and the identification of words in discourse context. *Memory and Cognition, 4*, 273–282.

Perfetti, Charles A. and S. Roth (1981). Some of the interactive processes in reading and their role in reading skill. In Lesgold, Alan M. and Charles A. Perfetti (Eds.), *Interactive Processes in Reading*. Hillsdale, NJ: Lawrence Erlbaum Associates.

Piaget, Jean (1976). *To Understand Is to Invent*. New York: Penguin Books.

Piattelli-Palmarini, Massimo (Ed.) (1980). *Language and Learning: The Debate Between Jean Piaget and Noam Chomsky*. Cambridge, MA: Harvard University Press.

Pierce, J. R. and J. E. Karlin (1957). Reading rates and the information rate of a human channel. *Bell Systems Technical Journal, 36*, 497–516.

Pillsbury, W. B. (1897). A study in apperception. *American Journal of Psychology, 8*, 315–393.

Pinker, Steven (1984). Visual cognition: An introduction. *Cognition, 18*, 1–63.

Pinker, Steven (1999). *Words and Rules: The Ingredients of Language*. London: Weidenfeld and Nicolson.

Pinnell, Gay-Su (1989). Success for at-risk children in a program that combines reading and writing. In Mason, Jana M. (Ed.), *Reading and Writing Connections*. Boston: Allyn and Bacon.

Piper, David (1987). Teaching story grammar: Some reasons for caution. *Canadian Journal of English Language Arts*, 10(1), 30–37.

Polanyi, Michael (1966). *The Tacit Dimension*. Garden City, NY: Doubleday.

Popper, Karl R. (1973). *Objective Knowledge: An Evolutionary Approach*. Oxford: Clarendon.

Popper, Karl R. (1976). *Unended Quest: An Intellectual Autobiography*. London: Fontana/Collins.

Potter, Mary C. (1975). Meaning in visual search. *Science*, 187, 965–966.

Potter, Mary C. (1984). Rapid serial visual presentation (RSVP): A method for studying language processing. In Kieras, David E. and Marcel A. Just (Eds.), *New Methods in Reading Comprehension Research*. Hillsdale, NJ: Lawrence Erlbaum Associates.

Potter, Mary C., J. F. Kroll, B. Yachzel, and C. Harris (1980). Comprehension and memory in rapid sequential reading. In Nickerson, R. (Ed.), *Attention and Performance VIII*. Hillsdale, NJ: Lawrence Erlbaum Associates.

Pritchard, R. M. (1961). Stabilized images on the retina. *Scientific American*, 204(6), 72–78.

Quastler, Henry (1956). Studies of human channel capacity. In Cherry, Colin (Ed.), *Information Theory*. London: Butterworths.

Rack, John P., Margaret J. Snowling, and Richard K. Olson (1992). The nonword reading deficit in developmental dyslexia: A review. *Reading Research Quarterly*, 27(1), 28–53.

Raphael, Taffy E. (Ed.) (1986). *The Contexts of School Based Literacy*. New York: Random House.

Rayner, Keith (1992). *Eye Movements and Visual Cognition: Scene Perception and Reading*. New York: Springer-Verlag.

Rayner, Keith (1997). Understanding eye movements in reading. *Scientific Studies of Reading*, 1(4), 317–339.

Rayner, Keith and Alexander Pollatsek (1987). Eye movements in reading: A tutorial review. In Coltheart, Max (Ed.), *Attention and Performance XIII: The Psychology of Reading*. Hove, UK: Lawrence Erlbaum Associates.

Rayner, Keith and Alexander Pollatsek (1989). *The Psychology of Reading*. Englewood Cliffs, NJ: Prentice-Hall.

Read, Charles (1971). Pre-school children's knowledge of English phonology. *Harvard Educational Review*, 41(1), 1–34.

Read, Charles, Zhang Yun-Fei, Nie Hong-Yin, and Ding Bao-Qing (1986). The ability to manipulate speech sounds depends on knowing alphabetic writing. *Cognition*, 24, 31–44.

Reber, Arthur S. (1989). Implicit learning and tacit knowledge. *Journal of Experimental Psychology: General*, 118, 219–235.

Reichardt, Konrad W. (1977). Playing dead or running away: Defense mechanisms during reading. *Journal of Reading*, 20, 706–711.

Reitsma, Pieter (1983). Printed word learning in beginning readers. *Journal of Experimental Child Psychology*, 75, 321–339.

Restle, F. (1970). Theory of serial pattern learning. *Psychological Review*, 77, 481–495.

Rhode, Mary and Bruce Cronnell (1977). *Compilation of a Communication Skills Lexicon Coded with Linguistic Information.* Los Alamitos, CA: Southwest Regional Laboratory for Educational Research and Development, Technical Report No. 58.

Rice, J. (1897). The futility of the spelling grind. *Forum,* 23, 163–172, 409–419.

Rice, Mabel L. (1990). Preschoolers' QUIL: Quick Incidental Learning of Words. In Conti-Ramsden, Gina and Catherine E. Snow (Eds.), *Children's Language (Vol. 7).* Hillsdale, NJ: Lawrence Erlbaum Associates.

Rieben, Laurence and Charles A. Perfetti (1991). *Learning to Read: Basic Research and Its Implications.* Hillsdale, NJ: Lawrence Erlbaum Associates.

Robinson, H. Alan, Vincent Faraone, Daniel R. Hittelman, and Elizabeth Unrah (1990). *Reading Comprehension Instruction 1783–1987: A Review of Trends and Research.* Newark, DE: International Reading Association.

Robinson, Ian (1975). *The New Grammarians' Funeral.* Cambridge, UK: Cambridge University Press.

Rogers, Rebecca (2002). Between contexts: A critical discourse analysis of family literacy, discursive practices, and literate subjectivities. *Reading Research Quarterly,* 37(3), 248–277.

Rosch, Eleanor and B. B. Lloyd (1978). *Cognition and Categorization.* Hillsdale, NJ: Lawrence Erlbaum Associates.

Rosen, Harold (1986). The importance of story. *Language Arts,* 63(3), 226–237.

Rosen, Harold (1988). Stories of stories: Footnotes on sly gossipy practices. In Lightfoot, Martin and Nancy Martin (Eds.), *The Word for Teaching is Learning: Essays for James Britton.* London: Heinemann.

Rosenblatt, Louise M. (1978). *The Reader: The Text: The Poem.* Carbondale: Southern Illinois University Press.

Rosenblatt, Louise M. (1980). What facts does this poem teach you? *Language Arts,* 57(4), 386–394.

Rosinski, Richard R., Roberta Michnick Golinkoff, and Karen S. Kukish (1975). Automatic semantic processing in a picture-word interference task. *Child Development,* 46(1), 247–253.

Rosset, Clement (1989). Reality and the untheorizable. In Kavanagh, Thomas M. (Ed.), *The Limits of Theory.* Stanford, CA: Stanford University Press.

Rottenberg, Claire J. and Lyndon W. Searfoss (1992). Becoming literate in a preschool class: Literacy development of hearing-impaired children. *Journal of Reading Behavior,* 24(4), 463–479.

Routman, Regie (1994). *Invitations: From Literature to Literacy.* Portsmouth, NH: Heinemann.

Rumelhart, David E. (1980). Schemata: The building blocks of cognition. In Spiro, Rand J., Bertram C. Bruce, and William F. Brewer (Eds.), *Theoretical Issues in Reading Comprehension: Perspectives from Cognitive Psychology, Linguistics, Artificial Intelligence, and Education.* Hillsdale, NJ: Lawrence Erlbaum Associates.

Rumelhart, David E. and Andrew Ortony (1977). The representation of knowledge in memory. In Anderson, Richard C., Rand J. Spiro, and William E. Montague (Eds.), *Schooling and the Acquisition of Knowledge*. Hillsdale, NJ: Lawrence Erlbaum Associates.

Sachs, Jacqueline S. (1974). Memory in reading and listening to discourse. *Memory and Cognition, 2*(1A), 95–100.

Sacks, Oliver (1989). *Seeing Voices: A Journey Into the World of the Deaf*. Berkeley: University of California Press.

Sadoski, Mark (1983). An exploratory study of the relationships between reported imagery and the comprehension and recall of a story. *Reading Research Quarterly, 19*(1), 110–121.

Sadoski, Mark, Ernest M. Goetz, and S. Kansinger (1988). Imagination in story response: Relationships between imagery, affect and structural importance. *Reading Research Quarterly, 23*, 320–336.

Saenger, Paul (1991). The separation of words and the physiology of reading. In Olson, David R. and Nancy Torrance (Eds.), *Literacy and Orality*. Cambridge, UK: Cambridge University Press.

Salmon, Phillida (1985). *Living in Time: A New Look at Personal Development*. London: Dent.

Salmon, Phillida and Hilary Claire (1984). *Classroom Collaboration*. London: Routledge and Kegan Paul.

Sampson, Geoffrey (1985). *Writing Systems: A Linguistic Introduction*. London: Hutchinson.

Samuels, S. Jay (1971). Letter-name versus letter-sound knowledge in learning to read. *The Reading Teacher, 24*, 604–608.

Samuels, S. Jay (1979). The method of repeated readings. *The Reading Teacher, 32*, 403–408.

Santa, Carol Minnick (1999/2000). President's message: High stakes, low benefits: An open letter to U.S. Secretary of Education Richard Riley. *Reading Today*, December 1999/January 2000, *37*.

Savage, Robert (2001). A re-evaluation of the evidence for orthographic analogies: A reply to Goswami (1999). *Journal of Reading Research, 24*(1), 1–19

Saxe, Geoffrey B. (1991). *Culture and Cognitive Development: Studies in Mathematical Understanding*. Hillsdale, NJ: Lawrence Erlbaum Associates.

Schatz, Elinore Kress and R. Scott Baldwin (1986). Context cues are unreliable predictors of word meanings. *Reading Research Quarterly, 21*(4), 439–454.

Schneider, Walter and Richard M. Shiffrin (1977). Controlled and automatic human information processing: I. Detection, search and attention. *Psychological Review, 84*(1), 1–66.

Scholes, Robert J. and Brenda J. Willis (1991). Linguists, literacy and the intensionality of Marshall McLuhan's Western man. In Olson, David R. and Nancy Torrance (Eds.), *Literacy and Orality*. Cambridge, UK: Cambridge University Press.

Schwanenflugel, Paula J. (Ed.). (1991). *The Psychology of Word Meanings*. Hillsdale, NJ: Lawrence Erlbaum Associates.

Scribner, Sylvia and Michael Cole (1978). Literacy without schooling: Testing for intellectual effects. *Harvard Educational Review, 48*(4), 448–461.

Seligman, Martin E. P. (1975). *Helplessness: On Depression, Development and Death*. San Francisco: Freeman.

Senner, Wayne M. (Ed.) (1989). *The Origins of Writing*. Lincoln: University of Nebraska.

Shallice, Tim and Elizabeth K. Warrington (1975). Word recognition in a phonemic dyslexic patient. *Quarterly Journal of Experimental Psychology, 27*, 187–199.

Shannon, Claude E. (1951). Prediction and entropy of printed English. *Bell Systems Technical Journal, 30*, 50–64.

Shannon, Patrick (1984). Mastery learning in reading and the control of teachers and students. *Language Arts, 61*(5), 484–493.

Shannon, Patrick (1985). Reading instruction and social class. *Language Arts, 62*(6), 604–613.

Shannon, Patrick (1989). *Broken Promises: Reading Instruction in Twentieth Century America*. Granby, MA: Bergin and Garvey.

Shannon, Patrick (1993). Critique of false generosity: A response to Baumann. *Reading Research Quarterly, 28*(1), 8–14.

Shannon, Patrick (1996). Mad as hell. *Language Arts, 73*(1), 14–19.

Sharkey, Noel E. and D. C. Mitchell (1985). Word recognition in a functional context: The use of scripts in reading. *Journal of Memory and Language, 24*(2), 253–270.

Shaywitz, S. E., M. Escobar, M. Shaywitz, J. Fletcher, and R. Makuch (1992). Evidence that dyslexia may represent the lower tail of a normal distribution of reading ability. *New England Journal of Medicine, 326*, 145–150.

Simon, Herbert A. (1974). How big is a chunk? *Science, 183*, 482–488.

Skinner, B. F. (1985). Cognitive science and behaviorism. *British Journal of Psychology, 76*(3), 291–301.

Slater, Wayne H. (1985). Revising inconsiderate elementary school expository text: Effects on comprehension and recall. In Niles, Jerome A. and Rosary V. Lalik (Eds.), *Issues in Literacy: A Research Perspective*. Rochester, NY: National Reading Conference, 34th Yearbook.

Smith, Frank (1969). The use of featural dependencies across letters in the visual identification of words. *Journal of Verbal Learning and Verbal Behavior, 8*, 215–218.

Smith, Frank (1976). Learning to read by reading: A brief case study. *Language Arts, 53*(3), 297–299.

Smith, Frank (1979). Conflicting approaches to reading research and instruction. In Resnick, Lauren B. and Phyllis A. Weaver (Eds.), *Theory and Practice of Early Reading* (Vol. 2). Hillsdale, NJ: Lawrence Erlbaum Associates.

Smith, Frank (1981). Demonstrations, engagement and sensitivity: A revised approach to language learning. *Language Arts, 58*(1), 103–112.

Smith, Frank (1983a). *Essays into Literacy*. Portsmouth, NH: Heinemann.

Smith, Frank (1983b). Reading like a writer. *Language Arts, 60*(5), 558–567.

Smith, Frank (1986). *Insult to Intelligence*. New York: Arbor House. Reprinted Portsmouth, NH: Heinemann, 1998.

Smith, Frank (1988). *Joining the Literacy Club*. Portsmouth, NH: Heinemann.

Smith, Frank (1989). Overselling literacy. *Phi Delta Kappan, 70*(5), 352–359.

Smith, Frank (1990). *To think*. New York: Teachers College Press.

Smith, Frank (1992). Learning to read: The never-ending debate. *Phi Delta Kappan, 73*(6), 432–441.

Smith, Frank (1993). *Whose Language? What Power?* New York: Teachers College Press.

Smith, Frank (1994). *Writing and the Writer* (2nd ed.). Hillsdale, NJ: Lawrence Erlbaum Associates.

Smith, Frank (1994b). Understanding Reading (Fifth edition). Hillsdale, NJ: Lawrence Erlbaum Associates.

Smith, Frank (1998). *The Book of Learning and Forgetting*. New York: Teachers College Press.

Smith, Frank (2003). *Unspeakable Acts, Unnatural Practices: Flaws and Fallacies in "Scientific" Reading Instruction*. Portsmouth, NH: Heinemann.

Smith, Frank and Peter Carey (1966). Temporal factors in visual information processing. *Canadian Journal of Psychology, 20*(3), 337–342.

Smith, Frank, Deborah Lott, and Bruce Cronnell (1969). Effect of type size and case alternation on word identification. *American Journal of Psychology, 82*(2), 248–253.

Snow, Catherine E., M. S. Burns, and P. Griffin (1998). *Preventing Reading Difficulties in Young Children*. Washington, DC: National Academy Press.

Sperling, George (1960). The information available in brief visual presentations. *Psychological Monographs, 74*(11), Whole No. 498.

Sperry, R. W. (1968). Hemisphere disconnection and unity in conscious awareness. *American Psychologist, 23*, 723–733.

Squire, James R. (Ed.) (1987). *The Dynamics of Language Learning*. Urbana, IL: National Conference on Research in English.

Staller, Joshua (1982). Neurological correlates of reading failure. In Singer, Martin H. (Ed.), *Competent Reader, Disabled Reader: Research and Application*. Hillsdale, NJ: Lawrence Erlbaum Associates.

Stanovich, Keith E. (1980). Toward an interactive-compensatory model of individual differences in the development of reading fluency. *Reading Research Quarterly, 15*, 32–71.

Stanovich, Keith E. (1981). Attentional and automatic context effects in reading. In Lesgold, Alan M. and Charles A. Perfetti (Eds.), *Interactive Processes in Reading*. Hillsdale, NJ: Lawrence Erlbaum Associates.

Stanovich, Keith E. (1982a). Individual differences in the cognitive processes of reading: I. Word decoding. *Journal of Learning Disabilities, 15*, 485–493.

Stanovich, Keith E. (1982b). Individual differences in the cognitive processes of reading: II: Text-level processes. *Journal of Learning Disabilities, 15*, 549–554.

Stanovich, Keith E. (1986). Matthew effects in reading: Some consequences of individual differences in the acquisition of literacy. *Reading Research Quarterly, 21*(4), 360–407.

Stanovich, Keith E. (1991). Cognitive science meets beginning reading. *Psychological Science*, *2*(70), 77–81.

Stanovich, Keith E. (1992). Speculations on the causes and consequences of individual differences in early reading acquisition. In Gough, Philip B., Linnea C. Ehri, and Rebecca Treiman (Eds.) *Reading Acquisition*. Hillsdale, NJ: Lawrence Erlbaum Associates.

Stanovich, Keith E., Anne E. Cunningham, and Dorothy J. Feeman (1984). Intelligence, cognitive skills, and early reading progress. *Reading Research Quarterly*, *19*(3), 278–303.

Stein, Dieter (Ed.) (1992). *Cooperating with Written Texts: The Pragmatics and Comprehension of Written Texts*. Berlin: Mouton de Gruyter.

Stevenson, V. (Ed.) (1983). *Words: The Evolution of Written Languages*. London: Methuen.

Suhor, Charles (1992). Semiotics and the English language arts. *Language Arts*, *69*, 228–230.

Sulzby, Elizabeth (1985). Children's emergent reading of favorite story books: A developmental study. *Reading Research Quarterly*, *20*(4), 458–481.

Sutherland-Smith, Wendy (2002). Weaving the literacy Web: Changes in reading from page to screen. *The Reading Teacher*, *55*(7), 662–669.

Tao, Liang and Alice F. Healy (2002). The unitization effect in reading Chinese and English text. *Scientific Studies of Reading*, *6*(2), 167–197.

Taylor, Barbara M. (1992). Text structure, comprehension and recall. In Samuels, S. Jay and Alan E. Farstrup (Eds.), *What Research Has to Say About Reading Instruction* (2nd ed.). Newark, DE: International Reading Association.

Taylor, Denny (1991). *Learning Denied*. Portsmouth, NH: Heinemann.

Taylor, Denny (1998). *Beginning to Read and the Spin Doctors of Science: The Political Campaign to Change America's Mind About How Children Learn to Read*. Urbana, IL: National Council of Teachers of English.

Taylor, Denny and Dorothy S. Strickland (1986). *Family Storybook Reading*. Portsmouth, NH: Heinemann.

Templeton, Shane (1991). New trends in an historical perspective: The "what" and "why" of skills instruction in literacy. *Language Arts*, *68*, 590–595.

Thompson, G. Brian. (1981). Toward a theoretical account of individual differences in the acquisition of reading skill. *Reading Research Quarterly*, *15*(4), 596–599.

Thompson, Richard A. (1992). A critical perspective on whole language. *Reading Psychology*, *13*(2), 131–155.

Thorndike, E. (1977). Reading as reasoning: A study of mistakes in paragraph reading. *Journal of Educational Psychology*, *9*, 77–110.

Thorndike, E. L. and I. Lorge (1944). *The Teacher's Word Book of 30,000 Words*. New York: Teachers College.

Tierney, Robert J. and J. W. Cunningham (1984). Research on teaching reading comprehension. In Pearson, P. David (Ed.), *The Handbook of Reading Research*. New York: Longman.

Tierney, Robert J. and T. Shanahan (1991). Research on the reading-writing relationships: Interactions, transactions and outcomes. In Barr, Rebecca, Michael L. Kamil, Peter Mosenthal, and P. David Pearson (Eds.), *Handbook of Reading Research, Vol II.* New York: Longman.

Tolchinksy, Liliana (2003). *The Cradle of Culture and What Children Know About Writing and Numbers Before Being Taught.* Mahwah, NJ: Lawrence Erlbaum Associates.

Torrance, Nancy A. and David R. Olson (1985). Oral and literate competencies in early school years. In David R. Olson, Nancy A. Torrance, and Angela Hildyard (Eds.), *Literacy, Language and Learning: The Nature and Consequences of Reading and Writing.* Cambridge, UK: Cambridge University Press.

Treiman, Rebecca (1992). The role of intrasyllabic units in learning to read and spell. In Gough, Philip B., Linnea C. Ehri, and Rebecca Treiman (Eds.), *Reading Acquisition.* Hillsdale, NJ: Lawrence Erlbaum Associates.

Treiman, Rebecca, Usha C. Goswami, and Maggie Bruck (1990). Not all nonwords are alike. Implications for reading development and theory. *Memory and Cognition, 18*, 559–567.

Trelease, Jim and Stephen D. Krashen (1996). Eating and reading in the library. *Emergency Librarian, 23*(5), 27.

Truax, Roberta R. and Richard R. Kretschmer, Jr. (1993). Finding new voices in the process of meeting all the needs of children. *Language Arts, 70*(7), 592–601.

Trushell, John (2002). Editorial introduction: The future of the book? *Journal of Research in Reading, 23*(2) 103-109.

Tulving, Endel (1985a). How many memory systems are there? *American Psychologist, 40*, 385–398.

Tulving, Endel (1985b). Memory and consciousness. *Canadian Journal of Psychology, 25*, 1–12.

Tuman, Myron C. (1987). *A Preface to Literacy: An Inquiry into Pedagogy, Practice, and Progress.* Tuscaloosa: University of Alabama Press.

Underwood, Geoffrey (Ed.) (1978). *Strategies of Information Processing.* London: Academic Press.

Urwin, Cathy (1982). The contribution of nonvisual information systems and language to knowing oneself. In Beveridge, Michael (Ed.), *Children Thinking Through Language.* London: Arnold.

Vaihinger, Hans (1952). *The Philosophy of "As-If."* London: Routledge and Kegan Paul.

van Dongen, Richard (1987). Children's narrative thought, at home and at school. *Language Arts, 64*(1), 79–87.

Vellutino, Frank R. (1987). Dyslexia. *Scientific American, 256*(3), 34–41.

Vellutino, Frank R. (1991). Has basic research in reading increased our understanding of developmental reading and how to teach reading? *Psychological Science, 2*(70), 81–83.

Venezky, Richard L. (1967). English orthography: Its graphical structure and its relation to sound. *Reading Research Quarterly, 2*, 75–106.

Venezky, Richard L. (1970). *The Structure of English Orthography.* The Hague: Mouton.

Venezky, Richard L. (1999). *The American Way of Spelling: The Structures and Origins of American English Orthography.* New York: Guilford.

Vincente, Kim J. and William F. Brewer (1993). Reconstructive remembering of the scientific literature. *Cognition, 46,* 101–128.

Von Sprecken, Debra, Jiyoung Kim, and Stephen Krashen (2000). The home run book: Can one positive reading experience create a reader? *School Library Journal, 23*(2), 8–9.

Vygotsky, Lev S. (1978). *Mind in Society: The Development of Higher Psychological Processes.* Cambridge, MA: Harvard University Press.

Walkerdine, Valerie (1982). From context to text: A psychosemiotic approach to abstract thought. In Beveridge, Michael (Ed.), *Children Thinking Through Language.* London: Arnold.

Walters, Gloria S., Melvin K. Komoda, and Tannis Y. Arbuckle (1985). The effects of concurrent tasks on reading: Implications for phonological recoding. *Journal of Memory and Language, 24*(1), 27–45.

Wasik, Barbara A. and Robert E. Slavin (1993). Preventing early reading failure with one-to-one tutoring: A review of five programs. *Reading Research Quarterly, 28*(2), 178–200.

Weaver, Constance (1988). *Reading Process and Practice: From Socio-Psycholinguistics to Whole Language.* Portsmouth, NH: Heinemann.

Weaver, Constance (1994). *Reading Process and Practice: From Socio-Psycholinguistics to Whole Language.* Portsmouth, NH: Heinemann.

Weintraub, Sam (1986). The fuzzy area of literature reviews. In Weintraub, Sam, Helen K. Smith, Nancy L. Roser, Walter J. Moore, Michael W. Kibby, Kathleen S. Jongsma, and Peter L. Fisher (Eds.), *Summary of Investigations Relating to Reading: July 1, 1984 to June 30, 1985.* Newark, DE: International Reading Association.

Wells, Gordon (1985). Preschool literacy-related activities and success in school. In Olson, D. R., Nancy Torrance and Angela Hildyard (Eds.), *Literacy, Language and Learning: The Nature and Consequences of Reading and Writing.* Cambridge, UK: Cambridge University Press.

West, Richard F., Keith E. Stanovich, and Harold R. Mitchell (1993). Reading in the real world and its correlates. *Reading Research Quarterly, 28*(1), 34–50.

Wheeler, D. D. (1970). Processes in word recognition. *Cognitive Psychology, 1,* 59–85.

Whorf, Benjamin Lee (1956). *Language, Thought and Reality.* Cambridge, MA: MIT Press.

Wildman, Daniel and Martin Kling (1978/1979). Semantic, syntactic and spatial anticipation in reading. *Reading Research Quarterly, 14*(2), 128–164.

Willinsky, John (1990). *The New Literacy: Redefining Reading and Writing in the Schools.* London: Routledge.

Willis, Arlette Ingram (2002). Literacy at Calhoun Colored School 1892–1945. *Reading Research Quarterly, 37*(1), 8–45.

Wilson, Stephanie Gray, Mike Rinck, Timothy P. McNamara, Gordon H. Bower, and Daniel G. Morrow (1993). Mental models and narrative comprehension: Some qualifications. *Journal of Memory and Language*, *32*, 141–154.

Wolf, Maryanne and Tami Katzir-Cohen (2001). Reading fluency and its intervention. *Scientific Studies of Reading, 5*(3), 211–239.

Wong, Bernice Y. L. (1982). Understanding learning disabled students' reading problems: Contributions from cognitive psychology. *Topics in Learning and Learning Disabilities, 2*, 43–50.

Yates, Jack (1985). The content of awareness is a model of the world. *Psychological Review, 92*(2), 249–284.

Yatvin, Joanne (1982). Learning to read at forty-eight. *Language Arts, 59*(8), 822–828.

Yatvin, Joanne (2002). Babes in the woods: The Wanderings of the National Reading Panel. *Phi Delta Kappan, 83*(5), 364–369. Reprinted in Allington (2002).

Young, Andrew W. and Andrew W. Ellis (1981). Asymmetry of cerebral hemispheric functioning in normal and poor readers. *Psychological Bulletin, 89*(1), 183–190.

Author Index

Subject Index